DATE DUE

DEMCO 38-296

THE NORTH AMERICAN
FREE TRADE AGREEMENT
AND THE
EUROPEAN UNION

R

THE NORTH AMERICAN FREE TRADE AGREEMENT AND THE EUROPEAN UNION

Nicholas V. Gianaris

PRAEGER

Westport, Connecticut
London

Library of Congress Cataloging-in-Publication Data

Gianaris, Nicholas V.
　　The North American free trade agreement and the European Union /
Nicholas V. Gianaris.
　　　　p.　　　cm.
　　Includes bibliographical references and index.
　　ISBN 0–275–96167–2 (alk. paper)
　　1. Free trade—North America.　2. North American Free Trade
Agreement.　3. European Union—North America.　4. Free trade—
European Union countries.　5. North America—Foreign economic
relations—European Union countries.　6. European Union countries—
Foreign economic relations—North America.　I. Title.
HF1746.G53　　　1998
382'.09407—DC21　　　　　97–34757

British Library Cataloguing in Publication Data is available.

Library of Congress Catalog Card Number: 97–34757
ISBN: 0–275–96167–2

First published in 1998

Praeger Publishers, 88 Post Road West, Westport, CT 06881
An imprint of Greenwood Publishing Group, Inc.

Printed in the United States of America

The paper used in this book complies with the
Permanent Paper Standard issued by the National
Information Standards Organization (Z39.48–1984).

10　9　8　7　6　5　4　3　2　1

To my grandson
Constantine Vasilis Gianaris

Contents

	Tables and Figures	ix
	Preface	xi
	Acknowledgments	xiii
1	Introduction	1
2	NAFTA	17
3	The European Union	41
4	Economic Organization: Similarities and Differences	61
5	Fiscal Policy	87
6	Foreign Trade	121
7	Monetary Policy and Exchange Rates	149
8	Investment and Joint Ventures in NAFTA	189
9	Cross-Atlantic and Intra-EU Acquisitions	207
10	Relations with Other Countries	229
	Notes	255
	Selected Bibliography	265
	Index	273

Tables and Figures

TABLES

3.1 Economic Indicators for the EU Countries, 1995   49

5.1 Government Expenditures, Budget Deficits, and Debts of the EU Countries   91

6.1 Trade of NAFTA with the EU Countries   123

6.2 Total Exports and Imports of Goods and Services of the NAFTA Countries   125

6.3 Total Exports and Imports of Goods and Services of the EU Countries, 1994   126

6.4 Total Exports and Imports of Goods and Services of the EU Countries, 1980–1994   127

7.1 Inflation in the NAFTA and EU Countries   165

FIGURES

5.1 Relationship of Per Capita GDP and General Government Expenditures as Percentages of GDP, 1994   89

5.2 National Income (Y) Determination with Government Expenditures (G)   96

5.3 The Public Sector in the United States and the EU   97

5.4 Tax Revenue of Main Headings as a Percentage of Total Tax Revenue of the NAFTA, EU, and Other OECD Countries, 1994   99

5.5   Receipts as Percentage of Total Tax Revenues for the
      NAFTA Countries, 1965–1994   100

5.6   Receipts as Percentage of Total Tax Revenues for the
      EU Countries, 1965–1994   101

5.7   Indirect Taxes as Percentage of GDP   111

5.8   Equilibrium Level of Income with Tax Cut   119

6.1   Trade Creation   131

6.2   Trade Diversion   131

7.1   Money Supply (M) and Velocity of Money (V = GDP/M)
      for Canada   153

7.2   Money Supply (M) and Velocity of Money (V = GDP/M)
      for Mexico   154

7.3   Money Supply (M) and Velocity of Money (V = GDP/M)
      for the United States   155

7.4   Money Supply (M) and Velocity of Money (V = GDP/M)
      for France   157

7.5   Money Supply (M) and Velocity of Money (V = GDP/M)
      for Germany   158

7.6   Money Supply (M) and Velocity of Money (V = GDP/M)
      for Greece   159

7.7   Money Supply (M) and Velocity of Money (V = GDP/M)
      for Italy   160

7.8   Money Supply (M) and Velocity of Money (V = GDP/M)
      for Spain   161

7.9   Money Supply (M) and Velocity of Money (V = GDP/M)
      for the United Kingdom   162

7.10 The Relationship of Interest, Income, Unemployment,
      and Inflation   170

10.1 Investment and Productivity Growth   231

Preface

Young America and aging Europe have had strong historical, economic, and sociocultural ties. From colonial times to their independence and gradual expansion and growth, the North American Free Trade Agreement (NAFTA) countries (Canada, Mexico, and the United States) maintained strong links with mother Europe through immigration, trade, and investment. Such links became stronger after World War II and remain strong today, especially on matters of capital formation, technological dissemination, and financial transactions.

The NAFTA and the European Union (EU) economies have great similarities in the relationship of the private and the public sectors, the degree of industrialization, and the elated fiscal and monetary policies. Such similarities, particularly in business regulations and taxation and market competition, make mutual trade and investment, as well as joint ventures and acquisitions, attractive and profitable on both sides of the Atlantic.

Present trends toward stronger economic cooperation of the Western Hemisphere and a united Europe are presenting new problems of worldwide dimensions. The immediate problem for the NAFTA countries, particularly the United States, is the impact of the continent-size market of the European Union on their economies. The expansion of markets for goods and capital and greater liberalization of the economies of the NAFTA and EU countries will create challenges and opportunities from the standpoint of capital investment, international trade, and economic growth. However, as the NAFTA and the EU eliminate internal barriers and move toward closer economic and political integration, the question is whether these blocs will turn to inward-looking groups or markets more open to the rest of the world.

The removal of physical, technical, and fiscal barriers, as well as the elimination of restrictions on trade, services, and capital movements within the NAFTA and the EU, would increase competition among their industries and between them and other outside firms. From this standpoint, the internal market program of the EU may be viewed as a potential opportunity for NAFTA (mainly U.S. firms) and vice versa, as long as it produces a more open market and liberalized business environment. However, in spite of possible broad trade benefits, certain industries may be adversely affected if NAFTA and the EU eliminate internal barriers only to create larger barriers around them. There are concerns that NAFTA and EU regulations and directives may create quantitative and qualitative restrictions, reciprocity requirements for other countries, and other provisions that may limit the benefits of liberalization to internal producers and traders, while outside firms and merchants may be at a disadvantage.

NAFTA and the EU are regions with markets that are fairly easy to enter compared to those of Japan and other places with high barriers. They have more or less the same business environment and similar market conditions. Therefore, they are evidently becoming more fertile markets for mutual trade and investment. Already large companies are well positioned both for individual and joint ventures and for transfer of technology on both sides of the Atlantic.

The purpose of this book is to examine trade and investment relations and related economic policies that affect developmental trends in NAFTA and the EU as a result of the economic integration of these large markets of the world. The insights and clarity of this book help the reader understand the complexity of present and future global issues. The book provides valuable resources and plausible alternatives for theorists and practitioners interested in the economic and political integration of NAFTA and the EU and their mutual trade and investment. It is a frank and pragmatic study that explores the dilemmas bedeviling the NAFTA and the EU nations as they try to introduce and foster new institutional arrangements to promote cooperation, stability, and growth.

After an introduction in Chapter 1, reviews of the historical trends and the past economic relations are presented in Chapters 2 and 3. Particular emphasis is given to intensive postwar and more recent efforts of integration of the NAFTA and the EU. Chapters 4 and 5 deal with the similarities in economic organizations and related fiscal policies as they affect trade and other financial transactions between NAFTA and the EU. Chapters 6 and 7 examine in more detail trade and monetary and exchange rates policies. Chapters 8 and 9 review the phenomenon of growing joint ventures in NAFTA and the EU and acquisitions across the Atlantic. Finally, Chapter 10 briefly illustrates economic relations with other countries, particularly the dramatic changes in Eastern European and Latin American countries.

Acknowledgments

I want to acknowledge my indebtness to Professors Janis Barry-Figueroa, Ernest Block, Clive Daniel, George Kourvetaris, Laurence Krause, Andreas Moschonas, Kostas Papoulias, John Roche, Dominick Salvatore, Shapoor Vali, and Paul Vouras, as well as to financial and legal experts Bill Gianaris, Michael Gianaris, Maria Kleine, Dimitris Lavdas, Constantine Papaconstantinou, and Christos G. Tzelios for their stimulating comments. Special thanks to Pauline Hamme for her tireless support in computer work and corrections of the manuscript. My final debt goes to Laurie Bath, Evangelos Karoutsos, Andre Pontual, Arifur Rahman, Aravella Simotas, Eleftherios Skiadiotis, Alexander C. Tzelios, and Victoria Varas for reviewing, copying, and other technical services.

Chapter 1

Introduction

HISTORICAL DEVELOPMENTS

Historically, after the conclusion of the Trojan War around 1200 B.C., Odysseus, the legendary ruler of Ithaca in ancient Greece (Hellas), sailed across the Atlantic to North America from Nova Scotia down the U.S. seashores, thence to Cuba and Haiti, and finally back to Ithaca. In his effort to return to his beloved wife Penelope, he was lost for ten years on the sea. He sailed through the straights of Gibraltar (or the Pillars of Hercules, as the Hellenes called them) and across the Atlantic to the unknown shores of the Americas.[1]

After the arrival of Christopher Columbus to the New World in 1492, many Europeans from Spain, Portugal, France, The Netherlands, Ireland, Germany, and England settled along the Atlantic coast from Canada to Florida and Mexico. In addition to the initial colonization, religious and political freedom and the hope of making a better living were the main reasons for immigration from many countries of Europe. In some cases, the custom of giving the newcomer fifty to one hundred acres of land and the achievement of independence attracted the poor people and the peasants of Europe to the new lands of opportunity.

The first English colony, established in 1607 by the London Company of Jamestown, Virginia, was ultimately changed into a royal colony because of mismanagement, starvation, and fighting with the Indians. Other English colonies sprang up to the north and south, started by commercial companies or by friends of the king. The expansion of the frontier, by pushing the Indian natives westward, and the use of indentured servants and imported Negro slaves, beginning in the seventeenth century, increased agricultural and handicraft production in the farms and cities. The business of a town, such as tax collecting, spending for roads, and other public projects, was decided by a "town meeting," a kind of direct democracy similar to that of ancient Greece. Trade among the colonies increased rapidly until the American Revolution (1776) and later, sociocultural relations and trade cooperation with mother Europe still continued, especially during the late nineteenth and early twentieth centuries, with the influx of capital and the new wave of immigration from Southern and Eastern Europe, mainly in the United States and Canada. The painful events of World War I, the Great Depression, and World War II brought Western Europe, the United States, Canada, and Mexico closer together, economically and militarily.

For a joint defense of the United States, Canada, and Western Europe, the North Atlantic Treaty Organization (NATO) was established in 1949. This treaty made the United States a military ally of Britain, France, Italy, Belgium, The Netherlands, Denmark, Portugal, and Luxembourg, along with Canada, Norway, and Iceland. Other Western nations later joined this mutual defense pact. In May 1952, five NATO countries (France, Italy, Belgium, The Netherlands, and Luxembourg), together with West Germany, signed a treaty to organize the European Defense Community (EDC), agreed to establish a six-nation army, and outlined plans to unite under a single constitution. In July 1952, the U.S. Senate ratified a "peace contract" with West Germany and indicated that it would approve a mutual defense treaty with the six countries of the EDC. Although France decided in 1954 not to ratify the treaty creating the EDC, the six nations did succeed in establishing Euratom and made plans for a common European market.

During the post–World War II period, strategic and military cooperation between the United States, Canada, and Western Europe for common defense overshadowed trade relations and economic policies. More or less the same relations prevailed between the United States and Japan. To avoid confrontations that would erode alliance relations, economic differences about steel, chickens, beef, and the use of hormones, as well as monetary disputes, were settled by national leaders and policymakers as secondary problems and byproducts of mutual defense protection, with the Untied States usually having the upper hand. However, the U.S. defense umbrella and its initial economic support stimulated trends toward the integration of the Western European nations.

The postwar rehabilitation of Europe—with American support, as well as technological dissemination and improvement—led to economic stabilization and growth to such an extent that Western European countries, along with Japan, became serious competitors of the United States. Moreover, the formation of the EU and the gradual economic integration of Western Europe made it a large economic group with a huge market and momentum toward political unification.

Moreover, the new economic and political reforms in the former Soviet Union and other Eastern Bloc nations, through economic restructuring, democratization, and openness, have reduced threats of conflict and thawed the ice of the Cold War between East and West. As a result, trade relations and economic policies have acquired more importance than defense considerations while economic competition across the Atlantic is growing. Therefore, a new system of Western economic cooperation that is independent of defense and military considerations and can stand on its own merits may be considered. Policymakers on both sides of the Atlantic should devise new harmonious ways to coordinate trade and defense relations and avoid open-ended threats for retaliation.

Making the NAFTA economies more stable and competitive requires the Spartan way of development; that is, frugality and hard work. Such an approach, used successfully by not only the Spartans of ancient Greece (Hellas) but also by present-day Japanese and Germans, would increase saving for financing productive investment and competitiveness in international markets. It would reduce the need to borrow from abroad and place more emphasis on new investments in technology-intensive plant and equipment.

For the NAFTA and some EU countries, this Spartan approach would mean further reduction or elimination of budget deficits as well as trade deficits, reduction in consumption, and an increase in savings and investment. Reduction in budget deficits can be achieved through increases in taxes and decreases in expenditures or through a combination of a "flexible freeze" in spending and economic growth. The last method, which is the least painful and objectionable, assumes a satisfactory rate of economic growth and zero real spending growth; that is, increases in spending for government projects are no greater than the rate of inflation, or increased expenditures in some programs are balanced by equal reductions in others. On the contrary, a substantial decline in the budget deficit would reduce the fiscal stimulus and cause a downturn in the economy, requiring a new round of deficits to stop the economy from moving into a severe recession or even depression. In connection with that scenario, the fact that the economies of some NAFTA and EU countries continued for years to be in an upswing brought forward arguments to maintain deficits for economic stimulation and prosperity.

As a result of the creation of a single European market, the economic stake of American investors is significant. Substantial economies would emerge in production, marketing, and distribution for American companies operating in a uniform EU market of more than $8 billion GNP with 370 million people, and even more with the eventual integration of other European nations.

The harmonization of the EU product standards, new testing and verification procedures, and the common technical and regulatory standards introduced to all member-nations would make trade and investment by NAFTA firms easier and less costly since they no longer need to modify their products according to the regulations and specifications of each EU nation. The same thing can be said for EU firms that trade with and invest in the NAFTA countries. However, NAFTA or the EU may try to shield some enterprises from competition for a transitional period of adjustment, especially in the automotive, textile, and electronics industries. Some reciprocity measures may restrict trade in goods and services, as well as direct and portfolio investment. These measures are of great importance for foreign banks and other firms expecting to expand operations in these regions.

The boom times of the 1980s pushed aside the unsolved problems left over from the turbulent times of the 1970s. Rapid growth of government expenditures and insufficient tax revenue generated large budget deficits and huge national debts in many NAFTA and EU nations. This domestic debt, together with the growing foreign debt, may be considered as an economic time bomb for these economies. Should a recession begin, the twin debts and their servicing may lead to high interest rates and ignite the bomb, generating financial and economic problems for the whole world.[2]

TRENDS FOR INTEGRATION IN EUROPE

Historically, Europe has played a vital role in the formation and development of economic and sociocultural world events. From the dawn of history to the present, changes in economic and sociopolitical conditions in this region influenced and shaped Western civilization as we understand it today.

From the Hellenic and Roman periods to the Middle Ages, the Industrial Revolution, and later, efforts for a united Europe were promulgated on many occasions. Writers and rulers in ancient Greece (Hellas) and Rome supported or enforced, from time to time, unions of city-states for parts or the whole of Europe. For centuries, emperors, kings, feudal lords, theologians, artists, and many common people vainly yearned for unity among the divided and, in many cases, belligerent nations of Europe. Writers and philosophers, such as Victor Hugo during the 1850s and Voltaire and Goethe before him, as well as Edward Kine and Andreas Rigopoulos, dreamed about a united Europe. Michelangelo, Rembrandt, and Reubens contemplated in their paintings a peaceful and prosperous united continent. Handel, Beethoven, Mozart, Wagner, and other composers advocated a harmonious and unified Europe, while Dante Alighieri, centuries before them (1300), supported the creation of a peaceful nation to engulf the whole of Europe. Although centuries have passed and unified Europe remains largely a dream, the near future may prove that this dream will become a reality. Victor Hugo once commented that a day will come when all nations of Europe will merge into a higher society.[3]

Even before the Great Depression, Eurocrats, or "Euroenthusiasts" such as Aristide Briand, the French Foreign Minister, proposed the creation of a United States of Europe to the League of Nations. His effort to unify Europe by peaceful means was interrupted by World War II, a war that can be characterized as a European civil war, as was World War I. After the bombing raids were over and animosity and hatred had been buried in the rubble, the centuries-old dream of the peaceful unity of Europe started slowly but surely to become reality. The hope is to create a multinational democratic community with a free flow of goods, people, and information, as well as a mutual and free exchange of ideas and culture.

The variety of European peoples with their different cultures and habits presents problems for a rapid movement of integration. Italians are considered to have a great respect for obscurity, while the French seem to be brittle and afraid of the future, with some degree of xenophobia and civilizing hypocrisy. On the other hand, the British are regarded as being preoccupied with a sense of economic and spiritual decline, while the Germans think about economic expansion.[4] Spain, Greece (Hellas), and Portugal, as less developed members of the European Union, as well as the Eastern European countries, which have only recently come out of long and painful dictatorships, try to catch up economically and politically with the rest of the community. In all these countries, there is a strong spirit of a united Europe, a "Euromania," pushing for rapid economic and political development.

After World War I and particularly at the beginning of the Great Depression, totalitarian fascist governments came into power all over Europe. The Depression of the 1930s finally burned out in World War II from 1940 to 1945. Thereafter, many labor parties came to power in Western Europe and introduced reforms regarding the distribution of income, the extension of welfare services by the state, and nationalization, particularly of railroads, power, coal, and other heavy industries.

The vision of a community of prosperous and unified Western European democracies, formed some four decades ago, has been realized. The devastation of World War II and the American economic and defense assistance thereafter helped extensively in the formation and growth of the EU. In addition, the end of the Cold War and the new spirit of cooperation between the former Soviet bloc and the Western countries are important elements of peaceful coexistence, under which economic and political cooperation can flourish.

An important issue considered by NAFTA and EU at present is the growing need for further political cooperation. Such cooperation may speed up and stabilize the long-run unification of the Western Hemisphere countries and Europe and prove the saying that "Politics may turn influence into affluence." Although politicians, in their effort to improve society, are said to go "One step forward, two steps backward, and one step to the side," the expected benefits from economic partnerships are forcing them to support a closer political cooperation among the nations involved.

The creation of a new Europe without borders and a single currency, the Euro, is the sine qua non for peace and prosperity in the continent. Failure to achieve a single currency would be a terrible blow to the fifty-year efforts for European unity. It is necessary to remember the bloody history of Europe in the first half of the twentieth century. After World War II, Konrad Adenauer of Germany, Charles de Gaulle of France, and other leaders, struggled to create the European Union, which has grown to fifteen members, with ten applicant countries waiting to join it. Moreover, improved East–West relations are renewing the hope of overcoming divisions in the European continent and deepening transatlantic relations with the United States, Mexico, and Canada, as the European Council reaffirms.

From a practical standpoint, intergovernment cooperation to combat terrorism, drug trafficking, and international crime has gradually been promoted. In implementing the provisions of the integration agreements on the completion of the internal markets, environmental problems are also to be considered. They include such issues as soil depletion, water resources, toxic wastes, acid rain and other forms of air pollution, depletion of the ozone layer, the "greenhouse effect," and nuclear contamination.

The NATFA and EU integration programs present challenges and opportunities to companies, not only for the American and European markets but for world markets. These challenges and opportunities are not only in the field of exports but in direct and financial investment. However, the Americans and the Europeans are expected to honor bilateral and multilateral agreements. They should not discriminate against other companies, particularly those of Japan; that is, other firms should have the same opportunities to compete in the market for goods and services and to invest in these markets.

From an investment point of view, many American firms are expected to enter the European markets, and vice versa, in the foreseeable future— establishing new enterprises and expanding old ones. At the same time, international competition requires preeminence in business and world-class quality in product trading. Familiarity with the legal aspects of trade and investment regulations is also necessary. The bottom line in our growing global economy is more exports and investment to improve the welfare of the countries involved. From a competitive standpoint, the U.S. annual budget deficits and growing debts are depriving it of its economic leadership in the twenty-first century. Within a few years, Germany and Japan are expected to be strong economic powers.

National interests, in the context of a rapidly changing world, are gradually subordinated to a common regional and eventually global system in which narrow national goals must defer to the optimization of common goals. The growing interdependence of trading nations requires a shift from hierarchical decision making to negotiations among partners and from sanctions and subsidies to persuasion. From that standpoint, the United States and the other NAFTA nations should be constructively involved to stimulate the growth of interdependence of the European nations to promote financial stability and economic progress, and vice versa. They should strengthen multilateral arrangements by solving trade disputes and try to harmonize domestic policies that facilitate international competition.

Furthermore, the economic and political reforms and the new trade initiatives of the former Soviet Union and the Eastern European countries as well as other Central and Latin American countries create new challenges and opportunities for both the EU and NAFTA. Such structural economic reforms and political openness or democratization could lead to further cooperation and integration. Policymakers then must be alert to tap potential resources and exploit investment and trade opportunities in both blocs and provide needed facilities and available information to entrepreneurs and business venturers.

Nevertheless, NAFTA skeptics and Euro skeptics think that a premature federalism could lead to a nationalist backlash. There are still different nations with different languages, and a rush toward integration might lead to a dangerous growing power of the far right (e.g., in France, Austria, or Mexico). However, more trade liberalization within the member-nations is a positive alternative with benefits for all the people involved.

ECONOMIC POLICY PROBLEMS

Privatization for Deficit Reduction

The privatization of state-owned enterprises has become of great importance in the recent past and is a significant theme at the present time, not only in the countries of NAFTA and the EU, but also in the previously centrally-planned economies of the Eastern European countries, including Russia and the Balkans. Private ownership, which largely prevails in NAFTA and the EU, works better than common ownership because it stimulates work incentives and increases productivity. As Aristotle said, "It is clearly better that property should be private," and that "common ownership means common neglect." On the other hand, John Stuart Mill, Jean Jacques Rousseau, and Joseph Schumpeter believed that greater democratization of property ownership advances human intellect and increases efficiency.

The transfer of government-managed firms to the private sector on a large scale, as practiced in the Eastern European countries, is a *nova terra* which needs further exploration and research. Such transfer of ownership may take place by giving low-price vouchers to citizens to buy shares of state enterprises (a policy implemented mostly in the Czech and Slovak republics, Poland, and Russia) or by selling shares to the public or foreign investors, as practiced in Balkan countries (including Greece, a member of the EU, which is in the process of privatizing its large public sector). Partial or total ownership may be given to the workers or employees of enterprises, a measure that is similar to the employee stock ownership plans (ESOPs) of the United States and the EU and the share economy of Japan.

In previous years, nationalizations were popular, particularly in public utility industries. Even banks were nationalized in Mexico and other countries. At present, sales of publicly-owned assets, and methods of government disengagements in general, occur in a number of countries.

There is currently a trend toward privatization and employee ownership not only in Eastern Europe but in the NAFTA and EU countries, which may lead to the spread of property ownership to more and more individuals and the eventual support of the theory of "people's capitalism." This economic system avoids extreme wealth accumulation and monopolization by individuals or the state. It generates a broader distribution of wealth which helps the stability of the economy.

Privatization and employee ownership may not be an elixir that always works on performance. Individual shareholders may lack the necessary training to appoint managers or may be apathetic to or influenced by political gimmicks on serious matters of enterprise decision making. That is why the stakes given to employees are normally lower than the majority in each enterprise, while big investment companies or mutual funds keep majority controls.

Monetary Considerations

A further EU monetary and political union which may be the forerunner of NAFTA's union was introduced by the Maastricht Treaty, which was signed by the EU government heads on 9–10 December 1991, and the respective Ministers of Finance and Foreign Affairs on 7 February 1992. It provides for the European Monetary Union (EMU) and the political union of the member-nations with their people being citizens of the EU. It also provides for a common foreign and security policy and increases the powers of the European Parliament. After its final ratification by all EU members, the Maastricht Treaty has been in force from September 1993. It aims to establish a single currency (the Euro) and a central bank by 1999 at the latest, a far-reaching phase of European integration. As soon as the finance and budgetary reforms are completed, negotiations for membership with other candidates, particularly the new democracies of Eastern Europe, will begin.

The EU nations face an imminent surrender of much of their sovereignty. The introduction of a common currency, the Euro, and the control of fiscal and monetary policy by a European central bank would reduce the ability of national politicians to set economic policy. Although the Euro has been advanced in part to counter the perceived American domination of the global economy and to make a more united Europe less dependent on the United States, the EU lacks a powerful federal government, such as that of the United States, to redistribute resources and coordinate related policies. France, Germany, Italy, Spain, the United Kingdom, and the other EU members may operate now like California, Florida, and New York, but without a federal government to deal with EU–wide measures.

Some Euro skeptics think that Germany, with the largest gross domestic product (GDP) in the EU ($2.32 trillion) compared to other member-nations (France $1.51 trillion, Italy $1.19 trillion, Britain $1.10 trillion, Spain $0.59 trillion, The Netherlands $0.28 trillion, and less GDP for the other members), will dominate the EU.[5] Neighbors, notably in France and Italy, argue that the integration of Europe and the introduction of the Euro as a common currency will "Germanize" the EU, not unite it. Although German officials argue that the EMU is not a German Diktat, other Europeans suggest that Germany should be a shareholder in the EU, not chairman of the board.

Regional Integration and Protectionism

Although the free trade system, in which consumer is king, is beneficial in theory to all countries or groups of countries, it seems to be difficult in practice. In all countries, governments represent to a large extent domestic producers who try to maximize their markets. However, to export more they have to permit more imports, thereby making concessions to gain concessions and benefits from the free trade policies of respective governments. Nevertheless, producers organize into broader coalitions to protect themselves in the case of loss from foreign competition, fostering a drift toward protectionism.

Similar coalitions of interest groups, which also push toward protection, can be observed in common markets or free trade agreements such as the EU and NAFTA. Thus, protection through EU or NAFTA subsidies in agricultural products, aircraft industry, and other sectors, is a drift toward esoteric or regional protectionism and a deviation from the free trade principles of international economics. Such esoteric or inward-looking policies, as well as a faceless bureaucracy which has slowly developed in the EU, may be responsible for neglecting the chaotic problems in Eastern Europe and Russia, as well as the ethnic, religious, and economic conflicts in the former Yugoslavia and Albania.

The new wave of regional trading arrangements, or the new regionalism, is criticized for hindering the existing multilateral trading system. Such regional trading arrangements include the EU, NAFTA, and the Asian–Pacific Rim, the de facto trading bloc in East Asia under the leadership of Japan. In addition, the Enterprise for the Americas Initiative (EAI) has been launched by the United States for a free trade area to include all of the Americas. With the arrangements of NAFTA and EAI, the United States gradually is moving away from its commitment to multilateralism and its staunch support of the World Trade Organization (WTO).

It seems that the world is moving toward a tripolar arrangement centered around the EU, NAFTA, and the Asian–Pacific Rim. However, Japan, the main partner of the Asian–Pacific Rim, is not moving fast, because of its large stake in the markets of NAFTA. If these blocs are complimentary to multilateralism or internationalism, trade creation would be higher than trade diversion and total welfare of all countries would increase. If they are benign or turn inward to "fortress" blocs, trade diversion would be higher than trade creation and total welfare would decline.

To succeed in the strategy of closer integration, currently the EU concentrates on internal economic and sociopolitical matters at the neglect of enlargement. This is so because to enter more members at this stage would complicate matters regarding monetary and budgetary issues. Moreover, poorer member-nations (Greece, Ireland, Portugal, and Spain) would object to the acceptance of other equivalent or lower-income countries, such as those of Eastern Europe and Turkey, because of the expected shift in development assistance.

The EU agreements with other European partners provide for the removal of tariffs and other restrictions on trade by both parties, though sooner by the EU. Also, provisions for the free movement of capital, labor, financial support, social reforms, and technical and scientific cooperation are included. For the Baltic and Balkan countries, longer-term cooperation agreements for the removal of quotas and other restrictions by the EU, the acceptance of the most-favored nation status and other conditions, and the promotion of mutual trade and investment are considered. Furthermore, the EU maintains cooperative agreements with sixty-six African, Pacific, and Caribbean (APC) countries.

The radical economic reforms in Eastern Europe and the former Soviet Union offer great opportunities for EU enlargement and the eventual creation of a United States of Europe. The dissolution of the former Soviet Union and the end of the Cold War present fertile ground for further economic and geopolitical cooperation among the European countries, as well as the United States and Japan. Economic development and democratization in the Eastern European nations, Russia, and the Balkan states may eventually lead to the integration of the entire European continent.

ECONOMIC INTERDEPENDENCE

Stabilization Policies

During the years after World War II, the economies of the NAFTA and EU countries become slowly but surely interdependent. From time to time, destabilizing factors have led to turbulence in the forms of inflation, exchange rate disturbances, and financial instability. On both sides of the Atlantic, the dilemma now is how to achieve economic stability with high employment and no chronic inflation. Current economic theories, including the dominant monetarism and orthodox Keynesianism, as well as counter-cyclical fiscal and monetary policies, seem unable to mitigate or eliminate inherent instability, especially in financial markets. From that point of view, one of the main problems of the economies of NAFTA and the EU is how to avoid stagnation and inflation.

Western Europe, Japan, and the newly industrializing nations are formidable economic competitors of the United States and other NAFTA countries. They sell products to the relatively open American economy and accumulate trade surpluses that force the dollar down and undermine the dominance of the United States as the world's largest economy. However, the fact that these competitors need the American market gives the United States leverage to pursue a policy of making them accept greater responsibility for defense and to make their markets more accessible to American products.

At present, it is difficult for any nation to grow alone. Without international cooperation and competitive adjustment, economic growth on a national and global level will stagnate. At the same time, some of the unfair trade practices, such as export subsidies, import restrictions, and unfavorable government policies, should be altered. Also, the adjustment of wages to labor productivity should be made so that competitive costs and fair factor price payments among trade partners prevail.

The costs of a fragmented European market in the past were high, while the benefits from a unified European market in the future are expected to be significant. Healthier competition, business and professional mobility, economies of scale, job creation, improved productivity, and better consumer choices are the challenges Europe faces. The political and economic future of the EU and Eastern Europe could be of great importance to foreign trade, investment, and international finance. It is a historical challenge which will change the global economy forever—it will enhance Europe's role in the world and effect the redistribution of power in the twenty-first century.

The United States, along with other nations, awaits the outcome of a Europe gestating with different sociopolitical traditions and economic institutions. The eventual European monetary union, with a common currency and a central bank and a strong European Parliament (with perhaps a European government in Brussels) present new and complex problems for American and NAFTA economic and foreign policies.

Brussels, where the EU headquarters is located, is gradually growing in importance in dealing with individual states similar to Washington, D.C. in the United States. It is expected that it will achieve interventional powers over national budget deficits, monetary cooperation, and trade transactions. The role of Brussels seems to be particularly important at a time when Eastern Europe is in the midst of economic reforms and political upheaval. From that standpoint, Germany is expected to play a major role regarding developments in both Western and Eastern Europe. The anti-Brussels arguments of some conservatives—that the EU tends to be bureaucratic and socialist— exist in imagination rather than in reality. However, the formation of a federal EU government in Brussels is expected to be beneficial to NAFTA and other countries, in that they would have to deal with one economic and political unit rather than fifteen different governments.

For NAFTA and the world economy, now is a promising moment in history, as Western Europe moves toward integration and Eastern Europe attempts to implement drastic economic and political reforms. The EU is in a better position now to share responsibility for providing resources and leadership to rebuild the global economy. Although it is the main rival of the United States, it is at the same time its closest ally. The main U.S. strategic goals in the postwar years—the economic reconstruction of Western Europe and its political cooperation—seem to have largely been achieved and now a further genuine partnership can develop.

Through bilateral and multilateral arrangements, risks of protectionism can be avoided and the economic pooling of the EU member-nations may be considered as an opportunity rather than a threat. As Europe tries to be on its own, taking care of itself, it does not mean the rejection of NAFTA. It does mean some degree of independence and some distancing from U.S. and NAFTA interests, particularly on economic and financial management and self-defense issues—because for Europe, defense security, which results in continental insecurity, seems to help the dollar more than the European currencies. However, there are calls for burden-shifting, leadership-sharing, and trade and investment policies which promote more international competition and economic growth. Some politicians and economists, seeing the chronic American trade deficits and the growing foreign debt, unwisely ask for protection and a return to neo-isolationism.

To raise the rate of productivity, increase competitiveness, and improve the living standards of their populations, both NAFTA and the EU must collaborate closely to achieve external trade and payment equilibrium and to foster greater stability on monetary and exchange rate matters. The formation and development of regional economic groups, such as the EU and NAFTA, should be supported, as long as it does not raise new trade barriers with the outside world.

To avoid trade wars and to further liberalize world trade, NAFTA and the EU are moving toward successful compromises on disputes such as the sale of hormone-injected beef and the refusal to scale back and eliminate trade-distorting subsidies in agriculture. The EU has become America's largest trading partner, and further economic cooperation is necessary for the improvement of the welfare of peoples on both sides of the Atlantic. The spirit of accommodation and compromise in trade relations should also aim to end barriers in financial, tourist, accounting, and other services and to protect trademarks, patents, copyrights, and other intellectual property.

There seems to be two main trends in the EU concerning a more or less open market for NAFTA and other nations. France and Italy, where nationalistic and protectionist elements are strong, present pressures for less openness to trade with countries outside the EU. Article 115 of the EU treaty allows individual members to limit trade with non-EU countries, as the French and Italians have already done for their automobile industries. However, EU countries with advanced industries competing effectively in international markets, such as Germany and Britain, reject protectionism and support an EU market open to the rest of the world in accordance with the rules of the WTO, especially the Uruguay Round. In any case, many American and other foreign companies are locating operations into the EU, as EU firms do into NAFTA to avoid possible projectionist measures in the future, such as those of Italy limiting Japanese automobile imports. Already there is skepticism that national quotas will be used as NAFTA or EU quotas, and the trend toward establishing protectionist regional trade blocs may intensify, to the detriment of free trade.

The immediate problem for NAFTA is the impact of the continental-size market of the EU on the NAFTA firms doing business in Europe. More specifically for NAFTA, the examination of business options available is critical regarding country-by-country or pan-European entry, joint ventures, and acquisitions. Furthermore, competitive assessment of various business sectors is needed for strengthening a strategic foothold in Europe in such industries as electronics, chemicals, telecommunications, computers and software, consumer products, and financial services. The same problem exists with EU firms doing business in NAFTA and involved in joint ventures and acquisitions.

International Position

As a result of the growing external debt, the volume of foreign assets in the United States exceeds that of U.S. assets abroad by more than one-half trillion dollars. However, U.S. assets in Europe were acquired primarily in the 1950s and 1960s at relatively low prices, whereas foreign assets in the United States were mostly acquired in the 1980s and recent years at high nominal prices. The evaluation of such assets shows how purchasing prices are partially responsible for the large net debt of the United States to the EU and other countries. Hence, the difference in the US. debt position may be smaller than it appears, in that the difference between the inflow and outflow of earnings every year is not as significant as statistical data indicate. Foreign assets in the other NAFTA countries (i.e., Canada and Mexico) and vice versa are not as significant in size as in the United States.

Nevertheless, continuation of trade deficits and growing external debt would result in a loss in the competitive position of the United States and a reduction in living standards for years to come. Regardless of the accounting gimmicks, the United States and the other NAFTA countries can rejuvenate their economy by better exploiting their vast resources and markets as well as their leverage throughout the world. At the same time, U.S. allies, particularly Japan, Germany, and other strong EU economies with trade surpluses, should be partially responsible in regard to defense, so that American rambo-style policies and the massive global burden of military expenditures can be reduced. Meanwhile, the NAFTA foreign economic policy should be redefined and unrealistic expectations should be changed to enable EU policies to be geared toward American steadiness and economic relevance. It seems that the main economic problem of the United States is not so much the trade deficit or the unwillingness of foreigners to treat it fairly, but rather the failure to invest in collective productivity and add value to the national and international economies, instead of borrowing for consumption. The United States borrowed heavily from Europe in the nineteenth century, but these loans were invested in railroads, factories, oil wells, inventions, and other productive assets. Now, the United States is consuming its way into economic oblivion.[6]

Europe is taking a historic step—it deserves support from other nations, especially the United States. Eventually, the European Common Market will become the largest integrated economy. The EU countries are recovering from the symptoms of nationalistic superiority and the sickness of Eurosclerosis and are moving gradually toward closer cooperation and eventual unification. They are trying to revive the unifying aspirations that emerged from World War II. The lesson of success of the United States of America may lead them to the formation of the United States of Europe.[7] The community of fifteen European democracies is winning a fine victory over national egoism and prejudice without much cost. It is moving from a bitter past to a better future, and the United States is expected to play a vital role in this movement as it has done in the past. Likewise, the Eastern European countries recently introduced drastic reforms to create a freer market and are preparing their economies for a closer cooperation and (why not?) a possible integration with the EU. Strategic regional expansion is expected to deliver new alliances and new partnerships through investment, joint ventures, and currency exchanges.

There seems to be a technological war among the Asian group (Japan, Taiwan, South Korea, and Hong Kong), the European group (the EU and probably the Eastern European countries), and the North American group (the United States, Mexico, and Canada). Each group is preparing its own economic bloc to face competition from the other groups. The key areas to improve technology and to increase productivity are research, industrial innovations, and advancements in education. From that standpoint, there is an outcry that the United States is becoming a nation of highly intelligent machines but ignorant people.

OVERVIEW

The potential effects of the integration of Canada, Mexico, and the United States, and the union of Western Europe at the onset of the rapid opening of Eastern Europe and Russia, are expected to "dramatically" change global economic, as well as political and cultural, relations. The removal of technical, monetary, and trade barriers within NAFTA and the EU and the liberalization of the economies of the Eastern European countries, including those of the Balkan peninsula and Russia, create challenges and opportunities from the standpoint of trade, investment, and economic growth. However, as NAFTA and the EU move toward closer economic and political integration, the question is whether these blocs will eliminate internal barriers only to create larger barriers around them.

The vision of unified and prosperous NAFTA and EU democracies, ready to face the growing competition between them and the Asian–Pacific Rim, can be realized through the enlargement and eventual integration of their neighboring nations.

The new trends toward privatization and democratization of property ownership in the economies of NAFTA and the EU and other neighboring countries facilitate the process of integration. Such measures of privatization, as well as employee participation and capital–labor co-management, prevail in almost all NAFTA and EU countries. Such economic organizations help stimulate further expansion and integration.

For more trade and investment in the Western Hemisphere, Caribbean and other Latin American countries should be incorporated into NAFTA, first as associates and eventually full members. The pursuit of such a policy would encourage the people of these countries to demand rapid changes toward democracy and economic progress.

The gradual enlargement of the EU, incorporating the developed nations of Western Europe and the less developed nations of southern and eventually eastern Europe, can be used as a successful example of closer cooperation and eventual integration of the Americas.

In our era of tripolar competition (EU, NAFTA, and the Asian–Pacific Rim), NAFTA should consider trade and investment expansion with neighboring countries, notably the Caribbean, the Central American, and eventually the Latin American countries. It is time the EAI take concrete measures to implement a policy of closer cooperation with the Caribbean and other EAI countries for mutual trade and development.

This study weaves together a historical framework with comparative case studies of NAFTA and EU member-nations. The result is an insightful analysis of how the interplay between politics and economics sets the stage for the dramatic events to come in the 1990s, and perhaps the twenty-first century. From that standpoint, this study is of great theoretical and practical use to students and scholars with a broad range of interests in the American and the European continents.

The following chapters focus primarily on the comparative issues common to the industrial societies on both sides of the Atlantic, as well as the main differences regarding economic policies, trade, joint ventures, and development trends between NAFTA and the common market of Western Europe.

Chapter 2

NAFTA

On 12 August 1992, the United States, Canada, and Mexico agreed on a plan for free trade that would gradually eliminate tariffs over fifteen years and stimulate trade and investment. While protecting the 1988 free trade agreement between the United States and Canada, this new agreement created the largest common market in total production, with 370 million consumers. It makes U.S. and Canadian industries more competitive by using low-cost Mexican labor, advanced U.S. technology, and rich Canadian resources.

Nevertheless, American labor unions and politicians argued that many American jobs will be lost, mainly in the automobile and textile industries. Japanese and European companies are also expected to manufacture goods in Mexico and ship them to the United States. Although it is estimated that about 100,000 jobs will be lost in industries displaced by imports, 300,000 new jobs are expected to be created in the exporting industries of the United States. Nevertheless, the net effects of NAFTA on jobs so far are negligible (about 30,000 jobs have been created and the same numbers eliminated from the beginning of 1994 until now).

A serious question regarding the effects of NAFTA on the American economy remains. What will the series of jolts on labor be, particularly during the first stages of the implementation of the agreement? The tasks of reconciling modern technology and economic integration press against many traditional jobs, especially in manufacturing. Instead of pandering to protectionist forces regarding trade and investment with Mexico, the United States and Canada should encourage a reduction in the population explosion in both Mexico and the other low-income countries that are expected to join NAFTA, as long as real economic growth remains low.

A gradual reduction of the demographic imbalances between the rich societies of North America and the poor and overpopulated societies of Mexico and the neighboring Central American countries that may join NAFTA in years to come would help the smooth integration of the economies of these nations. Moreover, the pressure from the more than one million illegal Mexican immigrants who stream across the Rio Grande every year would be reduced. In the meantime, the United States and Canada should introduce apprenticeship and retraining programs, similar to those of Germany and Sweden, to raise the skills of their workers and adjust them to the rapidly changing technology around the world. Such retraining should emphasize industries and services with extensive forward and backward linkages, in an unbalanced growth fashion, including computers, the use of robots in assembly plants, biotechnology, food processing, futures trading, and other financial and investment services.

There is strong criticism against NAFTA from politicians and economists, mainly in the United States. The main argument is that low wages in Mexico will send American jobs south because Mexican wages in manufacturing are about one-fifth of those in the United States. Moreover, under NAFTA, the flow of U.S. companies moving to Mexico could become a flood, particularly for American firms that assemble products in Mexico for duty-free exports back to the United States under the *Maquiladora* program.

The large difference in wages, though, may be balanced by the difference in productivity. It is estimated that American productivity is about five times that of Mexico. Furthermore, NAFTA would modify or abolish the advantages of the *Maquiladora* duty-free exports into the United States. It is expected that the average income of the Mexicans will increase as a result of NAFTA and that more American exports will flow into Mexico. It seems that even without NAFTA, American companies would continue to flow into Mexico because of cheaper wages and other advantages.

Minimum wages in Mexico are about $4.60 per day, compared to $5.15 per hour in the United States. Some 90 percent of workers are paid two to three times this minimum, or from $9.00 to $16.00 per day in Mexico. As the author of this book observed during a research trip to Mexico, workers in hotels and similar industries are paid on the average about $7.00 to $8.00 per day. According to the Labor Congress of Mexico, fifty-eight million persons live under poverty conditions. It is estimated that wages are expected to rise by 300 percent to meet the cost of living expenses.

Because of the big differences in wages, many factory jobs have moved to Mexico since NAFTA took effect, and the trend is expected to continue. For example, Key Tronic Corporation, a manufacturer of computer keyboards, moved about 300 jobs to Ciudad Juarez in Mexico where wages are one-fourth of those in its plant in Washington, D.C. As a result, sales increased because Key Tronic could lower prices to compete with Japanese manufacturers. At the same time, additional jobs were created not only in the Mexican plant but also in the Washington plant. Because of NAFTA, the company moved its manufacturing unit to Mexico instead of considering a low-wage Asian country. From that standpoint, corporate efficiency should also be considered in the measurement of NAFTA's effects.

Mexico joined the General Agreement of Tariffs and Trade (GATT)—now the WTO—in 1986. Mexico is also the third largest trading partner of the United States, whereas the United States absorbs the largest amount of Mexican exports. Trade between the two countries has more than doubled in recent years and is expected to increase even more in the future.

NAFTA, in conformity with WTO rules, will eliminate tariffs over a transition period. For import-sensitive U.S. industries, tariffs will be eliminated in ten years, and for particularly sensitive sectors, in as many as fifteen years from 1993. With NAFTA, half the Mexican tariffs on U.S. automobiles and light trucks were cut immediately and on three-quarters of parts within five years from the agreement. It is required that the imported vehicles in Mexico be 62.5 percent North American in content to benefit from tariff cuts. About 65 percent of Mexican imports from the United States were to be eligible for tariff cuts within five years. For about one-third of U.S. textile exports to Mexico, trade barriers were to be eliminated immediately, and for the rest within six years from 1993. Investment restrictions on telecommunications were to be eliminated by July 1995 and on banking and securities subsidiaries and financial services by 2000.

CANADA

A Brief Historical Review

Historically, Norsemen were the first Europeans to reach the shores of North America some five hundred years before Columbus, setting out to discover India, and founding the islands in the Caribbean Sea. From the Norse colonies in Iceland and Greenland, a mariner, Leif Ericson, landed in North America in A.D. 1000 in a region he called *Vinland*, probably on the coast of present-day Canada. Thereafter, John Cabot (of whom there is authentic record), another fellow Genoese of Columbus, persuaded King Henry of England to provide a ship and crew for a voyage westward. He reached Newfoundland in June 1497, and thereafter sailed from Europe again and again.[1]

In 1534, the French government commissioned Jacques Cartier to find a northwestern passage to Asia but, guided by fishermen's reports, he reached present-day Belle Isle Strait and later the Gulf of St. Lawrence. France dispatched more expeditions and granted a monopoly of the fur trade to members of the Cartier family in 1588, designating the discovered region *New France*. Later, fur monopoly rights were given to Sieur de Monts in 1608, who was helped by the French naval officer, Samuel de Champlain, and both the fur trade and the French colonies expanded. From 1615 onward, Franciscan missionaries arrived in Quebec and started to Christianize the Indians. In 1629, a relentless struggle commenced between Britain and France for possession of the Canadian territories. At that time and later, the feudalistic economic system, similar to that in France, prevailed in the region. Noblemen (*seigneurs*) had large tracts of land which were distributed to the common people (*habitants* or *censitaires*) in return for annual rentals of money, produce, or feudal services.

In 1672, Comte de Frontenac, governor of New France, and the explorer, Sieur de la Salle, discovered the Mississippi River, and in 1682 the entire Mississippi valley was claimed by France. After the prolonged struggle between the Anglo–Americans and the French and their allies, the Indians, the entire French domain on the North American mainland was ceded to Great Britain (Treaty of Paris, 1763) with the exception of territories west of the Mississippi and New Oreleans that had previously been ceded to Spain. The Quebec Act, enacted by the British Parliament in 1774, granted the safeguard of Catholics and other concessions to the French Canadians.[2]

Until the end of the eighteenth century, Canada was governed under the rivalries of France and Britain. After 1783, the country was influenced by its imposing neighbor, the United States, to the degree that Canadians used to say they felt as though they were sleeping in the same bed with an elephant. To a large extent, they still share the same sentiment. With the outbreak of the American Revolution, American troops captured Montreal in November 1775; but after their defeat at Quebec City on 31 December, they withdrew into New York State. In 1783, Canadian territories were ceded by Great Britain to the United States, including Wisconsin, Michigan, Ohio, Indiana, and Illinois.

After the French Revolution and during the Napoleonic Wars, British possessions in North America were not in danger as long as Britain had command of the sea and the United States remained neutral.[3] In 1854, the national legislation of Canada secularized the land reserves of the Anglican Church and abolished the seigniorial tenures.

Canada made significant contributions to the British war effort during World War I, dispatching 400,000 men overseas and suffering severe losses, with 210,000 casualties and 51,700 men killed. This accelerated Canada's progress toward full nationhood, and in 1931 it attained equal status in the British Commonwealth. The catastrophic stock market crash of 1929 affected Canadian foreign trade, mainly exports of grain and raw materials. The increase in tariffs in 1931, in retaliation for high tariffs in the United States, reduced Canadian imports and exports further. However, a treaty with the United States in 1932 concerning the projected St. Lawrence River waterway improved Canadian–American relations. Further development occurred with the reciprocity agreement of 1935, which revived trade between the two nations. This shows that cooperation agreements, such as the Cooperation Agreement of 1989 and NAFTA of 1993, help improve economic conditions for both Canada and the United States.

Canada's contributions to the Allies cause during World War II were impressive, both economically and militarily. Of Canada's 750,000 manned armed forces, there were 101,538 casualties and 37,476 men killed. In 1951, a Canadian brigade was assigned to duty in Europe with the NATO army. In 1954, the U.S. Congress approved the construction of the St. Lawrence Seaway and Power Project in joint efforts with Canada, which helped the economies of both countries and provided electricity to New York State.

Location and Resources

Atop the Western Hemisphere, Canada, a brooding geographic colossus, ranks third in area (after Russia and China) among the nations of the world. Officially known as the Dominion of Canada, it is the largest member of the Commonwealth of Nations. It is bound on the north by the Arctic Ocean, on the east by the Atlantic Ocean, and on the northeast by the Baffin Bay and the Davis Strait, which separate the mainland from Greenland. On the south it is bounded by the United States, and on the west by the Pacific Ocean and Alaska. With a total land area of 3,619,616 square miles, Canada has many islands, lakes (including the Great Lakes on the U.S. border), and rivers (including the St. Lawrence). Its population in 1995 was twenty-seven million. About three-quarters of Canadians inhabit a narrow belt along the U.S. frontier, mainly in Southern Quebec and Ontario.

Canada is comprised of ten provinces, each with its own parliament and administration in a federal system similar to that of the United States, and the Yukon Territory and the Northwest Territory, which are governed by commissioners assisted by councils. Ontario, Quebec, British Columbia, and Alberta are the most populated provinces. The other six provinces are Saskatchewan, Manitoba, Nova Scotia, New Brunswick, Newfoundland, and Prince Edward Island. The largest cities are Montreal (in Quebec), Toronto (in Ontario), and Vancouver (in British Columbia). Ottawa (in Ontario) is Canada's capital.

Canada, an Indian word meaning town, which appeared in the sixteenth century to describe the first French settlers along the north shore of the St. Lawrence River, is a geographically impossible and politically ridiculous country, as a prime minister once observed. It has been characterized as a manless land with landless men. The province of Quebec, which emerged after 1867, has maintained a French culture for over three hundred years. Its inhabitants are determined to survive as a distinct cultural enclave in a chiefly English-speaking continent, as they are suspicious of what they call English imperialism.[4]

Manufacturing industries, mainly foods and beverages, iron and steel, and wood and paper products, as well as exported goods, depend primarily on the raw materials supplied by domestic agriculture, mining, fishing, and forestry. Wheat, oats, other grains, and livestock are the main agricultural products.

Mineral and metal production comprise gold, platinum, copper, nickel, and other nonmetallics, including asbestos, coal, oil, and natural gas.

From the sixteenth century onward, the main Canadian exports were fur, fish, and forest products. More than one-third of Canada's land area consists of great forests. Recently, wheat and other grains, metals, and timber and other forest products have been the chief exports. Canada has the largest per capita export trade in the world, primarily with the United States. As John F. Kennedy said in a speech to Canadians, "geography made us neighbors, history made us friends, and economics made us partners."[5]

Economic Characteristics

Canada, the largest country in the Western Hemisphere, has a mix of private and government ownership, including federal and provincial. From that standpoint, it followed the British system, with a relatively large public sector, and the U.S. system, with a large private sector but extensive regulations. However, as a result of NAFTA, Canada is in the process of privatizing many public sector enterprises. Although it is considered as a mouse living next to an elephant, Canada is gradually merging its economy with the United States to exploit more efficiently its natural resources and to enjoy the huge market next to its borders.

Based on its peculiar political and geographic characteristics, Canada established or acquired a number of public enterprises (Crown corporations) so that a balance between the public and the private sector would be maintained. Thus, the Canadian Broadcasting Corporation was set up in 1932 for a nationwide service; Air Canada was established in 1937 to provide coast-to-coast air services; and Canada Mortgage and Housing Corporation was formed in 1948 to help finance housing, mainly for veterans. Also, the government used ownership to revitalize some key industries such as the Canadian National Railway (1919), the Cape Breton Development Corporation (1967), Canadair (1976), Fishery Products International, and National Sea Products (early 1980s). There are currently fifty-three parent Crown corporations with 169,000 employees and assets of about $58 billion. Moreover, there are some 233 provincial state firms, mainly in public utilities.

MEXICO

Historical Trends

The advanced culture of the Mayas, who inhabited Mexico during the first millennium B.C., attained its acme about the 6th century A.D. Thereafter, the Toltecs, another Indian group that migrated from the north during the early centuries of the Christian era, and later the Chichimecas, who dispersed the Toltecs, developed a great civilization until the fifteenth century, when the

Aztecs or Mexica, probably from the areas of present New Mexico and Arizona, achieved great political, social, and economic power, with corn as their main agricultural product.

In 1519 Hernando Cortes commanded a large force sent to Mexico by the governor of Cuba (which was governed under Spain at that time), and the Aztec capital fell to the Spaniards. In 1535 the colonial government was established with the appointment of Antonio de Mendoza (the first Spanish viceroy) and until 1821, Mexico was a colony of Spain.[6] Mendoza and some sixty successor viceroys expanded the area of New Spain to incorporate California, Texas, and New Mexico.

Florida also was largely under Spain until 1821. In March 1513, through an expedition led by Ponce de Leon, the Spanish Governor of Puerto Rico, the Spaniards established a settlement in a region which de Leon named La Florida, in recognition of its luxurious vegetation. In later expeditions and in conflicts with natives as well as French and British adventurers (mainly in St. Augustine), the Spaniards maintained their foothold in Florida. In 1763, Spain ceded Florida to Great Britain (Treaty of Paris), and in return the British evacuated Havana. But after twenty years, the British ceded Florida back to Spain in exchange for the Bahamas. In 1821, Spain ceded Florida to the United States in exchange for $5 million.

Many Indians were killed, and the rest, still a large majority of the population, continued to live in a feudalistic manner (*repartimiento* system) on tracts that were granted to nobles, soldiers, and the Roman Catholic Church. The Church became wealthy, holding about one-third of all property and land until its nationalization in 1859. The well-to-do prelates used to live in luxury, whereas the priests working in the Indian villages lived under poverty conditions, as did the Indians.[7]

Class distinction, corruption in the colonial administration, and the liberal ideas instigated by the French Revolution of 1789 generated periodic revolutions and weakened the link between colony and mother country. In July 1821, Mexico became independent (Treaty of Cordoba). Thereafter, a struggle mainly between rich conservatives (Centralists) and poor liberals (Federalists) continued. Because of friction between U.S. citizens and Mexicans, Texas rebelled and declared independence in 1836, and the United States declared war against Mexico. In 1847, a U.S. army occupied northern Mexico and Mexico City. On 21 February 1848, the Treaty of Guadalupe Hidalgo established the boundary of Rio Grande, and California and New Mexico became part of the United States.

As a result of the struggle between conservatives and liberals, from 1854 onward Benito Juarez, an Indian and great democratic leader of Mexico, emerged and influenced Mexican politics for many years. His government was supported by the United States. He introduced civil liberties, nationalized Church property, and suspended interest payments on foreign debt—a measure which led to a joint intervention of Britain, France, and Spain (1861–1863) and the arrangement of the debt repayment.

After a revolt in 1877, Porfirio Diaz became president and established a dictatorship that lasted until 1911. Under his rule, industrial plants, railroads, and other public works were established and foreign investment increased. Because he favored the rich by assigning them communal lands which belonged to the Indians, the spirit of revolt increased and a liberal president, Francisco Madero was elected in 1811. He was not a forceful leader, and rebel leaders such as Emiliano Zapata and Pancho Villa refused to obey. In 1913, Victoriano Huerta, the chief of Madero's army, seized control and killed Madero. New revolts were begun by Zapata, Villa, and Venustiano Carranza, who became president until 1920. Carranza introduced a new constitution in 1917, which provided for an eight-hour day, minimum wages, expropriation of all property of religious orders, restoration to the Indians of their communal lands, and limits on foreign ownership of land and mineral properties, including oil resources for which a tax was imposed. In a conflict with three leading generals, Carranza was killed and Alvaro Obregon was elected president in 1920. Obregon, Plutarco Elias Calles, and other presidents negotiated and arranged disputes with U.S. oil companies.

In 1932, the National Revolutionary Party (PRM) was in power, and put forward a six-year reform program which was put into effect in 1934 by President Lazaro Cardenas, detailing a cooperative economic system with distribution of land, public works, and seizure of foreign-owned oil lands. The National Railways of Mexico were nationalized in 1937 and properties of oil companies were expropriated in 1938. Because the sale of oil to the United States became difficult, Mexico turned to Germany, Italy, and Japan. However, with the outbreak of World War II, cooperation with the United States increased not only in trade but in military matters as well, including the use of Mexican airfields. After the sinking of two of its ships, Mexico declared war on Germany, Italy, and Japan in May 1942. Mutual tariff reductions and increases in trade developed with the United States, particularly after U.S. President Franklin D. Roosevelt visited Mexico in April 1943. In 1944, Mexico agreed to pay U.S. oil companies $24 million, plus 3 percent interest, for the oil properties that were expropriated in 1938. With the opening of the Falcon Dam and power plants on the Rio Grande on 19 October 1953, economic cooperation improved.

A serious problem existed, and still exists, with the seasonal farm workers from Mexico who illegally enter the United States by swimming the Rio Grande (*wetbacks*). This problem becomes less and less important with the provisions of NAFTA.

The Mexican *Ejidos*

In the Mexican countryside, a system of common ownership by groups (*calpulli*), usually with family ties, prevailed as early as the beginning of the sixteenth century when Spain conquered the Aztecs. Thereafter, concentration of private land ownership occurred, particularly during the period 1876–1910, and mostly under the presidency of Porfirio Diaz. After the Mexican Revolution, the First Agrarian Reform Act of 1915 created the common property system of *ejidos*, which resurged updated in 1922 and 1934 as well as during the 1960s and 1970s.

The *ejido*, a form of land tenure arrangement, is managed by elected persons: a president, secretary, and several council members. In this peculiar system of common property in agriculture, individual farmers are assigned small parcels of land for cultivation, but grazing areas are held in common. The *ejido*, as a legal entity, is the owner of the land. Some 40 percent of the agricultural land in Mexico is controlled by the *ejidos* and about 10 percent by other community groups (*comunidades*). Some *ejidos* have more than 1,000 members and control about 300,000 hectares; others have about 50 members and control about 100 hectares. Nevertheless, productivity in these common-owned lands is lower, varying from 30 to 50 percent of private farms, mainly because "common ownership means common neglect," as Aristotle said some twenty-five centuries ago. This has resulted in a movement toward privatization of the lands which belong to *ejidos* and *comunidades*, together with the privatization of the industrial and financial sectors of the Mexican economy. Moreover, such legal entities with common ownership do not internalize external cost and have no incentive to conserve resources. The result is the overgrazing and degradation of land.

Socioeconomic Changes

Mexico has recently privatized many state firms, including Aeromexico and Mexicana, reducing huge budget deficits and inflation and thereby somewhat stabilizing the economy.

From a socioeconomic standpoint, Mexico has had a turbulent history. Its population is composed of three main racial groups: white, Indian, and Mestizo (a mixture of the two groups and about 60% of the population). The Indians, who live primarily in South Mexico, are about 30 percent of the population (a sizable decline from 62 percent in 1900), and the whites (mainly of Spanish descent) and Negros comprise the remaining 10 percent. The old distinction of high-class whites born in Spain, *peninsulares*, and lower-class whites born in New Spain, *criollos*, or Creoles, gradually lost relevance to the current population.

After the conquest of Mexico by Spain in the sixteenth century, Spanish became the official language, and a large number of the more than 200 Indian dialects have become extinct. Illiteracy was at about 54 percent in 1940, but decreased to 30 percent in 1950, and even more thereafter. This means that, from an educational standpoint, adjustment to the commitments of NAFTA would not be difficult. An amendment to the constitution of 1917, ratified in 1953, gave women suffrage rights equal to those of men.

The political system of Mexico is more or less similar to that of the United States. The president is elected for six years by popular vote, and appoints his Cabinet, which is confirmed by the Congress. The Senate, or the Upper House, of 60 members, is elected for six years, and the Chamber of Deputies, or Lower House, of 161 members, is elected for three years. The governors are appointed by the president. The president, senators, and deputies are not immediately eligible for reelection. Unrestricted immigration from the Western Hemisphere, Spain, and the Philippines is permitted, though quotas exist for most European countries. However, immigration laws are expected to change as a result of NAFTA.

Mexico, which lies within the tropics and subtropics, is bounded by the United States on the north, the Pacific Ocean on the west, Guatemala and Belize on the south, and the Gulf of Mexico and the Caribbean Sea on the east. About one-fourth of the United States in size, it is the third largest country in Latin America with close to two million square kilometers.

About two-thirds of the population of Mexico (93 million in mid-1994) are of mixed Indian and Spanish descent (mestizos), and 96 percent of the people are Catholic. Family ties are strong and large families are most desirable. Average annual growth of population declined from 3.1 percent during the period from 1965 to 1980 to recently around 2.0 percent. However, the World Bank estimates that the population of Mexico will be 103 million by the year 2000.

The Mexican economy is more or less a mixed economy, also similar to that of the United States. Although the government participation in total output accounts for about 10 percent, a number of vital industries belong to the government, including petroleum, electric power, railroads, telecommunications, and some banks and warehouse facilities. In addition to petroleum and natural gas, important products are iron and steel, petrochemicals, glass, copper, and other mining products. Tourism is also an important industry from the standpoint of foreign revenue and seasonal employment.

The Mexican Constitution, which was adopted in 1917, provides for a Federal Republic which includes thirty-one states and a Federal District, where the capital, Mexico City, is located. Mexico entered the Organization of American States in 1980.

The rate of inflation in 1989 was 19.7 percent compared to 29.9 percent in 1990. It dropped to 11.9 percent in 1992 (the lowest in seventeen years) and continued to decline thereafter. Government revenue increased from 177.6 billion pesos in 1991 to 217.7 billion in 1993. As a result of NAFTA, fiscal policy measures have been taken to reduce the public sector and to lower inflation.

New economic reforms dealing with labor markets and the social security system, as well as further privatizations in the energy, transportation, communications, and other sectors, would help stabilize the peso and stimulate the economy.[8]

The international aid package of $50 billion, $20 billion of which came from the United States and about $18 billion from the International Monetary Fund (IMF), was used in 1994 to restore the confidence of foreign investors to continue their investment in the country. Mexico used part of this assistance (about $16 billion) to refinance and retire part of the $21.5 billion debt in outstanding dollar-linked securities (*tesobonos*). The debt of Mexico to the United States was paid in full in January 1997.

Although there was some skepticism regarding the instability of the Mexican economy as a result of the peso crisis in December 1994 and later, American companies such as General Electric, Farah, Allied Signal, and many others continue to invest and shift jobs to Mexico. An important reason for this trend is the low labor cost in dollars, mainly because of the sizable devaluation of the Mexican currency from 3 pesos to around 8 pesos per dollar. Such investment by U.S. companies in Mexico, which reached $3.3 billion in 1993, is expected to increase significantly in the future.

The main themes of current Mexican policies are free market reforms through privatization of state enterprises, adjustment to NAFTA commitments, and a more equitable income distribution. The expected new president, Luis Donaldo Colosio Murrieta, a forty-four-year-old U.S. trained economist and an activist of the ruling Institutional Revolutionary Party (PRI), which has been in power for decades, has proclaimed continuation of the reform program initiated by Carlos Salinas de Gortari, the Mexican president from 1988 to 1994, with emphasis on social programs for Mexico's poor villages (*pueblos*). The other main parties are the left-leaning Democratic Revolutionary Party (PRD), headed by Cuauhtemoc Cardenas Solorzano (the son of President Lazaro Cardenas who nationalized the oil industry of Mexico in the 1930s), and the centrist National Action Party (PAN), both of which put priority on social programs to lift millions of Mexicans out of poverty. Under the Salinas's government, the share of national wealth of the richest 10 percent of the population increased from 33 to 41.4 percent, whereas that of the poorest 40 percent declined from 15 to 12.3 percent.[9] As the writer of this book observed in his recent research trip to Mexico, there is a great difference between the rich tourist seashores and the inner provinces where very poor but very polite people live.

UNITED STATES

Colonial Times

Since America was discovered by Columbus in 1492, the Western Hemisphere has gone through many turbulent periods. However, through hard work and development, the United States has reached the status of being the most powerful economy in the world. Parochialism and economic groupings were prevalent during the colonial period. Sectionalism and division could be observed not only between individual colonies but also between the coastline and the interior, as well as between the North and the South, primarily up to the American Revolution (1776). There were the mainly British colonial aristocrats (landlords, merchants, and slave owners) with economic and political power, and the small farmers and poor people in the back country who paid relatively more taxes and other fees. They were the debtors to the creditor of the Eastern seaboard commercial establishment. Taxation was levied primarily on persons, not on property.

For years American patriots were engaged in a difficult war of independence from the British colonists, especially after the Declaration of Independence on 4 July 1776. Help came from France with an alliance in 1778. The war climaxed in 1781 when over 5,000 French soldiers with 9,000 American patriots under the command of George Washington besieged Yorktown, Virginia, and forced the surrender of the British troops and the loyalists under the command of General Charles Cornwallis. As a result, England acknowledged the independence of the thirteen states (Treaty of Paris, 1783) with the Great Lakes as a northern boundary and the Mississippi River as the western boundary, while Florida, on the southern boundary, was returned by England to Spain. The rest of the present-day United States, with the exception of an unexplored part in the Northwest, belonged to Spain at that time, as did Mexico and other Central and South American countries.

With the termination of the Anglo–American war in 1783, the estates of the loyalists were confiscated and land was redistributed. Recent research, however, indicates only slight effects on the economy from redistributed loyalist estates. More important were the vast lands the new nation obtained from the peace treaty of 1783. This national domain played a major role in American economic and political developments (notably in the Homestead Act of 1862) regarding religious freedom, the separation of church and state, and commercial expansion. Wages were determined primarily by the supply of and demand for labor, while the constant flow of immigration delayed the growth of labor movements for many decades.[10]

In 1803, under Thomas Jefferson's presidency, the United States purchased the vast area of Louisiana west of the Mississippi from France for $11.25 million, an area which Spain gave to France under the pressure of the powerful Napoleon Bonaparte in 1801.[11] In 1819, Spain sold Florida to the United States, and Mexico won independence from Spain in 1821, the same year of the Greek (Hellenic) revolution against the Ottoman Turks with the moral support of the United States and other countries. Texas, which had revolted from Mexico in 1836, was annexed by the United States in 1845, Oregon was divided with England in 1846, and a large area west of Texas and south of Oregon (California) was ceded by Mexico to the United States in 1848. In 1867, the United States purchased Alaska from Russia, got possession of the Samoan Islands in 1867, and annexed the Hawaiian Islands in 1898. At present, the United States is composed of fifty states and the District of Columbia.

Immigration from Europe

From the time of its discovery to the present day, the New World (America) has been populated mainly by immigration from Europe. The total number of foreign-born persons who came to the United States from 1790 to 1950 amounted to 106.4 million. The U.S. population increased from 3.9 million in 1790 to 5.3 million in 1800, and from around 76 million in 1900 to 150.7 million in 1950. At present the U.S. population is 264 million. Every time a census was conducted, it was found that some 7 to 15 percent of the population was foreign born, with 13 percent in 1790, about 15 percent in 1910, and 7 percent in 1950. The largest number of immigrants came in the decade of 1901–1910 (8.8 million), and the second largest followed from 1911 to 1920 (5.7 million).[12]

The main source of immigrants before 1890 was Northern and Western Europe, particularly from England, Ireland, and Germany. After 1890, Southern and Eastern Europe became the predominant source of the new wave of immigration, including Italy, Russia, Poland, Austria, Czechoslovakia, Hungary, and Greece (Hellas). Overpopulation, political or religious persecution and, at times, the avoidance of oppressive military service, as well as other depressive factors in Europe, were the main reasons for immigration across the Atlantic. American railway and shipping companies sent agents to Europe and subsidized fares to attract immigrants for the construction of railways, mining operations, and factory work in the rapidly growing cities. Also, before the Civil War (1861–1865), slave labor from Africa was used mainly on the plantations of the South. Mexico and Canada became additional sources of immigration after 1900. Mexico and other Central and South American countries are expected to continue to be the main source of immigration in the United States in the near future.

American workers, feeling the competitive pressure of cheap labor the flood of immigrants provided, opposed unrestricted immigration. As a result, Congress enacted legislation that prohibited employers from advertising in ways that stimulated immigration, and made immigration selective on grounds of nationality, with restrictions against undesirable aliens, such as criminals, prostitutes, and polygamists. Thus, the Chinese Exclusion Act was enacted in 1882. The emergency Quota Act, passed in 1921, permitted only a 3 percent immigration increase for each nationality. The quota system, as altered in a number of cases, prevailed until 1968. The main reasons for such restrictions were nativism, labor pressure, and the decline in the railroad industry due to the competition from shipping and particularly to the rapidly growing motor vehicle transportation of freight and passengers.

The influx of European capital, together with European workers and investors, helped the development of a large railroad industry, and the corporation form of business, which increased economic growth in the United States.

During the period between the Civil War and up to the end of World War I, railroad building boomed with a total mileage exceeding that of all of Europe. Afterward, because of unwise rail construction and overspeculation as well as new alternative means of transportation, many U.S. railways reached dismal conditions. Even today a number of railway lines are near insolvency and depend mainly on government subsidies.[13]

Tariffs

Because competition from Europe was strong and American industries were at an experimental stage, protection was needed until the infant U.S. industries matured and were able to compete with their European counterparts. Native and borrowed foreign capital plus labor and entrepreneurial skills were available, but foreign competition on a laissez-faire basis was severe. Alexander Hamilton, using the infant industry argument, proposed tariffs, and Congress approved them in 1789. Then, customs duties were required for industry, labor protection, and federal revenue to assist the newly established American government. However, Hamilton's tariff was primarily a revenue one and only mildly protective (at an average rate of 8.5%).[14]

During the years of colonialism and thereafter, U.S. trade relations with Europe and other countries continued to be important. Internal trade was largely governed by external trade. England and France, with strong economies at that time, were the main trading partners. However, after 1783, the United States was beyond the jurisdiction of the British Navigation Acts and foreign trade with England conducted by American vessels drastically declined. American merchants then turned to other countries for trade, mainly to China.

Before and after independence, American native investment was primarily directed toward domestic transportation (canals and trains), agriculture, and manufacturing, rather than to shipping and foreign trade. European merchants and shippers were the main competitors. By 1913, British ships carried about one-half and German ships about one-sixth of U.S. foreign trade, while American ships carried only about one-tenth. It was not until after World War II that the American merchant marine represented over 60 percent of the world's total foreign trade, compared to only 15 percent in 1936.

For government revenue and to some extent for industry and labor protection, 8.5 percent tariffs were imposed on imports in 1789. In 1792, the average rate of tariffs increased to 13.5 percent. Tariffs increased on a number of occasions, and the average level was over 47 percent in 1864 and 49.5 percent in 1890 (McKinley Tariff). The highest tariffs in American history were established in 1922 (Fordney–McCumber Tariff) allowing the president to lower or raise duties by 50 percent to equalize cost differences with competing Europe and other nations. Pig-iron, chemicals, cheese, butter, and other dairy and agricultural commodities were among the high-duty products at that time. With the changes of the Hawley–Smoot Act (1930), tariffs were at

33.6 percent for agricultural products, 35 percent for metals, and 59.8 percent for wool and woolens.[15] This protectionist policy of the 1920s stimulated monopoly at home and retaliations abroad, especially by Britain and France, and made it impossible for the European countries to pay their debts to America. This may be considered as an important reason for the world's economic depression of the 1930s.

Gradually, the United States became an exporter of primarily manufactured goods and a net creditor nation. Exports increased more than 20 times (from $400 million to $8,600 million) from 1860 to 1920, while imports increased by sixteen times (from $360 million to $5,730 million) during the same period. After 1911, America was no longer a main source of raw materials for European nations. Between 1911 and 1915, U.S. exports were composed of 46 percent manufactured products, 31 percent raw materials, and 23 percent foodstuffs, while imports were 40 percent manufactured products, 35 percent raw materials, and 25 percent foodstuffs. More or less, the same composition of imports can be observed in 1946 when exports of manufactured goods increased to 62.2 percent compared to a decline in foodstuffs to 23 percent, and only 15 percent in raw material exports.[16] Compared to the European nations, the United States has for decades remained a nation much less dependent on foreign trade. There will be more details on foreign trade in Chapter 6.

Western Europe has been, and still is, an important customer of the United States, although there were some setbacks. During the Napoleonic Wars and World War I, U.S. trade boomed with Europe. Likewise, the United States has been and continues to be Europe's best customer. Up to the 1920s, foodstuffs and raw materials were mainly exported from the new land to support the growing population and the expanding industrial plants of Europe. Manufactured and semimanufactured products were exported primarily from Britain and Germany in exchange for the imported raw materials.

With the use of the first transatlantic cable in 1866 and refrigeration on vessels after the 1870s, communications and shipments of products increased, promoting trade on both sides. Increases in prices, particularly between 1896 and 1920, reduced mutual trade somewhat, but the volume of commodities continued to be satisfactory. Cotton and grain exports played a major role in trading with Europe. U.S. imports exceeded the value of exports until 1875, but after that year U.S. exports were higher than imports for almost every year until the 1970s.[17] Currently, the value of U.S. exports of goods is lower than that of imports, and the resulting foreign trade deficit is a major problem for the economy of the country.

Banking Activities

Regarding early banking and monetary activities in the thirteen colonies, coins that European immigrants brought from their countries were used for transactions, along with wampum (beads made from certain shells strung together in belts or sashes), which were used as an ornament and for trade by the American Indians. Because such coins and wampum were limited and not well accepted, corn was made legal tender in Massachusetts, tobacco in Virginia, and rice in Carolina. In addition, wheat, rye, dried fish, and other commodies were used for barter exchanges. However, because much of colonial trade was conducted with Spanish colonies, Spanish coins in whole, half, or quarter pieces were extensively used.

Because coins were in short supply, paper money (bills of credit) was used by the governments of the colonies and property as collateral for meeting expenses. After 1775, the Continental Congress issued bills of credit to help pay for the War of Independence. By 1787, the severe depreciation of bills made them almost worthless, and for seventy years after the inauguration of George Washington as the first U.S. President in 1789, gold and silver coins were the major means of exchange.

Alexander Hamilton (1757–1804), son of a Scottish father and a French mother, became the first Secretary of the Treasury in 1789. He encouraged shipping, introduced tariffs and excise taxes, and implemented measures to protect American industry. He also persuaded Congress to charter the Bank of the United States (modeled on the Bank of England) in 1791. Although the Bank was opposed by state banks and small capitalists as a centralized institution favoring the rich, it survived (with a gap from 1811 to 1816) until 1836, playing a vital role in the U.S. banking system. Moreover, Thomas Jefferson (1743–1826), the U.S. President from 1801 to 1809, and his followers came into conflict with Hamilton's economic policy, especially regarding the Bank of the United States. Jefferson was influenced by the physiocrats in France, where he served as an ambassador from 1785 to 1789, and favored decentralization and the laissez-faire economic system.

In 1862, under the presidency of Abraham Lincoln, Congress authorized the issue of $150 million U.S. notes or *greenbacks* and another $300 million in 1863, making them legal tender. In 1863, gold certificates with 100 percent gold backing and, in 1878, silver certificates backed 100 percent by silver were placed in circulation. Also, in 1890, treasury notes (a temporary currency also backed by silver) were introduced, and both greenbacks and notes of private banks constituted the major monetary units. To charter and supervise national banks, the position of Comptroller of the Currency was established in the Treasury Department by the National Bank Act of 1863. National banks could also be established by the transfer from state charters.[18]

With the Gold Standard Act of 1900, gold and silver certificates were backed 100 percent by metal and were limited in supply, as were gold and silver coins and U.S. notes (after 1878). The amount of national bank notes was equal to the amount of government notes held by the banks. The inelasticity, or arteriosclerosis, of currency and credit to meet seasonal and cyclical changes ignited the crisis of 1907, the "rich man's panic." This crisis led to the creation of the Federal Reserve Bank (Fed) in 1913 which would control the economy's supply of money and credit and supervise the commercial banks. There are now twelve Feds with twenty-four branches in different regions of the United States. The main decision-making body is the Board of Governors, a body of seven members appointed for fourteen years. Unlike the central banks of Europe, the Fed is independent of the U.S. government. In addition to the currency already in circulation, the Fed added the Federal Reserve Notes backed by 40 percent in gold reserve and 100 percent commercial paper as collateral. During World War II, Congress reduced the gold reserve requirement from 40 to 25 percent.

European and other countries, more or less, followed the United States. However, Winston Churchill, then British Chancellor of the Exchequer, put England back on the gold standard at a wrong price level, leading the country to stagnation thereafter.

In the United States, the unit-banking system prevails compared to the branch system in Europe. That is why there are many independent commercial banks (14,700) in the United States, about one-third of which are national banks, while the rest, primarily small banks, are under state supervision. All national banks are members of the Fed as are most of the larger state-chartered banks.

Inter-War Period

The outbreak of World War I in Europe in 1914 helped the U.S. economy to grow mainly because of the heavy demand for American raw materials and war supplies for the belligerent European nations. By 1917, U.S. exports ($6.2 billion) exceeded imports ($3.3 billion) by about $3 billion. Gold poured into the United States and the value of European currencies, primarily the British pound, fell. U.S. loans were extended to Europe (about $2 billion by 1917) and for reasons of economic interest among others, the United States declared war on the German Empire on 6 April 1917. The United States became a strong economic power and the arsenal of democracy. U.S. trade with Europe increased significantly. U.S. imports from Europe increased from $896 million in 1914 to $1,128 in 1920, and exports rose from $1,486 to $4,466 million, respectively.[19]

The financial cost of World War I (April 1917 to July 1919) for the United States was about $33 billion, compared to over $360 billion for World War II, 31 percent of which was covered by taxation and the rest by loans. Although extensive government regulations, a mass of public agencies, and price controls were introduced to manage the war economy and to avoid inflation, the price index climbed from 100 in July 1914, to 187 in July 1917, and again to 206 in November 1918. Such control agencies, some of which proved useful later during World War II, dealt with fuel, transportation, finance, manpower, shipping, and other industries. Grain, raw materials, and other foodstuffs were bought from producers at minimum guaranteed prices, while the termination of immigration and demand for labor led to an increase in the membership of the American Federation of Labor (AFL), from two million in 1915 to more than four million in 1920. The eight-hour day, and half day on Saturday, both were introduced in the 1930s, and wages increased.

As a result of World War I, the United States was transformed from a debtor to a creditor nation, while European nations became debtors. Total private and government debts to the United States amounted to about $12.6 billion. Germany, with heavy reparation obligations, was in a dismal economic condition. The Europeans lost the income they had received from U.S. assets, and the condition of their economies worsened when the United States pressed them for loans and interest payments. Migration from Europe was reduced by U.S. quotas introduced in 1921, and European exports to the United States were substantially reduced due to very high protective tariffs (introduced by the Fordney–McCumber Act of 1922).

Moreover, gold payments drained reserves and crippled the European economies. Although in some cases interest payments were reduced from 5 to 3 percent and the installment period extended from twenty-five to sixty-two years (mainly for Britain), economies did not show significant improvement. Britain, which had lent more to the Allies than she had borrowed from the United States, advocated cancellation of all war debts with the hope of avoiding a worldwide financial crisis. Prices of U.S. farm products were reduced by about 50 percent, primarily because of the elimination of protective prices and the reduction in European demand, which significantly helped consumers on both sides of the Atlantic buy cheap agricultural products. However, the dollar shortage and the growing American investment in Europe intensified its dependence on the U.S. economy.[20]

To somehow mitigate the severe economic problems due to reparation payments, mainly to France and Britain, and the ongoing high inflation, the United States gave a gold loan to Germany in the 1920s. Also, American investments were flowing into Europe, mainly as the result of the Dawes Plan of 1924. By 1930, the U.S. net international economic position had improved from $3.7 billion in 1919 to $15.2 billion. With a short setback during the recession of 1920–1921, the U.S. prosperity of World War I continued through the 1920s. However, textiles, coal, mining, shipbuilding, and some other industries had not improved as much as the automobile, electrical, and construction industries. Foreign trade had not expanded significantly. The ratio of U.S. imports to national income was only 5 percent compared to 6 percent for exports.

After a minor recession in 1927, in which wages in construction, mining, and other industries declined, demand for durables and other goods also declined, and technological innovations continued to replace manual labor in the production process. Nevertheless, prices in the stock market continued to rise, from a total value of $27 billion in January 1925 to $87 billion on October 1, 1929, until the crash of 29 October 1929 (Black Tuesday), when stock prices declined by about 13 percent on the average and continued to fall thereafter. By 1932, average stock prices were only one-fourth their 1929 level. The stock market panic spread to other sectors of the economy. Investment and other spending declined; the wholesale price index gradually fell from 100 in 1926 to 95.3 in 1929, and again to 64.8 in 1932. Unemployment increased to about 25 percent, and the gross national product declined from $103.8 billion in 1929 to $55.8 billion in 1931.[21] The banking system nearly collapsed as borrowing declined drastically in spite of very low interest rates.

The policy of reducing imports and trying to export some of the joblessness to other trade partners made things worse. High U.S. tariffs that were imposed in 1930 by the Hawley–Smoot Act made loan payments by Western European nations difficult as export revenues severely declined. Total U.S. imports fell from $4.4 billion in 1929 to $1.3 billion in 1932, as did exports from $5.2 billion to $1.6 billion, respectively. England and other European countries were losing gold; and under the prevailing gold standard system, they had to devalue their currencies or face bankruptcy. By 1931, England went off the gold standard, devaluing its pound and encouraging internal expansion. Unlike France and Belgium, who abandoned the gold parity system later, England managed to recover from the Depression, while Germany, the United States, and other Western nations severely suffered from it. These dismal economic conditions contributed to Hitler's rise to power in Germany.

U.S. President Franklin Delano Roosevelt introduced the New Deal, a program of public works spending through the Public Works Administration and other agencies, and industrial self-regulation under the National Recovery Act of 1933. Also, a number of regulations were introduced to stimulate demand and to improve the economy through deficit spending, according to the Keynesian prescription. The United States abandoned the gold standard in April 1933, but gold could be used for international transactions with the dollar devalued by 50 to 60 percent. Federal Reserve member banks were not permitted to engage in stock market speculation, and insurance on deposits was provided. A personal Social Security System was introduced in 1935, much later than similar programs in Germany (in the 1880s), England, and other European nations. Furthermore, the Congress of Industrial Organizations (CIO), established in 1938, helped improve the position of labor unions.

Even before the Japanese surprise attack on Pearl Harbor on 7 December 1941, U.S. industries were partially transformed to the production of war material due to Lend–Lease and the defense commitments to European nations in 1940 and later. Wartime production contracts from European nations went to large U.S. corporations, primarily General Motors and other automobile companies. Total industrial production almost doubled during the war. American industry produced enough to equip the Allied armies and built harbors and airports in Britain and other countries.

Huge government spending, and a swelling demand, created inflationary spirals not only in Europe but in the United States as well, where prices had risen about 25 percent from April 1941 to January 1942. Price regulations and even the rationing of some products were used to curb inflation. Heavy taxation on personal and corporate incomes, excise and inheritance taxes, and the sale of war bonds were used in the United States to finance the approximate $300 billion cost of the war. However, the tax burden in Britain and other European countries was higher than that in the United States.

After the defeat of Germany and Japan in 1945 and the end of World War II, U.S. industry managed to switch to peacetime production without a severe recession or inflation. The United States continued to provide Europe and the rest of the world with vital materials and industrial products. As a result, the United States emerged as the richest and most powerful nation on earth. In June 1943, a U.S. proposal to form the United Nations Relief and Rehabilitation Administration (UNRRA) was accepted by forty-eight nations. From the $4 billion spent by this body, the United States gave $2,450 million, mainly to help feed much of occupied Europe. Lend–Lease stopped in 1945, while the UNRRA survived until 1947.

Post-World War II Period

When World War II was over, Europe was physically devastated, and the demand for U.S. dollars to finance badly needed imports was great. Although most of the European nations had to depreciate their currencies to attract inflows of dollars, international deficits with the United States remained sky high. Thus, the British pound depreciated from 4 to 2.80 pounds per dollar in 1947, and other national currencies followed suit, but the "dollar gap" or "dollar shortage" remained. Imports by Europe from the United States were four times greater than exports. There were widespread exchange and import controls, and American aid to Western European countries primarily went to help rehabilitate and stabilize their economies.

On 5 June 1947, George Marshall, then U.S. Secretary of State, in a speech at Harvard Univeristy, proposed a four-year program for the economic rehabilitation of Western Europe, initially known as the European Recovery Program (ERP), often popularly referred to as the Marshall Plan. The program was to be administered by the Economic Cooperation Administration (ECA), an agency of the United States, and the Organization for European Economic Cooperation (OEEC), representing seventeen European countries.[22] The former Soviet Union and other Eastern European countries refused to participate in this program. The OEEC was later named the Organization for Economic Cooperation and Development (OECD) and presently incorporates twenty-four countries, including the EU nations, the United States, Japan, Canada, and Australia.

The ERP, which had expended $12 billion in grants and loans, was liquidated on 31 December 1951, when the ECA was replaced by the Mutual Security Agency. About half of the money was used to buy industrial products, less than half for agricultural commodities, and $500 million for the

European Payments Union (EPU), a clearance agency created in 1950 to settle trade imbalances of the member-nations. As a result of American aid, the war-ravaged economies of Western Europe significantly improved, especially in the production of steel, cement, aluminum, coal, and foodstuffs. It can be argued, therefore, that the impetus for European economic cooperation came primarily from the United States, while the European countries were preoccupied with internal difficulties rather than utopian projects of unification.

The main goals of the OEEC were to allocate the U.S. financial assistance to its members and to coordinate economic development plans. Although it had no power of its own, the OEEC was successful in bringing its members closer together, since they had no choice but to agree among themselves to receiving U.S. assistance. From that point of view, the OEEC played an important role in creating a favorable environment for the formation of other intra-European organizations such as the EPU, the European Coal and Steel Community (ECSC) in 1952, the European Atomic Authority (Euratom), and the European Common Market or, officially, the European Economic Community (EEC) in 1957. However, the OEEC limited itself to economic research and publications of international character. The EPU, through multilateral exchange convertibility, increased trade and showed the necessity for a closer cooperation and eventual unification of Western Europe.

According to the U.S. Department of Commerce, aid to Western Europe from 1945 to 1962 amounted to $33 billion, out of $83.3 billion total worldwide aid. Some $17.3 billion were nonmilitary grants, $6.2 billion were government loans, and $15.5 billion were military grants.

In order to maintain friendly relations with Western Europe and other nations, as well as to preserve international stability, the United States promulgated these foreign aid programs. Moreover, the U.S. fear of the spread of communism intensified the reasons for such aid, particularly in the form of military grants. The main effect of American aid was to enable the economies of Europe to develop their resources and thereby stimulate foreign trade.

Greece (Hellas) and Turkey received military and other aid from the United States mainly to stop civil wars and prevent the Communists from taking over the government, as well as to avoid domination of the eastern Mediterranean by the former Soviet Union which could interfere with traffic through the Suez Canal.

Under the Truman Doctrine, the U.S. Congress appropriated $300 million for Greece (Hellas) and $100 million for Turkey in 1947. Both countries have been members of NATO since 1952, and continue to receive military and nonmilitary aid from the United States (about $350 million for Greece [Hellas] and $500 million for Turkey, annually). There are a number of U.S. military bases in Hellas and Turkey, as well as Voice of America facilities (VOA). As Walter Lippmann once remarked, these countries were selected for American aid "not because they are especially in need of relief, not because they are shining examples of democracy . . . but because they are the strategic gateway to the Black Sea and the heart of the Soviet Union."[23]

What were European weaknesses could be considered examples that could lead to long-run and advantageous policies. On the other hand, the U.S. emphasis on domestic economic autonomy and a disregard for its international implications could lead to disadvantageous policies concerning Atlantic and other economic relations. However, for American corporations, an integrated Europe may be the most open and profitable market in which to do business, similar to the Balkans in previous times. Yet critics argue that the EU could be a dog-eat-dog Darwinian nightmare, with American and Japanese companies enjoying large shares of business and profits, while workers get squeezed.

Important benefits of a single, unified European market can be achieved by cutting out red tape, breaking down protectionism, and removing obstacles on cross-border activities. This means economies of scale, more jobs, inflation-free growth, and healthier competition for EU and NAFTA, primarily with U.S. corporations.

U.S. Leadership in Technological Change

After the collapse of the Soviet Union, the United States has been moving gradually toward the transformation of much of its military-oriented industry into peacetime production activities, with emphasis on research and development, electronics, computers, steel, auto, and aircraft industries. Although the American economy has a high potential for success during change and adjustment, the fact that budget and foreign trade deficits continue and domestic and external debts grow deprives the country from utilizing its full potential and making its industry competitive in international markets. This requires emphasis on future investment, financed through higher saving and lower consumption.

To a large extent, the dramatic changes in computers and electronics affect labor employment in the production and distribution processes of the United States and other countries. Because automation was considered a major reason for the Great Depression of the 1930s, strategies such as a shorter work week were employed in order to avoid high unemployment and defective aggregate demand. Although some were afraid that this reduction in work hours would bring about severe crises, the U.S. work week was reduced from sixty to forty-eight hours, and later to forty hours, and productivity continued to improve.

Currently, there is discussion in the United States to reduce the work week to thirty-two hours, because of persistent unemployment and the growing use of computers, robots, and other modern technological devices which replace labor. A shorter work week would help mitigate recessions or depressions, reduce unemployment, and decrease welfare costs. Moreover, aggregate demand would not decline and economic stability would prevail. In this way, technological improvement would not be discouraged, machines would continue to produce more with less labor hours and workers, and employees would continue to earn constant and growing income with less hours of work. As a result, there would be sufficient effective demand, backed with income earned, to absorb the supply of goods and services produced by the machines, thereby avoiding the Sisyphus-type curse of economic fluctuations, preserving equilibrium in the U.S. economy.

Technological development and automation tend to grow by geometric progressions, though the chronic loss of jobs throughout the world continues. Productivity among manufacturing and white-collar workers increases through capital accumulation, mechanization, and technological innovations, but the growing amounts of goods and services may not have enough customers able to buy them. After all, production and economic growth take place to improve the standard of living of human beings and not just for the sake of numerical growth.

Many companies, large and small, lay off laborers mainly because of computerization and automation. For example, twelve people required to run a payroll department for a company of 2,000 employees are, after computerization, reduced to one individual. Even in public organizations and enterprises one can see the impact of computerization on employment. In a regional office of the Social Security Administration, a certain number of employees were required to provide information about retirement and disability. Currently, with a toll-free number one can have all the information one needs from a computer operator, regardless of the location within the country.

With greater growth and prosperity comes a greater demand for pensions and health care primarily for the ever-growing aging population, along with welfare, environmental protection, unemployment benefits, and other public goods for the general public. All these government services require higher expenditures and more taxes to finance them. However, regulations for certain natural monopolies, which work against free market capitalism, are expected to loosen, mainly because of technological improvement. Thus, the revolutionary technological progress in telephones, cables, radios, and other innovations in electronics, transportation, and finances, may increase competition and reduce the need for public sector controls.

After the death of command economics, there exists the challenge of solving the implicit or explicit conflict between politics and economics on an international scale. On the one hand, there is a trend of political decentralization or subdivision in different regions of the world and, on the other, an economic centralization movement à la EU or NAFTA in different parts of the globe.

The rapid transmission of information through electronic communication affects economic and political freedom. The power of governments and central banks to regulate economies and to control the value of their currencies is restricted by global electronic information. The knowledge of alternative economic and political systems, communicated electronically, increases expectations and changes people's preferences in the marketplace. Fiscal and monetary regulations, protectionist policies, and national censorship become largely ineffective and aggravate the migration of domestic wealth, when the largest portion of the news is received internationally through the mass media. The media also brings pressure on political leaders toward more freedom of choice and expression. From that point of view, totalitarian and authoritarian regimes are on a collision course with this new communication era, speeding up the process of economic and political convergence.

Chapter 3

The European Union

HISTORIC TRENDS

Euro–Hellenic Heritage

In ancient Greece (Hellas) (which, according to Nietzsche, provided the nucleus of European civilization), Kadmos, son of Aginora, lost his sister Europa. He searched for her in vain, then built a city as a model for people living together, and named it "Europe."

Almost all the varieties of speech used in Europe belong to the family of languages which include the Balto–Slavic (Russian, Polish, Czechoslovakian, Serbian, and Bulgarian), the Teutonic (English, German, Dutch, and Scandinavian languages), the Italic (French, Catalan, Spanish, Portuguese, Italian, and Romanian), the Hellenic (Greek), and the Celtic (Gaelic, Welsh, and Breton linguistic subfamilies).

According to archaeologists, the island of Crete was the place of European man's emergence from the Stone Age into the age of metals (iron and bronze). The Cretans (Minoans) were distinguished by their maritime and commercial activities along the Mediterranean shores (third millennium B.C.). The Greeks (Hellenes) (mainly Achaeans or Mycenaens, Ionians, Aeolians, Dorians or Spartans, and later Athenians) were the first to leave a record of themselves and their neighbors.[1] They were descendants of a branch of the European race living in the Alps and Central Europe to which Romans, Germans, Slavs, and other Europeans belonged.

Although the concept of European union gained significant attention and was implemented in the post–World War II years, previous attempts had been made throughout history toward a European economic and political integration. On a small scale, federations or unions of city-states that operated as independent economic and political units can be observed in ancient Hellas and Italy in the fifth century B.C. and afterward.

The first economic and political unions or confederacies in history were the Achaean and the Delian Leagues, developed in ancient Hellas from sixth century to third century B.C., established to formulate common economic and foreign policies on trade, coinage, and other matters.

In the Achaean League, which resembled modern federal systems and economic unions similar to the present EU and NAFTA, each member retained its independence, but all members participated in a council that met twice a year to formulate legislation and enact common economic policies. Moreover, a monetary union was formed between the city-states of Phocaea (close to Lydia where the first coins appeared in 640 B.C.) and Mytilene (on the island of Lesbos) in the early years of the fourth century B.C. Furthermore, the constitution of Solon (594 B.C.) introduced three classes of income taxes, abolished bondage, and gave citizens a share in the government in a democratic fashion. The income class of a person determined eligibility for public office.

The Delian League or the Confereration of Delos, with headquarters on the island of Delos in the Aegean Sea founded in 478 B.C., was mainly a military and foreign policy confederation designed to prepare its member-nations against possible aggression, mainly from Persia. Each of the member-nations, which at one time numbered over two hundred, made a contribution in proportion to its capacity, initially in men and ships, and later in money. After the Peace of Callias ended the war against Persia (449 B.C.), the treasury moved to Athens, which exercised significant economic and political influence until its defeat by Sparta in the Peloponnesian War (404 B.C.). The league was reconstituted in 377 B.C. under imperialistic Athens and continued until Philip II, Emperor of Macedonia, defeated the Athenians in 338 B.C. This organization of a federal alliance of sovereign states that maintained over long periods, resembles present NATO which includes the Western European countries, Canada, and the United States among some sixteen member-nations.

Phillip II and his son Alexander the Great, a student of Aristotle, unified the Hellenic city-states (338 B.C.) and other people as far as the Danube River, primarily to oppose Persia, the main enemy of the Hellenes at that time. During the Hellenistic Age, trade was greatly improved among the coast cities of the Mediterranean Sea by the seafaring Hellenes who traveled as far as Spain and Italy (Syracuse, Torrent, and Crouton) in their search for economic expansion. For many centuries after the division of Alexander's empire (323 B.C.), Hellenic culture had a profound influence on Europe, in the final phase of antiquity and the following medieval era.

In the meantime, the northern part of the Italian peninsula and the surrounding areas were colonized by the Etruscans (ninth century B.C.), a people who probably had originated in Asia Minor. The west central region, called Latium, belonged to a European tribe known as the Latins. This tribe, together with the related Umbrians, Samnites, Ligurians, and Itali, had moved from the north and settled in the entire region of present day Italy.

Roman Period and Middle Ages

After a century of Etruscan domination, a new power, Rome, originally a city-state of Latium, developed by 508 B.C. The Romans dominated all of Latium and conquered Etruria (309 B.C.). Gradually they expanded their sphere of influence to include the Mediterranean basin, conquering the Samnites, the Carthaginians in North Africa, the Iberian peninsula, and the Hellenic states (mainly between 264 and 146 B.C.). Also, they repelled repeated barbarian raids across the north and east frontiers. By A.D. 14, the Roman Empire embraced all of the continental mainland south of the Rhine and Danube Rivers, as well as Britain, Dacia, Parthis, Hellas, Asia Minor, and most of the northern coast of Africa.[2]

During the period of the Roman Empire (31 B.C. to A.D. 476) agriculture was given high priority over other sectors. Small landholders and free laborers left the countryside and crowded into the towns to increase the number of plebeians. The possession of large estates by the wealthy class and the nobles created the *latifundia*, which, together with the inefficiency of slave labor and the introduction of heavy taxation, accelerated the decline of the Roman Empire.[3] The creation of a new commercial class, the patricians, and the new landowners necessitated a body of laws which later had a profound influence on legal and economic institutions.

The recognition of juristic persons or legal entities, by Roman law can be seen as an important development from the standpoint of the modern invention and expansion of the corporation form of enterprise. The laws of contract and of private property, as well as our maritime laws and the systems of jurisprudence and jury duties, originated in ancient Rome. The importance of Roman law to the development of economic thought and institutions has been significant, particularly for Europe and the United States. Many of its principles influenced the legal systems of most of the Western countries, including those under English common law. The corporation form of enterprise and the Roman laws are valuable contributions to the long-term stability and growth of modern economies. Natural persons die and their enterprises are mostly dismantled but legal or juristic persons, such as private corporations and public enterprises, normally survive for many years and, in some cases, for centuries.

After the separation of the eastern section of the Roman Empire, cultural and commercial activities moved largely to New Rome (Constantinople) which became the capital of the Byzantine Empire (A.D. 326). The Emperors of Byzantium introduced a common language (Hellenic) and religion (Christian), and stimulated trade by reducing taxes and making administrative reforms in their dominions. Jewelry, pottery, silk production, and shipping were the main industries that flourished at that time, and Constantinople remained an international trade and intellectual center for about ten centuries, until Byzantium was occupied by the Ottoman Turks in 1453. With the increase in imperial expenses, the weight of taxation became greater, economic misman-agement increased, and after the eleventh century, the Byzantine Empire and its capital city began a slow process of decline. A number of scholars fled, or were summoned, to Western Europe, and carried with them Hellenic philoso-phy and culture, "the seeds" of which "grew into some of the finest flowers of the Renaissance."[4]

Venice, an Italian city situated on some 120 islands in a lagoon at the northern part of the Adriatic Sea, was founded in the fifth century by refugees from Northern Italy who were escaping the Teutonic invaders. Although nominally part of the Eastern Roman Empire (Byzantium), Venice became an autono-mous republic in A.D. 697 and, thereafter, a great commercial center for trade mainly between Europe and the Middle East. Rich Venice used mercenaries and local people to occupy important islands and ports in the Adriatic Sea and the Eastern Mediterranean to facilitate its shipping and trade operations. In 1204, when Constantinople fell to the Crusaders, Venice occupied Crete for over four centuries and later, in 1488, occupied Cyprus as well. In addi-tion, there were many other islands and coastlands occupied by Venice at that time, and many old Venetian fortresses can still be seen today. In competition with the Genoese and the Hellenes for the lucrative Mediterranean markets, Venice developed a prosperous commerce. In 1797, the Venetian republic was dismantled by Napoleon the Great, and many of its possessions were transferred to Austria, who finally ceded Venice to Italy in 1866.

During the Middle Ages (A.D. 476 to about 1350) and the Renaissance period (1350 to 1500), trade among European cities was limited. Agriculture, the main sector of the economy, declined and educational and technological advancement came to a standstill. It was thought that the Hellenic and Roman writers, particularly Aristotle, had provided complete scientific explanations for all subjects and no further improvement was possible. All over Europe ever greater administrative powers were given to the owners of large estates (the largest owner being the Church), who developed new political and eco-nomic units with their own laws and courts. Landlords acted as independent rulers over the serfs who worked for them. Merchants formed crafts and guilds in towns for protection, and from this, the capitalistic system emerged. Young serfs moved into the cities, as the Crusades stimulated trade in new markets. This led to a new economic climate that was favorable to trade and handi-crafts. Later in the Middle Ages, the Fuggers and other banking houses pro-vided financial services to merchants and handicraft guilds as well as to the Church of Rome.

In Western Europe, and particularly in Germany, the Protestant Reforma-tion initiated in 1517 contributed to the rise of capitalism, which first mani-fested itself in Italy in the thirteenth century. In contrast to the papal practice of indulgence, Protestantism supported individualism and considered worldly success to be a divine blessing, inspiring a work ethic that stimulated efficiency and economic development not only in Europe but also in the United States and other regions. This accelerated the rise of the merchant class and mercantilism in general.

The capitalistic system in the sixteenth and seventeenth centuries, and its spread throughout Europe and the Americas, was further developed especially by Calvinism, a Protestant system of thought that justified the pursuit of wealth, the payment of interest, and profit making. Yet today these teachings are criticized for not leading to the high economic growth of other religious creeds, such as that of Japan. Critics argue that the lagging growth of Scotland and the southern section of the United States is due to Calvinist and other Protestant religions.

Mercantilistic Colonialism

Under Mercantilism (1550–1776), emphasis was placed on foreign trade as a means of accumulating precious metals, the most desirable form of national wealth, and on the supremacy of the state over the individual. The state, being the locus of power, should support exports, create state monopolies, and establish colonies to increase national wealth. Commercial expansion by such monopolies as the Merchant Adventurers, the Eastland Company, the Muscovy Company, and the East India Company had initially as their main objectives the search for and the accumulation of precious metals (mainly gold and silver), which could be used to finance trade, pay large armies for foreign wars, or be retained as luxuries. As Columbus said in 1503, "With gold one can get everything he desires, even get souls into Paradise." This trade expansion led to colonialism. The mother countries of England, Spain, France, and other European nations expanded not only trade with the colonies (including present NAFTA countries) but also their political and military domination for purposes of exploiting natural resources, including the mining of gold. The search for minerals and other productive resources and the expansion of markets were the main reasons for establishing colonies. Navigation acts increased mercantile profits by confining the carrying of goods to the mother countries' own ships.

State and church financial facilities during the sixteenth and seventeenth centuries gave wealthy families, such as the Bardi, the Medici, and the Fuggers, the initiative to undertake commercial and financial adventures and thus displace the medieval feudal lords. This new system of commercial capitalism was characterized by economic freedom, technical progress, and profit seeking, regardless of the social consequences and communal relationships.

The quest for material wealth, self-interest, and liberalism by the rising merchant and industrial classes during the mercantilist period broke up the medieval controls, and replaced religious, noneconomic values with worldly, material ones. The gradual development of maritime commerce in most of the Mediterranean and other European ports, and the economic and other reforms introduced by the Renaissance, especially in Protestant countries, provided the necessary incentives for material success, technical advancement, and scientific progress. The discovery of new lands and the expansion of trade with the colonies led to the improvement of internal and external transportation, increases in food production, the accumulation of profits, and a gradual shift of power from the landowning nobility to the new merchant class. Low costs and high profits, used for further industrial expansion, were the economic objectives of the mercantilists. Low wages and the consequent suffering of the enlarged urban laboring class, as well as the exploitation of the less-developed colonial areas, were the outcomes. All these factors were conducive to the development of the capitalistic system that spread to the United States, Canada, Mexico, and other colonies.

Inventions and new technological methods of production in iron and textiles, particularly in the use of the steam engine (invented by James Watt in 1776) in England, increased industrial production and created a new capitalist or entrepreneurial class. Similar movements of industrialization and urbanization occurred in France, Germany, Spain, and other European nations. Specialization in production, competition, and the search for new resources and markets caused the spread of industrial development to the United States and other countries. As a result, living standards improved dramatically in Europe and in the Americas in the late 1800s and the beginning of the 1900s.

The doctrine of mercantilism in England, called *cameralism* (from Latin *camera* or chamber) in Germany, and Colbertism in France (from Jean Colbert, the French Finance Minister), supported the promotion of exports, and the protection of manufacturing and foreign trade, by active government intervention. This intensified the policy of colonialism by the European nations, particularly England, Spain, France, Holland, and Portugal.

With the end of colonialism approaching, the European nations turned against one another. The result was terrible destruction and crashing economic setbacks during World Wars I and II. Subsequently, aging Europe, having learned a harsh lesson from previous belligerence and destruction, turned toward cooperation and eventual economic and political integration by forming the successful EU, a dream that had been unrealized for centuries.

Efforts of European Unity

Europe, which stands today at momentous crossroads, has a history that radically changed both its face and the face of the world. To understand the current trend toward unification, a review of related historical trends in the continent is needed. The road to European unity goes far back into history.

The Hellenic and Roman dream of a united Europe, seen mainly through their many conquests, had permeated the continent for centuries. It prevailed during the Roman period (31 B.C. to A.D. 476) and the Byzantine period (326 to 1453), especially at the time of Justinian's rule (A.D. 554). Similar efforts were made during the years of the Frankish kingdom of Charlemagne, "King Father of Europe" (800); Otto the Great in 962, and later; the Austro-Hungarian Hapsburg Dynasty (mainly in the sixteenth century); and the period of the Austrian Chancellor Metternich (toward the end of the eighteenth and the beginning of the nineteenth centuries). Also, forceful attempts to unify Europe were made during the period of Napoleon Bonaparte (1799–1815); the new German Empire or the Second Reich (1871–1918) under the Kaiser and Otto von Bismarck; and in the 1940s by the alliance of Benito Mussolini of Italy and Adolf Hitler of Germany. However, Winston Churchill, the British Prime Minister, pointed out, "We must build a kind of United States of Europe," as the Hapsburgs also suggested centuries ago.

Probably the lack of success in unifying Europe through so many centuries was because of the reliance on forcible conquests by the European rulers. However, the Renaissance movement, begun in fourteenth century Italy and spread all over Europe by the late Middle Ages, incorporated a spirit of innovation and unity, a great reawakening of common interest in the literature, culture, and philosophy of ancient Hellas and Rome.

The Christian religion, under its main divisions (Catholic, Orthodox, and Protestant), played a significant role in stimulating efforts toward European unity. Nationalistic, economic, and political forces were powerful in leading European nations into conflicts and destructive wars throughout history, in spite of the fact that a number of patriarchs, popes, and other theologians appealed for unity and a reawakening of the European religious soul as the root of that unity.

From an economic point of view, the establishment of a German customs union (Zollverein, in 1834) under Prussian leadership, may be considered the closest attempt at a union similar to the present EU. It created a free trade zone throughout much of Germany, removed commerce restrictions, and demonstrated the importance of cooperation and unity on economic and political matters.

EVOLUTION OF THE EUROPEAN UNION

For several years, six European countries (France, West Germany, Italy, Belgium, Luxembourg, and The Netherlands) tried to strengthen their economic and political bonds. Belgium and Luxembourg created an economic union in 1921, joined by The Netherlands in 1944, creating the regional economic group known as the Benelux countries. Negotiations among these three nations began in 1943 when all three were under Nazi occupation.

After World War II, a ravaged Europe slowly set out on the path toward its crucial revival and eventual unification. The destruction of the war raised the question of how to avoid the European historic pattern of catastrophe, followed by revival, followed by catastrophe, *ad infinitum*. The consensus was that Europe should not be doomed to oscillation between order and chaos. Instead, new ways of establishing peace, stability, and prosperity should be found. A European supranationalism, or a European family of nations, was needed to submerge individual nationalism and historic enmities.

One of the first Europeans who wanted to promote Europe's recovery in the post–World War II years, and eventually its economic and political union, was Jean Monnet, a stocky French peasant figure. He pointed out that the people taking risks and offering innovative ideas for European integration deserve the laurels; however, emphasis should be placed on institutions (such as the EU), because of their ability to carry on to successive generations. Monnet wanted not so much to be somebody but to do something, especially to contribute to the union of the European peoples in liberty and diversity. He persuaded the United States, through President Franklin D. Roosevelt, to support the defense of Europe as "the arsenal of democracy." Also, he prepared the Schuman Plan, named for Robert Schuman, the French Foreign Minister (1950), for the creation of the ECSC in 1952, the forerunner of the EU. Italy and the Benelux countries, together with France and West Germany, signed the treaty that established the ECSC.

The Schuman Plan was designed to promote Franco–German reconciliation and to make it impossible for the European nations to fight against one another. The idea was to provide a practical basis for gradual concrete economic and political achievements. Europe, after all, is essentially compact and indivisible. Viewed from an airplane, the jigsaw frontiers make little sense.

The European Economic Community (EEC) was established by the Treaty of Rome in 1957 with six members: Belgium, Luxembourg, The Netherlands, France, West Germany, and Italy, commonly known as the "Inner Six." Formed to gradually reduce internal tariffs, the group was successful, and the United Kingdom and Denmark, as well as Ireland, joined the EEC in 1973. Hellas and Turkey became associate members in 1962 and 1964, respectively, and were allowed to export many of their products to the community free from duty while retaining tariffs during a transition period. Special arrangements and association agreements have been negotiated or signed with a number of countries in Africa, the Middle East, Asia, and Latin America, as well as Spain and Portugal. Hellas became the tenth member of the EEC in 1981, and Spain and Portugal the eleventh and twelfth members in 1986.[5] Because of political and other noneconomic integration movements, the EEC was later called the European Community (EC) and recently, the EU. Austria, Finland, and Sweden became members of the EU in January 1995. Table 3.1 shows the main economic indicators of the EU. High minimum wages, which exceed $10 per hour in affluent Northern Europe, are mainly responsible for high unemployment.

For Spain and Portugal, a ten-year transitional period (1986–1995) was provided for agricultural products, and a seven-year period was provided for fish, for which tariffs were gradually reduced by the EU. A similar five-year period was provided between the EU and Denmark, Ireland, and the United

Table 3.1
Economic Indicators for the EU Countries, 1995

Country	Population (millions)	Per Capita GNP (U.S. $)	Hourly labor cost,$	Current Account Balance ($bill.)
Austria	8.1	18,720	21.7	-5,113
Belgium	10.1	24,710	23.0	14,960
Britain	58.5	18,700	13.6	-4,632
Denmark	5.2	29,890	20.4	1,413
Finland	5.1	20,580	18.9	5,642
France	58.1	24,990	17.0	16,443
Germany	81.9	27,510	27.3	-20,976
Greece	10.5	8,210	6.9	-2,864
Ireland	3.6	14,710	12.2	1,379
Italy	57.2	19,020	16.2	25,706
Netherlands	15.5	24,000	20.9	16,191
Portugal	9.9	9,740	4.6	-229
Spain	39.2	13,580	11.4	1,280
Sweden	8.8	23,750	18.6	4,633

Sources: World Bank, *World Development Report 1997*, 215, 245; for labor cost, "Hourly Cost of Employing Labor," *Financial Times*, 24 October 1995, 6.

Kingdom. For industrial products, the transitional period was three years for Spain and seven years for Portugal. No time interval was provided for the introduction of value-added tax for Spain, and only three years for Portugal, compared to five years for Hellas (extended for an additional two years). Also, a seven-year period was provided for the free movement of the Spanish and Portuguese workers in the EU, as was initially provided for Hellas. Now, trade policy is dictated basically by Articles 110–116 of the Treaty of Rome.

There are four major institutions in the EU for the formulation and implementation of economic and other related policies: the Commission, the Council, the European Parliament, and the Court of Justice.

The Commission formulates and proposes related legislation and provides for the implementation of the EU's policies. The Commission comprises two members each from Britain, France, Germany, Italy, and Spain, and one member from each of the other member-nations, chosen for four-year terms by the EU member-nation governments. Jacques Delors, an energetic Frenchman, was president of the Commission for a number of years. Frans Andriessen, a former minister of The Netherlands is vice president, responsible for external relations and trade positions with the United States and other countries. Jack Sanders is now president of the EU. The rest of the commissioners have other assignments such as agricultural production and subsidy, financial affairs, budgetary problems, regional policies, transportation, cultural affairs, and environmental protection. The members of the Commission act not in the interest of their individual home states, but as representatives of the EU as a whole.

The Council approves the legislation of the EU and is its decision-making institution. In contrast to the Commission, its members act as representatives of the particular member-nation governments. For certain problems, the Council must consult with the Economic and Social Committee and the European Parliament. Under the revised procedures, a qualified majority is sufficient for the Council's decisions, not unanimous approval as before. Individual member-nations cannot exercise a veto anymore. This is a change that allows quick passage of EU proposals for further economic and political integration.

The European Parliament has existed since 1979. Its 626 members, representing the 370 million people of the fifteen EU member-nations, are elected by direct universal suffrage. There are 99 Euro–Parliamentarians from Germany, 87 each from Britain, France, and Italy, 64 from Spain, 31 from The Netherlands, 25 each from Belgium, Hellas, and Portugal, 22 from Sweden, 21 from Austria, 16 each from Denmark and Finland, 15 from Ireland, and 6 from Luxembourg. Plenary meetings are normally held in Strasbourg for one week each month whereas its Secretariat is in Luxembourg.[6]

The Parliament approves the appointment of the European Commission and can dismiss it by a two-thirds majority. It votes on the programs of the Commission and the adoption of the annual budget (around 80 billion ECUs in 1995). Also, it oversees the implementation of the EU budgets and it has the power to adopt regulations and directives on an equal footing together with the European Council and the active participation of the Commission, particularly after the increased power allowed by the 1986 Single European Act. Moreover, for international agreements, accession of new members, and other important decisions, the Council must obtain Parliament's approval. The members of the European Parliament are seated in political party groupings. These groups are not national, but rather, community groups, such as the Socialist Group, the European People's Party, and the Christian democratic group.

The Court of Justice acts as the Supreme Court of the EU regarding the validity and the correct interpretation of its legislation. It comprises 15 judges and 9 advocate-generals appointed for six years in agreement with the national gov-

ernments. Through its decisions, the Court helped rapid integration by eliminating barriers to free trade and other restrictions within the Union. Together
with other EU bodies, it has been a driving force behind the introduction of
the Single European Act, in 1986, and the gradual unification of Europe.

Of the total 626 Euro–Parliamentarians, the main winners in recent elec-
tions were Liberal or Free Democrats, the Environmentalist Greens, and the
Socialists. The Conservative Party and the Christian Democratic Party were
the main losers. However, the Europe's Peoples Party held a strong position
with 173 seats in 1995, compared to 221 seats for the Socialists and 25 for the
Green Party. In the United Kingdom, the Labour Party ended up with more
seats in the Euro–Parliament compared to the Conservative Party.

In accordance with the Single European Act, the EU reaffirms that it will
not be a fortress region, but a partner with outside nations, particularly the
United States and the other NAFTA countries. Moreover, more progress on
social aspects of the internal market is the intention of the EU Commission
and the union as a whole. Thus, two key directives, which will significantly
affect U.S. companies in Europe, are expected to provide for worker consultation and standard employment contracts. These directives will introduce
new rules that require firms to provide corporate information to workers and
to increase labor participation in matters of workplace, health, safety, training, and even transnational mergers.

Although the Treaty of Rome did not include explicit support of the social
and economic cohesion of the EU members, the establishment of the European Regional Development Fund (1975), the Structural Fund (1988), and
the Cohesion Fund (1993) did, as does Article 130a of the Maastricht Treaty
(1991) which states that "The Community shall aim at reducing disparities
between the levels of development of the various regions."

Regarding membership of other countries in the EU, Article 237 of the
Treaty of Rome provided that any like-minded state can apply for membership and, thus, the EU has been enlarged on a number of occasions since
1958. Also, Articles 131–136 of the Treaty provide that non-European countries can be brought into association with the EU. The usual EU practice of
enlargement is to enact agreements that include trade preferences for candidate member-nations. However, member-governments in the EU have concluded long-term agreements with other countries, without contesting the EU's
right to negotiate on matters of commercial policy.

Some serious questions remain concerning the future of the EU. What is
the relationship between enlargement and unification, or between widening
versus deepening of the EU? Are there conflicting interests in the process of
closer cooperation of the member-nations regarding foreign policy, defense,
and a single currency? The following sections attempt to answer such questions by reviewing the economic and geopolitical status of the countries and
regional groups involved.

EFTA AND THE EU

In 1960, three years after the formation of the EU, the European Free Trade Association (EFTA) was created in Stockholm. It included Austria, the United Kingdom, Denmark, Norway, Portugal, Sweden, and Switzerland. The EFTA (the "Outer Seven") as well as the EEC (the "Inner Six") formed to gradually reduce tariffs and encourage investment; however, EFTA permitted the retention of individual external tariffs and, in the process of closer cooperation, was not as successful as the EU. As a result, the United Kingdom, Denmark, and Ireland joined the EU in 1973, as did Portugal in 1986, and Austria and Sweden in 1995. Finland, which together with Liechtenstein had joined EFTA, became a member of the EU in 1995. Also, there are some sixty-six African, Pacific, and Caribbean (APC) countries with which the EU maintains cooperative agreements and provides financial aid.

Under the pressure of business and the fear of being left outside the single European market, Norway and Switzerland are expected to apply in the near future, although Norwegians had first voted in 1972 against EU membership, mainly because of the Norwegian fishermen's fear that EU trawlers would wipe the sea clean of fish.[7] Nevertheless, the severe loss of industrial competitivenes and the dissolution of the Warsaw Pact military alliance of the former Soviet Union and Eastern Europe intensified the desire of these nations for EU membership. It seems that these countries will soon join the EU as their preferential trade relations are approaching an end. Through bilateral agreements with the EU, these nations already export their products duty free to the EU and vice versa, without contributing to regional or agricultural programs and EU budget expenditures. Furthermore, the largest amount of their foreign trade is with the EU.

Encouraged by the drastic political and economic reforms in Eastern Europe and the former Soviet Union, Norway and other EFTA countries agreed in December 1989 to create a European Economic Space to abolish remaining tariffs and other restrictions. Also, industrial and other product standards would be harmonized and cooperation in environment, crime, and research and development would increase. These efforts were further intensified as a result of the Conference on Security and Cooperation in Europe by thirty-four countries in November 1990 and later. Democratization in Eastern Europe and the former Soviet republics removes political obstacles and opens the way for EU membership.

Fearing that it may lose its competitive edge and be isolated if it remains outside the EU, Switzerland announced plans to join the community. After the referendum on 24 May 1992 to join the World Bank and the International Monetary Fund with 56 percent in favor, Switzerland entered negotiations to participate in the EU. The seven-member Federal Council that governs the country decided to negotiate with the EU nations for closer relations and eventual membership in the union, with which Switzerland enjoys two-thirds of its trade. The end of the Cold War and the common problems of drug abuse, immigration, and economic fluctuations it shares with its EU neighbors has forced Switzerland to look afresh at its neutrality and to move toward integration with the EU. Recent openness in its banking system regarding secret foreign deposits would give Switzerland financial advantages in its economy and an increase in trade and investment transactions with other countries. In spite of this, on 6 December 1992, Swiss voters rejected the move toward economic integration with the EU, with 50.3 percent against and 49.7 percent in favor.

Liechtenstein is a tiny state of 28,000 people between Austria and Switzerland. Many international corporations have their headquarters there to take advantage of favorable tax and secret banking laws. Although it follows to a large extent Switzerland's economic policy, Liechtenstein voted to join the EU. Iceland, another small nation, is expected to apply for EU membership in the near future.

From economic and sociopolitical standpoints, Iceland, Norway, and Switzerland are largely at the same level as the advanced EU countries. In 1994, per capita GNP varied from $26,390 for Norway to $37,930 for Switzerland, which is higher than the average of the EU. This means that these countries present no adjustment problems in joining the EU. From that perspective, mutual trade and investment would increase with the many additional consumers added to EU's current 370 million, thereby enlarging the European markets.

Because of the expected close relationship between the EU and non-EU European nations, mutual investment and joint ventures will increase as entrepreneurs from both sides move into each other's territory. Furthermore, the predicted larger markets would facilitate mergers and acquisitions between them and other countries, notably the United States and Japan.

Norway's economy has been gradually interwoven with the economies of the EU nations, and as a result the country is a serious candidate for EU membership. Although in the past Norwegians voted against membership, the success of the EU is making joining the club attractive.

SOUTHERN MEDITERRANEAN CANDIDATES

Stronger linkages and closer ties have also been pursued between the EU and Cyprus, Malta, and Turkey, mainly through the Association/Cooperation Councils. These three southern Mediterranean countries have already applied for EU membership.

For Turkey, an associate member of the EU for more than three decades, membership may be further delayed because of reports of human rights violations, mainly against the Kurdish population, constant violations of the Hellenic sea and air space in the Aegean Sea, and the illegal occupation of nearly 40 percent of Cyprus since 1974. Moreover, the shift of EU attention to Eastern Europe and Russia, as well as the low level of development in

Turkey, hinder early membership in the EU. The per capita GNP of Turkey was only $2,520 in 1994 compared to more than $7,000 for Cyprus and Malta (which signed an association agreement with the EU in 1970).

Cyprus negotiated an associated agreement with the EU in 1972 and applied for membership in the summer of 1990. In the 1987 protocol, the EU signed another agreement for the establishment of a customs union over a ten-year period. However, the Turkish invasion in 1974 and the unlawful occupation of the island thereafter complicated the EU's relationship with Cyprus, and more so with Turkey. The main problem is that the Turkish Cypriots, who constitute 18 percent of the population, do not accept occupying less than 30 percent of the island's territory, including the region of Morfou, which generates about 40 percent of foreign earnings. In addition, over 80,000 Turks, implanted from Eastern Turkey, took over the property that Greek (Hellenic) Cypriots had been forced to abandon by Turkish troops. A peaceful settlement with the two communities could speed up EU membership. Cyprus, a tourist and offshore financial center, would see great improvement, and all Cypriots, particularly the Turkish Cypriots with a per capita income of less than half that of the Hellenic Cypriots, would be better off.[8]

EASTERN EUROPEAN CANDIDATES

Poland, Hungary, and the Czech and Slovak republics (CSR) are interested in joining the EU as soon as related institutional and economic reforms have been made. Similar aspirations prevail in Russia and other former Soviet republics.

The EU is on the verge of a monumental transition that will open up the economies of Eastern Europe to investment and trade in food, textiles, telecommunications, and other products and services as they have never been before. However, Eastern European countries, with weak economies and institutions, will not be ready for full membership for some time to come. Furthermore, they may fear colonization by their Western brethren, particularly Germany. Nevertheless, they continue to emphasize their connections with the EU and have started to negotiate closer relations.

Since the collapse of communism, trade of the Eastern European countries with the EU has increased sharply, accounting for more than half of their foreign trade. Recently each of the Eastern European countries signed an interim association agreement, aimed at preparing them for full membership in ten years. As a result, their products will have easier access to the EU, since few reciprocal obligations were imposed. Although full EU membership of the Eastern European countries is not expected soon, it will not take such a long transitional period as that of Turkey (since 1964) because there is not much difference in cultural, sociopolitical, religious, and economic conditions.

In the process of widening the union, the EU Commission proposed elimination of tariffs over six years for imports from Poland, Hungary, and the CSR. However, because of the expected competition, significant negative reactions, particularly from France, are expected from the opening of the EU markets to Eastern European commodities such as textiles, coal, steel, and agricultural and dairy products.

A joining of Poland, Hungary, CSR, and other neighboring countries with the EU may lead to a further postponement of using a single currency in all member-nations in favor of another important cause, that is the economic and political anchoring of these Eastern European states. However, the aspirations of these and other former communist countries have diminished somewhat because of the initial delays in the ratification or modification of the EU Treaty of Maastricht (1991) regarding the introduction of a common currency and the establishment of a European central bank before 1999. After the EU member-nations realign their currencies, it may be easier for the EU to reach out to Eastern Europe.

In almost all Eastern European countries and Russia, free market reforms, privatization of state enterprises, and political democratization are being rapidly enacted to make their systems similar to those of the EU. In the process of privatization, parts of ownership shares are usually given, or sold at low prices, to the employees working for these privatized state enterprises. Similar methods of employee participation prevail in almost all EU countries, such as employee stock ownership plans (ESOPs) in the United Kingdom, co-determination or co-management in Germany, and "popular capitalism" in France. Such similarities in economic organization help stimulate trends toward further EU expansion.

Standing in the way of employee participation is the fact that workers and individuals may not have enough money to buy shares of state enterprises, in auctions or otherwise. In some cases, enterprise executives (managers under the former communist system) and other domestic and foreign gangs have created phony joint ventures to get export–import licenses and loans to buy vouchers or shares from individuals, in order to control ownership. Some of these individuals are engaged in illegal activities, such as the trading of precious metals and uranium for nuclear weapons, car theft, even prostitution and drug trafficking. Such operations observed in Russia, Poland, and other Eastern European countries delay economic and political reforms and pose serious drawbacks to European integration.

The recent reforms in Eastern Europe have brought a severe increase in exchange rates and a decline in per capita GDP in terms of U.S. dollars. In Poland, for example, exchange rates have increased drastically (mainly after the "shock therapy" of January 1990) whereas per capita GDP has declined.

The per capita GNP of Poland, the former Czech republic, and Hungary is relatively low, whereas that of the EU is much higher. From that standpoint, it may be a number of years before these and other Eastern European countries can be ready for EU membership. Nevertheless, a transitional period of associated membership may be used for economic and sociopolitical adjustment for full membership as was given to other EU members in the past.

The Balkans and the European Union

In order to induce de-Balkanization, stimulate social and economic development, and reduce the danger of a wider conflict in the Balkans, the EU can move toward a closer cooperation agreement with the former Yugoslav republics and eventually the other Balkan countries of Albania, Bulgaria, and Romania. The cost to the EU from tariff reduction and regional development and other assistance would be less than the ongoing cost of military involvement through the United Nations and NATO, and other countries including the United States, Russia, and the Islamic nations.

An effective policy not only for the EU but for the United States and other countries may be to support an associated and even full membership of the former Yugoslav republics and other neighboring countries in the EU. This would help reduce ethnic and religious conflicts, rendering existing borders unimportant and giving hope for economic and sociopolitical improvement.

Closer EU cooperation with these republics would help increase investment and trade, particularly with Germany, Austria, and Hellas (a full member of the EU since 1981). Thereafter, investment and trade with other countries, mainly the United States and Japan, would also increase. The main obstacle the Balkan countries face in joining the EU is their low per capita income. However, Ireland, Hellas, Spain, and Portugal were in a similar condition before their entrance in the EU, and Turkey, with even lower per capita income, has been an associate member of the community since 1964.

Furthermore, Hellas, as a full member of the EU, can play a leading role in EU–Balkan relations. Nevertheless, like other EU member-nations, Hellas, as well as Italy, faced a serious problem of Albanian refugees in March 1991 and later, and more refugees are expected from other neighboring republics.

EU enlargement to the Balkan countries would be advantageous not only to Hellas, through more efficient transportation networks, but to all EU members which could use the Balkan Peninsula as a natural bridge for mutual trade and investment with the Middle East. Already, negotiations are being conducted between the EU and Romania, Bulgaria, and the former Yugoslav republics for tariff reduction.

Danube Basin or Euxene Common Market?

The establishment of a Danube basin common market as a buffer against a reunited strong Germany seems impractical in present day Europe. Such a union, including Austria, Hungary, the Czech and Slovak republics, Romania, and the former Yugoslavia, may be useful to the security interests of the EU, and particularly to a rejuvenated Germany, for some time to come. However, an economic association and eventual integration with the EU would be more effective and beneficial to all European countries, as opposed to departmentalizing the old continent into different fortress groups.

A similar intra-bloc common market for Balkan countries (Albania, Bulgaria, Hellas, Romania, Turkey, and the former Yugoslavia) is also impractical and not beneficial to the countries concerned. Intra-Balkan trade may impose costs upon the countries involved insofar as it means trade diversion. The beneficial effects of intra-bloc trade on balance of payments, industrialization, and economic growth may not exceed the detrimental effects of trade diversion of a Balkan common market. This may be so because the Balkan countries produce more competitive products than complementary products—the formation of a common market would make them poorer instead of richer.

The neighboring countries of the Black Sea, primarily Turkey, Romania, Hellas, Bulgaria, Armenia, and Georgia, agreed to create "the union of Euxene countries." Aristotle, in his writings about wonderful hearings, named a similar formation (fifth century B.C.) the common market of Euxene.[9] From an economic point of view, this infant union is not expected to have impressive results, mainly because these countries primarily produce competitive products. However, from a sociopolitical standpoint, such a union may prove beneficial for further cooperation, as a pioneering movement toward an eventual pan-European union under the auspices of the EU. Again, a closer cooperation with the EU may be more beneficial, though painful, for a transitional adjustment period. During the meeting in Athens in April 1995, as well as during other later meetings, the Euxene countries pledged further cooperation.

THE PROBLEM OF ENLARGEMENT

The Maastricht Treaty, signed by the EU member-nations in December 1991, provided for the creation of an EMU which aims at the establishment of a central bank (EuroFed) and a single currency by 1997, if a majority of members qualify; if not, by 1999 at the latest. It also calls for a move toward a political union and military cooperation. The Maastricht agreement revitalized Euro-optimism regarding closer cooperation and the deepening of the EU, which prevailed before the mid-1980s. It favors a deeper community with strict budgetary and monetary standards for inflationary controls and exchange rate stability.

Some EU member-nations oppose monetary and political union of the EU and express disagreement for the replacement of individual currencies by the common currency (Euro). Moreover, many farmers, particularly in France, object to certain EU directives concerning standardization of products as well as to the EU–U.S. agreement concerning the reduction of farm-product subsidies. Also, northern EU member-nations want to reduce their budget contributions regarding the support of the poorer southern member-nations.

There are cases though, in which EU member-nations follow different policies than those dictated by the Maastricht Treaty. Germany, for example, increased its interest rates in 1992 to avoid inflationary presures. As a result, funds were drawn to the deutsche mark, and severe pressures were put on the weak currencies of the other EU nations. This was particularly true for Britain and Italy, which left the European Monetary System (EMS, established in 1979). Moreover, Spain devalued its currency in 1993 and was permitted by the EU to devalue it again, as was Portugal. Other weak currencies, including the Danish krone, the Irish pound, and even the relatively stable French franc faced pressures of devaluation. Furthermore, Sweden allowed its currency to float against the EU. Such disturbances proved that the convergence of fiscal and monetary policies and the deepening of the EU would be difficult at least in the short term.

All these problems, and particularly pushing for an early monetary union, may dig a deep ditch between the EU and other candidate member-nations, especially those of Eastern Europe. Nevertheless, changes and compromises are expected to coordinate related policies and prepare the ground for further EU enlargement.

The dissolution of the Warsaw Pact and the gradual weakening of the American commitment to NATO increased the desire to broaden the EU eastward from the standpoint of defense as well. Thus, the thirty-eight nation Conference on Security and Cooperation in Europe (CSCE) decided to establish a small secretariat in Prague, an office in Warsaw, and a center in Vienna (Chapter of Paris, November 1990) to prevent ethnic and other conflicts. However, mainly because of the required unanimity, CSCE has not been effective regarding the disintegration and the ethnic and religious conflicts in the former Yugoslavia where echoes of World War I were heard. As the EU expands, difficult cooperation problems and pressures are expected from fragmenting tendencies by the absorption of the political and economic transformation of the Eastern European countries.

Nevertheless, Britain favors EU expansion as insurance against a supranational community and as a way of palliating workers' rights and socialist tendencies. Also, Germany, a federal state, favors EU enlargement in a federated form for trade and investment expansion although there is the serious problem of streams of immigrants expected to enter the country. Moreover, Germany may want to increase its political power by incorporating regions in the Czech and Slovak republics, as well as Slovenia, Croatia, Ukraine, and the Baltics, with which it has historical and ethnic relations.

The question of EU enlargement versus deepening is related to the specter of new immigration not only to Germany but to almost all other EU member-nations. In some cases, refugees and other immigrants have different cultural and religious backgrounds. For example, Muslims from Turkey and North Africa primarily enter Germany, France, Spain, Austria, and Britain. However, skin-heads and neo-Nazis in Germany, Jean-Marie Le Pen's National Front in France, and other conservative groups oppose such immigration "invasions." With the end to border controls in 1995, the immigration problem may intensify unless coordinated measures are taken. Such developments may delay EU enlargement.

Nevertheless, there are objections to the enlargement of the EU. France fears that EU enlargement would weaken an expected strong Europe that is necessary to counterbalance NAFTA and the Asian–Pacific Rim. Britain, which is considered mainly in France to be the "Trojan horse" of the United States destined to destroy the EU, seems to support enlargement for purposes of staving off a strong European federalism which it mistrusts. Others fear that an EU enlargement with Eastern Europe would make Germany a powerful economy that would dominate Europe.

From a practical standpoint, institutional reforms for effective decision making and policy implementation are needed to accommodate a growing EU. The EU Commission, with more and more members, would have a difficult time agreeing on important decisions and monitoring application of its directives by individual members. The same can be said for ministerial meetings and a swelling European Parliament with all the trappings of legislative delays. Pessimists fear that enlargement may lead to inflexibility and ever-growing crises.[10]

The resurgent economic nationalism and the difficulty in meeting the limits on budget deficits by a number of member-nations may lead to a two-track approach regarding monetary union. Countries such as France and Germany, with strong and relatively stable economies, can proceed faster in establishing a monetary union, whereas countries with weaker economies, such as Italy, Spain, and Hellas, can only proceed at a slower pace. To facilitate the transition to a central bank and monetary union, the EU established the European Monetary Institute in 1993. The exchange rate mechanism (ERM), already in operation, proved to be largely successful in currency realignment and exchange rate stability among the EU nations, thereby promoting intraregional trade and investment.

FUTURE PROSPECTS

As the EU moves toward common fiscal and monetary policies and political union, serious questions remain. Can the gradual deepening of the EU be combined with a gradual broadening to engulf eighteen, twenty-four, or even more European countries? Is the enlargement of the EU a recipe for its weakening, or is it a historical, economic, and political necessity?

For the EU to achieve its main goals, it should be enlarged to an ultimate membership of all the European nations. Although there are deeply rooted cultural and ethnic differences, and many doubts and quarrels may appear in the process of enlargement, the momentum should remain irreversible. Going back to a divided and belligerent Europe would be horrible, as history has proven repeatedly.[11]

To meet the challenge of the coming economic–political battle with NAFTA and Japan (and the preferential bloc it organizes, the Asian–Pacific Rim), Europe has to move fast to heal differences and enlarge itself to an effective producer-empire. By adding the other advanced EFTA countries and the educated and low-wage nations of Eastern Europe, it should not be obsessed with short-term obstacles but rather adopt advanced technology and cooperative policies that focus on long-term goals in the twenty-first century.[12]

Using short-term strategies for long-term goals, the EU should gradually engulf not only the Eastern European countries but also some of the republics of the Commonwealth of Independent States (the former Soviet Union). Because of the high degree of interdependence in these republics, it can be expected that they may form a new common market based not on Moscow's dictated policies, as in the past but on voluntary agreements and democratic procedures. Such an "Eastern Economic Community," if established, could be a serious competitor to the EU.

Rapid reforms and adjustments toward EU membership in Poland, the CSR, Romania, Bulgaria, Albania, and the former Yugoslav republics, as well as Cyprus, Malta, and Turkey, would strengthen democratic institutions and increase trade and investment, particularly in hotels, telecommunications, printing, financial, and other services. It should be recognized, though, that it is difficult for the former communist economies of Europe to break the chains of centralized controls and change the policies of subsidized prices and guaranteed sales. Furthermore, many state enterprises are run by Workers' Councils which face problems in the process of privatization and the spread of "people's capitalism" through the democratization of property ownership. Depending on future developments, the absorption of other European countries may transform the EU into a less cohesive Community. Already, there are arguments of a community of different speeds and tiers.

Specifically, the Eastern European countries, including those of the Balkan Peninsula and Russia, are in a stage of dramatic change from a command and bureaucratic economic system to a market system. However, they need Western help, not in the form of welfare, but in technical, managerial, and financial assistance, to revitalize their economies so they can join the EU club. By helping them to move forward, the West would be helped as well.[13]

For an effective European economic and, particularly, monetary integration, a convergence of price developments is necessary. This means that inflationary rates should converge and the budgetary deficits and public sector subsidies of inefficient enterprises should be reduced or eliminated. To achieve exchange rate and price stability, Eastern European countries and other EU candidate nations need to increase their exports to the EU countries which, in turn, should gradually open their markets for that purpose.[14]

Finally, an EU enlargement does not necessarily lead to a weak and chaotic Europe, particularly when there is a gradual acceptance of new members with certain adjustment periods. Assuming that the EU economic and political goals are accepted, other European countries may join the union, which could reach even fifty member-nations equaling the number of American states, and form the United States of Europe.

Chapter 4

Economic Organization: Similarities and Differences

PUBLIC VERSUS PRIVATE SECTOR

In the economies of NAFTA and the EU, there exists a serious question about the size of the public versus the private sector. In order to be efficient, a state should not be too large, nor too small, for it must be able to sustain itself. In some cases, though, when the state becomes very large, it tends to be similar to what Thomas Hobbes described in his *Leviathan*: a giant or monstrous technical person.[1] In such cases, frequently, governments collapse under their own weight as people try to regain their freedom.

About a century ago, Adolph Wagner promulgated the hypothesis that social progress causes a proportionately higher growth of the government.[2] Although Wagner's law of the expanding state activity explains important long-term trends in NAFTA and the EU, it was criticized as a self-determining theory of the state.

In addition to Adolph Wagner's predictions of a growing public sector as a result of economic development and the continued pressure for social progress, other economists seemed to expect growth in public sector expenditures and outlays for sundries. Arthur Pigou thought that the public sector, with increasing national income and wealth, would grow while empirical evidence supports a regular growth of government activity, mainly because of shifts of expenditures and revenues to new, higher levels in cases of wars and social disturbances, with no return to the previous lower levels (known as the displacement effect).[3]

In many countries, consumerism is rapidly growing, mainly because of government overspending. However, according to Stoic teachings, in order to be happy and have inner harmony, individuals should live in accordance with nature: *Akolouthos ti fisi zin*. Nevertheless, for a better quality of life and higher productivity, education and training of members of a society should become the "principle of utmost principles," as Plato mentioned some twenty-four centuries ago.[4]

Spending for public works or other investment generates a multiple increase in income (multiplier effect). Additional income, in turn, generates additional investment (accelerator effect). The interaction of the multiplier and the accelerator propel the economy forward when they are positive and backward when they are negative. It seems, though, that "public works . . . are always better maintained by a local or provincial revenue . . . than by the general revenue of the state."[5]

In addition to its social function, the public sector plays an important role in the performance of the overall economy. As a matter of practice, the public and private sectors are largely complementary and interdependent.

In both NAFTA and the EU a good proportion of economic activity is performed by public and semipublic enterprises. Such enterprises are, to a large extent, subsidized by government, and taxpayers have to bear the brunt of additional expense to cover the cost–revenue difference. Despite privileges in taxes and interest subsidies, which public enterprises enjoy in competing for scarce capital and materials, such entities are frequently hampered by political pressures and the weight of government bureaucracy which restricts work incentives and tends to reduce efficiency.

The economic role of government, which expanded during the last half of this century while social objectives were pursued in all NAFTA and EU countries, is under intense criticism. Mandated spending programs, such as interest payments, unemployment benefits, and other welfare costs, are difficult for governments to control because, whether explicitly or implicitly, they are indexed and increase with rising prices. Such spending based on indexed entitlements, which are considered in economic theory as automatic stabilizers, may on many occasions actually stimulate inflation. From that point of view, it becomes difficult for governments to exercise fiscal discipline, reduce budget deficits, and implement anti-inflationary policies.

Public enterprises in NAFTA and the EU are criticized as bureaucratic and inefficient. They are considered political creations that are influenced by pressure groups and politicians for more employment and lower prices. As the critics say, the private sector is controlled by the government, but the public sector is controlled by no one. On both sides of the Atlantic, poor management by political appointees and high costs from excessive union pressures, combined with low prices for social reasons, lead to frequent deficits and, therefore, to government subsidies.[6]

Some state-run enterprises, many of which exist in Mexico and the EU, are monopolies. Many enterprises sold to the private sector remain monopolies and, as such, resort to price fixing, supply restrictions and other anticompetitive and antisocial measures. They become sleeping monopolies with no interest in innovations and technological advancement. However, some state-owned enterprises may provide services that are socially efficient and economically viable through investment and determination of optimum prices. In that case, if there is a price change, nobody can be made better off without making somebody else worse off, according to the principle of Pareto's optimality. From that point of view, performance of state-owned enterprises may be equally or more socially efficient than private monopolies. In practical terms, this depends on the efficiency of the managers involved, regardless if they operate under public or private ownership.

To discourage monopolization of the market, special laws and regulations have already been introduced by NAFTA and the EU countries. They aim at the protection of the consumers from adulteration, pollution, resource depletion, and misrepresentation of quality and price. In the United States, such laws include the Sherman Act of 1890, which prohibits activities that restrain trade and monopolize the market; the Clayton Act of 1914, which forbids price discrimination and elimination of competition between corporations through interlocking directorates and other devices; the Trade Commission Act of 1914, which prohibits unfair methods of competition; the Robinson–Patman Act of 1936, which makes it illegal to try to eliminate smaller rivals by charging unreasonably low prices and using other supply discrimination techniques; the Celler–Kefauver Anti-Merger Act of 1950, which prohibits acquisition of real assets if such acquisitions substantially lessen competition; and other laws and regulations which were enacted to restrict monopoly and maintain competition. Similar antitrust laws prevail in the other NAFTA and EU countries that aim at protecting consumers from unfair trade practices.

However, in spite of such legislation, monopolization and oligopolization of the American and European markets continue to grow. This may be due to economies of scale, which large firms help create through the concentration of capital and modern technology. As long as large mononopolistic or oligopolistic firms can utilize mass production methods and reduce cost per unit, it is difficult to discourage their formation and operation through controls and regulations in the economy. The dilemma, therefore, is how to encourage competition and entrepreneurial innovation without hurting efficiency and economic progress.

Antitrust legislation may be considered as being, to a large extent, unrealistic, like the models of competition it aims to protect. Breaking down large enterprises or prohibiting mergers and other monopolistic formations does not seem to accomplish much from the viewpoint of optimal resource allocation and entrepreneurial innovations. The problems which antitrust laws face today resemble the heads of the mythological Lernaean Hydra, where, in the place of every problem solved, two others appear.

Consolidations and mergers may lead to better organizations and research and lower unit costs. To break or discourage such effective formations is to punish efficiency and success. Antitrust laws and related restrictions should probably discourage price fixing and employment malpractices rather than obstruct mergers that can improve quality and reduce the cost of production. One could argue in favor of replacing all antitrust laws with modern and simplified legislation that recognizes the present real conditions of the oligopolistic and monopolistic structure of the domestic and international markets. This is what can be observed in the EU, and to some extent in NAFTA, particularly with firms dealing with foreign trade and investment in the face of severe competition.

Public regulations and public enterprises appeared as alternatives to the short-comings of antitrust legislation. The responsibility of public utility regulations in the United States is mostly entrusted to state and local agencies. However, federal government commissions have also been introduced to reinforce lo-cal and state controls, mainly during and after the Great Depression. They include the Federal Power Commission (FPC), which regulates gas and elec-tricity; the Securities and Exchange Commission (SEC), which regulates stock and security markets; the Federal Communications Commission (FCC), which controls telephone and telegraph as well as radio and television services; the Interstate Commerce Commission (ICC), which regulates interstate and for-eign trade movements; the Federal Aviation Agency (FAA) and the Civil Aero-nautics Board (CAB), which are responsible for enforcing airline safety rules and economic aviation regulations, respectively. However, the CAB was abol-ished at the end of 1984 after forty-six years in operation, and the Depart-ment of Transportation assumed some of its remaining functions.

Parallel commissions or other business control institutions exist, or are at a development stage, in Canada, Mexico, and the EU. Thus, the European Court of Justice upheld the EU Commission's right to raid companies suspected of price fixing and other anticompetition practices. As a result, the Commission raided several European companies suspected of price fixing and inspected their books. The inspection included subsidiaries of the Dow Chemical Com-pany and other American firms.

Excessive government interventions in the market process, especially in the EU, through regulations and controls may, however, alter entrepreneurial investment decisions and, *ceteris paribus*, retard growth.[7] Thus, environment, health, and safety regulations may require the investment that might other-wise have been used in plant and equipment. They may also require a suffi-cient work force to operate needed control equipment and administer legal activities and office work without adding salable outputs. Nonetheless, pub-lic regulations are expected to yield contributions to total welfare, such as improvement in health and safety, that are difficult to gauge and cannot be fully reflected in reported output. Thus, further research is needed and more efficient measurement of the economic impacts of public regulations on a society to determine if their total beneficial effects overpass their detrimental effects on productivity. In general, NAFTA antitrust regulations and similar controls in the EU nations have indirect and modest influences on private sector allocations and free market operations.

Recent efforts to remove excessively burdensome regulations from the NAFTA and the EU economies have fallen short of the political rhetoric, and limited goals have been met. The bulk of deregulations on both sides of the Atlantic deal with transportation, financial services, environment, energy, and communications. Implementation of deregulations, however, has given more freedom to airlines and railroads to set prices, as well as to commercial banks to freely set deposit interest rates after the elimination of ceilings on such rates.

Government regulation of airlines, for example, was responsible for high labor costs and low efficiency. Since 1978, however, when the U.S. government's sheltering regulation of airlines ended, increased competition suppressed operational costs, including wages, which were reduced in a number of cases. Similar deregulation trends can also be observed in the EU countries, as well as in Canada and especially in Mexico. However, there is the danger that smaller companies will be swallowed up by larger ones, which may eventually control the market and charge higher prices. In addition, problems relating to proper maintenance and dangers of air accidents may appear.

PRIVATIZATION TRENDS

The main objectives of the economies of NAFTA and the EU include the increase of efficiency through competition and deregulation, the encouragement of employees to own shares in the firms in which they work, the spread of ownership in the general economy, the reduction of government expenditures to eliminate deficits, the need for more foreign trade, and the strengthening of the capital market and the economy as a whole. The spread of ownership and the democratization of property create a system in which the economy becomes more stable, as it is based on a large number of active participants relying on many feet.

Through the spread of ownership to many persons, there are better chances of environmental protection. As long as large segments of society are stockholders, decisions concerning depletion of scarce resources and environmental protection would be influenced by a general concern for the health and welfare of the population. This is a way to tame savage capitalism. In a global sense, democratization of property ownership would not only help reduce the danger of the growing ecological crisis and global population explosion, but it would lead to self-restraint and limitation of our desires and consumer demand, as Plato suggested twenty-five centuries ago.

To avoid or mitigate opposition to privatization of government enterprises by public employees, as well as from their elected representatives, a certain percentage of ownership stocks can be given to them. A number of countries, including Britain, France, Greece (Hellas), Italy, Mexico, Poland, and Russia, used such a measure to build support of privatization.

The government should encourage competition and use franchises and contracts, as well as apply users' charges for its services wherever possible. One way of privatization is through divestiture or gradual replacement of government activity, or load shedding. The selection of state-owned enterprises (SOEs) for privatization depends, among other things, on their viability, the political risk of the party in power, availability of managerial skills, and the revenue or foreign exchange expected to be collected from their sale to the private sector.

In order to preserve managerial competence with strong motivation and control, widely dispersed ownership may be foregone, although at the sacrifice of short-term distributional considerations. A large number of stockholders in privatized public enterprises with relatively small numbers of shares for each individual may be uninformed, ignorant, or apathetic. They may not have good knowledge of the position or operation of the enterprise and be unqualified to vote for efficient management, particularly during the early stages of transformation from the public to the private sector.

From the standpoint of efficient privatization, it is better to start with the liquidation or sale of small public enterprises and follow with more complex large state-owned firms, as Mexico did in the 1980s. Sales in cash are always preferable to accepting debt, because the liquidity provided can help to settle liabilities of the state firm under privatization, as well as to buy new machines and other technological instruments to modernize the firm. Moreover, it may be difficult for banks and other financial institutions to provide the needed funds.

Macroeconomic anti-inflationary and other stabilization measures taken before privatization would have positive effects on prices and demand for shares of the privatized firms and other state assets.

PRIVATIZATION IN NAFTA

Canada

The Canadian National Railway (CN), which operates some 18,000 miles of track in Canada and the northern United States, is under reorganization and privatization. As a result, about one-third (11,000) of its work force are expected to be laid off. Also, it is expected that, through the sales of assets and equity injection, half of its C$2.3 billion debt would be eliminated. With about C$4.3 billion revenue a year, CN, which is the sixth-largest railway firm in North America, is expected to collect about C$2 billion (U.S.$1.5 billion) from share offering, which would be coordinated by Goldman Sachs, Scotia McLeod, and Nesbitt Burns. No single shareholder may acquire more than 15 percent of the stake and no restrictions on foreign ownership are imposed by Ottawa.[8]

The Canadian government would sell most of its 70 percent stake (118 million shares) of Petro–Canada, the energy giant, in order to raise $1.2 billion. It is expected that the sale would reduce the government's stake to 20 percent. If the offering is oversubscribed, the government would set an over-allotment of 5.9 million additional shares.

Canada, with a large number of state-owned enterprises (or Crown corporations), is in the process of total or partial privatization of many of these enterprises. Already twelve of the Crown corporations have been fully or partially privatized, and others are in the process of privatization. Moreover, Crown interests in five mixed-owned corporations have been divested to the private sector. Privatized enterprises include Northern Transportation Co., de Havilland Aircraft of Canada Ltd., Canadian Arsenals Ltd., Canadair Ltd., Northern Canada Power Commission, Teleglobe Canada, and Air Canada (45%). Furthermore, CN Hotels, Terra Nova Tel Inc., Northwestern Inc., and all CN subsidiaries were sold to related private companies. Privatization initiatives underway include Eldorado Nuclear Ltd., Nordion International Inc. (formerly Radiochemical Company), Theratronic International Ltd. (formerly Medical Products Division of ACCL), and Air Canada (remaining 55% interest). From the sales of privatized companies, the government collected more than $1.5 billion. Nevertheless, a good number of enterprises dealing with transportation and communications, energy, construction, financial, and other services remain under government ownership, so that Canada maintains a tradition of balancing private and public sector initiatives to maximize the benefits to Canadians.

Canada, which appointed a Minister of Privatization, had, in 1980, more than 75 percent of state ownership in posts and electricity, 75 percent in railways and airlines, and 25 percent in telecommunications.

Mexico

Mexico increased the number of government nonfinancial enterprises from 175 to 520 during the period of 1960–1980 in which Argentina, Brazil, and several other developing and developed countries nationalized many enterprises. In 1980, the public sector of Mexico had more than 75 percent ownership in electricity, oil production, gas, coal, posts, telecommunications, railways, and shipbuilding; 75 percent in steel; 50 percent in airlines; and 25 percent in the motor industry. Among the privatized state-owned enterprises of Mexico were Aeroméxico Airlines and Mexicana Airlines, both of which became profitable after they were sold to the private sector. As a result of NAFTA's implementation, on 1 January 1993 and later, Mexico is expected to denationalize or sell many other industries to synchronize its public and private sectors with those of Canada and, primarily, with a very small number of U.S. state-owned enterprises.

Mexico has recently privatized more than 100 state firms, including Aeroméxico and Mexicana, and reduced huge budget deficits and inflation, thereby stabilizing the economy somewhat.

In less than five years, Mexico collected $22 billion from privatization of state firms, including two television networks and 126 theaters. From the sale of these networks and theaters, the government received $641 million from a group of investors, led by Ricardo Salinas Pliego, owner of a chain of appliance and furniture companies, and in competition with other groups including Paramount Communications and Capital Cities/ABC. These two networks pose a challenge to Televisa S.A., the huge Mexican media monopoly with four networks, which draws about 90 percent of the country's audience, radios, newspapers, magazines, and movie theaters.[9] Foreign (mainly American) equipment partners will be sought to participate in the networks.

In July 1992, Mexico sold its 66.3 percent stake in Banco del Centro, S.A., for $280.4 million. The bank has 130 branches, mainly in the central and western regions of the country. The government retained 8.88 percent of the shares to be sold at a later date. The total amount of money the government earned from the privatization program from eighteen banks, including five recently privatized banks, was $12.4 billion. Furthermore, the creation of new private banks has recently been authorized. International consultants, including CS First Boston, McKinsey & Company, and Allen & Hamilton, advised the Finance Ministry on the process of privatization.

Other important privatizations include Bancomer SNC (56% stake sold for $2.8 billion); Teléfonos de Mexico or Telmex (48.8% stake sold for $3.2 billion); and Altos Hornos de Mexico, the total shares of which were sold for $1.03 billion.

From the privatized giant Telmex, the workers acquired 3.3 percent of its capital, or 6,000 Telmex shares, with each worker receiving preferential terms. The shares were deposited in the trust funds of Banco National de Mexico S.A. and Multibanco Comermex S.A. However, the workers sold 41.5 percent of their shares because the banks failed to give them the preferential treatment they had been promised initially and are left with close to 2 percent of Telemex's capital.

The privatization policy and the liberalized investment laws of Mexico, initiated by President Maguel de La Madrid and deepened under President Carlos Salinas de Gortari, opened the way for U.S. manufacturers who moved their businesses south to enjoy cheap labor. As a result, the total number of jobs of U.S. affiliates in Mexico increased from 370,000 in 1986 to about 500,000 currently. During the 1980s, some 295,000 jobs moved to Mexico. If this trend continues, there are expectations that U.S. manufacturing jobs would decline to the point of turning the United States into a Third World nation, as has been the case for Argentina since the 1950s.

Since 1984 and up to the beginning of 1994, trade and investment reforms lowered average tariffs from 24 to 13 percent and liberalized the foreign investment code drastically. However, although extensive privatization has occurred, a large number of services such as oil, gas, electricity, railroads, radios, television, forestry, domestic transportation, and commercial, financial, and telecommunications remain under government control.

United States

The United States, with more than 75 percent federal government ownership in postal service and 25 percent in electricity and railways in 1980, has a very small public sector compared to other countries, followed by Japan with more than 75 percent ownership in postal service and telecommunications, 75 percent in railways, and 25 percent in airlines.

Since there existed no previous nationalizations, as was the case in Mexico and some EU countries, the United States has not been a big league player in the privatization movement. However, in the 1980s, the U.S. government sold Conrail and its minority shares in Chrysler. (More information on Conrail's problems is presented in a later section.)

Because of government budget restraints, it is proposed that private business operate parts of the 42,500 miles of U.S. interstate roads, collecting tolls and spending them for repairs. The states that own the highways can lease them to private investors for thirty or forty years with provisions that these investors would be entitled to charge tolls and be responsible for repairing decaying highways and bridges. This public–private partnership is expected to improve transportation, though tolls would be higher and more toll booths would be created. However, private companies may not provide the sufficient safety guarantees that the federal government does, and problems of pollution and road hazards may increase from the additional booths created. Nevertheless, a number of states have passed related laws, including California, Texas, Florida, Arizona, Minnesota, and Washington, and many other states are considering such legislation of public–private partnership. Also, Congress approved the privatization of Sallie Mae, which deals with student loans and college education financing.

The question of privatization versus public operation troubles many states and cities, including New York. New York City's subways, built mostly between 1900 and 1940, were publicly owned and privately operated (Interborough Rapid Transit and Brooklyn–Manhattan Transit lines) and publicly owned and operated (Independent lines). Because of reluctance to raise the nickel fare, and because of the Great Depression of the 1930s, the subway lines encountered severe financial difficulties; consequently, in 1940, Mayor Fiorello La Guardia brought all three lines under a single municipal system. Thereafter, high labor costs, competition from automobiles, and relatively low fares led to high deficits. In order to reduce deficits and take the subway out of politics, the municipal system was replaced by the Transit Authority in 1953. However, the turning of a public necessity into a business enterprise led to physical deterioration of the subways and the reduction of the accountability of elected officials. On the other hand, in the case of subway privatization, the tolls would be higher. Similar discussions on privatization have occurred regarding the public hospitals of New York.

Washington, London, Paris, and Moscow have better-run transit systems, but the governments pay huge subsidies. Similar questions have been raised for the privatization of the collection of parking fines and other public utilities that are natural monopolies and can raise prices as long as there is no competition or price controls by state or city commissions to protect the consumers. The dilemma of government inefficiency and private monopoly, which bothered Adam Smith and other classical economists, still remains and demands further research and reliable socioeconomic answers.

EU PRIVATIZATION

All EU and other Western European countries have large public sectors. In 1980, these countries (when statistical data were available) had more than 75 percent state ownership in postal service, railways, and telecommunications (except for Spain, with 50%). In electricity, Austria, Britain, France, Hellas, and Switzerland had more than 75 percent state ownership; West Germany, Holland, and Italy had 75 percent; Sweden had 50 percent; and Belgium had 25 percent. About the same proportions of public sector ownership prevailed in gas and coal. In airlines, Austria, Belgium, West Germany, Hellas, Italy, and Spain (with a stake in 747 companies in 1983) had and still have more than 75 percent state ownership; France and Holland had 75 percent, as had Britain before its privatization program of the British Airways was enacted; Sweden had 50 percent; and Switzerland had 25 percent. In steel, Austria had more than 75 percent state ownership; Britain, France, Italy, and Sweden had 75 percent; Belgium and Spain had 50 percent; and Holland had 25 percent. In the motor industry, Austria had more than 75 percent state ownership in 1980; Britain, France, and Holland had 50 percent; and West Germany and Italy had 25 percent. All these countries and many others are in the process of selling state-owned enterprises to reduce inefficiency and large deficits.

In almost all EU countries there is a trend toward privatization, that is, the selling of part or total government control in inefficient enterprises to the private sector to avoid additional debt from accumulated annual deficits. In some cases, such enterprises raise capital by issuing equity rather than borrowing. In other cases, they are encouraged to replace debt with equity. If investors overvalue such enterprises, it is proper for their managers to try to tap the market for sales of shares. A serious problem, though, appears when a government enterprise for privatization is not expected to be efficient in the future, in which case no investors are willing to buy shares or to accept replacement of debt by equity and the enterprise may be declared bankrupt. Governments also may give foreigners and especially expatriates incentives to buy shares.

The EU governments received some $43 billion from privatization of state enterprises in 1996, already a 30 percent increase from the previous year, bringing the total value of privatization to $230 billion. The privatization proceeds of 1997 are estimated at $53 billion, with about 40 percent from foreign investors. The Italian government, which collected $5.9 billion from sales of shares in Erni Oil Company, expects to receive some $20 billion in 1997 from sales of utilities, energy, telecommunications (Telecom Italia), and banks.

Likewise, France expects to collect $11 billion, Spain $8.6 billion (mainly from Endesa, the electricity group), and Germany, who received $13.5 billion from sales of Deutche Telekom in 1996, plans to collect $5 billion from privatization.[10] Also, the Greek Telecom (OTE) is in the process of privatization, as is the Portuguese Telecom from the sales of shares, of which Portugal has already raised $2.03 billion.

In EU and other countries, in which family ownership of private companies is more common, debt is a valuable tool for financing because it allows growth without forgoing the benefits of concentrated ownership. However, in large manufacturing companies equity financing is more common. For example, in Turkey, financing of manufacturing firms is about two-thirds equity financing, and the rest is mainly long-term debt (about 17%) and internal financing (about 13%). Around the same proportions of equity and internal financing can be observed in Mexico, whereas in the United States, internal financing accounts for about three-fourths and in Germany about two-thirds. Nevertheless, the right mix of equity and debt depends on many factors, including the growth of the market and the existing indebtedness.

In its efforts to denationalize industries, the Italian government sold its remaining 84 percent stake in Dalmine S.p.A. steel company to Techint Finanziaria S.p.A. and Siderca S.p.A. companies, both controlled by the Rocca family. Moreover, Banca di Roma, Italy's second largest banking group, is in the process of privatization.

BAA PLC, formerly the British Airport Authority, was privatized in 1987. It operates Heathrow, Gatwick, and five other British airports. Also, it has a contract to manage retailing at Pittsburgh International Airport and all operations at the Indianapolis International Airport, and it has its eyes on other countries as well.[11]

The French government plans to put on the market at least part of the company that will result from the expected merger of the aerospace concerns Aerospatiale SA and Dassault Aviation SA.[12] Moreover, it plans to sell shares of the France Telecom S.A., worth $8.82 billion, the biggest initial public offering ever.

Although the European Commission has sought to prevent bailouts of inefficient state companies, Alitalia, the Italian state carrier, which is in the process of privatization, would receive some $1 billion to be kept afloat by its corporate parent, the state holding company IRI. In an agreement with its unions, Alitalia would cut costs so that it would be efficient while employees would take at least 20 percent stake in the firm and would have three seats on the board.

EMPLOYEE OWNERSHIP

Many large and small companies around the world realize that employees are the key to better performance. Creative human resource management, with increasing employee involvement, is vital in promoting quality performance in the present highly competitive world. Through greater employee responsibility, continuous on-the-job training, teamwork production, and work motivation, economic performance is improved. This is a successful way of investment in human capital and organization which has been implemented in many countries.

In order to increase employees' involvement, some companies offer a certain number of stocks at lower than market price, with the option to keep or sell them after a number of years. This and similar partial ownerships of stocks increase the motivation and the productivity of the employees because they feel that good performance by the company will eventually increase their monetary return.

Employee ownership is rapidly growing in both NAFTA and the EU. For example, in the United States, employee stock ownership plans (ESOPs) increased rapidly during the last two decades. Also, in the European Economic Area (EEA), which includes the fifteen EU countries and the EFTA countries, labor participation in enterprise decision making is growing. Employee ownership also takes the form of ESOPs in Britain, Italy, Hellas, and other European countries, while in France and Sweden it takes the form of workers' consultation, and labor–capital co-management or co-determination in Germany.

There are questions as to whether ESOPs constitute an innovation or a sham that offers employees no real representation in the companies in which they work and as to whether they lead to labor–management cooperation and the improvement of competitiveness and productivity.[13]

In order to avoid economic and social downsizing and euthanasia through its own "creative destruction," as Joseph Schumpeter observed, the capitalistic system of NAFTA and the EU should be modernized. The recent spread of shareholding, through ESOPs or otherwise, is a process which reforms and improves the system. For example, total equities outstanding in the United States increased from $1.9 trillion in 1984 to $6.3 trillion in 1996, about half of which belong to households, whereas individual shareholders increased from 8.6 million in 1956 to 51.3 million Americans in 1992, and the number continues to grow.

Although automation and foreign competition exercise heavy pressure on the middle class, modern or democratic capitalism based on private ownership and self-interest, which is essential to promote wealth, as Aristotle and Adam Smith argued, will prevail through innovations and reforms. The government can encourage such ownership diffusion by providing tax and other incentives, thereby discouraging wealth concentration and monopolization.[14]

Several terms are used to express widespread share of ownership, or split of shares, and a number of divestiture modes are utilized to privatize state-owned enterprises. Such modes include traditional capitalism, institutional capitalism, popular capitalism, and labor or employee capitalism.

In traditional capitalism, shares of the SOEs are sold through the Stock Exchange or in auctions in which foreign investors can participate. Stocks of the SOEs may be sold to such institutions as pensions or similar funds of the workers and employees. This is the case of institutional capitalism in which the workers and employees become owners indirectly through stocks acquired by their pension funds. There is a risk, however, of decline in stock prices or complete loss from weak SOEs, and certain legal conditions must be fulfilled before such transactions are made. Normally, a certain portion of the stocks of the divested SOEs, usually up to 30 percent, is acquired by pension funds, depending on the economic standing of these enterprises. In any case, pension funds became an important source of financing the privatization process in the EU, NAFTA, and other countries, and expectations are that they will become more important in the future.

There are cases in which the government permits taxpayers to deduct the total amount of the money they spend to buy stocks from their taxable income. In order to spread ownership to large segments of population, some limits of deductible income per person can be instituted. Privatization of SOEs through selling shares to the general public in this fashion, known as popular capitalism, is attractive and popular. Although some taxpayers may sell their shares, ownership usually remains widespread and effective control is exercised by the management.

In order to stimulate production incentives and to gain support of the workers and employees of the divested SOEs, the government normally offers a portion of the stocks of the enterprises to them at preferential terms, usually lower than the market prices. Such spread of equity to employees and workers, or labor capitalism, may depend on the wage bill to equity ratio, but in the first stage of privatization, the percentage of labor may be small (less than 20%). Nevertheless, the workers and employees may use their stocks as collateral to acquire loans from banks and buy additional shares to the point of becoming owners of all the stocks of the firms in question. The fact that the payment of the workers for the stocks is frequently less than their market value (sometimes at 50%) make such purchases attractive. Also, the firm may offer to repurchase the stocks at retirement or before, if their prices are lower, say by 50 percent of what the workers pay initially.

U.S. ESOPs

According to the National Center for Employee Ownership, there are about 10,000 U.S. companies that are partially or totally owned by more than eleven million employees through ESOPs, which have been growing year after year. Such employee ownership varies from less than 1 percent to 100 percent, but mostly below 50 percent ownership of the company. It seems that the decline of the trade unions from 33 percent in 1975 to less than 14 percent at present encourages the creation of ESOPs. It is estimated that there are 1,500 majority employee-owned U.S. firms with more than one million employees and workers.

In 1992, there were 9,764 ESOPs with 11.2 million employees, compared to 7,402 ESOPs with 7.4 million employees in 1985, and only 1,604 ESOPs with 248,000 employees in 1975.

Expectations are that the number of ESOPs will increase, mainly because of the tax breaks provided for both employees and company owners. Thus, if employees own 30 percent or more of a company stock, they can sell their stocks at retirement without paying capital gains tax on their profits. More attractive tax reforms are expected to provide additional incentives for forming ESOPs, including the deduction of more of the cost of borrowing money.

The largest companies in which the employees have a majority ownership include Publix Supermarkets, Epic Healthcare, Avis, Science Applications International, The Parson Corporation, Amsted Industries, Avondale Shipyards, the Journal Company, Morgan Stanley, Austin Industries, and Weirton Steel Corporation. The number of employees per company varies from 65,000 for Publix, 13,500 for Avis, 8,000 for the Parsons, 7,500 for Avondale, 6,700 for Morgan, and 6,100 for Weirton. If the United Airlines (UAL) unions, with 82,000 employees, conclude their six-year effort to acquire the firm, then UAL would be the largest employee-owned company. Employees in other airlines, including Eastern, Republic, Western, and T.W.A., have stakes varying from 12 to 45 percent with seats on the board of directors.

Avis, Inc., which established employee ownership in 1987, is a successful company with the value of its stock growing from $5 in 1987 to $18 recently. It seems that the monthly meetings of the employee empowerment groups with the management help introduce innovative suggestions about running the firm. It can be said that making employee ownership work is difficult but largely beneficial.

In some cases, employees initiate stock ownership proposals and even offer concessions-for-equity swaps, as was the case with T.W.A. where the employees, primarily the pilots with salaries of more than $100,000 a year, accepted $660 million concessions in exchange for 45 percent ownership in 1992. Thereafter, T.W.A. proved to be a successful airline in the United States. Unions need to put aside their animosities and avoid the disagreements like those of the pilots, machinists, and flight attendants of Northwest Airlines.

A number of American, European, and other airlines try to save themselves by gaining labor concessions in return for some level of employee ownership. Thus, T.W.A. recovered from huge losses and moved toward profitability after the restructuring of its ownership. Northwest Airlines avoided bankruptcy in 1993 by using a similar restructuring program. The pilots and other employees of Southwest Airlines have 12 percent ownership and are paid only for the time they fly. KIWI International Airlines is owned by pilots and other employees who paid $50,000 each to create the company. However, troubles have appeared because of severe competition. Moreover, United Airlines and its employees continue to talk about a buyout offer of 60 percent of shares of the pilots, engineers, and flight attendants. It seems that free market rewards, efficiency, improvement, and growth are achieved with high production incentives and no labor disturbances as employee owners cannot strike against themselves.

The International Business Machines Corporation (IBM) filed a registration statement with the Securities and Exchange Commission for 6.5 million shares, worth of about $44 each, to be contributed to its employee retirement plan. IBM, which is using stocks instead of cash for pension obligations, plans also to contribute 15 million shares, from time to time, to its employee retirement plan.

The Todd Products Corporation, which designs and manufactures power supply units and electronic equipment in Long Island, New York, established an ESOP in order to motivate employees and avoid new outside owners. Chemical Bank provided advice and financial support for this ESOP, as it does for other mobile market companies. Because more than 30 percent of the company's stock is sold to an ESOP, capital gain taxes can be deferred until death. Also, the principal and the interest on the loan are tax deductible. Each employee who stays five years with the company is allocated shares worth a certain percentage of his or her salary. Until the company is taken public, vested employees can sell their shares back to the ESOP when they leave. There is a danger, though, that when the company is taken public, the employees may be unhappy when the stock prices decline.

Publix Supermarkets, Florida's largest chain, is owned by the employees and is expanding to Georgia and other states. As the author discovered in related research, the employees have high incentives. Other firms with employee ownership include Morgan Stanley Company, which deals with financial operations, and Thermo Electron Corporation, a successful company in which 95 percent of the 5,000 employees are shareholders. In the steel industry, in addition to Weirton Steel Company, which is wholly owned by employees since 1986, the LTV Corporation, the second largest steel company, sold its storage and steel bar divisions to employees in 1985 and 1989, respectively. Also, the USX Corporation's plant in Geneva was bought by workers in 1987, as was 80 percent of the McClouth Steel Company in 1988. The main reason for these sales is to reduce employee costs and pension liabilities by having the workers take some risk to preserve their jobs. However, Cyclops Industries turned down the employees offer of $50 million to buy Cytemp Specialty Steel.

Phone companies, such as Ameritech, Bell Atlantic, and Southwestern Bell, adopted a poison pill by giving shareholders the right to buy stocks at half price and established ESOPs to make a hostile takeover very expensive and to save taxes.

The Bureau of National Affairs Inc. in Washington, D.C., a publishing firm competitive with the Lawyers Co-operative Publishing Company, is owned by the employees. They both publish business law, tax, and other legal research products.

Dun and Bradstreet Corporation, a business information company in New York, authorized the repurchase of more than 3 million shares for employee stock options and compensation plans. Charles Schwab Corporation of San Francisco sold 10 million common shares to an ESOP; and Houston Industries, an electric utility holding company, adopted an ESOP which bought about 10 million of its 128 million shares.

The Consolidated Rail Corporation (Conrail), which evolved from six bankrupt Northeastern railroads, was taken over by the government in 1976, and sold to the public in 1987, announced a plan to establish an ESOP worth $300 million and to buy back more than one-third of its outstanding shares of about $1.3 billion. In addition, a debt increase was announced to make itself a less attractive candidate for a takeover. Currently, CSX Corporation offered $8.5 billion to acquire Conrail, in competition with Norfolk Southern Corporation, which came with a more lucrative offer of $10 billion, and the competition continues with higher offerings.

East Rock Partners L.P. recently established an Employee Stock Ownership Trust. Kerr–McGee Corporation, an energy company, sold more than 2.6 million shares to its ESOP and received $125 million, while American Medical International Inc. and Domino's Pizza Inc. are considering the creation of ESOPs. Tribune Co. expanded its employee ownership from 1 to 10 percent through a $350 million ESOP, while Polaroid Corporation's employees have acquired 20 percent of the company.

In Avis, Inc., an ESOP owns most of the stocks on behalf of 12,500 employees, through a $1.7 billion leveraged buyout. This made Avis a successful enterprise and its stock ownership a catalyst for better performance in paying back debts and making profits.

Other companies that created ESOPs for better performance or tax-shelters include PPG Industries Inc., U.S. West Inc. (a telephone company), Delta Airlines, and Merck and Co. Inc. Also, the New York Times Company and the Kimberly–Clark Corporation offered to give a paper mill that they own jointly in Ontario to its employees.

U.S. Tax Benefits For ESOPs

The rapid growth of ESOPs is primarily due to the tax incentives provided by legislation. The Employee Retirement Income Security Act of 1974 gave legal sanction to ESOPs and allowed tax breaks on the loans made to them. The Tax Reduction Act of 1975 allowed for tax deductions on owner contributions to ESOPs, while the Small Business Employee Ownership Act of 1980 permits the Small Business Administration to lend money to ESOPs. Moreover, the Economic Recovery Act of 1981 permitted tax credit for the money contributed to an ESOP by an employer, while the Deficit Reduction Act of 1984 allowed banks to exclude from reported income 50 percent of interest earned on loans to ESOPs.

Section 542 of the Tax Reform Act of 1984 allows corporations to deduct cash dividends paid to a tax credit employee stock ownership plan. It is required, though, that the dividends must be received by the ESOP within ninety days of the close of the plan year. Also, Section 543 of the Act adds Section 133 to the tax code and permits a 50 percent exclusion from tax payment of interest on loans used to finance the acquisition of employer securities by an ESOP. The loans must be made by a bank or other financial institution. The loan can be made to an ESOP or to a corporation that lends the money to the ESOP.

Tax laws providing benefits to employee ownership should exist for a substantial time so that the system can be given a chance for a real trial and to determine its workability. However, such laws should not be so attractive that they create an artificial short-run euphoria with long-term discouraging effects.

Through ESOPs, companies can provide employees and themselves with tax-favored benefits. Also, new ownership shares can be allocated to the employees without cash spending. A significant benefit for companies is the contribution they can make to an ESOP that is totally tax deductible. Such a contribution can be up to 25 percent of the payroll of ESOP participants. For example, if the payroll of ESOP participant employees in a company is $100 million, the company can contribute up to $25 million to an ESOP that is tax deductible. This can take place through issuing new shares of the company's stock to an ESOP, and these shares are allocated to individual employees. However, the voting rights of the ESOP participants may present problems to the existing shareholders, especially when employees' holdings may approach or achieve majority control. Also, problems of cash liability may be created when the company buys back shares of large numbers of departing ESOP participants.

Criticism of ESOPs

Although the law encourages employee ownership, the ESOP movement may not always boost productivity. For example, encouragement was given to owner–farmers by the Homestead Act by the U.S. Congress in 1862, but not many farmers remained with the agricultural sector. A similar "industrial homestead" act through ESOPs, which Congress enacted in 1974, may not always assure high productivity. As economies become more advanced, productivity may decline in the industrial sector; therefore, more emphasis should be given to ESOPs in the service sector. From that standpoint, the term "workers' ownership" would be gradually replaced by "employee ownership."

For some executives, employee ownership may be an anathema. They may not be willing to involve the new owner–employees in decision making. Furthermore, they may abuse tax-advantaged ESOPs, covering their actions with the mantle of employees' capitalism to retain control. Managers may theoretically support employee ownership and compensation according to productivity, but they may hesitate to implement such measures in practice. Therefore,

employee ownership may not be an elixir that always works on better performance, especially if employees do not have a voice in the conducting of company business. ESOPs make capitalists out of people with voting rights for
work incentives and anti-takeover defense, but there may be cases in which
employee owners may vote in favor of a corporate raider as well.

To counter plant closings, particularly in the antiquated U.S. steel industry,
workers and employees are offered the alternative of ownership and operating the firms themselves. High labor cost (around $40,000 per year for a
typical production worker) and heavy pension liabilities make steel products
noncompetitive. Such cost disadvantages lead steel companies to consider
complete or partial shutdowns or, as labor unions argue, to play one plant off
against another. As a result, the pressure upon labor unions to accept sizable
wage reductions and other concessions becomes obvious. In serious cases,
plans are presented for the closing of plants permanently, or have the workers
accept ownership.

Weirton Works, a division of National Steel Corporation (the fourth-largest
producer of steel in the nation), was transformed into the largest employee-
owned enterprise in the nation. The workers accepted 32 percent pay cuts and
reductions in pensions in return for stockholding of the company. The plant,
with some 7,000 workers and business worth $1 billion per year, was bought
at about 20 percent of the $322 million book value. A large portion of the
purchase price was in the form of notes to be held over fifteen years. Weirton
Works of West Virginia, which produces rolled steel for automobiles and house-
hold appliances as well as tin plates for beverage and food containers and
other steel products, raised the rest of the money on the financial markets.
Also, U.S. Steel Corporation contemplates similar labor concessions or transfer
of ownership to employees to avoid shutdowns.

Labor unions in airlines are trading wage concessions for equity. The UAR
Corporation, the parent company of United Airlines, is negotiating labor concessions in wages and other benefits in exchange for a stake in UAR ownership by the unions of pilots, machinists, and flight attendants. Similar trading
of concessions for equity were made in T.W.A. and Northwest Airlines.

Although previous attemps by the unions of United Airlines to buy the
company failed, the need for long-term viability of the carrier and the security of
the workers' jobs necessitate reconciliation instead of confrontation. In the negotiations, the unions would exchange 15 percent wage cuts with a 60 percent stake
in the carrier. The stockholders would retain the remaining 40 percent of the
shares and would receive $20 a share for the other 60 percent to be financed
by the cash reserves of the company plus new equity. In the end, the employees obtained 55 percent ownership. However, lenders may have reservations
for the support of a company in which labor unions have a majority stake.

On both sides of the Atlantic, modern enterprises in many cases require
higher performance from their employees and workers than they are able to
offer. This may lead to mistrust and conflicts between labor and manage-

ment. To overcome such problems and maximize efficiency, some form of cooperation and collaboration is necessary through the creation of ESOPs or other forms of employee participation. In any case, ESOPs make the fates of companies and employees more intertwined.

Facing the problems of plant closings and layoffs, labor unions began to support worker purchases of the companies in which they work and also provide funds for such purchases. Thus, U.S. labor leaders established the Employee Partnership Fund to help workers buy factories. With the workers' concessions, additional loans can be solicited from commercial banks and other investment institutions for enterprise expansion.

Some enterprises merge into newly formed companies owned by employees, management, and certain institutional investors. Full-time employees are usually eligible for stock ownership. Shareholders approve the percentages of shareholding among the new owners in such mixed schemes which are formed to avoid bankruptcies or buyouts by other companies. Cone Mills Corporation, a textile firm, entered this scheme to prevent a takeover by Western Pacific Industries, a former railroad company that makes thermosplastics, counting devices, and other precision parts. Also, Dan River, Inc., voted to sell the firm to its employees to avoid a takeover by Carl Icahn, an investment company in New York.

Because of the extensive split of shares in a large number of shareholders, stock ownership by the employees makes it difficult for buyouts by other companies. This is the case with U.S. News and World Report, Inc., which is owned by its employees. Other companies, primarily competing advertisement magazines, openly or secretly, offer higher prices per share than those in the stock exchange markets or than the book value, in order to acquire majority of stocks and thereby reduce competition in related industries. Such related companies include Atlantic Monthly, Capital Cities Communications, and the Times–Mirror Company.

Chemical Bank bought Chase Manhattan Bank for $10 billion in 1995. As a result, 12,000 jobs would be eliminated in three years. The new bank, which has the name Chase Bank, recently introduced a plan of employee stock ownership. Each full-time employee has the option to buy up to 400 shares with a fixed price of $35.50 per share, up to the year 2000. If the price per share in the stock market reaches $50.00, the employees can sell 200 shares, and if it reaches $60.00 they can sell the remaining 200 shares, or they can sell the option itself for the price difference (e.g., $60.00 minus $35.50). This means that on the average there would be about a $10,000 gain per employee. Part-time employees can buy up to 200 shares under the same terms.

Trade Winds, a hotel resort group in St. Petersburg, Florida, with 577 suites and hotel rooms, established an ESOP in December 1995. In interviews with the employees, their enthusiasm and eagerness to serve the clients is visible. As shareholders, they feel the company belongs to them and its good performance preserves their jobs and good wages.

Radio Shack gives the option to the employees to buy shares after ninety days of work. They can use up to 7 percent of their salary annually, matched with 40 percent by the company, for stocks that can be sold any time. The net gain for the employees is the 40 percent contribution by the company when they buy stocks.

Toys-R-Us Company also provides stocks to its employees with some benefits.

In WINN DIXIE, a food chain, employees can receive 50 to 100 shares a month at a sizable discount. Such an option is determined periodically and the shares can be sold back to the company after five years. The company lends money to the employees to buy such stocks and the loans can be repaid monthly over three years without interest.

WORK RULES AND PRODUCTIVITY

In the capitalist economies of NAFTA and the EU, a legal framework into which market institutions and free enterprises can develop is required. A system of civic and business law is needed to protect property rights and free transactions. Ownership of property includes the rights of acquisition and the use and disposal of property. These rights are above government or other infringement.[15] The legal system, with its complex series of rules, should protect personal and group rights against incursions and give individuals the right to enter any business so that efficiency is promoted through competition and entrepreneurial innovations. To be effective, contracts made by individuals and enterprises should be enforced by law and, in cases of nonperformance, a system of adjudicating damages should be provided.

Compared to the United States, the EU is over-regulated on matters of labor. If regulations concerning no weekend work and other restrictions were eliminated, machinery, which does not know holidays, can be run with additional labor, thereby increasing productivity and creating jobs. It is estimated that the EU real economic growth has totaled 73 percent since 1970, but employment has risen only 7 percent.

According to the U.S. Labor Statistics Bureau, the EU Statistics Office, and the International Labor Office in Geneva, the average work week varies from 43.6 hours in Britain, 40 in the United States, 39 in France, 37.9 in Japan, and 37 in Germany, whereas the vacation days per year vary from 30 in Germany, 27 in Britain, 25 in France, and only 12 in the United States and 11 in Japan.

French legislation approved a four-day week for 1996 and thereafter, but wages were to be reduced by 5 percent on the average (from 3% for low wages up to 8% for higher wages) and employers must employ 10 percent more workers. In addition, the government would abolish the 8.8 percent unemployment payroll tax to offset increased employer costs. Furthermore, with the expected higher productivity from the reorganization of work shifts and more working people, as well as the introduction of profit-sharing schemes, the French government expects a widening of the tax base and an increase in tax revenue.

In the United States, labor unions promote the introduction of a thirty-hour work week so that work would be spread to those unemployed. To that effect, Representative Lucien Blackwell of Philadelphia introduced a bill in 1993 (now in U.S. Congress for approval) for a government-mandated thirty-hour work week. Because of health and other benefits, employers hesitate to employ new workers and instead use part-time employees (who accounted for 5% of the total work force of 120 million in 1993) or overtime to do the work.

The 500 big industrial companies reported in *Fortune* magazine reached a peak at 16.3 million employees in 1979, but with a steady decrease thereafter, declined to 11.8 million in 1992. Large corporations such as General Motors, AT&T (and its computer unit, NCR), Philip Morris, IBM, Boeing, Sears, Coca-Cola, and many other companies are laying off thousands of employees to reduce production costs and be competitive.

Increased global competition, and the advancement in computer and other technology, transform production from labor to capital intensive, generating more structural unemployment in both blue-collar and white-collar workers. Moreover, big investment funds, such as employee pension funds, put pressure on corporate boards to reduce cost and increase profits. This trend of massive layoffs is expected to lower the employee morale, as employees fear the next round of layoffs, and is detrimental to productivity incentives.

The reduction of the work week without raising production costs and cutting workers' remuneration may be difficult in practice. It may be based more on optimistic expectations than on real evidence. More flexible work shifts, higher employee morale, and more employee participation may boost productivity and generate additional employment. However, less work hours by skilled personnel and no reduction in wages are expected to lead to higher costs, at least for a period of initial adjustment. In any case, part-time employment still increases rapidly. According to the U.S. Department of Labor, it increased by about 50 percent from 1977 to 1986 in the United States, Japan, and Italy, 40 percent in Canada and Germany, and 72 percent in Britain.

Advanced free market or capitalist economies of NAFTA and the EU, with heavy capital accumulation and growing automation, resort to shorter work weeks to avoid extensive unemployment and decline in aggregate demand. Computers, robots, and other machines are replacing workers, and the average unemployment rate is currently about 11 percent in the EU countries and around 6 percent in the United States.

People do not care if they are governed by the right or the left. What they are concerned about is unemployment. Jobs are disappearing fast. Industry giants such as Philips, Michelin, Fiat, Volkswagen, B.M.W., Daimler–Benz, and many other large- and medium-sized companies, not only in Europe but in Japan, the United States, and many other countries, continue to lay off workers and replace them with machines. Many people feel insecure and become conservative in their spending. Such symptoms, which have similarities with those of the pre-Depression years of the 1930s, may result in pessimism, defective demand, and a severe economic crisis.

In order to avoid mass dismissals, some firms switch to four-day work weeks, some reduce the hours of work per day, and others use extended vacations or early voluntary retirement through severance payments and similar devices to mitigate the problem of unemployment and loss of income. Also, the policy of working less but with more flexibility, including night and weekend work so that machinery can operate for longer periods, seems to attract attention. However, a key element in the growing fascination of a shorter work week is the avoidance of substantial reduction in worker income and the consequent decrease in their overall demand.

Even an exchange of slightly lower pay for a reduction in work week hours would give the workers more freedom to enjoy the benefits of automation and to use more leisure time for education and cultural activities. However, reduction in wages is not necessary, and more people may be hired if productivity gains offset related costs. Otherwise, domestic and foreign competition would lead to losses and layoffs.

Employers argue that a major reason for high unemployment is extensive regulations, which are associated with inflexible job markets, mainly in Europe, and costly welfare programs, especially in the United States where employers pay all or a large part of the health benefits for their employees. This is why they resort to overtime work, which has increased significantly in recent years, or use short-term contracts with no benefits.

LABOR–MANAGEMENT SHARING

For American and European industries to compete in the global marketplace, greater sharing of management and information with employees is needed. By giving greater responsibility to employees, workplace innovations, competitiveness, and productivity increase. A healthier workplace is created through a policy of providing information to the employees who participate in company affairs.[16]

Nevertheless, some labor leaders, including the president of the International Brotherhood of Teamsters, are against the new trend of labor–management cooperation. This type of opposition justifies the public perception that big labor unions are obstructionists. Others think that many companies lay off employees and cut wages and benefits instead of sharing management with employees.

At the Conference on the Future of the American Workplace in Chicago on 26 July 1993, labor–management and government representatives, including U.S. President Clinton, agreed to make efforts for cooperation of all groups for the creation of jobs, increase in efficiency, and implementation of common work practices. They pointed out that labor–management frictions undermine productivity and competitiveness and lead to job shrinkage. In order to reverse the steady decline of union membership over the last twenty years, a cooperative workplace, extensive skills training, and profit or revenue sharing should be encouraged. Instead of raising wages, gain-sharing in the form of bonus payments based on workers' achievement is favored by many companies.

The Wheeling–Pittsburgh Steel Corporation, with nine plants in Pennsylvania, West Virginia, and Ohio, introduced an example of union–management cooperation that gave the workers a significant role in running the company and cutting labor costs. The aim of this new "partnership" agreement of stockholders and workers is to improve work life and production. In addition to profit sharing and workers' participation on the board of directors, strikes and other labor disturbances are expected to be reduced while a more humane management would utilize all the skills and knowledge of workers. Four company and four union representatives constitute the Strategic Decisions Board and meet monthly to oversee product quality, machinery utilization, new investment and technology, and work performance from the shop floor to the board room. Average labor cost in wages and benefits was reduced from $21.40 to $17.50 per hour, some workers began leadership training, and productivity improved. Furthermore, the LTV Steel Company set up a similar profit sharing and stock plan in return for labor concessions while six other major steel companies use the same framework for union negotiations to be more competitive in domestic and international markets.

In some firms, including Ford Motor Company, there is a trend to replace the cash bonuses for executives with a form of rights to shares of stock that are earned over a period of several years. The cash bonus system focuses attention on short-term performance rather than long-term growth. To attract and retain executive talents, a proper reward for long-run management performance is needed. This can be achieved through granting rights to common stock issued at the end of a performance period (e.g., three or five years). According to such a compensation plan, executives can sell the shares after the end of a specified performance period or when they retire.

"Management by stress" is a team method used by Ford, Mercedes, and Volkswagen. However, it is criticized as resembling Taylorism, a time and motion study introduced by Frederick Taylor, which reverts workers into hired hands, disregarding their knowledge and innovative talents.

To avoid strikes and other labor disturbances, steel companies negotiate with steel workers' unions and offer seats on their boards of directors as well as better pensions. Bethlehem Steel Corporation offered a seat on its board of directors to the United Steelworkers of America, which would entitle them to liens or second mortgages on valuable assets if the corporation does not honor its offer. Similar benefits and collaterals were offered by other steel companies including the USC Corporation, Armco, Inc., National Steel, Inland Steel (which promised profit sharing and a minimum pension of $1,200 per month to its workers), LTV Corporation, and Wheeling–Pittsburgh Steel Corporation. All these concessions are the result of the implicit or explicit interest of management to give benefits and to share power with the workers in order to insure uninterrupted operations and to increase incentives and productivity.

The Web Converting Company, a Massachusetts-based manufacturer of video and audio cassette tapes, is a 25 percent employee-owned firm and plans to become a fully employee-owned company in the near future.

As in the capitalist firm in the markets of NAFTA and the EU, and likewise in the labor-managed firm, the paragon of efficiency is the maximization of net revenue or value-added per worker. Here the operating rule is to add workers until the income per worker is equal to the marginal value product of the last person employed. If the firm is not operating under conditions of perfect competition, where profits are zero, but it makes more than normal profits, the wage rate will be lower than that of a worker in the labor-managed firm. If other cooperative factors (primarily capital and raw materials) are fixed, additional workers would reduce the capital–labor ratio and, *ceteris paribus*, diminish income per worker. Therefore, for additional workers, investment should be made so that the capital labor ratio will at least be the same. Such invested capital should be expected to be recovered.

With the co-management system, labor and management become more partners than opponents. Although critics say laborers may fall into a tender trap, and have less control than bargaining methods provide in practice, labor in Germany and elsewhere seems to feel comfortable with that system, and losses from strikes and other labor disturbances have been reduced.

Although bargaining with rather than participation in management was used to gain control over wages, hirings, firings, and other labor matters, slowly but consistently worker ownership and participation have been gaining ground in recent years. This is because unionism can primarily be blamed for high absenteeism, incessant strikes, and slow economic growth.

Some form of capital–labor co-management, or co-determination, has prevailed for decades in a number of countries, including Germany (*Mitbestimmung*) and Sweden. Depending on the size of the firm, labor is participating in management and comprises up to 50 percent of the decision-making board of directors in Germany. In Sweden, elected work councils participate in enterprise decision making regarding wages, hiring, firing, and other labor matters, as well as investment and mergers.

Moreover, employee investment funds were established recently in Sweden. Such funds are financed by contributions of employees and employers, and aim at acquiring stock ownership for labor unions and enterprise expansion.

In order to motivate part-time workers and make them more productive, attractive benefits including stock options and medical insurance may be offered by management. This has the advantage of increasing the longevity and commitment of part-time workers in the companies where they work; and because of the lower labor turnover, the companies save in training costs. Although it is an expensive and administrative nightmare to include part-time workers in a full-scale benefits plan, increase in productivity is expected to outweigh the additional cost, particularly when a reward/vesting system is structured in a way that workers receive new stock options each year. The Starbucks Coffee Company introduced such a system by providing stock options to its part-time workers annually, but the workers gain ownership rights to those options at rates of 20 percent per year. Also, Starbucks Coffee provides medical benefits, as well as a free pound of coffee each week per worker.

The Virginia-based United Mine Workers and the coal industry introduced rules in their recent contract to change the relationship between management and labor toward closer cooperation in resolving labor problems early on. Also, the contract provides for the strengthening of workplace democracy and for the miners to have a say regarding work performance and remuneration. Moreover, new proposals call for the establishment of a labor–management cooperative committee to deal with labor problems before the expiration of related contracts. Similar five-year contracts are expected to be enacted by other coal companies and labor unions.

As unemployment persists and budget deficits and government debts inhibit adequate fiscal responses, a shorter work week may provide the answer. With the surge of technology, unemployment is expected to increase significantly. The options of using tax cuts or public sector expenditures to stimulate the U.S. economy run up against large budget deficits every year and a growing debt of more than $5.4 trillion with an interest burden of more than $220 billion a year.

The contention of management that a shorter work week would increase the cost per unit-product, and the fears of workers that their weekly pay would be cut, can be mitigated by reducing work week hours by less than productivity gains so that wages would not be reduced and decent profits gained. Then, both labor and management would share the benefits of productivity, with additional workers hired and greater leisure realized.

Bell Canada, the largest telephone company of Canada and a subsidiary of BCE, Inc., asked employees to work four days a week instead of five and accept a 20 percent wage cut. It is expected that other employees would accept such measures to avoid layoffs. Also, Bell Canada, with more than 46,000 employees, plans to freeze management salaries and cut vacation pay to slash costs.

The individualistic system of capitalist ownership is gradually replaced by administrative or managerial capitalism. The individual ownership of the means of production in advanced societies has been largely transferred to institutional investors, primarily pension and mutual funds. The executives or managers (or boards of directors) of these institutions, as well as other national and multinational corporations who are elected by their members or shareholders, decide about investment directions and the process of production and distribution of goods and services.

In the economies of NAFTA and the EU, managers try to maximize profits by satisfying consumers' desires in the domestic and foreign customer-oriented markets. Under competitive conditions, they may try to increase production using natural resources, without much consideration of depletion of these resources and environmental protection, as the demand of over-consuming societies grows. The hope is that investment in research and development and technological improvement would lead to quality growth; that is, increases in the production of goods and services, with protection of scarce resources and no deterioration of the environment.

Managers of transnational companies face the challenge of changing traditional organizations structured along geographic or product lines, and integrating assets and resources around the world. Some of them are previous raiders (the "barbarians at the gates") who acquired quick profits from mergers and acquisitions, particularly in the 1980s, but recently moved into the board rooms of transnational corporations.

Regardless of the economic system, there is a trend of labor moving out of agriculture, first into industry and then into services. With the new technological developments in computers and electronics, this trend is moving faster in both NAFTA and the EU countries.

In the United States, workers have moved in large numbers from the agricultural sector to the manufacturing and finally into the service sectors. The size of the labor force engaged in agriculture declined from more than 50 percent in 1840 to about 30 percent in 1910, and 12 percent in 1950 to only 3 percent presently. In the EU, where industrialization started earlier, this structural change in labor occurred earlier and continued thereafter, but at a slower pace.

With the introduction of the steam railway in 1828, industrial growth was enhanced. Gradually, and mainly from the early 1900s, workers moved rapidly into services such as trade, communications, education, health, finance, and computer and other business services. Since more women have entered the labor force during the postwar years, primarily in the service sector, and more manufacturing jobs have been lost to foreign competition, the labor movement to services has intensified. The transformation of labor from agriculture to industry and services is expected to increase in Mexico and other developing countries.

Chapter 5

Fiscal Policy

GOVERNMENT EXPENDITURES

Fiscal policy deals with government expenditures and taxation. General government expenditures include federal or central, state, and local government spending. As the federal system of government in the United States has a number of independent state governments, with regional diversity and preservation of freedom, likewise the EU is moving toward a similar system of federation of the European member-nations.

From 1950 to the present, general government expenditures, as percentages of GDP, have increased. This trend seems to verify the law of rising public expenditures mentioned by Adolph Wagner, a German political economist, who said that social progress in industrializing nations causes a proportionately higher growth of government, or the public sector, than growth in the overall economy.[1] Such growth is partially the result of wars, inflation, and other disturbances that push government expenditures to successively higher plateaus. However, high government expenditures are associated with large budget deficits and inflationary pressures. That is why NAFTA and, more so, the EU countries are engaged in austere policies to reduce deficits and stabilize their economies.[2]

With a large public sector in the NAFTA and EU economies, fiscal policy acquires great importance not only in matters of financing government expenditures but also in matters of counter-cyclical policy. The federalism of the United States, and to some extent Canada and Germany, establishes a division of powers between national and state governments in contrast to other nonfederal countries such as Britain, France, Italy, Spain, Greece (Hellas), and Portugal. Government spending involves payments for goods and services and other transfers and intergovernment activities.

In the European nations, power is concentrated mainly in the central government, but the U.S. federal system of government has a number of independent state governments which provide for regional diversity and preserve liberty. Canada and Mexico tend to follow the U.S. system. Except for some important federal government activities such as creating money, collecting taxes, regulating trade, and conducting wars, all other powers and controls were given by the U.S. Constitution of 1788 to the individual states, who developed their own constitutions, collected their own taxes, and exercised their own policies and controls.

According to Adam Smith, "Public works . . . are always better maintained by a local or provincial revenue . . . than by the general revenue of the state." However, to encourage specialization, promote positive externalities, and lower production costs, some restrictions on the U.S. state governments have been introduced regarding freedom of trade across state lines. A similar policy of free trade movement across member-nations is presently followed by the EU for larger markets, economies of scale, and diffusion of technology.

In the long run, the NAFTA and EU public sectors have grown proportionately at a faster rate than the overall economy. General government expenditures increased significantly during the postwar years. The expansion of the public sector, or the growing average propensity to spend, is the result of ever-increasing demand for government services, including those of regional and local units of government which, in turn, lead to high elasticities of government expenditures with respect to national income. Such elasticities, that is, the percentage of change in government expenditures over the percentage of change in national income, were high (varying from 1.2 to 1.4), meaning that for each percentage increase in national income there was a higher than 1 percent increase in general government expenditures for NAFTA and the EU, particularly after 1965.

With economic development, public expenditures on goods and services, such as defense and internal security, social security, post office operations, sanitation, health, education, fire fighting, parks, environmental protection, and other urban and social services, increase more than the overall economy. However, because of the bureaucratic and inefficient government activities, almost all countries started denationalizing or privatizing a number of national industries.

Although there is a great gap in the per capita GDP among the EU countries, the differences in government outlays are not as large. As Figure 5.1 shows, Spain, Greece, and Portugal, with relatively low per capita GDP, have lower general government expenditure compared to Germany, France, and Sweden. The ratio of general government outlays of the EU (average of Britain, France, Germany, and Italy) is close to 45 percent, and that of NAFTA is 35 percent. The EU countries, with a larger public sector than the United States, are taking measures of denationalization and relative reduction of gov-

Figure 5.1
Relationship of Per Capita GDP and General Government Expenditures as Percentages of GDP, 1994

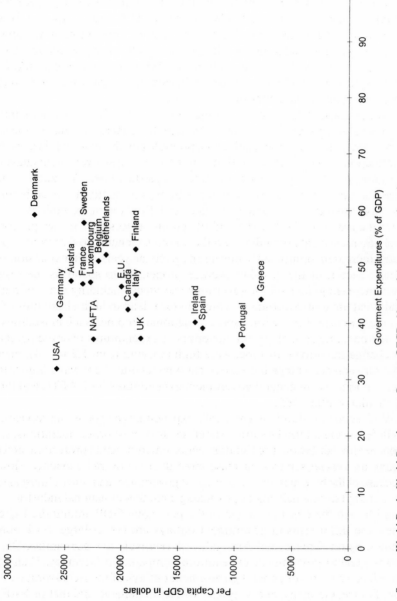

Sources: World Bank, *World Development Report*; OECD, *National Accounts*, various issues.

Note: In some cases closest years' data available were used for NAFTA, Canada, and the United States.

ernment expenditures. As a result, the proportion of GDP spent by the government is expected to decline in the near future.

To decrease intervention and spending and increase competition, the EU reduced and even abolished government subsidies that were given to some industries in accordance with Article 92 of the EU. They represent more than 100 billion ECUs or $120 billion per year. Italy holds the first place in such subsidies, followed by Germany, France, and Britain. However, subsidies are still permitted for poor regions, for social policy, for programs of economic importance to the EU, and for cases in which free trade is not interrupted.

Table 5.1 shows central or federal government expenditures, budget deficits, and debts for the EU countries. All these countries, except Denmark, had relatively high budget deficits in 1995, with Greece (Hellas), Sweden, and Italy being in the front line. In 1995, federal or central government expenditures were 21.6 percent of GDP for Canada, 11.7 percent for Mexico, and 22.2 percent for the United States; whereas deficits were 3.7 percent, 0.7 percent, and 2.2 percent, respectively. Regarding defense spending, Britain, Canada, Germany, Hellas, Portugal, and the United States spend high percentages of their budgets for military purposes. U.S. government debt was 71.2 percent of GDP in 1996. Belgium, Italy, and Hellas had far higher government debts than required by the Maastricht agreement (60% of GDP).

Central government expenditures, as percentages of GDP, are lower in the NAFTA than in the EU countries. Social services absorb the largest part of budget expenditures, varying from 36 percent for Mexico and around 52 percent for Canada and the United States. For the EU nations, they vary from 31 percent for Greece, to 52 percent for Britain, 59 percent for France, 69 percent for Germany, and 70 percent for Austria. Spending for defense absorbs 18 percent of the budget expenditures for the United States, 7 percent for Canada, and only 2 percent for Mexico. For the EU nations, defense spending varies from around 2 percent of budget expenditures for Austria to 3 percent for Italy and Spain, 6 percent for France, 9 percent for Germany and Greece, and 10 percent for Britain. Greece has relatively high military spending in the NATO alliance, mainly because of conflicts with Turkey, another member of NATO, over the occupation of some 40 percent of Cyprus by Turkish troops for more than twenty years.

The twin deficits in the federal budget and the balance in foreign trade increased U.S. claims concerning the share of military spending by the EU and other NATO member-nations. The argument is that the United States spends more for common defense than all members of NATO together, including the EU countries, Japan, and Canada. It is suggested by the U.S. policymakers that all partners share in the expenditures of mutual defense according to their economic conditions, which have lately been largely improved. Each American spends for common defense twice as much as any allied citizen in the EU and the other partners in NATO.

Large EU nations such as Britain, France, and Germany are able and willing to work toward a defense cooperation that could reduce the burden of

Table 5.1
Government Expenditures, Budget Deficits, and Debts of the EU Countries (as Percentage of GNP)

Member Countries	Central Gov't expenditures 1995	Budget deficits 1996	1997	Debt 1996	1997
Austria	39.5	5.1	3.0	69.3	73.3
Belgium	50.4	3.4	2.9	132.7	127.2
Britain	39.5	3.8	3.7	49.3	56.5
Denmark	42.2	1.0	0.4	81.6	70.4
Finland	39.2	3.0	1.7	62.5	60.2
France	45.4	4.2	3.2	55.0	56.6
Germany	24.6	3.9	3.4	60.1	63.2
Greece	66.2	7.9	5.7	113.3	104.5
Ireland	47.5	2.6	1.1	80.0	76.0
Italy	51.6	6.8	3.7	121.4	122.9
Netherlands	52.8	3.5	2.3	79.5	76.0
Portugal	44.3	4.5	2.9	72.6	67.6
Spain	34.2	4.7	3.4	65.5	68.9
Sweden	47.5	4.5	2.5	79.5	78.5

Sources: World Bank, *World Development Report*, various issues; Stathis Efstathiadis, "I Siglisi kai to Enieo Nomisma" (Convergence and the Common Currency), *To Vima*, 10 March 1996, E5 (from Statistics of Deutsche Bank, January 1996); *Selides* 3, 34 (1996) 35; "Kritiria Siglisis" (Criteria of Convergence), *National Herald*, 22–23 February 1997 (for 1997 projections of the OECD).

Note: In some cases, previous years' data were available.

Canada and the United States and strengthen the EU. At the same time, a shift in the balance of decision-making power in favor of the EU could take place in the future, while the United States and Canada could divert more attention to the economic development of Mexico and other Third World nations. Such a geopolitical reorientation is also greatly supported by the new economic and political reforms implemented in the former Soviet Union. Almost all the countries considered have high proportions of central government expenditures going toward housing, social security, welfare, and health. In education, the proportions are about 2 percent for the United States, Britain, and Germany, 7 percent for Italy, more than 11 percent for Ireland and The Netherlands, and 15 percent for Belgium.

Because overcentralization and bureaucratization kill initiatives and create unhealthy economic dependencies, decentralizing trends continue and local governments are strengthened, particularly in the United States, France, Greece, and Italy. Countries with decentralized public sector activities or federations have large proportions of state and local government expenditures as a proportion of total government spending. They vary from 40 percent for the United States and Germany, to 32 percent for Italy, and 28 percent for Britain. France and Belgium have low levels of state and local government expenditures (13 and 11%, respectively) and therefore a proportionately larger public sector mainly because of their institutional structure. Also, for countries with relatively lower per capita income, such as Mexico, Portugal, Spain, and Greece, these expenditure ratios are low, varying from 4 to 10 percent.

AUSTERITY AND UNEMPLOYMENT

As the European continent moves toward economic and political union, problems of unemployment and social discontent appear in almost all the EU nations. Anti-integration movements from both the left and the right and disaffections with EU membership are growing in many parts of Europe, particularly in Austria, France, Greece, Italy, and Sweden, in addition to Britain's Euro skepticism.

The reduction in public deficit, that is, the gap between government expenditures and tax revenue, is costing blue-collar jobs and eroding social well-being. As a result, right-wing parties in Austria, a land that welcomed Hitler's annexation in 1938, and other EU member-nations are growing, opposing the import of immigrants, mainly from Turkey, who take away work or live on welfare.

Although there are high unemployment rates all over Europe (in 1996, 12.3% in Italy and 12.6% in France, the highest in fifty years), plans to trim public expenditures are widespread. More jobs would be lost, mainly through attrition, but it is expected that there would be an economic big bang in the EU by the new money system. Moreover, in Italy, the legal work week was reduced from forty-eight to forty hours, and the minimum age for leaving school was increased from fourteen to sixteen years. Similar plans are considered by the other EU countries. Nevertheless, higher taxes to cover parts of deficits are expected to refuel discontent in northern Italy, where the secessionists argue that the industrial north pays a high price to support the less-developed south.

Nevertheless, other countries desiring to enter the EU, such as Hungary, Slovakia, Romania, and eventually the republics of former Yugoslavia, avoid ethnic conflicts and resolve border disputes in order to prepare for EU and NATO membership. As a result, Hungary signed cooperation treaties with

Romania and Slovakia, which pledged to respect the human rights of two million Hungarians living in Romania and 500,000 living in Slovakia.

THE PROBLEM OF AGING

A serious problem of fiscal policy in the future is the graying or aging on both sides of the Atlantic. Today in the United States, a newborn girl is expected to live past seventy-nine, more than six years longer than a boy, compared to only forty years for a newborn girl in 1850, and two years longer than a boy. In 1790, the average American could expect to live for 47.3 years. Moreover, in 1790, half the American people were under sixteen, but in 1990, the medium age rose to thirty-three. The same phenomenon can be observed more or less in the EU. In Canada and Japan, life expectancy is seventy-seven and eighty, respectively. In Mexico, the life expectancy is seventy for men and seventy-seven for women. It has been estimated that 30 percent of the world's population will be over the age of sixty-five in the 1990s.

The social security programs, which Otto Von Bismarck first introduced in Germany a century ago, may be unsustainable over the coming decades. From that standpoint, adjustments such as later retirement, cutbacks in benefits, or higher taxes to finance such programs would be needed. This is expected to be a serious problem for the United States when the baby boomers (those born from 1946 to 1963), accounting for 31 percent of the U.S. population, reach the age of retirement. On the average, the U.S. government spends about nine times as much on every elderly person as on every child, mainly because of the elderly's political influence.[3]

This trend might lead to intergenerational conflicts, and the class warfare might not be between the poor and the rich but between the young and the old. Regarding the argument that aging might mean less entrepreneurial and creative societies, it can be said that the benefits of old age are experience and the accumulation of knowledge, which in turn is related to creativity and innovation, as the examples of Socrates, Thomas Edison, and many other elders in history indicate.

Perhaps one of the reasons for the creation of the EU and NAFTA is to attract young immigrant workers from the poorer southern EU countries to more industrialized northern EU countries, and from Mexico to the United States. Other problems of aging may be the expected reduction in savings, mainly by the baby boomers. Investments in mutual funds and bull markets would be reduced, and pressure on economic performance would increase.

The ratio of retirement-aged people to working-age adults (in 1990, 22.3% for the United States, 18.8% for Canada, 28.8% for France, 29.5% for Britain, and 29.6% for Germany) continues to increase all over the world. This trend is particularly evident in the more industrial countries of the United States and the EU, where in 1990, the average retirement age was 65.1 in Canada, 63.5 in the United States, 62.9 in Britain, 62.4 in France, and 61.4 in Germany.

With ideological walls crumbling all over the world and the evolution of Western Europe toward a unified market, greater competitiveness in production and distribution, less government spending, and sustained economic growth for higher standards of living are the objectives of national economies. Socialist governments in some EU and other countries adopted programs geared to free market economies and international competition. Although in these and other Western European countries government expenditures are higher than those of the United States, emphasis is placed more and more on the private sector as the main driving force of employment and growth. Similar policies of reduction in government expenditures and privatizations are implemented more emphatically in Eastern Europe and the former Soviet Union.

As nationalistic and ideological differences wither away, more productive investments are financed by worldwide reduction in defense spending. Moreover, the gradual elimination of traditional borders in capital markets between NAFTA and EU stimulates transactions and increases interdependence. From that point of view, domestic fiscal and monetary policies should be formulated within a global framework while national security and economic policies should be interwoven with international policies. This is particularly so for the United States, with large domestic and foreign debts that lead to a gradual loss of the preeminent role the country has played in this century.

As life expectancy has improved steadily, the social security and medicare benefits have increased drastically. As a result, payroll taxes, starting from 2 percent on earnings in the United States in 1937 (Social Security Act, 1935), increased gradually to 15.3 percent (with half paid by the employer and half by the employee), as did the taxable payroll ceilings (from $3,600 in 1951, to $42,000 in 1986, and $62,500 in 1996). In the EU, payroll taxes are high (around 30% of earnings), as are benefits (receiving about basic salary at retirement), compared to about $700 monthly, on the average, in the United States. The current trend of increasing life expectancy, along with declining birth rates, leads to what is known as the graying of America and Europe. Some 35 million Americans (30% Hispanic, 22% black, and 14% white) lack any kind of health insurance, though almost all people in Europe are covered by national health insurance. The largest proportion of insured population in the United States (about 75%) has private health insurance.

RELATIONSHIP OF GOVERNMENT SPENDING AND EMPLOYMENT

At times, the governments of NAFTA and the EU use investment and public employment programs or subsidies to provide employment as a means of alleviating both general unemployment and particular distributional inequalities in depressed sectors and regions. On many occasions, when lagging demand tends to stagnate the economy, in order to avoid high unemployment, these governments may resort to investment and income policies.

It would seem that job creation subsidies for hard-to-place persons, used mainly in the EU, have limited success. From a distributional point of view, government expenditures through supported work programs might have the same impact as through existing income maintenance systems. In many cases, though, governments in NAFTA and the EU resort to unproductive increases in spending to reduce unemployment. However, when taxes or other revenues are available, government programs should be selected on their efficiency rather than their redistributive effects. Such a policy is expected in the long run to reduce the income gap ratio and the Gini coefficient of income distribution among the poor, as well as the rate of unemployment, which exerts strong influence on the popularity of parties and politicians.

Fiscal measures to stimulate the economy include increases in government expenditures and decreases in taxes, and are used on both sides of the Atlantic. A rise in government expenditures in the form of investment, transfer payments, or other kinds of spending will increase autonomous demand and stimulate the economy. A reduction in taxes will leave taxpayers with a larger income to spend. Again, a rise in spending by taxpayers will increase aggregate demand and stimulate economic activity. In both cases, if there is unemployment in the economy, one can expect employment and production to rise. The opposite holds true when expenditures are reduced and taxes are raised.

Additional spending generates a multiple increase in income (multiplier effect). Additional income, in turn, generates additional investment (accelerator effect). The interactions of the multiplier and the accelerator propel the economy forward when they are positive and backward when they are negative.

Figure 5.2 shows that a $5 trillion spending for consumption (C) leads to an equal amount of national income (Y), as the consumption function (line C) indicates. An additional spending for investment (I) of $0.4 trillion creates a new equilibrium of spending and income (Y = C + I) and pushes national income or output to $6 trillion. That is, each dollar invested adds $2.50 more income to the economy, which means that the multiplier (k) is equal to 2.5 (or $k = \Delta Y / \Delta I = 1.0/0.4 = 2.5$).

Full employment (F) in the economy can be achieved at an income or production of $7 trillion. The difference between actual income and potential or full-employment income $(7 - 6 = 1)$ is lost income or output because of unemployment. If there is no additional spending, the economy faces what Keynes called chronic unemployment, which is equal to this difference. The resultant gap, *ab*, is called the deflationary gap. An additional spending by government (G) to point *a* will push total spending to $7 trillion and lead the economy to a full employment equilibrium of aggregate demand and supply, where C + I + G = Y, or total spending is equal to total earning. This will be the ideal position of the economy, with full employment and stability.

However, if government spending is more than that required for the full employment level, an inflationary gap *ac* would be created and the increase in national income from $7 trillion to $8 trillion means an increase in prices, or inflation. That is, it is an increase in nominal, not real, income and production.

Figure 5.2
National Income (Y) Determination with Government Expenditures (G)

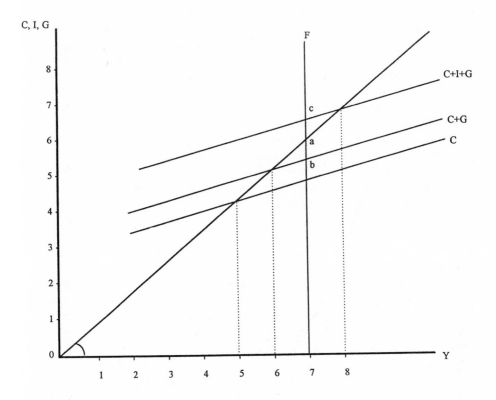

The NAFTA and the EU countries use fiscal policy for counter-cyclical policy. *Ceteris paribus*, a change in government expenditures (/ G) would produce a change in income (/ Y) larger than the initial spending, depending on the marginal propensity to consume (c).

$$\Delta Y / \Delta G = 1/(1 - c) \text{ or } \Delta Y = \Delta G/ (1 - c).$$

For example, if the marginal propensity to consume is 0.80, a change in government spending of $10 billion for transfers or other expenditures would change income by $50 billion; that is, $10/(1 - 0.80) = 10/0.2 = 50$ and the spending multiplier is equal to 5. This means that each additional dollar spent by the government would create $5.00 of additional income through the respending process in the economy by consumer groups receiving additional income. Figure 5.3 shows the growing public sector of the EU and the United States in the post–World War II years.

Figure 5.3
The Public Sector in the United States and the EU

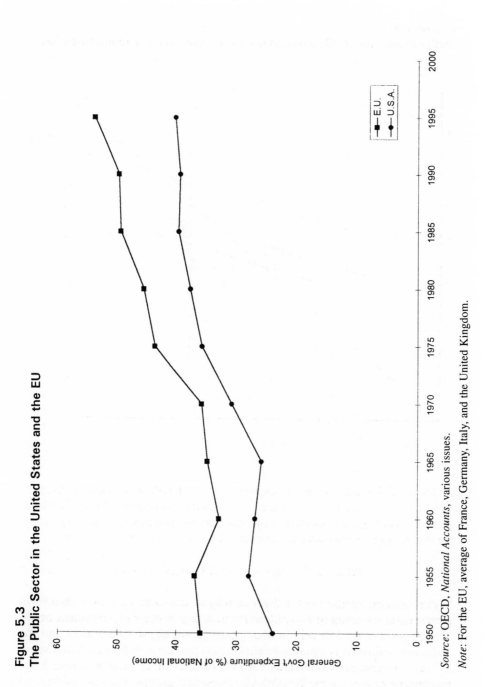

Source: OECD, *National Accounts*, various issues.

Note: For the EU, average of France, Germany, Italy, and the United Kingdom.

However, a change in taxation (T) of the same amount as a change in investment or government expenditure is expected to result in a smaller change in income and in an opposite direction. A part of the rise in taxation would be absorbed by a decrease in saving and the remainder by a decrease in consumption or aggregate demand. Thus, an increase in taxes would reduce demand by c times the rise in taxes, or

$$\Delta Y = -c\Delta T/(1-c)$$

and the tax multiplier ($\Delta Y/\Delta T = k_t$) is

$$k_t = -c/(1-c) = -c/s$$

where c is the marginal propensity to consume and s the marginal propensity to save. Thus, a decrease in taxes by $10 billion, assuming a marginal propensity to consume (c) equal to 0.80, would increase income by $40 billion, not $50 billion (as the equivalent increase of government expenditures would do).

TAXATION

Direct and Indirect Taxes

This section deals with the similarities and differences in tax policies of NAFTA and the EU countries. It concentrates on the distinction between direct (or income and profit) and indirect (or consumption) taxes.

Regarding the question of whether direct or indirect taxation is better from the standpoint of incentives to work and productivity, it seems that direct taxes, imposed primarily on individuals, are associated with disincentives to work and invest. Although the best tax is no tax, indirect or commodity (*in rem*) and service taxes discourage overconsumption and encourage saving for investment financing. However, they are largely regressive (their proportions decline with increases in income), taking a large fraction of their revenue from the low-income groups. From that standpoint, it is proper to make them progressive.[4]

In the United States and Canada, indirect taxes are levied principally by individual states and localities, but in the EU countries taxes are levied mainly by the central governments. However, U.S. income taxes are levied by the federal government, as well as by most states and some cities, which follow by and large the federal tax pattern. In the EU countries, the central governments provide localities with some, though relatively small, portions of tax revenue in the form of financial aid.

The main source of budgetary revenue is taxes on income and profits for all advanced economies of NAFTA and the EU (except France). However, for the less-developed economies of Mexico, Greece, Portugal, and to some extent Ireland, the main source of budgetary revenue is indirect taxes on goods and services. Figure 5.4 shows the composition of tax revenue for all OECD countries, and Figures 5.5 and 5.6 show the trends for such tax revenues for NAFTA and the EU countries, respectively.

Figure 5.4

Tax Revenue of Main Headings as a Percentage of Total Tax Revenue of the NAFTA, EU, and Other OECD Countries, 1994

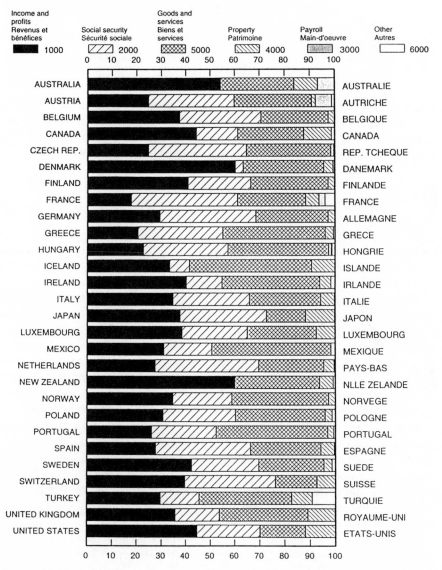

Source: OECD, *Revenue Statistics of the OECD Member Countries* (Paris: OECD Publications, 1996), 15.

Figure 5.5
Receipts as Percentage of Total Tax Revenues for the NAFTA Countries,
1965–1994

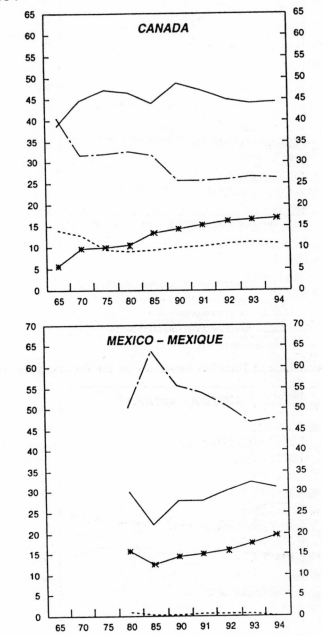

Figure 5.5 (*continued*)

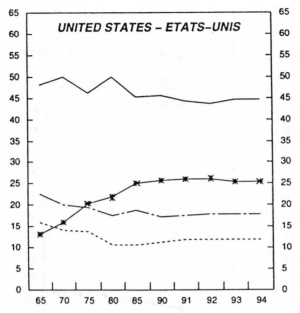

Source: OECD, *Revenue Statistics of the OECD Member Countries* (Paris: OECD Publications, 1996), 19–25.

Key:

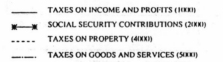

TAXES ON INCOME AND PROFITS (1(XX))

SOCIAL SECURITY CONTRIBUTIONS (2(XX))

TAXES ON PROPERTY (4(XX))

TAXES ON GOODS AND SERVICES (5(XX))

Figure 5.6
Receipts as Percentage of Total Tax Revenues for the EU Countries, 1965–1994

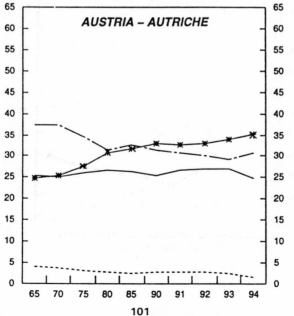

Figure 5.6 (*continued*)

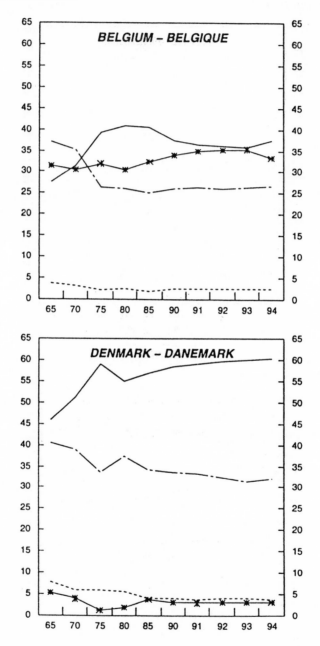

Figure 5.6 (*continued*)

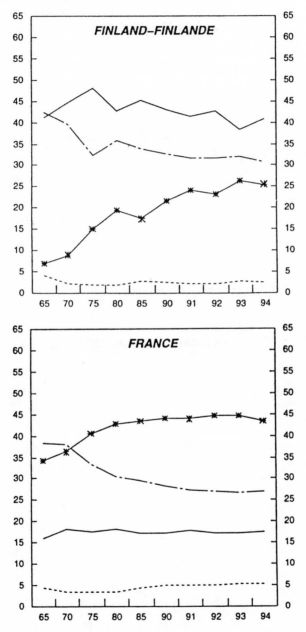

Figure 5.6 (*continued*)

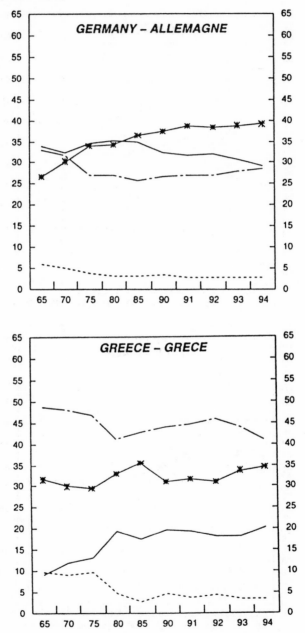

Figure 5.6 (*continued*)

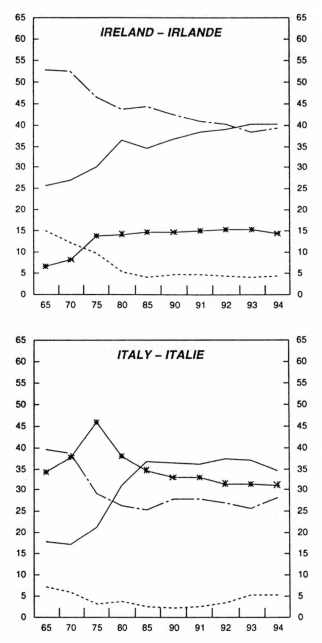

Figure 5.6 (*continued*)

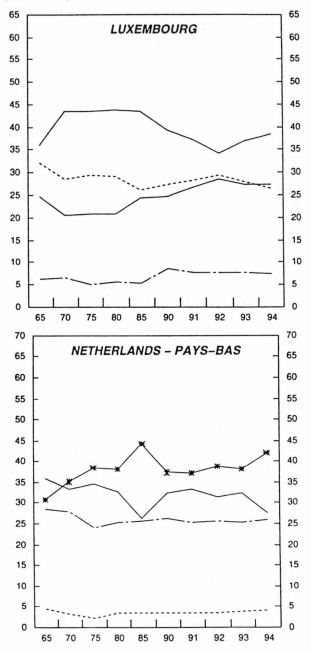

Figure 5.6 (*continued*)

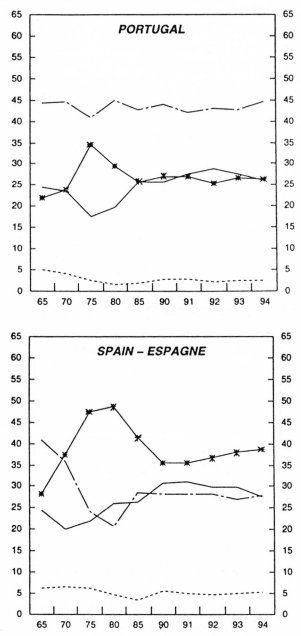

Figure 5.6 (*continued*)

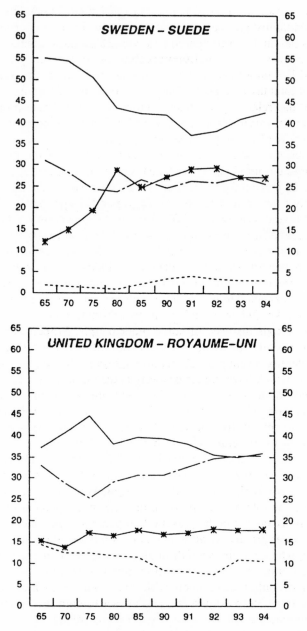

Source: OECD, *Revenue Statistics of the OECD Member Countries* (Paris: OECD Publications, 1996), 19–25.

Key:

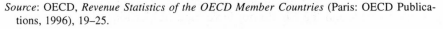

——— TAXES ON INCOME AND PROFITS (1(XX))

✳——✳ SOCIAL SECURITY CONTRIBUTIONS (2(XX))

- - - - TAXES ON PROPERTY (4(XX))

—·—·— TAXES ON GOODS AND SERVICES (5(XX))

For the last three decades, Canada and the United States have had relatively high and constant taxes on income and profits as proportions of total tax revenues (about 45%) compared to lower (30%) and growing proportions in Mexico. Likewise, Belgium, Denmark, Finland, Ireland, Italy, Luxenbourg, Sweden, and Britain all had high taxes on income and profits, varying from 35 percent of total tax receipts for Italy to 60 percent for Denmark. The other EU countries had relatively low taxes on income and profits as proportions of total tax revenue, varying from 18 percent for France, 20 percent for Greece, and 30 percent for Germany and Spain.

Tax revenue from social security is relatively low for the three NAFTA countries, varying from 17 percent of total tax revenue for Canada, 20 percent for Mexico, and 25 percent for the United States, whereas for the EU countries it varies, mainly from around 15 percent for Ireland, 20 percent for Britain, 25 percent for Finland, Portugal, and Sweden, 30 to 35 percent for Austria, Belgium, Greece, and Italy, and as high as 40 to 45 percent for France, Germany, The Netherlands, and Spain. Nevertheless, in addition to the inflationary rate, social security benefits should include the productivity rate or the real rate of return of the previous contributions to the system. Although partial or total privatization is expected to incorporate such real rates of return, the volatility of the stock market (where social security contributions would be invested), might create serious distress for some older people. Property or real estate taxes, which are collected mainly by local authorities, are mostly 5 percent or less of the total tax revenue for all countries, except Britain, Canada, and the United States, which have higher property taxes (around 10%).

National corporate tax rates in 1995 varied from 28 percent for Sweden, 33 percent for Britain, 33.33 percent for France, 35 percent for Spain and The Netherlands, 36 percent for Portugal, 37 percent for Italy, 38 percent for Ireland, 39 percent for Belgium, and 45 percent for Germany.

There is a trend in the EU countries to reduce income tax rates, as the United States did in the 1980s. Germany, where the income tax system is considered too complex and socially unjust, plans to introduce reforms and reduce the top tax rate on income from the present 53 percent to 35 percent and the initial tax rate from the present 25.9 percent to 20 percent.[5] After the proposed tax rates are discussed with business lobbies, the trade unions, and the churches, which are financed through taxation, the Christian Democratic Union (CDU) aims at massively cutting personal income and corporation taxes. Germany could then compete with other countries, which have top tax rates varying from 35 to 40 percent, and attract foreign investment to boost jobs and economic growth. However, expectations are that the tax base would be broadened, tax breaks eliminated, and the tax system simplified.

Both NAFTA and the EU do not have high proportions of indirect taxes relative to GDP. Indirect (or consumption) taxes are imposed initially on objects (*in rem* taxes) and include excises (mainly on fuel, beverages, tobacco, and travel), sales taxes, value-added taxes, stamps, and tariffs, and are levied against goods and services independent of the owner's ability to pay. In the

United States, these taxes are levied primarily by individual states and localities; in the EU, mostly by the central governments. Figure 5.7 shows that indirect taxes were constant at around 10 percent of national income for NAFTA and 14 percent for the EU from 1968 onward.

Indirect taxes as percentages of total taxes are higher in low-income countries such as Mexico, Greece, Ireland, and Portugal than in the advanced EU countries, Canada, and the United States. From that standpoint, and as a result of the EU integration, a relative decrease in indirect taxes and structural changes in both direct and indirect taxes are expected to occur in the near future in the above low-income countries. In EU countries with high indirect taxes, reduction or elimination of excise taxes and tariffs, according to the directives of the EU, would reduce tax revenue and exert pressure on domestic industries producing the same goods or close substitutes to imported goods. The same thing is expected in Mexico. However, such a competitive process would reduce inefficiency despite the expected detrimental effects on employment conditions.

The elasticities of indirect taxes with respect to private consumption, imports, and GDP for the periods of 1950–1960 and 1960–1970, were greater than one. In the 1970s and later, however, the elasticities were less than one and lower in the United States than in the EU. These results indicate that during the 1970s the relative growth of indirect taxes in the United States was lower than the growth in the other variables (private consumption, GDP, and particularly, imports). The dramatic increases in the value of oil imports without a similar increase in tariffs on imported oil (and contrary to what is customary in the EU and other countries where oil prices are more than double of those prevailing in the United States) seemed to be responsible for the differences. In the 1980s and later, the elasticities of indirect taxes with respect to private consumption, imports, and GDP were all close to one.

Sales Taxes

Consumption or transaction taxes include general sales taxes, excise taxes, severance taxes, turnover taxes, and value-added taxes. In the United States, sales taxes produce about 50 percent of state and 10 percent of federal consumption or expenditure taxes imposed on sellers' gross receipts of product transactions and paid by households or consumers. They are impersonal taxes and can be placed at one or more than one stage. They may be based on GDP; that is, on both consumer and capital goods, or more usually, on consumption expenditures.

Excise taxes are selective taxes on specific products such as liquor, gasoline, tires, tobacco, telephone services, air transportation, customs duties, and pollution costs. When they are used to penalize extravagant or harmful consumption, especially regarding alcoholic beverages and tobacco, they are called sumptuary taxes. They are levied primarily by the U.S. federal government on a unit-of-product basis (unit tax) or as a percentage of price (*ad valorem* tax).

Figure 5.7
Indirect Taxes as Percentage of GDP

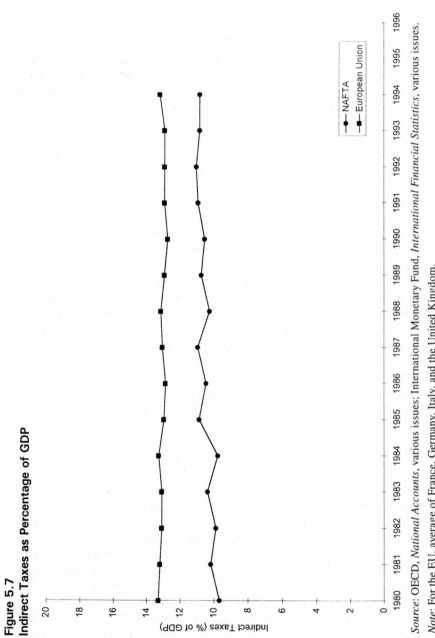

Source: OECD, *National Accounts,* various issues; International Monetary Fund, *International Financial Statistics,* various issues.

Note: For the EU, average of France, Germany, Italy, and the United Kingdom.

In place of excise taxes, user charges can be levied. In this case, fees are collected to finance particular public services such as urban mass transit and highway and road construction, for which a special trust fund can be established. Although it is difficult to match benefits and user charges, even an approximation of cost–benefit analysis can be beneficial, especially from a political point of view. Another related tax is the severance tax, used by thirty-three states in the United States, and usually on gross receipts from natural resources such as minerals, fish, and timber. It may also be used to replace property tax and has the advantage of helping resource conservation.

Value-Added Taxes

The value-added tax (VAT) is primarily a consumption tax and, as such, is included in indirect taxes. The VAT, introduced by the EU member-nations, is a proportional tax on the value of all goods and services included in a firm's invoices, reduced by the amount of previous VAT liability. As the supporters of the VAT argue, this tax is simple. It reduces consumption expenditures, decreases tax evasion, improves the flexibility of the tax structure, and stimulates investment and economic growth. As a tax on the difference between the total value of output minus the value of purchased material input, it helps policymakers determine whether demand for consumer goods is growing in an inflationary way. Thus, the VAT can be used to regulate demand. However, additional value-added taxes, when first introduced, would more than likely be passed on to consumers in the form of rising prices.

The revenues of the EU member-nations as a group come primarily from the VAT (1% of the VAT collected by the member-nations goes into the EU common pot), customs duties, and special levies on agricultural imports (including sugar duties). Revenue from the VAT is about 50 percent of total EU revenue, as a unit separate from that of the individual member-nations. Most of the collected revenues (about two-thirds) are spent for the support of prices of agricultural products by a special EU fund known as the Fond European d'Orientation et de Garantie Agricole (FEOGA); around 10 percent for the regional development of backward areas; and the rest (about 6%) for social policies, research, energy, and aid to Third World countries. Greece, Italy, Portugal, Spain, and to some extent France are the main recipients of subsidies for agricultural products and regional development.

Serious financial problems have appeared in the budget of the EU with the two-thirds of its annual receipts spent for farm subsidies. The countries of the north, primarily Britain, and to some extent Germany, object to farm subsidization and have asked for a revised farm policy to eliminate food surpluses that are then sold on world markets. Australia, the United States, and other countries that export farm products complain that the agricultural policy of the EU leads to unfair competition against their own products.

Policymakers and economists in the United States and other countries have started contemplating the introduction of the VAT as a substitute for personal income taxes. Shifting the nation's tax burden away from taxes on income and profits and toward the VAT, supporters believe, would stimulate production incentives and discourage consumption expenditures. However, they argue, care should be taken to avoid burdening low-income and middle-income consumers upon whom such taxes primarily fall. This can be achieved by providing tax exemptions for the necessities of life, such as food, modest rental payments, or a small home. Also, a VAT can be coupled with a rebate on low incomes and exports.

With the introduction of the VATs, there would be less confusion over tax legislation that the mass production of laws and regulations have created in the already saturated legal profession. They, like sales taxes, are simple and fair and catch both tax evaders and tax avoiders.

The VAT, a form of which was adopted by the State of Michigan in 1953, repealed in 1967, and reenacted in the mid-1970s, is levied on the increments of the value of goods and services at each stage of production and distribution. It extends to the retail stages of virtually all sectors, including services. It covers more taxpayers than other forms of taxation and, because it usually increases revenue and reduces evasion, many countries have introduced it.

Although it is argued that the introduction of the VAT leads to inflation, empirical research has shown that in the majority of the countries that have introduced it, the VAT has a minor or no impact on inflation. This has been particularly so in countries such as Austria, France, and The Netherlands, where authorities imposed temporary price controls to offset an expected once-and-for-all increase in prices due to the introduction of the VAT, or where the VAT replaced other forms of taxation. In a few cases, the anticipation of the introduction of a VAT acted as a trigger for wage increases and credit expansion, which led to inflationary pressures. The uncertainty induced by the tax change might have a major effect on the vicious circle of wage–price increases although the direct effect of the VAT might probably be trivial. Furthermore, when the VAT is introduced at times of economic slowdown or recessions, traders are expected not to pass the tax on to consumers in the form of higher prices, as happened in Germany.

In the United States, most states levy sales taxes at widely different rates. However, in other countries, circumstances are different because VATs have either replaced inefficient turnover or cascade taxes (e.g., in France, Germany, and The Netherlands) or been required for EU membership (as in the case of the United Kingdom, Greece, Spain, and Portugal). In France, the VAT was introduced in 1954 where presently it raises about 50 percent of tax revenue. In Germany, the VAT was proposed in 1918 and introduced in 1967. There it provides 13 percent of government revenue. In Britain, it provides 15 percent and in the EU 10 percent of the overall tax revenue.

One of the major criticisms against consumption taxes, and particularly VATs, is that they are hidden sales taxes and that they absorb higher proportions of income from the poor and lower proportions from the rich. Income taxes are open so that people can see them better than the VAT. However, the unequal results of consumption taxes come from the higher inequality of the distribution of income and wealth. A better distribution of income makes the difference between consumption and income taxes less important and makes the VAT more attractive. As long as there is high income inequality, income taxes of some progressive form or a combination of consumption and income taxes is required. Moreover, some form of progressivity can be introduced in consumption or indirect taxes.

It is argued that federal or central government VATs would interfere with state and local sales taxes in decentralized federations like the United States. However, this can be arranged through the proper coordination of the different forms of consumption taxes (the VAT, sales and excise taxes, customs duties, etc.).

A VAT is a proper fiscal measure to reduce budget deficits and stimulate investment. Such a consumption tax, which is paid for by the manufacturers at each stage of production and ultimately by the consumers, can partially replace income and other taxes.

A European-style VAT for NAFTA can be progressive, with low rates for widely used basic goods and services and high rates for luxury and unhealthy goods (tobacco, alcohol, and gasoline). To ease the burden on the poor, food and housing, as well as other necessities, can be excluded from VAT, as they are presently excluded from state and local sales taxes.

Eventually, the VAT can partially replace personal and corporate income taxes and encourage work incentives. Thus, U.S. private savings is currently low, about 2 to 4 percent, compared to other countries such as Europe and Japan. Therefore, private consumption, which is the tax base for the VAT, is high (about 96 to 98% of income) and it does not make much difference if income or consumption is taxed. However, an average 3 percent VAT in the United States can generate more than $100 billion a year in revenue, discourage excessive consumption and waste, encourage savings for investment financing, and depending on the elasticity of imports, improve the balance of trade. This indicates that sooner or later the VAT will infiltrate the American, and eventually the NAFTA, tax systems. It has been used successfully for years in the EU.

Revenues of the EU member-nations from the VAT, as a percentage of GDP, vary from around 6 percent for Italy and Spain, 7 percent for Germany and Britain, 8 percent for France, 9 percent for Denmark, and 11 percent for Greece.

Regarding coordination of the tax system, the EU Commission proposed in March 1996 to create a VAT rate ban, with a minimum rate of 15 percent and a maximum rate of 25 percent. However, for certain categories of goods and services, member-nations can apply one or two lower rates which may not be less than 5 percent. Such rates were projected to be in force for two years (from 1 January 1997 to 31 December 1998) but their application can be extended later.

From a fiscal standpoint, the arrangement for common fixed VAT rates for all EU members would consolidate the smooth functioning of the single market and facilitate economic and monetary union. Also, it would eliminate distortions in the internal market, stabilize tax receipts, promote employment, and reduce or eliminate tax evasion and fraud, which have increased mainly because of the liberalization of the financial markets.

Taxes and Economic Growth

On both sides of the Atlantic, and notably in the United States, tax policies have been used from time to time to counter economic fluctuations. In order to promote saving and investment and stimulate economic growth, tax reductions were used on a number of occasions. However, one may be skeptical that lower taxes have always had a significant impact on long-run economic growth. Moreover, high marginal tax rates may not always have distortionary effects.

In the long run, economic growth can be achieved through increase in the factors of production, technological improvement, and net gains from foreign trade. Although the developed countries of NAFTA and the EU have a huge capital stock, new investment, in which improved technology is normally embodied, matched with increase in the labor force, can produce a boom in economic growth. Such a boom can be achieved through lower marginal tax rates, which stimulate work incentives and encourage investment in human and physical capital.

In order to boost economic growth, two other forms of taxes may be considered: a flat tax and a consumption-based tax. A flat tax is a single rate tax beyond a certain level of income, for example, 17 percent on income earned from wages and pensions. Also, the same tax rate could be paid on the profits of businesses, though interest payments could not be deducted as an expense in computing such profits. Net rental income would also be taxed. In a flat tax, no taxes would be imposed on interest and dividend income received by households, but deductions for home mortgages and charitable contributions would be eliminated.

It is expected that a flat tax would stimulate the economy and divert investment from home ownership to other more productive activities. However, it would be sharply regressive, as it would tax lower-income people at higher rates than the wealthy, a large part of whose income comes from interest, dividends, and capital gains.

A significant reform to boost economic growth is to impose taxation on consumption. One method is to keep the current tax system but to exempt all savings from taxation and to replace current income taxes altogether with consumption taxes. Another method, widely used on a local level, is a sales tax; that is, a flat tax rate on consumption expenditures. Finally, the VAT is another form of consumption-based tax.

It is estimated by Dale Jorgenson of Harvard University that a consumption-based tax rate of 15 percent in the United States would match the revenues generated by the current income tax system. Moreover, it would increase investment which in turn would increase output by about 9 percent in the long run.[6]

The federal government of the United States is using budget deficits to stimulate the economy and reduce unemployment. In order to reverse recent huge layoffs, additional spending should be sizeable. However, the question is how to finance such spending without significant increases in budget deficits.

A gradual and sizable increase in consumption-based or value-added taxes for investment financing would stimulate the economy without igniting inflation and discouraging technological improvement. This measure, which can be considered as a hybrid of the Keynesian demand side (increase in investment spending) and the neoclassical supply side (increase in production) economics, and would also reduce foreign trade deficits and thus make the dollar stronger.

Particularly for gasoline taxes, it is time for the American consumer to reconsider one of the popular symbols of American life, "Mom, apple pie, and cheap gasoline." In almost all other countries, the price of gasoline is higher (up to $4.50 per gallon) than in the United States (about $1.50 per gallon), and a higher tax would reduce budget deficits, pollution, accidents, and the dependency of Americans on other oil-producing countries.

STABILIZATION AND GROWTH POLICY

The problem of economic stabilization has preoccupied many EU and NAFTA governments and economists throughout history. Some two centuries ago, Adam Smith thought that a more equitable distribution of income was necessary for a large market so that the whole economy could take full advantage of specialization and economies of scale. "No society can surely be flourishing and happy, of which the far greater part of the members are poor and miserable."[7] However, it is doubtful that Smith wanted to stress the social aspect of the distribution of income or the problem of defective demand, which Malthus, Marx, and Keynes emphasized later, or that he wanted government intervention to bring about a more equitable distribution of income through taxation or other fiscal and welfare measures. Along these lines, Thomas Malthus argued that, in a competitive economy, overproduction or a general glut of the market could occur when an effectual demand for produce becomes less than the supply. To this argument of partial market failure, which was contrary to Say's law that supply creates its own demand and there can never be shortages or gluts in a competitive market, no suggestions for public sector intervention or other remedies were made. It was John Keynes who later introduced the policy of government spending to stimulate income and employment and avoid economic crises.

John Stuart Mill, on the other hand, thought that the laws of production are physically determined, whereas the laws of distribution are manmade. From that point of view, the role of government may be considered as more effectual on matters of economic stabilization and income distribution than production. He felt the government should take upon itself the function of protecting the general interest and that the best state for human nature is one in which, while no one is poor, no one desires to be richer.[8]

Many fiscal and monetary measures Keynes suggested in this system of government intervention were applied in several countries, including NAFTA and the EU member-nations, but it is questionable whether these measures and tools are responsible for the inflationary bias these and other countries practiced during the post–World War II years. However, in some instances, lack of cooperative factors, market limitations, and bottlenecks in particular sectors and industries make such policy prescriptions result in increases in money incomes and prices instead of in real output and employment. One cannot use public sector spending to increase consumption and stimulate development in economies where there are inelastic supplies and scarcity of available resources.

Moreover, the public sector or government spending may be needed for reasons of economic stabilization. In the NAFTA and EU economies, a high proportion of national income is expected to be saved, primarily because of increases in the institutionalization of savings in the form of contractual obligations, such as pension fund contributions and insurance premiums, as well as increases in corporate savings. Such a trend to save more (*ceteris paribus*) would lead to less private spending, less demand, less income, and less employment unless offset by public sector spending. In addition, generous incentives and different measures to stimulate investment and other forms of spending are provided by the EU and NAFTA governments during periods of sluggish demand.

The use of tax and expenditure policies by these governments to achieve full employment, price stability, and economic growth have attained great importance in the past three decades. Under-utilization of the labor force and of the capital stock involves waste and inequities. One of the main goals of fiscal policy is to avoid such waste and inequities through demand stimulation, production incentives, and replacement of welfare by workfare.

However, changes occur in the structure of the labor force with the addition of larger proportions of females and young people. Therefore, a certain rate of unemployment of up to 5 percent may be permitted. Such a "natural" rate of unemployment may be the result of job changing or frictional unemployment; that is, when people are in a transitional period seeking new employment. Also, retraining may be required because of structural changes in the economy. Likewise, a reasonable rate of inflation of up to 3 percent may be considered as desirable for purposes of discouraging hoarding and encouraging investment. Therefore, economic policies aiming at less than 5 percent unemployment and no more than 3 percent inflation are more reasonable and realistic than a simultaneous zero unemployment and zero inflation. As explained earlier, though, this is difficult to achieve, and a tradeoff between unemployment and inflation usually takes place.

Fiscal policy as a stabilization tool often conflicts with other objectives in the economy, primarily with those of monetary and growth policies. Moreover, coordinating the timing of government policies is a difficult task in the political process. It takes time to recognize a fiscal problem and time to implement needed actions, as well as to observe and evaluate related responses. In a decentralized economic system, such as that of the United States and some EU nations, there are administrative and legislative delays in implementing tax and expenditure measures in stabilization and growth policies, as there are in monitoring the effectiveness of such measures. However, there are certain fiscal parameters with built-in flexibility that work automatically, independent of time and magnitude. Such built-in or automatic stabilizers include unemployment benefits, progressive taxation, indexing, retirement benefits, pensions, and similar fiscal variables that exist and work alone in the NAFTA and the EU countries without having the governments change them through new legislation or regulations. As such, they cushion the amplitude of cyclical fluctuations and tend to stabilize the economy.

A distinction between the long-run roles of government policies and their short-run stabilizing roles in the economy seems to be absent in popular and political discussions. In the short run, cyclical measures may be used to reduce the market failures of recessions and help adjust disposable and spendable income to permanent income. To reduce inflationary pressures, easy fiscal policy may be accompanied by tight monetary policy in a fine-tuning process, so that real interest rates and currency appreciations would not be excessive, domestically and internationally.

On the contrary, to keep high employment targets, tight fiscal policies may require easier monetary policy and increases in exports. Nevertheless, disciplined fiscal management should recognize structural budget deficiencies and accept the need for pursuing "natural" rates of unemployment and reasonable inflation rates. Moreover, stimulative budget policies and counterbalancing monetary policies should encourage investment in the human and physical capital for long-run growth in the economies of NAFTA and the EU.

Successive changes of income (ΔY) are generated in the economies of the EU and NAFTA by an initial amount of government expenditures (ΔG). Additional income created is partially spent for additional consumption and partially saved and presumably invested through financial institutions. Depending on the marginal propensity to consume (assumed to be 0.80), the initial government spending generates a multiple amount of income. This is known as the government-spending multiplier ($\Delta Y/\Delta G$), which in our example is equal to 5 (or $\Delta Y/\Delta G = 1/1 - 0.80$). This means that each additional dollar of government spending generates an additional \$5.00 of income. Moreover, assuming that the resulting savings are channeled into investment, an additional amount of capital investment from the incremental incomes (induced investment) is generated. This is known as the accelerator ($\Delta I/\Delta Y$), which in our example is equal to 0.20. This additional investment would bring into

Figure 5.8
Equilibrium Level of Income with Tax Cut

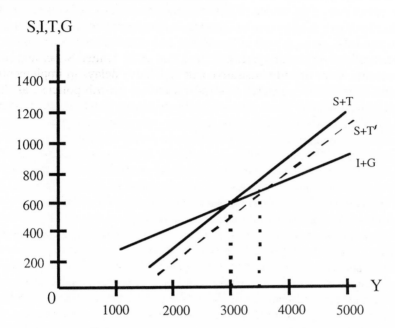

operation a similar multiplier and another accelerator and so on. The interactions of the multiplier and the accelerator contribute to economic fluctuations, resulting in booms when they are positive and slumps when they are negative. However, in the case that these tools are positive, real income and employment would increase up to the level of full employment. Thereafter, additional spending would increase only nominal income, generating a rise in prices or inflation.

Similarly, a change in taxes will lead to a multiple change in national income. Figure 5.8 shows that a tax cut leads to higher national income. The shift of the S + T (saving plus tax) curve, through a tax cut of $100 billion, to a new S + T' curve results in an increase in national income (Y) from $3,000 billion to $3,400 billion. The tax multiplier, therefore, is equal to 4 (or $\Delta Y / \Delta T = 400/100$). The opposite result is expected in the case of an increase in taxes, through a shift in the S + T curve to the left and the establishment of a new equilibrium at a lower level of income. Such tax reductions were practiced in a number of cases in some EU member-nations, and more so in the United States.

Chapter 6

Foreign Trade

EXPORTS AND IMPORTS

This chapter deals with the trade relations between NAFTA and the EU. The possibilities and the difficulties of closer cooperation are also examined. Trade and other relations between the two have been strong throughout history. It can be said that the relations of old Europe and young America have been and still are similar to those of a mother and a daughter, not only on economic but also on sociocultural and other matters. However, the integration movement of the EU presents problems of trade and investment adjustment between NAFTA and the EU. In the short run there may be conflicts regarding exports of certain products and services, but in the long run their mutual needs for trade and investment will necessitate closer cooperation and mutual dependence.

Subsidies and other measures are frequently used by the NAFTA and the EU countries to stimulate production and to increase exports, as well as to protect certain domestic industries or products. In many instances, though, agricultural and industrial expansions create unneeded duplicate projects with idle capacity that threaten to initiate slumps on both sides of the Atlantic. To grasp foreign markets and increase employment and income at home, the governments of the EU and NAFTA resort from time to time to protectionist measures that stifle competition and restrict free trade between them.[1]

As in 1492 when Christopher Columbus expanded European trade by discovering North America, so more than 500 years later a new European *Odyssey* of economic expansion is in the making. The new integrated Euromarket of the EU nations, as Jean Monnet and Robert Schuman advocated in the 1950s, arose high hopes about the great opportunities expected to be opened to domestic and foreign enterprises. Although member-nations are slow in yielding sovereignty, the pressure for economic improvement via the free movement of people, goods, and money, generated cooperation in removing nationalistic and other obstacles and creating a single market and a closer partnership.

Europe realizes that it cannot compete with the United States and Japan without dismantling trade barriers and restructuring its economic and political institutions. The complete economic unification of the EU countries and eventually all of Europe is an ambitious plan, similar to that of Napoleon the Great, but it must be voluntary, not forced. A united Europe will reduce internal national conflicts and strengthen democracy. Extreme right or left governments will be discouraged as resources and investment will quickly move to other EU and Eastern European countries. However, there is skepticism in NAFTA and other nations that European enterprises, exposed to greater competition internally, may press for protection from their American and Asian counterparts. There is a risk that restrictions on trade, investment, services, and other economic activities may then take place.

Some American economists and politicians feel that the European integration may lead to protectionism, introducing preferences for European firms and European goods and services and adversely affecting NAFTA companies and products. This may be particularly so for food products, pharmaceuticals, and services. Although the European policymakers argue that there is a commitment not to create additional barriers, some NAFTA companies, particularly in the United States, invest inside Europe to hedge against probable protectionism. Nevertheless, free trade arrangements between the NAFTA and the EU can be made, before the "European train leaves the station," or at least at the next station, without challenging the EU integration and identity. Until recently both groups were slow to react; now they are trying to catch up by working a more equal Atlantic relationship.[2]

The fear of reciprocity would force Europe and America to promote trade liberalization and more openness. It would seem that for more trade and investment, Europe needs America as America needs Europe. Through negotiations and mutual concessions, less protection and more cooperation could be forthcoming under the umbrella of the World Trade Organization (WTO). Both NAFTA and the EU are large markets, and an American–European corporate alliance can further promote economic prosperity on both sides of the Atlantic.

As Table 6.1 shows, NAFTA (mainly the United States) has had mostly trade deficits with the EU in recent years. However, for almost all post–World War II years until 1983, it had trade surpluses. On the average, U.S. exports to the EU are about one-fourth of its total exports, whereas its imports from the EU are about one-fifth of total imports. After World War II the devastated economies of Europe needed the American consumer and particularly capital goods for their development. In recent years, though, with the exception of 1991, the EU has managed to advance enough to sell more products to the United States, Canada, and Mexico annually than it buys. Canadian exports

Table 6.1
Trade of NAFTA with the EU Countries (at Current Prices and Current Exchange Rates, in Billions of U.S. Dollars)

Years	Exports				Imports				Overall Balance
	USA	Canada	Mexico	Total	USA	Canada	Mexico	Total	
1980	52.5	8.0	2.4	62.9	33.0	4.7	2.9	40.6	
1981	50.0	7.3	3.6	60.9	43.6	5.2	3.5	52.3	8.6
1982	50.8	6.4	4.5	61.7	46.4	4.8	2.6	53.8	7.9
1983	47.4	5.5	4.0	56.9	47.8	5.0	1.4	54.2	2.7
1984	49.0	5.8	4.4	59.2	63.0	6.6	1.6	71.2	-12.0
1985	48.1	4.8	4.2	57.1	71.3	7.9	1.7	80.9	-23.8
1986	52.1	5.5	3.5	61.1	78.7	9.2	1.9	89.8	-28.7
1987	84.6	6.8	3.0	94.4	59.4	10.2	2.1	71.7	22.7
1988	89.0	8.9	2.7	100.6	74.1	13.1	2.9	90.1	10.5
1989	85.9	9.7	2.6	98.2	88.7	12.6	2.7	104.0	-5.8
1990	102.2	10.5	3.4	116.1	103.3	14.8	5.0	123.1	-7.0
1991	107.3	10.6	3.3	121.2	96.3	14.0	5.9	116.2	5.0
1992	106.2	9.9	3.4	119.5	104.5	13.1	7.3	124.9	-5.4
1993	97.0	8.4	2.6	108.0	109.2	12.6	7.3	129.1	-21.1
1994	105.4	8.6	2.6	116.6	123.9	14.4	9.0	147.3	-30.7

Source: United Nations, *Yearbook of International Trade Statistics*, various issues.

Note: After 1989, trade with 15 member-nations of the EU.

to the EU vary from 5 to 9 percent and imports from 10 to 14 percent of the total, whereas Mexican exports to the EU vary from 5 to 17 percent and imports from 11 to 16 percent of the total, respectively.

Trade among NAFTA Countries

As expected, the largest proportion of Canada's trade is with the United States. Out of the total exports of Canada ($183 billion in 1994) about 80 percent goes to the United States, and out of the total Canadian imports ($178 billion in 1994) around 70 percent comes from the United States.

Of the total world imports to Mexico (about $100 billion in 1994) around 70 percent comes from the United States, 2 percent from Canada, and 11 percent from the EU, whereas of the total Mexican exports ($62 billion in 1994) about 85 percent goes to the United States, 3 percent to Canada, and 5 percent to the EU. Before the creation of NAFTA, Mexican imports from the United States, Canada, and the EU as proportions of its total imports were about the same as in recent years, whereas exports have been lower. This means that, through the NAFTA treaty, Mexico is increasing its exports to the other NAFTA members, notably the United States, and is reducing them from the EU.

The U.S. exports to Canada amount to $133.7 billion in 1996, or around 22 percent of total U.S. exports, whereas U.S. imports from Canada are around $156.5 billion in 1996, or 20 percent of total U.S. imports, and growing. In 1996, the U.S. deficit to Canada was $22.8 billion, compared to $16.2 billion with Mexico, $47.7 billion with Japan, and $39.5 billion with China. Table 6.2 shows total exports and imports for the NAFTA countries from 1980 to 1994.

Recently, the General Motors of Canada Ltd., a unit of General Motors Corporation based in Ontario, was awarded a contract by the Canadian Government for 240 armored cars, worth $552 million (Canadian), or U.S.$407 million.

Trade of the EU Countries

Table 6.3 shows total trade of the EU countries with the rest of the world and trade proportions with the rest of the EU nations. Germany has consistently more exports than imports, ending up with large surpluses. The Netherlands, Italy, and Sweden have relatively smaller trade surpluses, but Austria, Britain, Hellas, Spain, and Portugal have trade deficits. The other EU nations have small surpluses, while the EU as a unit has sizable annual trade surpluses.

Trade between the EU nations has increased significantly more than trade with non-EU nations. Britain, France, Germany, and Spain have slightly higher proportions of exports to the rest of the EU nations than proportions of imports. Hellas, Italy, and Sweden have higher proportions of imports than exports from the other EU nations.

These trends indicate that as the EU moves toward integration, trade between member-nations increases at the expense of the non-EU nations, including the

Table 6.2
Total Exports and Imports of Goods and Services of the NAFTA Countries (at Current Prices and Current Exchange Rates, in Billions of U.S. Dollars)

| Years | Canada | | | Mexico | | | U.S.A. | | | Overall |
	Exports	Imports	Balance	Exports	Imports	Balance	Exports	Imports	Balance	Balance
1980	74.9	70.1	4.8	20.8	25.2	-4.4	277.5	293.9	-16.4	-15.9
1981	80.8	77.6	3.2	26.0	32.4	-6.3	301.4	317.7	-16.3	-19.4
1982	78.3	67.0	11.4	26.6	17.9	8.7	280.2	303.2	-23.0	-2.9
1983	83.9	72.9	11.1	28.3	14.0	14.3	272.7	328.1	-55.4	-30.1
1984	97.3	85.4	11.9	30.5	16.8	13.8	297.8	405.1	-107.3	-81.7
1985	98.8	90.4	8.5	28.4	19.1	9.4	296.4	417.6	-121.2	-103.4
1986	99.4	96.0	3.4	22.5	17.4	5.1	313.1	451.7	-138.7	-130.2
1987	109.7	106.0	3.7	27.4	18.8	8.6	356.6	507.1	-150.5	-138.2
1988	129.4	127.1	2.4	28.9	26.2	2.7	436.4	552.2	-115.8	-110.8
1989	138.4	140.3	-1.8	33.0	33.3	-0.4	500.4	587.7	-67.3	-89.5
1990	144.8	146.8	-2.0	38.5	41.4	-2.9	548.9	628.5	-79.6	-84.4
1991	143.9	150.8	-7.0	39.6	48.8	-9.2	592.3	620.9	-28.6	-44.8
1992	149.9	154.9	-5.0	41.5	59.8	-18.3	628.2	668.4	-40.2	-63.5
1993	162.3	164.8	-2.5	44.9	60.3	-15.4	647.8	724.3	-76.5	-94.3
1994	182.6	178.5	4.1	47.9	66.9	-19.1	706.4	816.9	-110.5	-125.4

Source: OECD, National Accounts, various issues.

NAFTA nations. From that point of view, the United States and other nations' fears of lower exports to the EU are justified, at least for the short term.

In the long run, though, a unified common market of Europe would increase trade opportunities not only among EU member-nations but between EU and non-EU countries, primarily with the NAFTA countries. Free movement of goods and services, without national regulations and border restrictions, a uniformed business code, and a more homogeneous consumer population would facilitate transactions between the EU and NAFTA.

Table 6.4 shows total exports and imports of the EU with the rest of the world from 1980 to 1994. Although there were trade deficits in a few recession years of the 1970s and early 1980s, mostly trade surpluses prevailed in the EU during the last three decades. However, large surpluses can be observed after 1982. This trend encourages rapid integration of the European Common Market as well as closer cooperation with non-EU trade partners, particularly NAFTA and the Eastern European countries.

The U.S. trade deficits, mainly after 1980, are primarily due to big increases in imports compared to comparatively lower increases in exports. For more than fifty years before 1971, U.S. exports were higher than imports, leaving surpluses in the balance of payments. The steep rises in oil prices in the 1970s were a severe burden on the economies of the United States and the EU. Moreover, the appreciation of the dollar in the first half of the 1980s and

Table 6.3
Total Exports and Imports of Goods and Services of the EU Countries,
1994 (in Billions of U.S. Current Dollars)

Countries	Exports		Imports		Balance
	Billions of $	% with the E.U.	Billions of $	% with the E.U.	
Austria	73.1	65.6	73.7	68.4	-0.6
Belgium	175.2	75.4	162.2	75.1	13
Britain	267.6	56.4	278.3	54.9	-10.7
Denmark	51.3	58.7	41.8	75.9	9.5
Finland	34.7	56.8	28.7	54.7	6
France	303.3	63.2	274.3	62.6	29
Germany	463.8	57.8	453.1	55.5	10.7
Greece	16.9	57	25.8	67.8	-8.9
Ireland	37.4	73	30.3	58.1	7.1
Italy	258.2	57.2	217.2	61.8	41
Netherlands	171.5	70.7	153.7	62	17.8
Portugal	24.8	73.8	32.2	73.3	-7.4
Spain	107.2	70.6	106.5	64	0.7
Sweden	72.1	59.2	63.8	62.5	8.3
Total	2057.1		1941.6		115.5

Sources: OECD, *National Accounts*; United Nations, *Yearbook of International Trade Statistics*; and International Monetary Fund (IMF), *International Financial Statistics*, various issues.

Note: In some cases, data from earlier years were available. Exports and imports in national currencies were changed to dollar values at year-end exchange rates.

the federal budget deficits may be considered the main reasons for the large deficits in the U.S. balance of trade. However, the depreciation of the dollar thereafter was expected to reduce trade deficits, though with a delay. This is indicated by the lower trade deficits that can be observed in recent years.

Efforts of the U.S. monetary authorities to drive the dollar down aim primarily at reducing imports from and increasing exports to the EU and other countries. For instance, there is a decline in U.S. car imports, mainly because of the depreciation of the dollar. Depressed sales can also be observed in German cars, such as Audi, Porsche, and even Mercedes-Benz, which has had a near monopoly in luxury cars for some thirty years with an annual production of 550,000 cars. However, BMW is maintaining increasing sales in NAFTA and other countries including Japan. It seems that increases in discount interest rates in Germany and Japan would curb inflationary pressures, though they would also reduce somewhat the huge industrial expansion these countries achieved previously.

Depending on the price elasticity of imports, the amount of imports would be determined by the percentage of currency depreciation:

Table 6.4
Total Exports and Imports of Goods and Services of the EU Countries,
1980–1994 (at Current Prices and Current Exchange Rates, in Billions
of U.S. Dollars)

Years	Exports	Imports	Balance
1980	940.7	977.6	−36.9
1981	870.6	876.8	−6.2
1982	837.3	835.5	1.8
1983	817.8	797.1	20.7
1984	832.2	804.5	27.4
1985	871.8	835.9	35.9
1986	1079.4	1005.2	74.2
1987	1303.9	1242.3	61.6
1988	1449.3	1408.9	40.4
1989	1536.5	1513.1	23.4
1990	1853.6	1827.7	25.9
1991	1844.9	1850.1	−5.2
1992	1991.2	1976.5	14.7
1993	1844.9	1748.8	96.1
1994	2057.3	1941.6	115.7

Source: OECD, *National Accounts*, various issues.

$$Em = \frac{\Delta Qm/Qm}{\Delta Pm/Pm}$$

Countries with surpluses in their trade balances, such as Germany, often
do not want their currencies to appreciate much because it makes their products more expensive abroad and foreign products cheaper at home. On the
other hand, countries with trade deficits, such as the United States, Canada,
and Mexico, frequently do not want their currencies to depreciate much because it can stimulate inflation as prices of imported products are rising. Although the demand and supply mechanism of currencies should be free to
correct imbalances, in many cases coordinated policies of concerned mon-

etary authorities may intervene in money markets to influence currency prices one way or another.

The establishment of pan-European standards and regulations in product testing and certification, safety and quality requirements, telecommunications and marketing, financial services, and public sector procurement would harmonize and reduce national differences and encourage internal and international competition. Thus, wasteful duplication would be avoided and investment and trade would rise on a European-wide scale.

To take advantage of this large European market and the liberalized trade regulations, the United States, and to a lesser extent the other NAFTA countries, are proceeding aggressively with plans to improve exports to and investment in Europe. Thus, the "Europe Now" and "Export Now" programs have been initiated to highlight the advantages of exporting to and investing in Europe. To support these programs, and to help NAFTA companies, particularly in the United States, penetrate the European markets, a number of services are offered by such institutions as the United States and Foreign Commercial Service (U.S. and FCS), which provides information on customs and exchange rate (with about 250 trade professionals in Europe); the International Trade Administration (ITA) of the U.S. Department of Commerce, offering counseling services; and the Trade Development (TD) unit, assisting exporters and investors to promote exports through successful marketing and competition. Also, trade fairs and exhibitions (or pavilions) in Europe are used to promote products and to attract potential customers, qualified distributors, and trade agents.

Competition between the EU and NAFTA is becoming strong not only in commercial goods and services but also in military weaponry. The EU is successfully challenging the U.S. arms industry in the area of weapons and military hardware, such as missiles, aircraft, and tanks.

U.S. financial deregulation, though a meritable idea, has not proven effective in correcting unbalanced transactions between NAFTA, the EU, Japan, and other countries. Perhaps its timing and implementation were inappropriate, exposing financial markets to great uncertainty and risk. Thus, the weaker dollar has not done much to improve the U.S. trade balance, probably because of the existing inflexibility of trade and financial markets.

Business fluctuations and other external factors affect economic trends in the EU. Since 1945 and until the oil crisis in 1973, Western Europe had a satisfactory economic expansion. Thereafter, a severe recession followed until the mid-1980s, when an upturn in economic growth and foreign trade could again be observed. Recently, high unemployment and low rates of economic growth prevail in the EU.

In the process of harmonizing rules and removing barriers, there have been complaints—mainly from Britain and Germany against France and Italy—that they favor maintenance of trade barriers to outsiders. There is a serious question, though, whether American or Japanese cars and other goods with European content be considered as foreign and therefore subjected to tariffs, quotas, and other restrictions. Thus, executives of Fiat S.p.A. in Italy, and Renault and Peugeot in France, maintain that if the EU content of Bluebirds (cars) are more than 50 percent Japanese and less than 50 percent British they must be subject to import quotas (no more than a certain percentage of the domestic market in France). The same thing can be said about the EU imports of Honda cars assembled in Ohio. It is argued, however, that this policy would reduce or discourage American, Japanese, and other foreign investment in the EU.

In the European countries, entrepreneurs and businesspeople in the automobile and other industries have expressed their solid support for the single European market, expecting to increase trade and investment. They have begun to overcome their earlier indifference to the expected European integration, and are grasping its implications on their enterprises. The feeling is that they have to adapt rapidly to the new economic and political environment in order to survive in a more competitive, larger market. This is particularly so because of the new conditions created in the reformed economies of Eastern Europe.

There are complaints in Europe that American performance in restraining demand to reduce imports and increase savings has been inadequate. Excessive spending and the rise in exports lead to pressures on productive capacity and feed inflationary expectations and growing domestic and foreign debts. On the other hand, the United States criticizes Germany for not doing enough to stimulate demand and increase its rate of economic growth, which would encourage investment, reduce unemployment, and increase tax revenue. From that point of view, a better coordination of economic policy between NAFTA and the EU that would prevent them from turning into fortress groups, preserve open economies on both sides of the Atlantic, increase free trade, and keep the EU and NAFTA from turning against each other—with all the consequent detrimental effects for their economies and their people.

The percentage increase of imports related to increases in income (income elasticity of imports) was higher in the NAFTA than in the EU countries for the last three decades. For example, the income elasticity of imports was, on average, 1.97 for the United States from 1960–1980 and 1.29 for the EU during the same period. Later it was around 1.1 for the United States and only 0.8 for the EU. This means that the United States spent proportionally higher percentages of income increases for imports than the EU did during the last three decades.

COMPETITION AND PROTECTIONISM

Historically the U.S. economy, which is the largest in NAFTA, has had high tariffs. The duties collected, as a percentage of dutiable imports, varied widely at various times in U.S. history: 45 percent in 1820; 64 percent in 1833 (Compromise Tariff Act); about 25 percent in 1857; 18 percent in 1860; around 50 percent in 1900; 12 percent in 1920; 60 percent in 1930 (Smoot–Hawley Act); about 15 percent in 1967 (Kennedy–Round Reductions); and around 7 percent later after the Uruguay Round.[3] Recently it seems that the United

States, along with other members of GATT (now WTO), took a number of steps to promote free trade by reducing tariffs and eliminating trade barriers.

However, there exist quotas on certain products, based mainly on voluntary restraint agreements among the NAFTA and EU countries as well as other nations. Thus, to protect the American steel industry against imports from other nations, imports are limited by the United States to 20 percent of domestic steel consumption. Such quotas are the result of the flood of imports and the big losses by steel companies especially in the 1980s. Steel companies argue that foreign governments subsidize steel that can be sold in American markets at prices lower than the cost of production. Similar voluntary restraints prevail for cars, textiles, and other products that are considered to be under conditions of unfair competition. There are complaints, though, by some U.S. companies which buy steel that, as a result of protection, shortages appear and prices go up. This is why there are efforts to influence Congress not to extend such protective measures. Also, imported vehicles classified as trucks are subject to higher duties than other imported cars, a measure that affects U.S. imports mainly from Germany, Britain, and Japan.

Trade Creation and Trade Diversion

Theoretically, the creation and enlargement of trade groups like NAFTA and the EU are expected to lead to the creation of trade because part of the domestic production by some member-nations would be replaced by lower-cost imports from other member-nations. This, in turn, leads to greater specialization based on the principle of comparative advantage which in turn leads to the increase in the welfare of the member-nations.

On the other hand, trade diversion, which reduces welfare, is not expected to occur to a significant extent as long as lower-cost imports from outside the community are not replaced by higher-cost imports from EU member-nations. Likewise, the association and eventual integration of Eastern European and other neighboring countries with the EU, as well as NAFTA with Chile and other Latin American countries, would lead to trade creation rather than to trade diversion, as long as domestic tariffs among members would fall and tariffs on imports from the rest of the world would not rise. Therefore, the greater the number of NAFTA or EU member-nations and the larger their size, the lower the cost of production and the higher the welfare of the countries involved, particularly when they are geographically close.

The effects of trade creation in a customs union such as the EU or NAFTA, when a part of domestic production of a member-country of the union is replaced by lower-cost imports from another member-country, are shown in Figure 6.1. The vertical axis shows the price in dollars ($) and the horizontal axis shows the quantity (Q) of a commodity as related to demand (D) and supply (S) curves, whereas point E indicates the equilibrium of supply and demand. With tariffs, total consumption of the country before the formation

Figure 6.1
Trade Creation

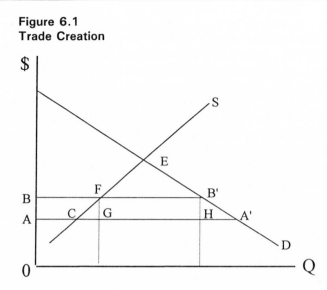

of the customs union is shown by the line BB', domestic production is represented by BF, and imports are represented by FB'. The tariff revenue collected is the rectangle FGHB'. After the formation of the union, consumption is AA', domestic production AC, and imports CA'. The revenue from tariffs disappears and the net gains of the country are equal to the sum of the two triangles CFG and A'B'H.

Figure 6.2 shows the effects of trade diversion when lower-cost imports from outside a customs union, such as the EU or NAFTA, are replaced by

Figure 6.2
Trade Diversion

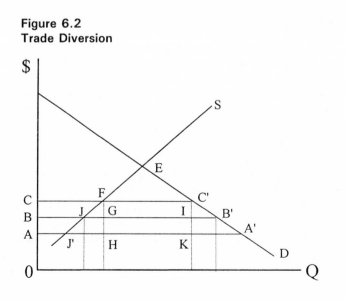

higher-cost imports from union members. Line AA' shows the position of the country under free world trade, with J'A' representing imports. A nondiscriminatory tariff shifts line AA' to CC', with FC' imports. After reducing or eliminating tariffs among EU or NAFTA members, the imports of the country in question are JB'. The welfare of the country is the summation of the two triangles FGJ and B'C'I, whereas the welfare loss from trade diversion is the rectangle GHIK. Thus, the net welfare loss is the difference between the rectangle GHIK and the two combined triangles FGJ and B'C'I.

In a customs union like NAFTA and the EU where tariffs or other barriers on trade among members are reduced or eliminated and trade policies are harmonized with the rest of the world, trade creation and trade diversion may occur. Trade is normally created and welfare increased among member-nations of the customs union. But trade diversion and welfare reduction can be expected to occur in nonmember-nations because of the less efficient use of their resources as a result of the formation of a customs union.

When part of domestic production is replaced by cheaper imports from another member of a customs union, then trade creation occurs. Moreover, the welfare of nonmember-nations may increase through higher imports as a result of the increase in real income of the members of the union. As long as a customs union, like NAFTA or the EU, does not raise tariffs or other trade barriers to outside nations, then the reduction of barriers among members would normally increase trade and welfare, not only for members but for nonmembers as well. Nevertheless, there may be reductions in the union's demand for imports from, and its supply of exports to, the nonmember-nations and an improvement in its collective terms of trade depending on the relative elasticities.

Trade Barriers

Since 1980, protectionist barriers have gone up in both the EU and the United States. A real appreciation of the currency of a country, *ceteris paribus*, leads to a worsening of the balance of foreign trade and therefore to the economic and political pressures for protection. On the contrary, a real depreciation of a currency leads to the improvement of the balance of trade and the relaxation of protectionist pressures or even the reduction of trade restrictions. Thus, the sizable depreciation of European currencies in the 1980s improved the EU trade balance accordingly. Also, the depreciation of the dollar in the early 1990s helped the U.S. trade balance. Deregulation in air and surface transportation, financial markets, communications, oil prices, and stock exchange brokerage has intensified price competition and spurred efficiency on both sides of the Atlantic. Moreover, proposals for regulatory reforms have been made in the NAFTA and EU countries for further deregulations in banking and natural gas prices, deposit insurance and private pensions, nuclear licensing, trucking and railroads, and environmental restrictions. However, in some cases deregulations led to overlapping markets, turbulent entry of new firms, and maneuvers toward price discrimination.

Through the elimination of border controls and harmonization of product standards, the EU production and market would expand for both domestic and foreign companies. It is estimated that the removal of internal barriers would result in a 5 percent increase in NAFTA and EU GDP.

By establishing new NAFTA and EU rules and eliminating conflicting procedures of individual member states, the two groups may offer good opportunities for business firms located in, or exporting to, the EU and NAFTA countries. However, in implementing internal market reforms, it is expected that the EU would not discriminate against foreign companies by transforming internal barriers into external barriers around the whole community. The new rules should not impose limits regarding fair competition from other external firms; rather, they should introduce a true liberalization spirit for trade and investment for outsiders as well.

The Internal Market Directives (more than 200 of them already adopted by the EU and others to be adopted soon) deal with the removal of physical, technical, and fiscal barriers, border controls on vehicle safety, and veterinary or phytosanitary controls. Technical barriers removed or to be removed include restrictions on capital movements and trade services as well as differences in industrial and competitive standards. Removal of fiscal barriers means harmonization of tax systems, particularly value-added and excise tax systems. Already customs documents have been the same in all member-nations so that duplications and bureaucratic confusion for goods shipped to or within the EU are reduced or eliminated. However, variations on health and product safety requirements by member-nations are allowed within certain limits. Similar measures are expected to be introduced by NAFTA countries in the near future.

NAFTA exporters and affiliates producing in the EU should be familiar with EU common trademark and copyright laws, the EU-wide standards of testing and certification, common public procurements, new rules on pollution (air, water, land, and noise), and a variety of other regulations and directives relative to their operations. Likewise, EU exporters and affiliates producing in NAFTA should be familiar with related policies in Canada, Mexico, and the United States.

Fair Trade Practices

Maintaining fair trade between NAFTA and the EU and any other group or country may require countervailing duties and antidumping measures. NAFTA shows a reliance on both antidumping actions and countervailing duties, but the EU is resorting mainly to antidumping actions. These measures, which have been accelerated substantially lately, are used by pro-trade governments, such as the United States, Australia, Canada, and some of the EU member-nations, to cope with domestic protectionist pressure.

Because of the large trade deficits and the unfair trade practices from some partners, certain trade provisions have been introduced in the United States, such as the Omnibus Trade and Competitiveness Act of 1988, which provides methods for the trade representatives to negotiate reduction of unfair practices with other counterparts. Once a country is put on the list, negotiations must be made within a specified time. If an open market does not result, the country which claims damages may close its market to the offending country for certain products. However, retaliation should occur against products with an alternative domestic supply and not against imported products that have significant claimant's content. Being backed up by a significant stick and carrot policy, it would seem that this is a useful provision. Under such conditions, it is difficult for trade partners to circumvent related measures. Because of the accumulation of trade disequilibria, disputes and negotiations between the EU, NAFTA, and Japan continue. As a result, U.S. trade policymakers are after the EU on Airbus subsidies and the restrictions on beef with hormones, Canada for fish exports, and Japan for using U.S. technology.

Strict implementation of the U.S. Omnibus Trade and Competitiveness Act would constrict the EU not only for Airbus but also for European practices in the trade of oilseeds and other products. Moreover, Japan's unfair trade practices regarding intellectual property (patents, copyrights, and trademarks) are under review.

The EU warned, however, that if the United States persists in accusing it of unfair trading practices, it would challenge the U.S. law before the WTO, which serves as a global trade charter for the member-nations and an agency resolving trade disputes. However, despite the disagreements, the representatives of both sides agreed to arrange a serious dispute over EU subsidies that limit imports of American soybeans as well as U.S. restrictions on sugar imports. This is the proper way to avoid retaliations and re-retaliations that cause the contraction of world trade.

The U.S. Omnibus Trade and Competiveness Act stipulates that sanctions can be imposed if other nations restrict imports of American products. As a result, the EU and South Korea were considered for reprisals for restricting imports of U.S. telecommunication products such as digital switching devices, big switchboards, and many other related products for which the United States has a comparative advantage.

If foreign products are sold in the United States at less than their fair value, the U.S. Department of Commerce can impose antidumping duties to eliminate the price differential. If such imported products harm, or threaten to harm, American firms producing similar products, duties could be collected by the Customs Service to eliminate the difference between the cost of foreign products and the lower prices at which they are sold in the United States. However, the EU is not considered as an unfair competitor probably because the EU may, in retaliation, name the United States as a trade violator for a number of products, or because of political and strategic reasons.

There is a great deal of criticism against these U.S. measures on the grounds that they were used to divert attention from the macroeconomic responsibilities of the United States which have led to budget and trade imbalances. It is argued that the United States is shifting from a policy of economic internationalism to a more parochial economic nationalism. In the name of free trade it moves more and more toward protectionism. Specifically, the EU argues that such unilateral measures violate the WTO, are against the global negotiations of the Uruguay Round for trade liberalization, and may be used by NAFTA as a group.

The main purpose of citing countries for unfair trading is to encourage free trade by cutting barriers in finance, insurance, construction, and other services, as well as ending restrictions on foreign investment, imports through licensing and procurement, and other policies that suppress international transactions. To achieve this goal, the United States, and eventually all of NAFTA, are prepared to cut restrictions on steel, textiles, sugar, and dairy products. If negotiations for mutual reduction of trade barriers fail, then world trade may be organized under preferential blocs such as the EU, NAFTA, and perhaps a Pacific trade group.

Similar efforts of reducing import restrictions are made by some U.S. steel-using companies, organizations, and political groups lobbying to eliminate steel import quotas and other barriers. The group of companies that oppose import quotas include Caterpillar, Inc., which makes machines, White Consolidated Industries which produces home products, National Refrigerator and Air Conditioning Products, Inc., Baker's Pride Oven Company, Inc., and many other firms that complain that such quotas raise cost prices. On the other side of the argument, there are steel-producing companies that support the import quotas or the voluntary restraint agreements that limit the amount of imported steel to about 20 percent of domestic consumption. Currently, imported steel by the United States is about 18 percent.

The main U.S. steel companies that support the maintenance of restraints are USX Corporation, Bethleham Steel Corporation, and LTV Corporation. Many other steel companies argue that they need import quotas and protection from competition with subsidized EU and Japanese steel producers to continue making progress and maintaining profitability.

The EU complains that the new U.S. trade law that permits the president to order 100 percent tariffs on imports from countries considered as practicing "unfair" trade restrictions is risky. It is an arrogant and dangerous policy that makes the United States an almighty judge of what is fair trade. The EU may use the same technique to curb U.S. products entering their markets. Already, the EU has published a list of unfair U.S. trade restrictions. They include high tariffs on textiles, shoes, onions, and other agricultural products, export subsidies and import quotas for certain products, "buy American" rules for a number of goods, and other restrictions, including the unfair practices procedures mentioned previously. The Europeans argue that what Washington is doing is contrary to its international obligations.

A related study of the IMF revealed that U.S. nontariff restrictions were equivalent to 25 percent tariffs on such products as textiles, cars, and steel. There are many U.S. "voluntary" restraints on imports, including trade barriers listed by the EU that are estimated to cost American consumers $50 billion. In spite of the free trade rhetoric, U.S. barriers on imports increased during the last decade. However, the overall level of protection for agriculture is higher in the EU and Japan than in the United States and the other NAFTA countries. The producers subsidy equivalent is around 35 percent for the United States, 50 percent for the EU, and as high as 75 percent for Japan.[4]

As mentioned earlier, the EU absorbs the largest amount of U.S. exports. Out of a total $816.4 billion U.S. exports in 1996, 23.7 percent went to the EU, compared to 21.6 percent to Canada, and only 11.8 percent to Japan. Not only in commodity exports is the EU important to the United States and other NAFTA nations, but also in such services as television programming, for which American producers have increased their revenue from sales in the EU six times in this decade. However, there are complaints that the largest eight EU countries require that some degree of programming be European produced, and there are plans to set quotas on American television programming in the entire EU. Although there are no restrictions in the United States, some countries, including Canada, have such limitations to preserve their cultural sovereignty by limiting foreign films and television material. About two-thirds of foreign program sales of American entertainment producers, such as Fox, Columbia, Paramount, Warner, and Universal, are made in the EU.

The EU is restricting U.S. and other television programming, not only for the commercial protection of European producers but perhaps to preserve its society's culture. The Europeans seem to value culture much more than Americans and they allocate larger amounts of public funds for its maintenance compared to those of the United States. It is argued that some form of protectionism is needed to resist the rapidly expanding U.S. cultural imperialism in the EU. The United States, though, is fighting such EU cultural protectionism via the WTO, arguing that it is a violation of its regulations.

There is a trend and even a war among mass media firms for the domination of markets on both sides of the Atlantic. Mergers, acquisitions, and friendly or hostile takeovers lead to the monopolization of the information markets. Fewer and fewer people control radio and television stations, satellite channels, videocassettes, cable systems, movies, theaters, book publications, magazines, newspapers, and other media that influence and even direct public opinion. This concentration of media, that is, the monopolization or oligopolization of producing and distributing information, reduces critical reporting and public access to independent production and endangers the democratic process. The relaxation of antitrust legislations and even the support of cartelization and concentration of media in NAFTA, and more so in the EU, reduce diversity and genuine competition and may misdirect information that feeds the human mind.

Spending for research and development (less than 2% of GNP in the United States, Britain, and France, and close to 3% in Japan) is responsible for innovations and new patents. It seems though in recent years many firms emphasize short-term profits, not long-term research and development.

The EU, with a higher percentage of farm population (8%) compared with the United States (3%), presents objections to substantial cuts in farm support programs. That is why it seeks a slower pace of change and not drastic reductions of agricultural support programs in the form of subsidies or the use of variable levies that curb imports. EU farmers (mainly in France, Italy, Spain, Hellas, and Portugal) are expected to present severe oppositions to cuts in or elimination of farm support. Similar opposition to the curbs of agricultural support is expected by U.S. farmers, chiefly by the producers of dairy products and sugar, as well as by Japanese rice growers for which high prices and tough barriers to market access are maintained.

TRADE PROBLEMS

Because of the rapid growth of the EU and the reduction of tariffs as a result of the negotiations under WTO, trade between the EU and NAFTA is expanding. However, there is some trade diversion in agricultural products because of EU tariffs that equalize import prices to the common farm prices established by the EU (variable import levels). The high prices of supported agricultural products lead to large surpluses of these products in the EU.

A serious dispute between NAFTA and the EU involves the agricultural support programs, guaranteeing prices above markets levels, buying surplus products and sometimes dumping them at lower prices. Such programs cause distortions in the world markets and lead to retaliations. During the WTO negotiations, the EU proposed a freeze in state support prices. Cereals, dairy products, beef, vegetable oil, sugar, and rice are the main products included in this proposal. The United States, Canada, Australia, and other producers suggested that all subsidies stop by the year 2000. However, the EU proposed that reductions can gradually be negotiated but rejected complete elimination of subsidies. On the other hand, U.S. payments to farmers to reduce land cultivation or herds, as well as output quotas, are not included in the freeze proposal.[5] Although consumer-oriented subsidies help the increase in the production of food and other agricultural products, they also contribute to slow economic growth and increased inflation through rising government expenditures.

Serious financial problems appeared with the EU budget with about two-thirds of its annual receipts spent for farm subsidies. The countries of the north, primarily Britain and to some extent Germany, object to farm subsidization and ask for a revised farm policy to eliminate food surpluses which are then sold on world markets. Australia, the United States, Canada, and other countries that export farm products complain that the agricultural policy of the EU leads to unfair competition against their own products.

Moreover, Britain wants to reduce its net cost of EU membership, as does Germany, which pays about $2 billion a year more than it gets, and also wants its share of EU expenditures to be kept under control in the future. The southern EU countries, including southern Italy, Hellas, Spain, and Portugal, press for better agricultural subsidies. Northern EU countries, such as Denmark, Belgium, and The Netherlands that produce large amounts of cattle-raising products, also collect sizable subsidies. For milk alone, subsidies amount to about 30 percent of the total agricultural subsidies.

The EU provides subsidies to various agricultural and dairy products, mainly by guaranteed minimum prices. Essentially, it buys such products at determined prices and sells them to the manufacturers and sellers at auction. Because of the complaints of people who process these products that the guaranteed minimum prices arose over time and are no longer competitive outside the EU, subsidies are provided primarily on the sale of these products.

Olive oil, along with seed oils from corn and soybean, are important products included in the EU subsidies. Mediterranean oil producers, primarily in Italy, France, Spain, and Hellas, are the main receivers of olive oil subsidies. Berio and Bertolli are the largest producers of olive oil imported to the United States from Italy.

Farm support policies are wasteful, inefficient, and damaging to the economies of the countries involved. The origins of agricultural protectionism are primarily caused nationally by domestic pressures to provide support to farmers. The impact of a reduction or elimination of agricultural protectionism is expected to be beneficial to NAFTA and EU economies. It is estimated that the ending of such protectionism will reduce the U.S. trade deficit by more than $40 billion and create about three million new jobs in the EU. Moreover, it would increase incomes in developing nations and reduce their debt by 5 percent annually.[6] However, to avoid sharp ups and downs in prices of farm products in a cobweb fashion, some form of protection or other kind of price support may be needed.

In its efforts to liberalize global trade in farm products, the United States proposed a system of fixed tariffs, instead of quotas, licensing, and variable levies. U.S. producers in highly protected sectors such as dairy products, peanuts, and sugar became uncomfortable, but American farmers in general offered their cautious support to the proposal. The EU Commissioner for Agriculture, though, expressed opposition to the idea while Japan, with rice prices ten times higher than the world level, is not enthusiastic about the proposal.

Moreover, to avoid increases in budget spending and reduce overproduction of milk and other agricultural products, the EU Farm Ministers periodically urge the Commission to draw up rules concerning quotas and price determination for such farm products. France and other member countries support such rules of fixed prices and quota packages as long as they do not send the wrong signals to EU farmers. These measures bring some relief to Germany which allocated high quotas to its farmers.

Hormones and Trade War

As part of the serious battle against possible European protectionism from the EU internal unity, the United States used trade sanctions against European food products in retaliation for the EU ban on imports of meat that contain growth hormones. The ban is universal and is justified on the grounds of health, especially for children. It applies to all countries outside the EU. Also, European farmers are not permitted to use hormones that increase the normal weight of animals by as much as 20 percent. The movement against hormones was started by consumer activists in Germany and Italy who argue that they are carcinogenic. Already Australia, Argentina, Brazil, New Zealand, and other meat producing countries have agreed to ship to Europe only hormone-free meat.

The United States, though, objected to this ban and retaliated by imposing 100 percent tariffs on such EU products as tomatoes and tomato sauce, boneless beef, instant coffee, certain alcoholic drinks, fresh and concentrated juices, pet food, and certain pork products. Similar objections were expressed by Canada. The U.S. trade sanctions against the EU were estimated to cost about $100 million, an amount about equal to the loss of U.S. exports to the EU because of the ban. The EU retaliation included sanctions on American walnuts, dried prunes, peaches, papayas, and apricots. There were fears that this might lead to a trade war, as Brussels threatens counter-retaliation and Washington re-retaliation, *ad infinitum*.

The United States argued that there is no scientific basis for such claims. Although there is not agreement among scientists regarding health hazards from growth hormones, there is a desexing, calming effect on animals that leads to unnatural, quick growth, especially when the hormones are overused. It is estimated that a single $1 hormone can save $20 in quick-fattening cost.

The problem started in Italy in 1982 (and later in Germany and Holland) after the carcinogenic synthetic estrogen diethylstilbestrol, or DES, was found in baby food. As a result, infants of both sexes developed breasts and DES was banned. American breeders are permitted to shoot the hormones into cows' ears but Europeans used to inject them into the skeletal parts of the cattle.

The EU ban on beef raised with growth hormones (imposed on 1 January 1989) forced U.S. meat producers to seek alternative markets, primarily in Japan, Mexico, and Egypt. Livers, hearts, kidneys, tongues, and other specialty meats are more popular in Europe, Japan, Mexico, and other countries than in the United States. Meat manufacturers, packers, and exporters searched for other markets. The Japanese market has an increasing taste for processed meats and hot dogs while the Mexican government made meat imports easier by lowering tariffs. Thus, American beef producers expect to replace part of the EU beef sales in these and other countries. However, the Europeans accept hormone-treated meats for pet food, but not for use by people because it is harmful to humans. The United States reduced import restrictions on British pork and pork products because of the elimination of the danger of hog cholera, a contagious disease of swine.

On the other side of the Atlantic, European farmers and policymakers present proposals to ease the dispute by allowing larger import quotas for American meat free of hormones. Otherwise, there is fear that retaliations and counter-retaliations can seriously damage the sizable annual trade between the EU and NAFTA, mainly the United States. It is better to negotiate than to fight. That is why the EU postponed for some time any retaliation against American tariffs on its food products.[7] At the same time, American beef producers, especially from Texas, put pressures on Washington to comply with the EU directives and certify meat for exports to be free of hormones, accordingly.

This dispute of the United States versus the EU over American beef with hormones resembles a similar dispute a century ago. In the 1880s, the German Empire, under Chancellor Otto von Bismarck, and other European nations banned U.S. pork products because of the presence of trichinae worms. American pork raisers and other pressure groups argued that this was a protectionist measure. The Germans counter-argued that they required inspection of their own pork for public health purposes. Finally, threats of retaliation and re-retaliation stopped when the U.S. Congress passed a microscopic inspection law in 1891. The Europeans lifted the ban and the 1880–1891 pork war was over.

The U.S. Omnibus Trade and Competitiveness Act, and especially Section 301 under which the beef retaliation was justified, is used as an instrument to harass European and other trading rivals. It urges the U.S. president to respond to unreasonable and unfair trade practices of other nations. However, it is argued that this leads to unilateral decisions, regardless of contractual rights and obligations under the WTO, and in practice makes the above competitive act anticompetitive and protectionistic.

It seems that with the rapid growth of international transactions it becomes inevitable that other nations would rise and share prominence in world trade. The acceptance of this principle would save the WTO international trade talks on agricultural subsidies and it would not jeopardize the EU common agricultural policy (CAP), protecting consumers all over the world, and especially in Japan where farm products are very expensive.

A serious problem in beef trading appeared recently, not so much between NAFTA and the EU but between Britain and the other EU member-nations. British cows contracted bovine spongiform encephalopathy, which may be contracted by humans through beef and other byproducts from the so-called "crazy" cows. In order to lift the EU ban on British beef exports, the British government decided to slaughter more than 1.2 million cows and other cattle born to cows. However, it is expected that the EU would not lift the ban for years, because of the danger of mad cow disease.[8]

U.S. banana exporters, mainly Chiquita Brands International and the Dole Food Company, appealed to the U.S. government to urge the EU to cancel its decision of 1993, imposing import restrictions on bananas, with the exception of those from former EU colonies, which supply about 15 percent of the EU banana market. Some seventy members of the U.S. Congress, including Bob Dole, advocated trade sanctions against Costa Rica and Colombia unless they pulled out of the EU's banana quota program.

Steel Problems

On both sides of the Atlantic, the steel industry has been in difficulty particularly since the peak production of 1974. Whereas in 1950, the United States produced about half of the world's steel, today its share is only about 10 percent. U.S. net imports are around 25 percent of its steel output. On the other hand, steel production in the EU tripled from 1950 to 1970, but it decreased thereafter, though net exports have been and still are realized. Out of a world total annual steel production of about 800 million tons, the United States is producing around 85 million tons, while the EU is producing about 140 million tons, or 18 percent, compared to 26 percent in 1950. Germany, with about 40 million tons of steel production, is the main EU producer, followed by Italy (15 million tons), France (20), Britain (15), Belgium (11), The Netherlands (6), and Luxembourg (4). Other nations, primarily Japan (with about 15% of the world's production and net exports of more than 30 million tons annually), Brazil, and South Korea have emerged as major steel producers.

Comparatively speaking, total cost per ton of steel is higher in the United States than in the EU and Japan while the cost of coal and ore is about the same. Relative decline in U.S. productivity and a rise in wages are mainly responsible for labor cost differences. In the mid-1960s, the average American steel worker produced twice as much steel per hour as his German, French, British, and Japanese counterparts. However, after 1982, the productivity of the German steel worker was 108, compared to an index of 100 for the U.S. worker, 100 for the French worker, 71 for the British worker, and as high as 141 for the Japanese worker. Wages of U.S. steel workers increased to about double those of the average manufacturing workers in the 1980s, compared to less than 50 percent higher in the 1960s. The differences in the EU nations are not as great. Thus, hourly compensation costs for production in iron and steel manufacturing are higher in the United States than in Japan, Germany, and Britain.[9] For the other EU countries, hourly labor cost is between that of Germany and Britain. With the unification of Germany and the reforms in Eastern Europe, related EU labor costs were not significantly increased. With the closer cooperation of the NAFTA countries, labor cost in steel and other products would be suppressed.

To protect the domestic steel industry until it becomes competitive, the United States introduced protective trade measures such as the voluntary restraint agreements (VRAs) with the EU and Japan and the trigger-price mechanism (TPM). As a result, U.S. imports from the EU and other countries decreased from around 25 percent to 18 percent, thereby protecting jobs in the steel industries which neglected to do their part regarding reinvestment and modernization. Moreover, the TPM, not permitting imports below an established minimum price, led to a relative increase in steel prices, estimated at about 10 percent.

This increase in steel prices induces the use of alternative materials and increases imports of manufactured products with steel as their component. In addition, such quotas and restrictions encourage companies that use steel to operate outside the country with restrictions and controls. Therefore, in the long run, such restrictions are expected to turn against the steel industry they aim to protect.

The Commission of the EU has primarily imposed domestic controls on steel output, investment, mandatory minimum prices on steel bars, and guidance prices for other steel products in the 1970s and 1980s. Moreover, a regulation of national subsidies was initiated to stimulate reorganization and modernization of the EU steel industries. Nevertheless, efficient steel industries, primarily in Germany, objected to minimum prices and quantity controls on the grounds that they deprived them of market competition by prohibiting them from charging lower prices, thereby turning them into sleeping monopolies.

In addition to domestic controls on prices and production, the EU introduced import price controls on steel similar to the trigger-price mechanism of the United States. This means that import prices could not be less than the basic prices established by the EU. Otherwise, antidumping procedures were to be enacted and imports were to be excluded from the EU. However, exemptions were permitted for countries that negotiated with the EU through VRAs. Some fifteen countries negotiated and achieved such exemptions which have been renewed periodically.[10]

After many complaints from U.S. steel producers, an antidumping and countervailing investigation was started by the Department of Commerce in the 1980s. Many large steel companies in almost all EU countries were charged for subsidization and dumping operations as were some Japanese companies as well. This was particularly so for Italian, French, British, and Belgium steel companies with subsidies varying from 11 to 26 percent. Most German firms, though, were found not to be subsidized were opposed to subsidies by other EU nations. Some big EU steel producers, such as Urino and Sacilor of France, Italsider of Italy, Cockerill–Sambre of Belgium, and the British Steel Corporation, did not like to lose their U.S. market and pressed their governments to enter into agreements with the United States to arrange the antidumping and countervailing duty problem.

The agreements and arrangements between NAFTA (mainly the United States) and the EU as well as other countries reduced price controls and quotas and encouraged competition in favor of the consumers of the countries concerned. On the contrary, restrictive measures protect inefficiency, discourage productive investment, and penalize consumers concerning prices and quality products. Moreover, reduction or elimination of subsidies reduces budgetary deficits and stabilizes the economies on both sides of the Atlantic.

A serious problem for the German economy is the declining steel industry. The huge Krupp steel plant in the Ruhr Valley near the River Rhine, which was established in 1894, has been deemed uneconomical. High labor cost and stiff international competition are mainly responsible for the decline of the steel industry which once was the pride of Germany's economy. The Rheinhouse Mill, for example, operates at about half of its annual capacity of four million tons and a labor force of about one-sixth of that before World War II. The number of employees in the steel industry declined from 400,000 in 1965 to about 66,000 at present. To solve its problems, Krupp–Hoesch seeks to buy its competitor Thysen A.G. with 111,000 employees for $8.1 billion.

Other steel mills such as Mannesmann A.G. and Thyssen A.G. face similar problems and together with Krupp are in the process of reconstruction through labor cuts or readjustments. It is a phenomenon similar to that in Pittsburgh, Pennsylvania, where some 100,000 jobs have been eliminated. The hope though is that additional jobs will be created in service industries. Nevertheless, Chancellor Helmut Kohn and other politicians promised to support the redevelopment of the Ruhr Valley and other regions which suffer because of the declining steel industry. However, less expensive labor from East Germany and other neighboring countries would reduce cost and make the German steel industry more competitive.

As a result of the U.S. quotas against imported steel, import market share was reduced from 30 percent in late 1984 to less than 20 percent today. At the same time, through industry's reinvestment and restructuring, man-hours per ton were reduced to a lower level than in Germany and Japan and labor productivity was improved. It is estimated that U.S. auto companies pay less per ton for domestic steel than their counterparts pay in Japan. However, this is mainly because of the significant depreciation of the dollar and not so much to higher productivity and lower cost in the U.S. steel industries.

It is argued, though, that a robust demand for steel, in addition to cost cutting and the declining dollar, made the U.S. steel industries competitive and profitable. Nevertheless, steel-using manufacturers complain they face higher costs, delays, and shortages, and they expect damages in their international competitiveness and eventual losses. Quotas are considered medicine: boosting one industry in the short run but making many others sick in the long run.

In a serious effort to end subsidies to all industries, the United States agreed with the EU and six other countries (Japan, South Korea, Brazil, Mexico, Australia, and Trinidad and Tobago) to terminate subsidies to steel producers. A similar agreement to end subsidies is pursued with other steel producing countries.

At the same time, the United States ended its old quota program which kept imports below 20 percent of the quantity sold in the country. Under the new quotas, the EU and sixteen other countries would export to the United States 19 percent of its domestic market and Japan's share would be only 5 percent. Each percentage point involves about one million tons of steel and the total amount permitted in the United States is around eighteen million tons.

Such agreements of cuts in subsidies are the result of the Uruguay Round of talks and the adjustments that the IMF works out with Mexico, Brazil, and other countries. These steel-producing countries realized that trade liberalization would reduce the cost of taxpayer support of industry and benefit the consumers.

There are complaints, though, in recent WTO reports that, although the United States and the other NAFTA economies are generally open to imports, certain parts of their sectors, including steel, textiles, sugar, dairy and other agricultural products, semiconductors, automobiles, and machine tools enjoy protection. Even among the NAFTA members, the United States enjoys protection for some products. For example, the Clinton administration bludgeoned Mexico recently into a settlement to keep Mexican tomatoes out of the American market.

TRADE LIBERALIZATION

The liberalization of trade among the United States, Canada, and Mexico creates a regional block that is expected to reduce consumer prices, stimulate competitiveness, and increase exports for all three members of NAFTA. Already, U.S. exports to Mexico more than doubled in the past four years to more than $50 billion a year. The historic trade agreement of NAFTA would stimulate ambitious merchants and investors to exploit opportunities in all member-nations.

Customs duties were to be eliminated on about half of the U.S. products when the NAFTA pact became law, and tariffs for other products would be eliminated over ten to fifteen years from an average of about 10 percent. Nevertheless, conflicts appear from time to time. The United States complained that Canada protects domestic dairy products (eggs and poultry) with quotas and tariffs running as high as 300 percent. However, a free trade panel decided that Canada has neither violated the NAFTA treaty nor the WTO by protecting those products. But, under the trade accord, all tariffs between the United States and Canada must be eliminated by 1998.

In order to make sure that big trade partners, including Canada, Japan, and the EU, are abiding by trade deals, the United States established a special office to coordinate foreign trade with the Department of Commerce. With this office, the U.S. government expects to beef up enforcement of trade agreements with its main partners who are supposed to honor them.

As a result of NAFTA, the 113 United States–Canada border crossings became more accessible. U.S. President Bill Clinton and Prime Minister Jean Chrétien of Canada signed an accord to ease border crossing back and forth and to increase air travel between the two countries. The United States and Canada have the world's largest trading relationship (some $300 billion a year).

Because of the reduction in tariffs under NAFTA, U.S. exports to Mexico are expected to increase significantly. However, U.S. imports from Mexico may increase even faster. Some of the increase in exports to Mexico come from items that boomerang back to the United States in the form of imports, including such items as automobiles and other high technology goods. This is because component parts are shipped to Mexico for assembly into finished products, which are exported back to the United States. Also, infrastructure equipment may be exported to Mexico for use in the building of factories and then returned.

After NAFTA was ratified by Congress in November 1993, the optimistic projections that it would create hundreds of thousands of jobs in the United States have not materialized during the first years of its implementation. On the contrary, according to the Department of Labor, more than 40,000 jobs were lost in a two-year period. Even within Mexico there was a failure to create jobs in the period of 1994–1995. However, the main reasons for the failure of sizable job creation in both countries was the deep recession of the Mexican economy because of the peso crisis which started in December 1994.

The severe devaluation of the peso accounts for the disappearance of the U.S. trade surplus with Mexico and the loss or no creation of jobs in the U.S. economy. Nevertheless, the drastic peso depreciation to more than 100 percent is expected, *ceteris paribus*, to improve the balance of trade and the labor market of Mexico for the coming years as Mexican exports became cheaper and imports more expensive for Mexicans who are less able to buy American goods.

There is no doubt that there will be setbacks along the way, but the net result of NAFTA should be beneficial for the United States, Canada, and Mexico, as well as for the whole hemisphere of the Americas. With the peso now at market rates, and not artificially overvalued as it was up to the end of 1994, both economies across the Rio Grande are expected to be in an advantageous position from the standpoint of mutual trade. However, the pressure on the U.S. labor force is expected to continue, particularly in labor intensive industries, because of the great differences in wages. Already, the average wages in Mexico are about one-fourth of those in the United States, and many U.S. and Canadian companies are expected to relocate to Mexico for lower labor costs.

Canada has accused, from time to time, the EU and other countries of catching undersized turbot (a large, edible European flatfish) outside Canadian waters and even chased Spanish and other trawlers with warships (*Turbot War*). In order to avoid further disputes, Canada reached an agreement on this matter with the fifteen members of the Northwest Atlantic Fisheries Organization in September 1995, which took effect on 1 January 1996. As a result, Canada can place independent observers on board the fishing vessels in international waters off the Atlantic Coast to monitor catch levels and fish sizes.

Enforcement measures also include satellite tracking to observe cheating regarding turbot fishing. In order to make the agreement practical, Russia and Japan agreed to turn over some quota to allow the EU to catch about 11,000 tons of the disputed fish per year, or 55 percent of the total harvest.

In December 1995, the United States and the EU designed a wide ranging transatlantic trade and security accord to cut trade barriers, cooperate for peace in the Balkans, fight international crime, and be more open to do business on both sides. In a sense, "what is made in Europe must be good enough for America and vice versa." The accord solved differences on television programming, agriculture, and other trade issues that would benefit both parties in the future. Moreover, the appointment of Spanish Foreign Minister Javier Solana as Secretary General of NATO, aims at shaping U.S.–European relations in the post–Cold War era.

Dumping and antidumping policies, ruled by Article V of GATT, which was recently replaced by WTO, are used from time to time by both NAFTA and the EU. Dumping is perceived as the international dimension of antitrust legislation which encourages competition. The formation of NAFTA, which can be considered as a counterpart of the EU, is helping the convergence of antitrust and antidumping policies of these two groups through negotiations.[11]

The enlargement of the EU may create problems for Third World countries regarding tariff changes. If tariffs of new members were lower than those of the EU for nonmember trading partners, related compensation might be claimed. For example, the United States, Canada, and Australia reached a compensation agreement with the EU to cover the tariff increase as a result of the accession of Austria, Finland, and Sweden on 1 January 1995. Other EU trading partners such as Argentina, Chile, New Zealand, and Thailand are expected to follow. This was the result of the rules of WTO and Washington argued that the losses were about $1.7 billion in trade, mainly in semiconductors, chemicals, seafood, pet food, cherries, and rice. However, Hellas, Italy, and Spain objected to such concessions, particularly on almonds and rice. Nevertheless, the EU pledged to reduce tariffs on a number of products, especially on semiconductors, wheat, corn, and other goods.

TOURISM

Improvements in transportation and communication help increase travel and tourism not only between NAFTA and the EU but between these and other countries. The seashores of Canada, Mexico, and the United States are attractive places for tourists as are those of the EU countries. Impressive beaches of the NAFTA countries in the Atlantic and Pacific oceans, as well as in the EU Mediterranean countries, are places that attract tourists from all over the world. Florida, the Cancun Province in the Mexican Gulf, and Acapulco in western Mexico hold the front line for vacations as do the Hellenic Islands and other places in the Mediterranean Sea, mainly in Italy, France, and Spain.

Ancient monuments and old places help improve tourism and cultural development. In Hellas, for example, in addition to the Olympic games in Olympia which started in 776 B.C. and are the largest and oldest, of interest are the Nemean Games, started in 573 B.C. in Nemea, near Mycenes, and took place every other year. Other games were those at Delphi and Isthmia, near Corinth. The Nemean festival was one of the four pan-Hellenic competitions in ancient times in which wars and killings would cease voluntarily. The winners were garlanded with laurels and sometimes were provided with free food for life. No distinction was made between professionals and amateurs in this one-day festival which was used as funerary games, common from the days of Homer (around 1200 B.C.) to Alexander the Great (325 B.C.). There is a long entrance tunnel with limestone blocks on which names of ancient competitors can be seen even today. The tunnel was sealed by silt in the first century A.D. and opened a few years ago. Many sprinters from a number of countries (some 500 from 28 nations in June 1996) emerge from the ancient tunnel into the stadium which was used more than 2,000 years ago.[12]

Major cities with museums and other monuments, such as New York, San Francisco, Paris, London, Vienna, and particularly Athens and Rome, attract people from many other countries and provide revenue for tourist and other related services. However, there seems to be conflict between clean environment and rapid economic growth. Other EU member-nations such as Italy and Hellas, as well as Mexico City, Los Angeles, and to some extent Montreal among the NAFTA cities, face the most serious environmental problems.

Many marble columns, cathedrals, and statues in the NAFTA and the European cities (particularly Athens and Rome) are sickly gray because of air pollution, chaotic traffic, and public indifference. This is particularly so with the fifth century B.C. Acropolis in Athens, the second century statue of Marcus Aurelius in Rome, and many other monuments. It is suggested that some original statues be stored in museums and copies be put in their place for public display. Other measures include protecting the statues with glass screens. In any case, keeping Athens, Rome, Paris, Washington, D.C., and other tourist cities and their monuments in shape requires a *Sisyphean* task and heavy public sector expenditures.

Most of the large cities in America and Europe show signs of physical and spiritual uniformity. As a result, urbanists and tourists have begun to look toward smaller, neglected cities for a sense of history, continuity, and old world cultural and social manners. Primarily because of economic backwardness and political neglect, many of these lesser cities remain intact. Gradually, economic development and the process of NAFTA and European integration is expected to change the old characteristics of many of these cities. Nevertheless, measures should be taken to preserve and even to improve their historical and tourist elements through environmental protection rules and quality city planning.

Chapter 7

Monetary Policy and Exchange Rates

HISTORICAL TRENDS

Europe

Money, which is anything generally accepted as a medium of exchange, has been a useful instrument for transactions throughout history. Different societies used many objects as money, including human skulls, elephants, cows, bread, wine, slaves, shells, women, and primarily, metals. Even today in the Yap island of the Pacific, large stones, with a hole in the center to carry them (fei), are used as money.

Cattle, the meaning of the Latin *pecus* from which the word pecuniary is derived, was used as money in ancient times in Homeric Greece (Hellas), Persia, Egypt, China, and primitive Italy, Ireland, and Britain. Even today in southern Sudan, people use cattle and goats as a standard of value. Thus, "a reasonably sound wife costs about 40 head of cattle, with perhaps a few goats and chickens thrown in."[1]

The Greeks (Hellenes), to whom the Western world owes its democracy according to Nietzsche, were first to democratize money or be democratized by it. As Herodotus (5th century B.C.) mentioned, money gave people freedom of movement and leisure.

During the Homeric period (around 1200 B.C.), the Hellenes measured money by goods (cows, metals, or other barter units), not goods by money as we, being dominated by money illusions, do now. Even before the time of Homer, all values were expressed in terms of cows and oxen, especially during the Minoan (Cretan) and Mycenaean civilizations, as well as in other areas of Europe, Asia, and Africa. Thus, in Mycenae, southwest of the Isthmus of Corinth, a copper ingot of 2.5 feet long in a shape of ox-hide, as old as the fourteenth century B.C., was found that suggests a transition from the live ox unit to metals. Moreover, certain pieces of gold called *talents* were in circulation but were expressed in terms of cows.

In the discussion for using Euro as a new name for the EU currency in place of the previous European Currency Unit (ECU), an alternative name suggested was the talent, which was used in ancient Hellas and classical Rome, considered the common roots of the EU member-nations. It was easily pronounceable in all languages and was considered as a hard currency with a value of 26 kg of silver. Finally, the name Euro was accepted by the EU members.

In ancient Sparta, "scientific" money units were introduced by Lycurgus, the tough ruler, in about the ninth century B.C. They were large iron discs that when red hot, were dipped in vinegar to make them unmalleable and useless for other purposes. Later, gold and silver were deposited by the Lacedaemonians with the Arcadians for safekeeping.

The iron discs had a face value higher than the intrinsic or metal value ("debased money"). The Spartan monetary system fell into disuse after the Lacedaemonians were compelled to relinquish the hegemony of Hellas to Athens in 479 B.C.[2] This system of debased money was used later and even today by advanced money societies. However, Greek (Hellenic) money was free of debasement with two spectacular exceptions under Solon (sixth century B.C.), the Athenian lawmaker, and Dionysus (fifth century B.C.), the tyrant.

From the middle of the seventh to the end of the fifth century B.C., coins replaced previous tortoise-shell currency in Lydia and in the island of Aegina. Athens used silver (from the mines of Laurium) coins (*drachmas*), which were stamped to indicate their value, according to Aristotle, who also mentioned that commodities have a use value and an exchange value. Aristotle further distinguished the difference between wealth and money, which can be used for exchanges and storage of wealth.

Plato referred to money as a "symbol or token" and proposed that token-money be used for domestic trade and gold and silver be restricted to transactions with foreigners.[3]

Not long before 405 B.C., Aristophanes noted in *The Frogs* and other plays, that in "our Republic bad citizens are preferred to good, just as bad money circulates while good money disappears," a concept very near to Gresham's Law, named after Sir Thomas Gresham, Queen Elizabeth's Chancellor of the Exchequer (1559). Moreover, money was internationalized by the Hellenes.

The main reasons for the desire to issue common currency lay sometimes in the need for military cooperation, and sometimes in the recognition of the advantages of free economic intercourse.[4] These reasons were and still are important for using common currency by American states, the dollar, in the past and by the European Union, the Euro, at present.

During the period of the Roman Empire (31 B.C. to A.D. 476), money and credit opened new freedoms and opportunities, and financiers and profiteers flourished while peasants and workers complained. Trade enterprises were growing and interest from money began to play an important role similar to that of today. The first metal money of Rome was copper in bars or ingots, fractions of which weighing a Roman pound were named *asses*. Later, silver coins called *denarii*, similar to those previously used in Hellas and mostly debased, were used. The fall of the Roman Empire was partially due to the decline of the silver and gold mines of Spain and Hellas, in addition to slavery and moral corruption. More or less, the same conditions prevailed in the Byzantine Empire (395–1453), which primarily used gold currency.

In post–Roman Europe, early financial operations were carried on by monasteries, which also accepted articles of value for safekeeping. Interest is *tokos* in Hellenic, which means a child, and interest from money was considered immoral by the church and unnatural by Aristotle (two dimes cannot beget a baby dime).

Frequently, Jews who were outside the pale of the church were active in money changes and money lending with interest. In England, William the Conqueror allowed lenders to charge up to 45 percent interest, collecting vast taxes and borrowing freely from them. However, gradually the Jews were persecuted and, in 1290, were ordered to leave the country under penalty of death.[5]

Later, the Lombard bankers from Italy extended their operations all over Europe, including England, where they gave their name to a financial street in London. Financial houses such as the Bardi, the Peruzzi, the Medici, and the Strozzi in Italy, as well as the Fuggers and the Rothschilds in Germany, were exempted from the ban on usury and made loans to kings, merchants, and even to the Pope during the Medieval and Renaissance periods. In the seventeenth century, goldsmiths or jewelers on Lombard Street and other places in England such as monasteries, accepted deposits for safekeeping, giving the proper receipts. Gradually, the depositors asked the goldsmiths to pay others, originating the modern check. Later, these receipts were payable to the bearer, making the transfer of funds easier as the depositors could hand the receipts over to their creditors, performing the same functions as in modern banking. Gradually, the goldsmiths were overshadowed by great chartered banks. Among the first important banks were the Bank of Sweden (1656), the Bank of England (1694), the Bank of France (1800), and the German Reichs Bank (1873).

United States

In the American colonies, coins brought over by European immigrants and Indian wampums were initially used as money. Beaver skins were also used as a medium of exchange. Corn was mainly used as legal tender in 1631 in Massachusetts, and tobacco and rice were used in the South. Because much trade was with the Spanish colonies, the Spanish silver "milled" dollars, or fractions of them, were also used until 1857. However, the shortage of coins led to paper money in the form of *bills of credit,* either as notes against land as security or as unbacked, gradually depreciated bills. After George Washington's inauguration in 1789 as the first President of the United States, gold and silver full-bodied coins were used.

The gold standard, first introduced in Britain in 1821, was adopted by the United States in 1900 to avoid relative price fluctuations in the prevailing bimetallic system of gold and silver. The gold standard, by which the supply of money was determined by the amount of gold, and anyone could get it, was abandoned by Great Britain in 1931 and by the United States in 1933. In its place, the gold reserve system was introduced in which a certain percentage of the money supply was kept in gold. The price of gold was determined to be $35 per ounce, and no one could get it. In practice, it was used for the settlement of international trade balances. In 1971, the price of gold was left to the free market mechanism (or floating dollar).

The first U.S. banks were the Bank of North America established by the Continental Congress in 1781, and the Bank of The United States, established by Alexander Hamilton, the first Secretary of the Treasury, in 1791. State banks were in operation as early as 1784. On 23 December 1913, the Federal Reserve Act established the Federal Reserve Bank (Fed), independent from the federal government, to manage money and credit.[6]

The seven members of the board of governors of the Fed are appointed for fourteen years by the president, with the consent of the Senate. On the contrary, the central banks of the EU nations are mostly under the control of the government and the political party in power. The managers of these banks are appointed by the government and are largely following its policy directives. The main economic problems of the central banks are the financing of budget deficits in a noninflationary way and the stimulation of the economy in cases of recession.

MONETARY AND FINANCIAL POLICIES

Of the three NAFTA countries, Canada had a relatively high growth of money supply, whereas Mexico had a big increase in money supply in 1990–1993 but normal growth for the other years, as Figures 7.1 and 7.2 show. Mexico had a similar instability in the velocity of money, and Canada had a declining velocity up to 1985 and a constant velocity of money thereafter.

As Figure 7.3 shows, the United States experienced a significant increase in the money supply after 1980, which is related to the increase in the nominal GDP, that is, the real GDP plus inflation. Velocity of money, the speed by which the average dollar changes hands in a year, was declining or relatively constant around 6 in the period of 1980–1995. However, there was a gradual increase in velocity during the 1960s and the 1970s.

The U.S. velocity of money, that is, the ratio of GDP over money supply, increased gradually from 3.5 in 1960 to 6.8 in 1981 (by 94%) but remained

Figure 7.1
Money Supply (M) and Velocity of Money (V = GDP/M) for Canada

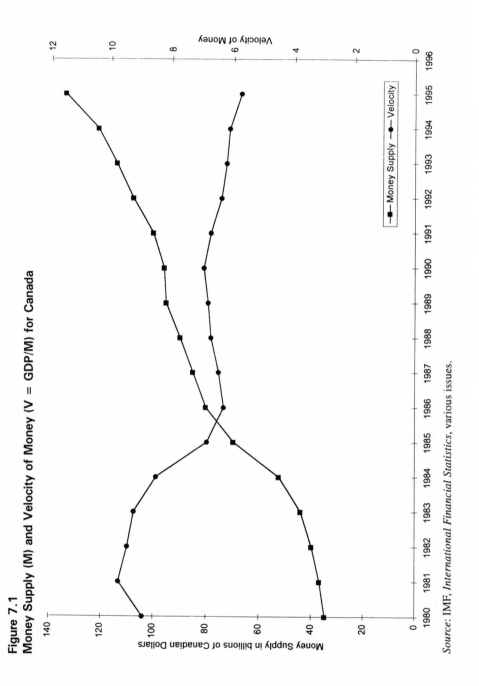

Source: IMF, *International Financial Statistics*, various issues.

Figure 7.2
Money Supply (M) and Velocity of Money (V = GDP/M) for Mexico

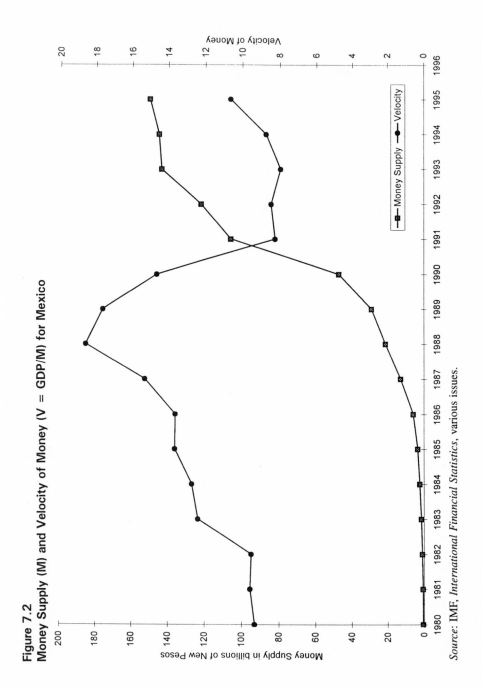

Source: IMF, *International Financial Statistics*, various issues.

Figure 7.3
Money Supply (M) and Velocity of Money (V = GDP/M) for the United States

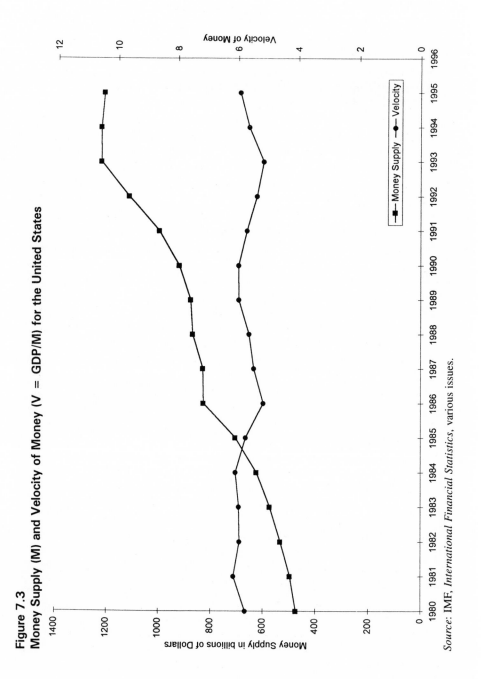

Source: IMF, International Financial Statistics, various issues.

155

relatively constant thereafter. This supports the argument that the velocity of money is not constant over time as the monetarists argue. From that standpoint, inflation, particularly in the 1970s, was largely due to the increase in velocity of money, which is mainly the result of fast spending promoted by advertisement and the U.S. advanced monetary system.

What happened to the relationship of the U.S. money supply and the velocity of money in the 1960s and 1970s can be observed in other EU countries as well. In Britain, the velocity of money increased from 3.9 in 1960 to 7.4 in 1980 but declined thereafter. Likewise, money supply increased slowly from 1970 to 1985 and rapidly thereafter. However, velocity of money remained relatively constant for France, Italy, Spain, and to some extent Hellas for the last three decades and declined for Germany and Italy, as Figures 7.4 to 7.9 show. This means that all these countries financed their nominal GDP through increases in money supply.

On 27 June 1989 in Madrid, the then twelve EU nations accepted the first stage of the monetary union plan, which would end exchange controls and other restrictions in banking and insurance services. The first stage, which started on 1 July 1990, would be followed by two more stages, which would involve the acceptance of a common currency and the establishment of the Central European Bank. Prime Minister Margaret Thatcher of Britain, at that time, and the Tory Party, under pressure of a possible election defeat and not to be left out of the trend toward a European integration, accepted the first phase of the plan but still presented objections regarding the other two phases.

Intergovernment conferences would deal with the other two phases of the EU monetary union. Also, they would consider modifications of the initial charter of the EU (the Treaty of Rome of 1957) toward full economic union. In the process, Britain, Italy, and Sweden are expected to join the European Monetary System while other EU nations eliminated foreign exchange controls and restrictions on capital movements after 1990.

The EU controls about 20 percent of world trade, the United States 15 percent, and Japan around 10 percent. Although Japan controls around 47 percent and the United States 32 percent of the financial capital of the world, a significant expansion of related EU companies is expected to increase European financial controls on an international level.

The U.S. addiction to domestic (public and private) debt, as well as to external debt, affects the economic power of the country and increases its financial dependence upon the EU and other countries. Internal U.S. government debt increased from $1 trillion in 1980 to $5.2 trillion currently, while the U.S. net international investment position changed from a positive balance of $106 billion in 1980 to a foreign debt of more than $1 trillion now. At the same time, NAFTA and nonfinancial companies, particularly in the United States, rely more and more on borrowed money, including Eurodollars and sometimes junk bonds, while their equity to debt ratio is under pressure. Presently, U.S. banks and corporations are at a disadvantage compared to the

Figure 7.4
Money Supply (M) and Velocity of Money (V = GDP/M) for France

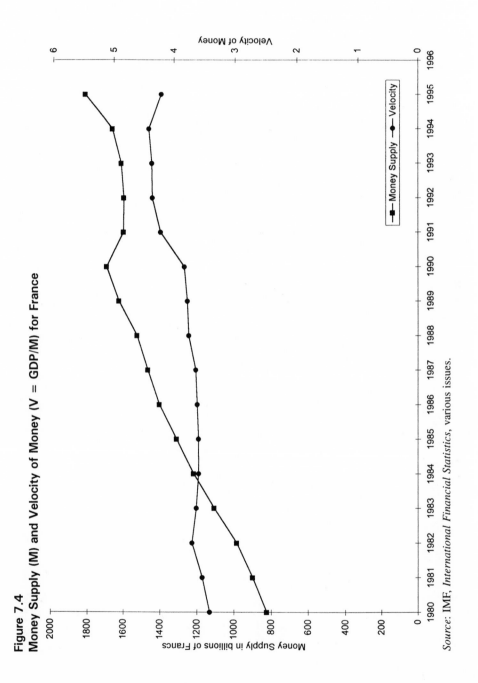

Source: IMF, International Financial Statistics, various issues.

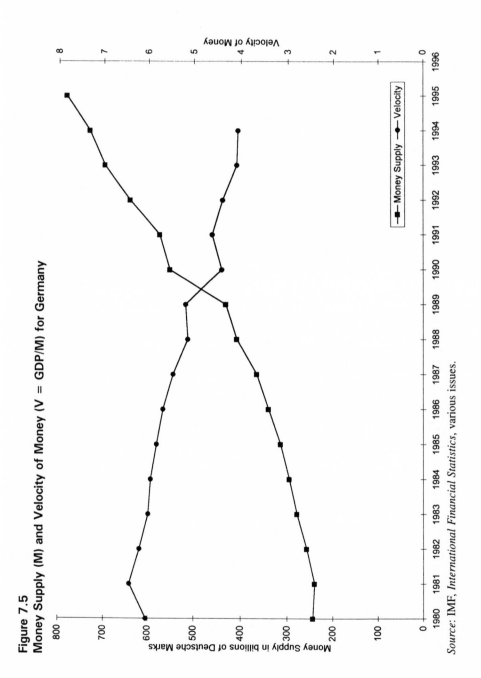

Figure 7.5
Money Supply (M) and Velocity of Money (V = GDP/M) for Germany

Source: IMF, *International Financial Statistics,* various issues.

158

Figure 7.6
Money Supply (M) and Velocity of Money (V = GDP/M) for Greece

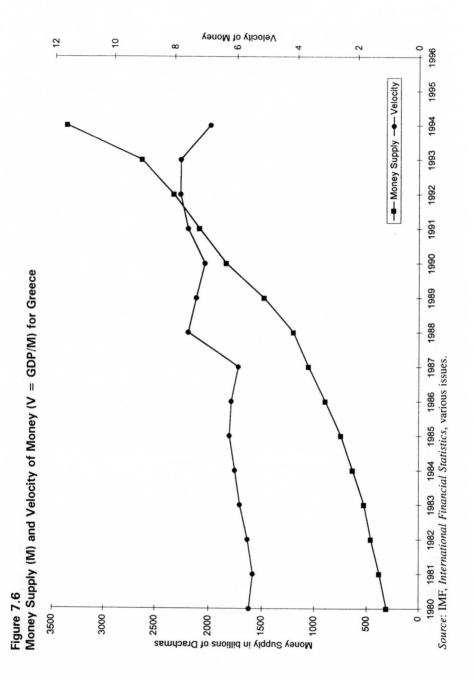

Source: IMF, *International Financial Statistics*, various issues.

Figure 7.7
Money Supply (M) and Velocity of Money (V = GDP/M) for Italy

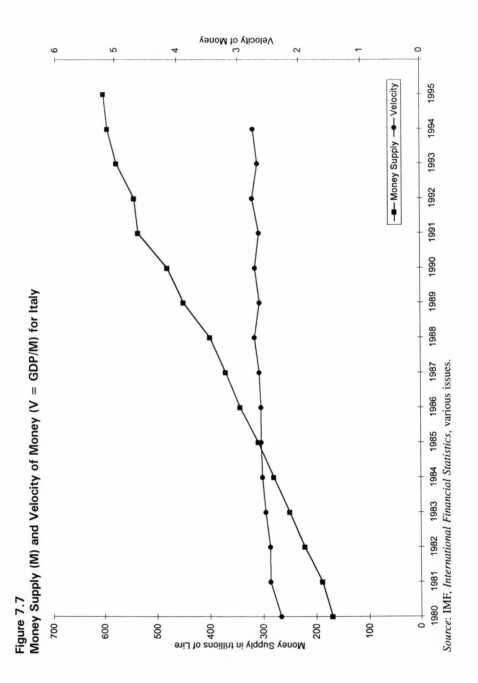

Source: IMF, *International Financial Statistics*, various issues.

Figure 7.8
Money Supply (M) and Velocity of Money (V = GDP/M) for Spain

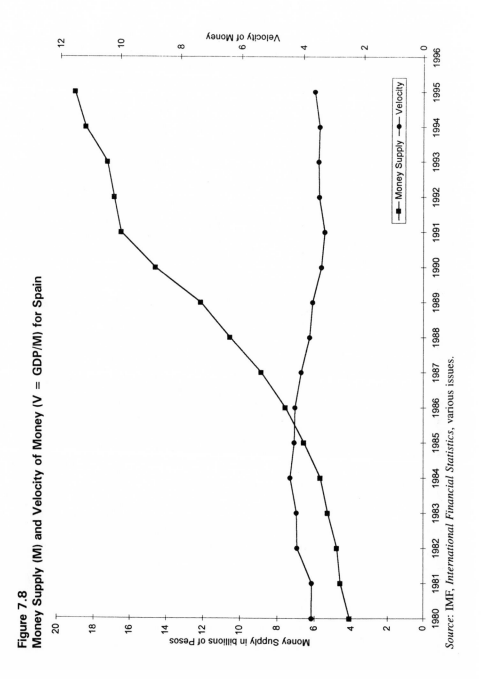

Source: IMF, *International Financial Statistics*, various issues.

161

Figure 7.9
Money Supply (M) and Velocity of Money (V = GDP/M) for the United Kingdom

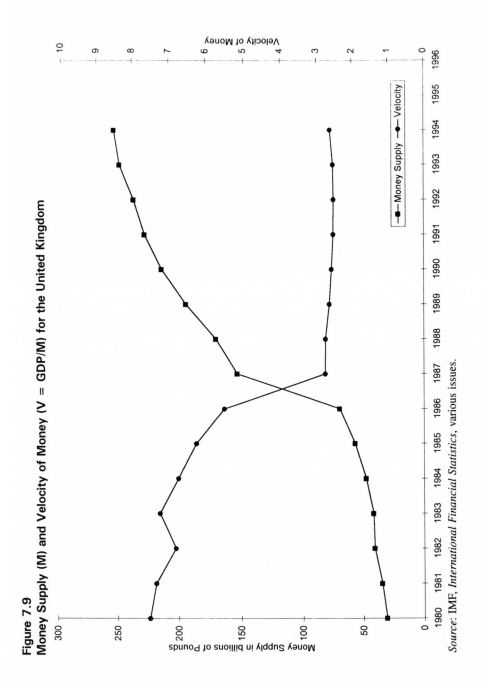

Source: IMF, *International Financial Statistics,* various issues.

European and Japanese banks and corporations, mainly because of the previous depreciation of the dollar. For the EU and other foreign corporations, American assets are cheaper in terms of their currencies than are European assets in terms of dollars. In connection to that, the Eurocurrency market plays a significant role in acquisitions and transfer of assets.

In addition to the serious debt exposure with developing countries, major American banks from time to time face another important exposure with leveraged buyouts (LBOs). So far, similar LBO exposures with EU banks are limited because of related controls by central banks and governments in Europe. However, as such transactions are expanding rapidly in the old continent, LBO exposure of EU banks may appear.

An additional reason for the continuation of the large U.S. trade deficits and the sizable depreciation of the dollar is the lack of vigorous expansionary policies in countries with large trade surpluses, such as Germany and Japan. If fiscal stimulative measures are not undertaken, easy monetary policy may be implemented through short-term increases in money supply and reductions in interest rates. It is estimated that a reduction of interest rates by 1 percent increases real GDP by 0.5 to 1.5 percent in Europe and Japan and by approximately 0.5 to 1 percent in the United States, after some two to three years. However, it must be recognized that monetary easing should be temporary because extended monetary growth, *ceteris paribus*, may lead to a rise in inflation.

High interest rates in one country attract capital inflow from other countries and affect exchange rate fluctuations. Typically, interest rates are raised to keep inflation checked. Recently, Germany raised the discount rate which is still lower than that of the United States. This is the rate commercial banks pay for borrowing from central banks. Also, the short-term (Lombard) rate was raised. The main reason for these raises in interest rates is to keep inflation at the present rate (2–3%) although it is still lower than in other countries. Other EU countries such as Denmark and The Netherlands joined Germany in raising interest rates and Britain and France are expected to follow.

As a result of interest rate increases, the value of the dollar is expected to decline while that of the German mark and other related EU currencies are expected to increase. Although a similar increase in interest rates by the Bundesbank was criticized for contributing to the crash of the stock market in October 1987, the new increase is not related to the same variables of that time, the main one being over-inflated prices of stocks, a current phenomenon in the U.S. stock market.

The drastic reforms in Eastern Europe and the economic union of West and East Germany attract capital investment and financial aid that put strains on the EU and the U.S. credit markets. Competition for funds raises interest rates in Europe and the United States and reduces bond prices. For example, interest rates on ten-year German bonds rose above U.S. rates in the recent past but they tend to be equal now.

Countries with trade deficits such as Britain, France, Greece, Portugal, and the United States would face more serious problems in financing their deficits and external debts. Funds previously headed for these and other countries in financial need would shift to east bloc nations, particularly Hungary, the Czech Republic, and Poland. The drain of capital from the West would lead to fears of inflation, higher interest rates, and lower economic growth across Western Europe and the United States. It is estimated that the cost of rehabilitation and development of east bloc nations would be $300 to $500 billion over the next few years.

Inflationary Pressures

Comparatively speaking, inflation in the EU on the average was higher than in the United States and Canada during the last two decades but was far higher in Mexico, as Table 7.1 shows. From the EU member-nations, Greece and Portugal had high rates of inflation, followed by Spain, Italy, Sweden, and Britain. The Netherlands, Ireland, Germany, Belgium, Denmark, and France had low rates of inflation in recent years and the other EU members were somewhere in-between. In the two decades before 1986, the United States and the EU countries had relatively high rates of inflation, but due to disciplinary economic policies on both sides of the Atlantic, those rates were reduced significantly. Presently, inflation (the Consumer Price Index) has been reduced again for all countries of NAFTA and more so for the EU member countries as they try to achieve the Maastricht goal of less than 3 percent of the GDP.

A coordinated monetary policy and eventually a single currency with a central bank in the EU, along with a common economic policy, would reduce inflation differentials in the EU countries and help stabilize their economies. Although this would involve a transfer of national sovereignty, as the British officials argue, it would stop substantial differences in economic policies by individual EU member-nations and reduce frictions on exchange rates among European currencies as well as between them and the U.S. dollar.

In the market economies of the EU and the NAFTA countries, increase in prices is primarily the result of excess demand over supply (demand-pull inflation) or increases in wages or other factor prices at rates higher than the rates of productivity (cost-push inflation). An increase in spending, stimulated by budget deficits, may be considered as an important reason for demand-pull inflation in these countries. On the other hand, because of the strong labor unions in Greece, Portugal, Spain, and to a lesser extent, Italy, Britain, France, and Germany, increases in wages and labor benefits result in cost-push inflation. In the United States, though, where ESOPs include more than ten million workers (approaching the numbers in labor unions), sharing in corporate decision making reduces the pressure for increases in wages higher than productivity rates. A similar expansion of employee sharing in decision

Table 7.1
Inflation in the NAFTA and EU Countries (Average Annual, Percentage, GDP Deflator)

Country	1973-84	1984-94	1995	1996
NAFTA				
Canada	9.2	3.1	2.2	2.7
Mexico	31.5	40.0	35.0	34.4
USA	7.4	3.3	2.8	2.9
EU				
Austria	5.3	3.2	2.3	2.2
Belgium	6.4	3.2	1.5	2.1
Britain	13.8	5.4	3.4	2.4
Denmark	9.4	2.9	2.1	2.4
Finland	10.7	4.2	1.0	0.6
France	10.7	2.9	1.8	2.0
Germany	4.1	3.0	1.8	1.5
Greece	17.3	15.5	9.3	8.5
Ireland	14.4	2.0	2.5	1.7
Italy	17.2	6.2	5.2	4.0
Luxembourg	n.a.	n.a.	1.9	1.8
Netherlands	5.9	1.6	1.9	2.3
Portugal	20.5	12.0	4.1	3.5
Spain	16.4	6.5	4.7	3.6
Sweden	10.2	5.8	2.5	2.8

Sources: World Bank, *World Development Report*, various issues;
    IMF, *International Financial Statistics*, various issues; *SELIDES*,
    Athens, Winter 1996–1997, 33.

making and co-management of labor and capital (mainly in Germany) is partially responsible for anti-inflationary trends in the EU. Another reason for less pressures of wage increases, especially in the United States, is the dwindling power of labor unions, which lately behave like tamed dogs. Also, cheap labor in Mexico is suppressing wages in the other NAFTA countries, notably the United States.

Although both fiscal and monetary policies are used to curb inflation by the governments considered, more emphasis is placed on monetarism and supply-side economics. Sometimes, though, reduction in government expenditures or tax increases are used to reduce inflation. This is particularly so in countries with large budget deficits such as the United States and most of the EU countries. The idea is to reduce spending and aggregate demand, thereby suppressing inflation.

Tight monetary policy by the central banks of the EU and NAFTA countries to fight inflation usually pushes yields of short-term debt securities above those of long-term bonds and produces a slowdown in the economy. Such a policy, which was implemented in the early 1980s when rates of inflation were high, pushed real interest rates up high and produced a severe recession in the United States, the EU, and other Western economies.

The NAFTA and the EU monetary authorities have to seriously consider these developments in determining money supply for financing real GDP and for reducing inflation. When the velocity of money (V) and the money supply (M_1) grow over and above the real production (Q), prices (P) grow accordingly. This is because, according to the classical equation of exchange, the percentage change in money supply $(\Delta M_1/M_1)$ plus the percentage change in velocity $(\Delta V/V)$ is equal to the percentage change in the price index $(\Delta P/P)$ plus the percentage change in real GDP, or the change in the quantity of production $(\Delta Q/Q)$, that is, $\Delta M_1/M_1 + \Delta V/V = \Delta P/P + \Delta Q/Q$. For example, if money grows by 8 percent, velocity by 2 percent, and real production by 4 percent, then inflation is 6 percent $(0.08 + 0.02 = \Delta P/P + 0.04$ and $\Delta P/P = 0.10 - 0.04 = 0.06)$.

Unlike some EU countries with high inflation, notably Greece and Portugal, which finance public sector deficits in an inflationary manner, the United States and other countries borrow money from the general public to finance budget deficits. It does not increase the money supply for that purpose. From that point of view, there seems to be a close relationship between budget deficits, changes in money supply, and the rates of inflation in countries that finance budget deficits by printing additional money. In such cases, public sector deficits, including those of public enterprises, should be responsible for inflation.

Although financial markets are efficient in transforming savings into investment, lately savings have been channeled into financing acquisitions and takeovers, and not much in financing investment in new plants and equipment. Moreover, the governments and the central banks of the industrial countries can cause a new surge of inflation by bailing out savings banks or other enterprises. Such bailing out of troubled banks, with uncovered large debts, occurred in the United States.

To deal with inflation and recession, central banks or monetary authorities on both sides of the Atlantic, explicitly or implicitly, use the following version of the quantity equation of exchange to forecast inflation:

$$P^* = (M_2 \times V^*)/Q^*$$

In this equation, M_2 stands for the money supply that includes not only the cash in the economy and deposits in checking, but also travelers checks, savings accounts, and deposits in money market and mutual funds. V^* stands for the long-run velocity of M_2; that is, the speed with which money changes hands in the economy. Q^* is the potential value of production or real GDP. Finally, P^* stands for expected future prices.

Since velocity is considered constant, according to monetarists, and Q* is regarded as a predictable figure, the eventual price level will depend on the manipulation of the money supply by the central bank. If P* is compared with P (the current price level), then inflationary trends can be predicted. If P* is higher than P, then future inflation will exceed current inflation and vice versa. For example, P* = ($2,200 billion × 3)/$6,000 billion = 6,600/6,000 = 1.1 That is, if M_2 (money supply) is $2,200 billion, V* (velocity) is equal to 3, and Q* (predicted real GDP) is $6,000 billion, then P* (expected inflation) will be 10 percent. Although additional measures of fiscal and income policies are also important, monetary measures based upon the above equation play a vital role in dealing with inflation or deflation, particularly in the United States and Britain, and to a lesser extent, France, Germany, and other EU countries. However, our empirical findings do not always support constancy in money velocity over time, making predictions about inflation unreliable (see Figures 7.1 to 7.9).

As the dollar becomes stronger, the EU monetary authorities are under pressure to raise interest rates to avoid an increase in inflation. The question is: What are the causes that determine the value of the dollar and how it affects trade balances? It seems that psychological reasons affect the ups and downs in the short run, while interest rates, inflation, savings rates, budget and trade deficits, and economic growth affect the value of the dollar primarily in the medium term. However, in the long term, the purchasing power of currencies plays an important role in the determination of their relative values. It may be argued, though, that all these factors, one way or another, affect the dollar up or down regardless of the longevity of time.

In the process of monetary adjustment and policy harmonization, some flexibility should be allowed for the EU member-nations to adjust their fiscal and monetary policies to new conditions of monetary integration. Individual governments should be permitted, within specified limits, to finance budget deficits through domestic credit creation, that is, through their central banks. Nevertheless, budget deficits should be financed primarily by selling securities (bonds or bills) to an EU-wide market. Thus, each member-nation can achieve monetary expansion by selling government securities to other member-nations with available capital, thereby curbing inflationary pressures and contributing to regional economic stabilization and growth. Such securities can also be sold in local currency and guaranteed by Euros, as happened recently in some cases. However, the EU should develop a mechanism for effecting transfers of funds among its different regions, supplemented by related subsidies.

Currently, problems of monetary stability are appearing regarding the inconvertibility of the currencies of the Eastern European countries. For example, questions are raised as to the exchange rates of the currencies of Eastern European nations in terms of German marks, U.S. dollars, or other hard currencies and their effects on interest rates, inflation, and economic growth.

COUNTER-CYCLICAL POLICY

Monetarism and classical economics alone may not solve the problems of inflation or recession in the NAFTA and EU countries. Fiscal policy and Keynesian demand-side measures and, at times, wage and price controls may also be needed to limit severe recessions or fight inflations and propel these economies toward real growth. Monetary policy relies heavily on velocity, the movements of which are difficult to predict, as explained earlier, as well as on interest rates, which may easily plunge and lead the economy to severe recessions. Classical economists assume a perfectly competitive economy, with no long-term contracts, no unions or other restrictions, in which prices and wages dance to the market drumbeats of supply and demand toward full employment. From a Keynesian perspective, though, there are doubts that the economy operates in an auction-like or competitive fashion. On the contrary, there exist institutional features or bottlenecks that prevent the market from regulating itself smoothly and reliably.

When people are trying to save a lot but investors only want to invest a little, a downturn in the economy and an increase in unemployment is expected. In such cases, the government can fill the gap by stepping up spending by increasing the budget deficit. However, easy money may be preferable because it reduces interest rates and stimulates investment, while large budget deficits will increase interest rates and discourage new investment. An easy-money policy may be implemented through buying government securities by the central banks of the EU and the NAFTA countries in an open market. This provides the banks with more money available for loans, reduces interest rates, and stimulates investment. The opposite is true when securities are sold to the general public to cool off high demand in the economy and reduce inflation. Likewise, when the central bank increases interest rates, demand for loans declines, and inflation is reduced, but unemployment rises. Empirically, such economic changes occurred in the U.S. economy during the period of 1980–1982 when interest rates increased to 21 percent and a severe recession followed, increasing the unemployment role from 7 to 12 percent, and reducing inflation from 13.5 to around 5 percent.

The U.S. tax cuts and other stimulative measures introduced before 1987 led to the rapid growth of the stock market at rates far higher than the growth of the economy. This illusory growth of the stock market provoked the market plunge on 19 October 1987. The Dow Jones Industrial Average fell 508 points, losing 23 percent of its value in one day, compared to 12.6 percent loss in the crash of 29 October 1929. Financial deregulation, the domination of stock trading by mutual funds and pension funds, program trading, and the growing corporate buyouts have encouraged quick return and discouraged long-term productive investment. Thus, the over-optimistic euphoria resulted in the crash of the stock market and the subsequent pessimistic expectations of a recession or even depression. Similar conditions may occur again in the

United States and in other NAFTA and EU countries unless corrective counter-cyclical measures are taken by fiscal and monetary policymakers.

Also, aggregate demand is affected by the functions of liquidity preference. According to the Keynesian prescription, if people prefer less liquidity, they will release and use idle cash balances, and aggregate demand will increase. This is another form of stimulation of the economy. If people prefer more liquidity, they will reduce spending, and so aggregate demand will decline.

The relationship between interest rates and national output or product when planned spending equals income when aggregate supply equals aggregate demand, can be seen with the IS curve in Figure 7.10, which explains the goods market equilibrium schedule. The IS curve shows the equilibrium points of investment (I) at different rates of interest, and saving (S) at different levels of income. Thus, the lower the interest rate, the more the investment and the higher the income. The higher the income, the more the saving for investment financing. The steepness of the negatively sloped IS curve depends on how sensitive investment spending is to changes in the interest rate or return to investment.

The money market equilibrium, or the upsloping LM schedule (liquidity preference function) is derived by the demand for money (L) curve at different levels of the interest rate, the money available at various levels of income and a given money supply fixed by the monetary authorities. With the level of income rising, the need for transactions money rises and the amount left over (supply of money, M) declines.

At the equilibrium level of income, saving (S) is equal to investment (I) while at the money market equilibrium, supply of money (M) and demand for money or loans (L) are equal. The investment-saving (IS) curve in Figure 7.10 shows the level of national income when intended (*ex ante*) saving and intended investment are adjusted to be equal. The lower the interest rate, the less people want to save and the more corporations and entrepreneurs want to borrow and invest. The demand for loans and supply of money (LM) curve shows the equilibria of the money market at different interest rates and income levels. Different interest rates are associated with different income levels.

At equilibrium point b, the shift in the IS curve to a new position IS', mainly because of government spending, leads to a higher interest rate and higher income, compared to equilibrium at point *a*. Depending on the labor-intensive method of production introduced, this leads to more employment and, *ceteris paribus*, to less unemployment but higher inflation. This is shown in the Okun's law curve, which relates income or production and unemployment, and the Phillips curve, which relates unemployment with inflation.

The points where the IS and LM curves meet indicate the interest rates and the levels of income at which both the savings–investment market and the money market are at equilibrium. Expansionary fiscal policies, through an increase in public expenditures or a decrease in taxes by the governments of NAFTA or the EU nations would shift the IS curve outward, increasing in-

Figure 7.10
The Relationship of Interest, Income, Unemployment, and Inflation

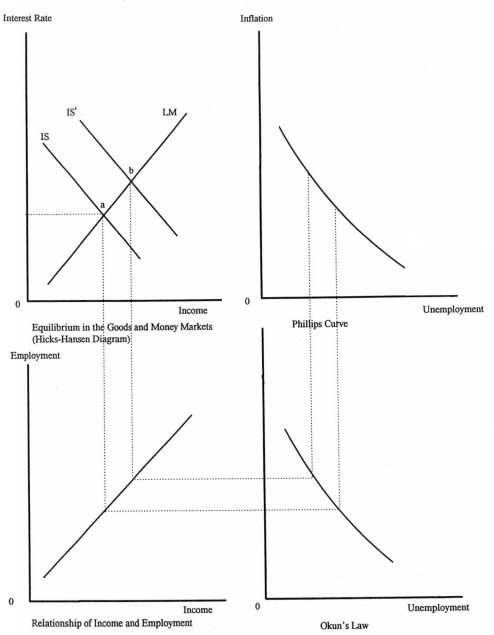

Interest Rate

IS'

IS

LM

b

a

0

Income

Equilibrium in the Goods and Money Markets
(Hicks-Hansen Diagram)

Inflation

0

Unemployment

Phillips Curve

Employment

0

Income

Relationship of Income and Employment

0

Unemployment

Okun's Law

come but also raising interest rates. However, an expansionary monetary policy would shift the LM curve outward but then interest rates would be lower and national income higher. Therefore, all things being equal, a monetary easing would keep interest rates down, stimulate investment, and increase income and employment toward the full employment level of the economy.

Banking Activities

Strong ongoing competition between the EU and NAFTA is expected to continue, particularly after the welding together of the fifteen European national economies into a single currency and a closer cooperation with the east bloc countries. The 1986 Single European Act provides for the free movement, not only of goods and persons, but also of services and capital. Although financial and banking services have not benefited to the same extent as manufactured goods, they are expected to play a major role in the improvement of other sectors of the EU economy. Already direct and portfolio investment have been liberalized and similar measures were adopted for deposits and credits. The EU financial sector accounts for about 7 percent of the GDP and represents more than three million jobs, or 3.5 percent of total EU employment. Projected harmonization of national laws concerning banks, insurance policies, and stock exchanges, as well as expansion in Eastern Europe, will greatly improve the services sector.

In spite of the fact that a number of banks and financial institutions operate on both sides of the Atlantic, there remain important obstacles in serving foreign markets, primarily because of different national regulations of banking and financial operations. The next frontier for trade liberalization is international services in general and financial services in particular. This is important because of the growth of trade between the EU and NAFTA as well as investment and other transactions that require the development of banking and financial services to facilitate such transactions. As the services sector is rapidly growing in domestic economies, likewise financial and other services are expected to grow rapidly in a global scale so that capital movements, information and security services, as well as other activities can move quickly between continents. Already, many securities are listed on the stock exchanges of both the EU and NAFTA, mostly from the United States.

The spirit of harmonization of financial regulations includes the reciprocity provision concerning banking services, portfolio management, and stock transactions. The banking directives allow banks which pass guidelines to receive a single banking license and enable them to operate throughout the whole EU. However, foreign banks should receive these rights on the basis of reciprocity only if EU banks have equal access to other partner countries' markets. This reciprocity principle includes life insurance and investment services, particularly portfolio management activities. On these grounds, the Shareholder Disclosure Directive stipulates that an owner who sells or buys at least

10 percent of a company's total stock must notify that company and the company, in turn, must inform the public through the responsible authorities.

With a unified European monetary system linking domestic money markets, the stronger EU countries would largely influence monetary conditions in other member countries. The Eurodollar market played a similar role in affecting, directly or indirectly, national monetary policies in Europe and linking such policies with those of the United States and Canada. Thus, a policy to tighten monetary conditions in a country would lead to an increase in borrowing by commercial banks or individuals from other countries. This money would then be converted into local currency and affect money supply and credit policy, thereby nullifying, partially or totally, the restrictive policy of the country in question. However, flexible exchange rates are expected to correct the situation through adjustment in par values. Also, tax and expenditure policies can be used to supplement monetary policies toward domestic economic stability. Moreover, coordination of national policies and cooperation among central banks can prevent large-scale movements of capital in the short run, in response to changes in monetary policies and interest rate differences.

The introduction of a European monetary system could eliminate large fluctuations in exchange rates and enhance convertibility in national currencies. Even common rates of money growth could be established. If member-nations attempt a divergent monetary policy, this will result in payment imbalances that will force them back to monetary harmony. Again, coordination of national economic policies is required to avoid disturbances from budgetary deficits and other misguided financial policies. A limited pooling of reserves with some form of joint management would provide the first step of an EU monetary union and facilitate credit extension among members and between the EU and NAFTA countries. The First EU Banking Directive of 1977 provided for the coordination of national laws and regulations, and the Second Banking Directive of 1988 introduced a single banking license valid across the EU.

With amendments to the Second Banking Directive of the European Commission, the European Parliament introduced controls regarding banking permits for new banks and takeover of EU banks by other banks outside the union. The controls refer to the suitability of the shareholders who hold more than 5 percent of the assets of the banks. Such supervisory controls cover branches of nonunion banks as well. However, some exemptions from the regulations of this directive were extended for Greece and Portugal.

In the banking sector, the EU permits the establishment of banks by other countries under the principle of reciprocity. Also, EU banks can participate in other nonfinancial companies with up to 25 percent of their own capital.

To make the banking sector more competitive with other European and international banks, Spain approved the merging of Banco Espanol de Credito and Banco Central to create the biggest commercial bank in Spain and the twentieth largest in the world in capital and reserves. The combined profits of the two banks are more than 60 billion pesetas (120 pesetas to the U.S. dollar) per year. Their total assets are more than 7 trillion pesetas, with deposits of about 5.5 trillion, and equity at 530 billion pesetas.

Under pressures for growing world trade, many countries such as Germany, France, Britain, The Netherlands, and other industrialized countries reduced, or are in the process of eliminating, obstacles to foreign banking activities. However, requirements of national or reciprocal treatment still remain in force for most of the countries. The NAFTA governments prefer national treatment for their subsidiaries in other countries, though the common EU rules on banking operations would be easier and less costly than adjustment to each of the different EU nations. Then, serving the United States and other multinational companies on their efforts to increase trade and investment in continental Europe would be more efficient and less expensive.

Financing growing stock market operations in the EU is another field that needs attention, especially in Britain, The Netherlands, and France. The removal by France of the last foreign exchange controls on businesses and its successful policy of disinflation would make the Eurofrank market an important source of credit and investment. Moreover, individuals are permitted to have foreign currency accounts or to hold a foreign account in France. With a high withholding tax on investment income, France is expected to adjust to the harmonizing EU investment rules and remove related controls and regulations.

To raise funds quickly, aggressive corporate raiders prefer syndicated loans mainly in the Eurocurrency market. Lenders also prefer to give acquisition-related loans because the average spread of Eurocurrency loans is about 0.5 percent above LIBOR, the rate at which British banks lend to each other. Moreover, loans for acquisitions and leveraged buyouts in NAFTA can bring up to 3 percent more than those in Europe. Such syndicated loans, associated mainly with mergers, are expected to be higher in the future, considering the number of loans and the selling of them enacted by such big leveraged buyouts and buy-ins in the NAFTA and EU countries.

In relation to that, the banks that lent money to Kohlberg Kravis Roberts to buy RJR Nabisco for $25 billion sold sizable loans mainly to European banks. Also, European firms use the syndicated loan market to buy other European or American companies. For example, Grand Metropolitan, a British hotel group, borrowed some $6 billion to acquire Pillsbury, a food and restaurant company. Syndicated loans have become common, and new issues of Eurobonds are growing. American and European investors are lining up to use such syndicated loans, although more and more European companies are moving toward leveraged buy-outs and buy-in deals as the EU gradually becomes integrated into a single market. However, extensive use of junk bonds for leveraged buyouts may be risky, as happened with the bankruptcy of Drexel Burnham Lambert Inc., a large U.S. investment firm that laid off 5,400 employees in the United States and Europe.

In order to discourage takeover on both sides of the Atlantic, it may be suggested that short-term capital taxes be raised. But for long-term investment, indexation of capital gains is needed so that the effects of inflation can be eliminated. Such measures would discourage leveraged buyouts and mega-mergers for short-run profits and stop the unhealthy and superficial growth of the markets involved.

To encourage more banking business in the United States and to attract capital inflow, the Federal Reserve approved in 1982 the creation of international banking facilities (IBFs) which accept foreign deposits. Because they were not subject to domestic regulations and taxes, they became successful in attracting large amounts of foreign deposits. They are treated like foreign branches of U.S. banks and are not subject to reserve requirements and other restrictions. They are mostly exempted from state and local taxes as well.

There are more than 600 offices of foreign (mainly European) banks in the United States with over 20 percent of total U.S. banking activities. They may operate as agency offices of foreign banks that are not subject to U.S. regulations or as branches of foreign banks bearing their names and usually enjoying full-service offices. Or, they may operate as subsidiary U.S. banks which are subject to U.S. regulations but are owned by foreign banks. Foreign banks can form IBFs and Edge Act corporations, which are special subsidiaries created by the Edge Act of 1919, engaged mainly in international banking and exempted from certain regulations such as those not permitting the opening of branches across state lines.

Liberalization of banking and financial services is also required to speed up monetary unification of the EU member-nations. In the process, painstaking negotiations may be needed to reconcile differences and to avoid embarrassing interest groups that may feel threatened. It is difficult though to completely eliminate banking and financial regulations on a national level and achieve a complete free banking on the EU, NAFTA, or international level. Restrictions exist even on interstate levels as in the United States, for example, and more so on an international level. Thus, in Britain, banks based outside the EU must include a warning in their advertisements about the absence of deposit insurance and transfer risks. Also, The Netherlands requires certain conditions for non-EU banks to use the word "bank" in their titles. In many cases permission for establishment is required, and certain activities, such as deposits and loans, managing securities issues, or underwriting bond issues, are prohibited.

As the U.S. external trade deficits shrink, imbalances within the EU continue. While trade deficits in Britain, Hellas, and other EU members worsen, Germany's surplus is growing. If such imbalances continue, the planned monetary union of the EU may be in jeopardy. To reduce or eliminate imbalances, surplus countries like Germany should stimulate their economies and import more from their deficit partners. However, differences in inflation and competitiveness, and therefore in real exchange rates, seem to be the main reasons for trade imbalances. Nevertheless, it is expected that adjustment in the related currencies, together with flexible monetary and fiscal policies, would reinforce monetary stability in the European Monetary System and help achieve monetary integration, along with trade and eventual political integration among the European nations. It seems, though, that barriers in financial and banking services have not generated as much concern as trade transactions.

EURODOLLAR TRANSACTIONS

Although the Eurodollar market began its expansion in the late 1950s, even before World War II, some form of foreign currency existed in London which was the international financial center at the time. In 1957, the Moscow Norodny Bank of the former Soviet Union deposited dollars in its branch in London and in another bank in Paris (the Banque Commerciale pour l'Europe du Nord) whose telex was "Eurobank." The main reason for the removal of the Soviet balances from New York to a British-chartered Russian bank and to Paris was the fear of a possible freeze or confiscation of Soviet funds by American authorities during the Cold War. The example of the Soviet Union was followed by other Eastern European countries and later by American and other banks and corporations. These Eurobank dollars, or continental dollars, were and still are called Eurodollars.

The first Eurodollar business involved an $800 million loan on 28 February 1957 by the Moscow Norodny Bank in London and was repaid in dollars outside the U.S. banking system without any interference. The Sterling Crisis of 1957 encouraged the British banks to turn to such dollars for the financing of foreign trade. Other Western European banks continued the practice of accepting dollar deposits and lending them out to other European banks and corporations, thereby financing world trade in dollars outside the United States. The European banks are able to take deposits and lend out dollars with more attractive interest rates compared to their American counterparts because they are not under restrictions and regulations, such as reserve requirements or exchange controls.

The development of the Eurodollar market, particularly after 1963, was the result of the efforts of banks to escape national controls whenever their cost outweighed benefits. In order to regulate the participation of U.S. banks in this market, the Kennedy administration tried to enforce the Interest Equalization Tax, taxing the differences in interest, but the result was the opposite with a large outflow of dollars from the United States to Western Europe. Similar outflows of dollars occurred in the 1960s as a result of exchange controls introduced by the Voluntary Foreign Credit Restraint Program and the Foreign Direct Investment Regulations. Such controls and regulations required foreign investments to be financed mainly from abroad. As a result, U.S. banks increased their operations in Europe, where they established branches to tap the Eurodollar market. Although these regulations and controls were removed in 1974, exchanges in dollars in Europe continued to thrive. The same thing can be said about Regulation Q of the Fed, requiring that member banks pay the lower interest rate on time deposits fixed by the states where they operate. But Regulation Q did not apply to deposits outside the United States, and investors looking for higher interest rates deposited and redeposited their money in the Eurodollar market.

There are arguments that the Eurodollar market may be responsible for stimulating world inflation. Although the Eurodollar multiplier is not expected to be large, there is some influence on inflation depending on the velocity or the speed of Eurodollar transactions. However, it is difficult to measure such a velocity and the related influence on inflation because, among other reasons, controls and supervisions of the market by central banks are limited or nonexistent. Moreover, domestic monetary policies become to some extent ineffective, especially in the countries whose currencies are involved. Such countries include the United States with dollars (Eurodollars), Germany with marks (Euromarks), France with francs (Eurofrancs) and eventually Euros, and Japan with yens (Euroyens). Thus, if the Fed attempted to absorb dollars by selling bonds domestically, this policy might be undermined by domestic banks through loans from the Eurodollar market, thereby nullifying partially or totally the results of contraction of money and credit. In addition, more and more American corporations and investors become foreign holders of dollars and this means less business and profits for American banks and other companies. To such fears, expressed mainly by some bankers, one can advance the argument that deposits of dollars abroad are to a large extent transfers to the same or another American bank, or even to a non-American bank, that these dollars remain primarily within the American banking system. Overall, in spite of some problems with the central banks, the Eurodollar market is beneficial to the world economy, particularly to the EU, making loans accessible, facilitating transactions among nations, and advancing the international financial markets.

A growing Eurodollar market in a more unified Europe would make EU banks stronger than their American counterparts while their influence on the World Bank and other international institutions would be more significant. However, the establishment of NAFTA banks or their subsidiaries and other industries in the EU would enhance their ability to influence events on the old continent and help avoid serious impediments to economic and defense policies in this part of the world.

The real political power in the world is related to economic, technological, and financial power. Banks and other financial intermediaries, along with advanced telecommunications, play a significant role in the transmission of such power from country to country and from continent to continent.

Foreign exchange markets, where monies are traded, exist to facilitate currency transactions and international payments. The terms "Eurocurrency market" and "Eurobanks" signify international monetary exchanges, deposits, loans, and credit in general, not only in Europe, but also in offshore banking activities in the Bahamas, Hong Kong, and elsewhere. The reserve status of the dollar and the dollar deposits in the EU banks created the sizable Eurodollar market. Because of controls and regulations in domestic banks, Eurobanks or offshore banks are able to offer higher deposit and lower loan interest rates, thereby narrowing the difference (spread) in dollars.

The European countries, and perhaps the entire world, have an interest in preserving the health of the U.S. economy. At the same time, the United States should encourage saving for investment. Its policy of dependence on Eurocurrencies and foreign savings to finance budget and trade deficits and domestic investment is gradually wearing away its economic strength and world influence. Although this policy is not expected to lead to a collapse or a "heart attack" of the U.S. economy in the short run, it may lead to a gradual weakening or a "cancer" in the long run.

There are large amounts of Eurodollars deposited in European and other banks that affect the economies of NAFTA, the EU, and other countries. At present, many multinational corporations deposit their surplus funds into European and other banks instead of U.S. banks. Eurodollar deposits became more attractive because European banks are permitted to pay interest on very short-term deposits, and no reserve requirements and other restrictions exist. This new money supply outside the United States makes the U.S. monetary policy less effective and the dollar an important component of the international monetary system. Therefore, a synthesis of domestic monetary policy and international monetary and trade transactions would improve economic stability at home and abroad.

Banks and trust companies from the United States, Britain, and other countries have moved operations to Bermuda, the Bahamas, and the Caribbean Islands, among other offshore centers. They are now looking to the EU to pick up more business, particularly as closer integration advances. Instead of farming investment management out to managers in Europe or North America, they increasingly offer it to their global investors in these places, where they enjoy more freedom and flexibility regarding taxation and other restrictive measures.

There are more than 1,300 captive insurance companies, offshore banks, or trusts in Bermuda alone, representing about half of the world's captives, which resemble their competitors in Luxembourg and Switzerland.

The U.S. Tax Reform Act of 1986 taxes all investors, wherever they are, and does not allow exceptions for investment in Eurodollars. This reform act and the easing of related regulations by some states made it more attractive for onshore captives. International companies partly owned by a U.S. company can use Eurodollars and enjoy previous benefits. From that point of view, the Europeans are expected to make up for the offshore operations lost because of the new U.S., and eventually NAFTA, regulations.

COMMON CURRENCY IN THE EUROPEAN UNION

During the Middle Ages, feudal rulers frequently tried to have common currency with trading partners. In 1865, the Latin Coin Union was created among Belgium, France, Greece, Italy, and Switzerland but was undermined by policy conflicts and so disbanded in 1927. The Scandinavian Coin Union (Denmark, Norway, and Sweden) of 1872–1924 worked smoothly for a time but eroded with World War I.

The old European dream of creating a single unified currency seems to be gradually becoming a reality. The European Community's founding of the Treaty of Rome in 1957 provided for coordination of economic and monetary policies of the then six member-nations (France, West Germany, Italy, and the three Benelux countries, Belgium, Luxembourg, and The Netherlands). In 1972, the six member-nations linked currencies in *snake* to limit fluctuations, and in 1979, the European Monetary System, which tied exchange rates but permitted slight changes, and the ECU were established by the then nine member-nations (Britain, Denmark, and Ireland became members of the European Community in 1973, Greece in 1981, Spain and Portugal in 1986, and Austria, Finland, and Sweden in 1995).

The ECU, now the Euro, was created by the EU to deal with international trade and finance instead of having to deal with several separate and often volatile national currencies. It is based on a currency-basket that includes the currencies of the EU member-nations, but with different weights, and is adjusted every five years. In terms of dollars, it is worth about $1.30. The German mark carries the most weight (30%), followed by the French franc (19%), the British pound (13%), and the Italian lira (10%). Less weight has been assigned to the currencies of the smaller member-nations, according to the share of every member to the GDP of the EU. It is expected that the Euro would have a higher value after the single EU currency is established.

Articles 108 and 109 of the Rome Treaty of 1957 provide for a special committee that suggests measures of mutual support and possible deviations from certain obligations of the member-nations who have serious problems with the balance of payments.

In 1987, the Single European Act fixed the objective of monetary union for the first time, and in 1989 the Delors Report outlined a three-stage plan for a single currency. In 1991, the heads of the twelve member-nations agreed in Maastricht to create a monetary union in 1997, or at the latest, in 1999.

One of the serious problems of the EMU would be the arrangements of exchange rates to link the non-EMU currencies to the Euro and the related provisions for credit facilities. The external debt-service needs of the EU member-nations would be a major factor in determining the level of national reserves and the exchange rates.

After the 1992 currency turmoil, Britain and Italy left the EMU and the exchange rate mechanism. Then, fluctuation bands were widened. The European Monetary Institute (EMI), as a forerunner of a European Central Bank, was founded in Frankfurt, Germany on 1 January 1994.

The timetable for the transition to the new currency, set by the meeting of the fifteen member-nations of the EU in Madrid on 13 December 1995, determined that during 1996 and 1997 governments should reduce deficits, and in early 1998, the EU will rule which nations qualify to participate in the monetary union. Also, in 1998 a new European Central Bank will be created.

On 1 January 1999, parities of currencies of qualifying countries will be irrevocably fixed, the European Central Bank will take over monetary policy, and governments will issue debt in Euros. In 2002, Euro notes and coins will be issued and begin to circulate, stores will price goods in Euros, and national currencies will be replaced by Euros, which will be the only legal tender.[7]

In order to achieve these goals, most member-nations are required to practice economic belt-tightening because their annual budget deficit must be no more than 3 percent of GDP and the consumer price index (annual inflation) 1.5 percent per year, and currency exchange rates and long-term interest rates must be no more than 2 percent of the average of the three best-performing members. Moreover, total government debt must be no more than 60 percent of GDP. However, for countries like Belgium, Greece, Italy, Portugal, Spain, and Sweden, with higher budget deficits and government debt than is required by the Maastricht Treaty of 1991, there would be pressure for cuts in social programs such as health, education, unemployment benefits, pensions, and other welfare programs which may lead to economic and social disruption.

The unanimous vote of the fifteen EU member-nations in Madrid in December 1995 committed governments to slash spending or raise taxes by the end of 1997 in order to reduce budget deficits and debts and to create a single unified currency for the twenty-first century. This means that generous social programs will be cut for many Europeans in two years (instead of the seven that U.S. Congress considers), and economic and political strains may appear. Furthermore, some countries fear that, with the new currency, they will give up sovereignty over their monetary policy, and that Germany's dominance will be enhanced. Others fear that they will not be able to qualify for membership for years because of their high debt levels.

Regarding the name of the common currency, the Europeans accepted Euro as the least offensive, though the Germans preferred their mark, the French their franc or ECU, and the British the crown or the shilling. Moreover, the Greeks (Hellenes) noted that the name Euro is very close to their word urine. Nevertheless, its root is from the name "Europa" in ancient Greece which, according to Nietzsche, provided the nucleus of European civilization.

SINGLE CURRENCY PROCEDURE

The most important and difficult problem of the EU is the monetary union, that is, the establishment of a single currency and a central European bank. In order to preserve stability, it was agreed by the member-nations of the EU that, in case of fluctuations of member currencies beyond a certain margin (2.25%, with some exceptions), the EU would intervene. Furthermore, a committee of Central Bank presidents and experts was established in June 1988, and the twelve member-nations of the EU at that time reached an agreement to allow free capital movements. Then, the most advanced members agreed to lift foreign exchange restrictions by mid-1989. However, Greece, Ireland, Portugal, and Spain, being at a lower level of development, were permitted to remove restrictions later. This was considered as the largest deregulation program in history.

On 27 June 1989 in Madrid, the EU member-nations accepted the first stage of the monetary union plan to end exchange controls and other restrictions in banking and insurance services. The first stage, starting on 1 July 1990, would be followed by two further stages (1 January 1994 and 1 January 1999, respectively) that would involve the acceptance of a common currency and the establishment of a central European bank. During the second stage of EMU, the member-nations are supposed to work on convergence of their systems regarding price stability, public deficits and debt, exchange rates, and long-term interest rates.

In order to achieve these strict measures which were put forward by the Maastricht Treaty of 1991, severe austerity measures are needed by a number of EU members. Such measures would further increase EU unemployment, which already is more than 10 percent. Only Denmark, Ireland, and Luxembourg currently meet the Maastricht Treaty's criteria on budget deficits and on public debt, though France, Germany, and Austria are close. Italy (with the lira currently floating outside the EMS), Greece, and Belgium have large public debts, and the other members are in between. In addition to Italy, Britain has not been part of the European exchange rate system since the turmoil of 1992, and neither has Sweden. That is why EU governments, notably France and Italy, face increasing pressure to avoid a slowing of their economies and prefer an extension of the timetable for introducing a single currency or the establishment of special, intermediate brief stages to meet the fiscal criteria. Further negotiations on this subject occurred among the heads of state in the Madrid Summit in December 1995, and among the finance ministers in Dublin in September 1996. The European Council would decide by December 1997 which member-nations meet the convergence criteria and confirm the beginning of stage three by 1 January 1999.[8]

It is difficult for many EU members to meet the Maastricht requirements. Even Germany and France have public deficits higher than 3 percent of GDP (3.5% and 6% of GDP, respectively, in 1995). Some other members are in worse positions regarding budget deficits and more so regarding public debts, and the rates of economic growth are relatively low all over Europe. It seems that further belt-tightening by the governments of the EU member-nations is required if these economies are to generate enough savings to reverse these trends. Yet, with high unemployment rates in these economies, enacting spending cuts will be very difficult politically.

Nevertheless, Article 104-C of the Maastricht Treaty states that if there are exceptional circumstances, the public deficit ceiling shall be considered satisfied when an EU member temporarily exceeds the limit and makes substantial progress toward compliance. From that standpoint, a broad interpretation of this Article may accommodate certain deviations.

PROBLEMS REGARDING THE USE
OF COMMON CURRENCY

Many Europeans, particularly the British, disagree with the introduction of a common currency by all EU member-nations. They feel this would be a big step toward a complete subordination of national sovereignty to the bureaucracy of Brussels. At the same time, the European Court could exercise excessive power over monetary and other matters of the member-nations.

Because of the strict convergence criteria of the EMU, many EU citizens, in opinion polls, reject such a union in the short run. There is skepticism in the northern EU countries that a more flexible interpretation of the Maastricht criteria might allow their southern neighbors, particularly Greece, Italy, and Spain, to squeeze into the EMU and then tear it apart if their budget deficits persist. Nevertheless, all the members of the European Banking Federation are in favor of the EMU, and optimism is growing among EU businesses and citizens on the eventual success of a single currency, the Euro. Already, the Bank of England is making preparations toward the EMU, from which it expects growing benefits for itself and other banks and industries, even if Britain stays outside of it.

Almost all the EU members take measures to meet the Maastricht targets and to make their currencies strong enough to be ready to switch to the new single currency. The Italian government introduced, among other measures to cut public debt, a one-year tax on incomes to raise $3.6 billion (5,500 billion lire) to reduce its budget deficit to 3 percent of GDP, in order to join the EMU. As a result, the EU finance ministers allowed the Italian lira to rejoin the currency grid of the group (at 990 lire to the German mark), which had been previously forced out during the crisis of 1992, as was the British pound. However, it is required that any currency of the EU must meet the grid's fluctuation margin of 15 percent for at least two years before it can qualify for the Euro (lately at 2.25%). Out of the fifteen EU currencies, eleven are currently in the grid. The Greek drachma and the Swedish krona have never been part of it.[9]

Regarding the future EU payments-interlinking system, through the Trans-European Automated Real-Time Gross-Settlement Express Transfer (TARGET) system, there is a dispute mainly between Britain, France, and Germany. Britain argues that member-nations outside EMU should have access to TARGET, whereas France and Germany insist that they should be restricted from linking their currencies within the pan-European system. However, the Euro may be used in the countries outside the EU at the wholesale level in the payments system and across markets.[10]

For the reinforcement of the role of London as a leading financial center in the EMU, the London International Financial Futures and Options Exchange and the London Commodities Exchange are now operating as a merged market, known as LIFFE. The idea is to ensure that London will be the world center for Euro derivatives trading, in addition to its importance as trading center in futures and options on financial, agricultural, and other products, as a result of the EMU. The Bank of England, with its history of experience, is expected to continue to play a significant role in these matters under the new financial system in Europe.

In order to accommodate the existence of a single currency alongside non-participating national currencies, a two-speed system, in which France and Germany would participate in the first place, is proposed. The remaining national currencies outside the Euro could float within certain boundaries and the EU could coordinate their variations. The replacement of the current ECU, which is mainly used by the EU for internal accounting and for loans and bonds, by the Euro can be arranged by the Commission or the EMI regarding union as well as nonunion parties.

Countries with large budget deficits and heavy debt, such as Italy and Greece, should take measures to cut expenditures on state payrolls, health care, subsidies, and other government spending so that they would not be left behind the rest of Europe. Italy's goal is to cut its budget deficit from 7 percent of GDP a year to less than 3 percent. Likewise, Greece takes measures to reduce its budget deficit from 8 percent to less than 3 percent. France also plans a budget freeze to keep the government deficit at around $55 billion, or 3 percent of GDP, by spending cuts and increase in taxes on alcohol and cigarettes. In comparison, the budget deficits of the United States are about 2 percent of the GDP.

It was proposed, mainly by Theo Waigel, the German Finance Minister, in the meeting of finance ministers in Dublin in September 1996, that EU countries with fiscal deficits of more than 3 percent of GDP would make noninterest paying deposits which could then turn into fines (0.25% of GDP for each percentage point of deficit over the 3% ceiling). The Dublin meeting endorsed the creation of the European Stability Council for the coordination and supervision of budgetary policy in each member-nation.

To pave the way for the monetary union, the European system of central banks would include the European Central Bank (ECB) and the national central banks. As mentioned previously, the ECB would replace the EMI which was set up in 1994 to prepare the ground for issuing EU bank notes and promote payments across countries' borders. Its main goals would be to maintain price stability, promote open markets and competition, and harmonize monetary instruments and techniques so that uniform policy can be achieved across member-nations.

Instruments to be used for these goals include reserve requirements (RR), that is, percentages of deposits which banks are required to hold with the central bank to back their deposit liabilities, and the related money multiplier (1/RR), as well as the open market operations (buying and selling government securities to achieve stability and economic growth).

Financial institutions which accept deposits and extend credit may include, in addition to banks, mutual funds and postal financial services. The ECB would control the money supply and set a corridor within which interest rates could fluctuate, similar to the bounds the Bundesbank and other national banks practice presently. The ECB and the national control banks could provide or withdraw liquidity and steer interest rates through open market operations. Moreover, they could intervene in the market and make repurchase agreements (repos), which would allow repurchasing or reselling securities at a specified time in the future at a specified price, as well as entering into foreign exchange swaps.[11]

DISPARITIES AND PRIORITIES IN THE EU

At the EU summit meeting in December 1995, member-nations confirmed that 1999 would be the year of monetary union. However, as long as differences among members persist, it is questionable if the monetary merger would be smooth in practice. The convergence criteria set by the Maastricht Treaty regarding inflation, budget deficits, and government debt would be difficult for some members. To achieve the happy marriage of monetary union, the fiscal house of each member should be in order. However, high unemployment, disparities in living standards, and social unrest might appear as a result of the strict measures required by the Maastricht Treaty. Moreover, if the ceilings of the public sector deficits of 1 percent instead of 3 percent prevail, as proposed by Germany, more difficulties would appear.

Potential benefits of the EMU include the elimination of the trouble of doing business in many currencies and the increase in cross-border investment due to the establishment of a single monetary unit. This would eliminate instabilities from devaluations that price out of the market the goods of countries with stable currencies. It is estimated that about $30 billion is wasted annually from shuffling and exchanging different currencies. However, member-nations with uncompetitive industries would not have the potential of becoming more competitive through currency depreciation, thereby facing industrial deterioration, which could lead to large cross-border movements of capital and labor. This might drive some member-nations out of alignment. In any case, it is too late to retreat, and through a monetary union, expectations are that Europe would swallow Germany, not the other way around.

In a six-day conference at the World Economic Forum at Davos, Switzerland, on 5–11 February 1996, world financial leaders put less priority on the EMU than on economic growth through reduction in interest rates. They feared that the severe slash of budget deficits, in accordance with the Maastricht agreement, would lead to severe recessions. The question is if the goal of a common currency, the Euro, is worth the sacrifice. As mentioned previously, only Luxembourg meets the standard of keeping budget deficits at no more than 3 percent of the GDP.

In order to avoid the economic stagnation of Europe and the large spillover effects across the Atlantic, postponement of the single-currency in Europe on 1 January 1999 and the replacement of national currencies (coins and notes) by June 2002 have been suggested. Moreover, the introduction of the Euro could delay plans to bring other Eastern European countries into the EU.

EFFECTS OF THE STOCK MARKETS

Transactions in equities among NAFTA, the EU, and other nations are growing rapidly. Thus, foreigners' purchases of U.S. stocks were around one-half trillion dollars in 1995, compared to $173 billion in 1990, whereas sales of foreign stocks to Americans were around $400 billion in 1995, compared to $132 billion in 1990. The enormous development of telecommunications leads to the opening of overseas markets and the overhaul of transatlantic transactions. From a financial standpoint, the whole planet is shrinking rapidly.

The New York Stock Exchange (NYSE), founded on 17 May 1792 by twenty-four stockholders and merchants, is a leader in the global marketplace where more than 2,675 companies list their shares, more than 230 of which are non-U.S. companies, and of those, mainly EU companies. Similar stock markets have been established in the other NAFTA and EU countries and are rapidly growing. They are providing companies with visibility and investors with opportunities and success through sharing in economic growth worldwide. This is an efficient way to transform saving into investment and to participate in the economic development of the countries involved.

Seven Canadian companies joined the NYSE in 1995, bringing that country's total to thirty-nine, with a market capitalization of $78.6 billion. Barrick Gold Corporation (ABX), Seagram Company Ltd. (VO), Newbridge Networks Corporation (NN), Placer Dome, Inc. (POG), Northern Telecom Limited (NT), and Alcan Aluminium Limited (AL) are some of the big firms of Canada listed in the NYSE.

Mexico had twenty-two companies listed on the NYSE at the end of 1995, including Telefonos de Mexico, S.A. de C.V. (TMX); Grupo Televisa, S.A. (TV); Grupo Tribasa, S.A. de C.V. (GTR); Empresas ICA Sociedad Controladora, S.A. de C.V. (ICA); Coca-Cola Femsa, S.A. de C.V. (KOF); and Grupo Financiero Serfin, S.A. (SFN). Three of these companies are under Global Depository Receipts/Shares and the rest under American Depository Receipts/Shares.

Stock and bond diversification between the large markets of NAFTA and the EU can yield higher returns with less risk than investment in one of these economic groups, mainly because of a broad range of opportunities and lower volatility. This is so because of different endowments of natural resources, cultural differencies, and independent regulations and economic policies.

In order to avoid listing requirements on trading in the United States, American Depository Receipts (ADRs) have been created. ADRs are issued by an American bank and represent the ownership of foreign stocks held in custody by the bank issuing them. Global Depository Receipts (GDRs) can be issued on stock exchanges of a number of countries. The EU stocks listed in the NYSE are under ADRs.

At the end of 1995, there were ninety-three European companies listed on the NYSE, with a market capitalization of $104.3 billion, eighty-nine of which were EU companies, primarily from the U.K. (39), and Italy and The Netherlands (11 each). The value of the stocks traded in 1995 in the NYSE were $48.9 billion for U.K. companies, $30.4 billion for The Netherlands, $13 billion for Finland, $8.5 billion for Spain, $4.9 billion for France, $2 billion for Denmark and Italy each, $1.9 billion for Ireland, and $0.9 billion for German companies.[12] Some of the important EU companies listed in the NYSE are: Daimler-Benz AG (DAI) of Germany; Tele Danmark A/S (TLD); SGS-THO-MSON Microelectronics N.V. (STM), and Elf Aquitaine (ELF) of France; Nokia Corporation (NOKA) of Finland; Elan Corporation, PLC (ELN) of Ireland; Royal Dutch Petroleum Company (RD), and Unilever N.V. (UN) of The Netherlands; Repsol, S.A. (REP), and Telefonica de Espana, S.A. (TEF) of Spain; and Vodafone Group PLC (VOD), Hanson PLC (HAN), British Petroleum PLC (BP), Smithkline Beecham PLC (SBE), and Glaxo Wellcome PLC (GLX) of the United Kingdom.

Sometimes the growth of the stock markets is high compared to other economic variables. For example, the Dow Jones Industrial Average (DJIA) in the United States rose from 3,000 in 1991 to more than 6,500 in 1996, and to 6,877.68 on 19 March 1997. The average daily value of trading in the NYSE in 1995 was a record $12.2 billion, or $3.1 trillion for the whole year. The GDP in current prices rose from $5,723 billion in 1991 to about $7,300 billion in 1996, or 28 percent. To a lesser extent, similar trends can be observed in the other NAFTA and EU countries. Thus in the Toronto Stock Exchange, the 300 composite index rose 25 percent in 1996, matching the Dow Jones in the United States. In the EU, Finland's stock market jump was the highest (47%) followed by that of Spain (41%) during the same year.

From a macroeconomic point of view, the growth of the stock market would be expected to follow, more or less, the growth of the economy as a whole. But the ratio of DJIA growth to GDP growth (the DG ratio) rose far above 1 (1.00/0.28 or 2.8 times) during 1991–1996. Also, the ratio of the DJIA to the value of all the companies' assets (the Q ratio of Professor J. Tobin, 1981 Nobel Prize winner) rose substantially above 1.

There are numerous reasons for the ups and downs of stock and bond markets. They include movements of interest rates, extensive involvement of mutual funds and pension funds, cost-cutting and short-term profits through corporate reorganization, mergers and acquisitions, exchange rate fluctuations, and internationalization of the stock and bond markets. Information processings of improved computer equipment, as well as the World Wide Web and the Internet, reduce cost and attract profitable investment, globalizing portfolio transactions.

Now foreigners own more than 30 percent, or more than $1 trillion, U.S. treasury bonds not held by U.S. government agencies (mainly the Federal Reserve and Social Security), compared to less than 20 percent in 1992, whereas Americans cut their investment in treasury securities in favor of stock funds.[13]

The mutual fund industry plays a significant role in financial policies of NAFTA and the EU. It crashed with the stock market in 1929 and developed again in the 1960s to be almost destroyed in 1973–1974 with the market collapse at that time. Helped by the creation of money market funds in the 1970s, the assets of the U.S. mutual funds industry increased from $45.9 billion in 1975 to about $2 trillion currently, compared to about $1.5 trillion held by domestic banks in mortgages and commercial loans. According to the Investment Company Institute, there are more than 600 retail money market mutual funds with total assets exceeding $400 billion. Dreyfus, Fidelity, Kidder Peabody, Merrill Lynch, Vanguard, Paine Webber, and hundreds of other firms are in the mutual funds business.

Lately, investment banks, young urban professionals (yuppies), and other financial gurus advise people to invest in short-term speculative stocks for quick profit. However, when the overinflated stock market drops as a result of adjustment to the real performance of the economy, savings of the shareholders evaporate, as happened in similar cases in the past with the leveraged buy-outs and junk bonds. The obsessive concentration of the NAFTA and EU stock markets on short-run gains, through program trading, index options, triple witching hours, portfolio insurance, and other arbitrage devices may lead to the creative destruction or the euthanasia of the financial system.

Presently, many brokers, lawyers, bankers, investment gurus, and other speculators lead the stock markets to artificial growth, generating unnecessary economic fluctuations or business cycles. The same thing can be said for many financial markets which pursue their casino instincts. From that standpoint, macroeconomists tend to think that money coming from mutual funds is suspect but money coming from banks is reliable.

The dramatic increase in mutual funds, on both sides of the Atlantic, and the huge accumulation of money from them, has generated concerns about needless market volatility and deep periodic fluctuations in the economy. However, the transfer of funds from banks to equity market via mutual funds, mainly because of low interest rates, may add to short-term volatility of the market, but it also provides diversity and increases the spread of corporate ownership among many shareholders, not only in the NAFTA and EU countries, but all over the world. Such shareholders are introduced to the operations of the equity markets and are expected to invest more in individual stocks themselves. As a result, many more people become stock owners, and more funds are available for productive investments, thereby making mutual funds a great contributor to the marketability of corporate equity.[14]

The number of new foreign stock listings on the NYSE is rising fast, from less than five per year before 1985 they increased to close to sixty in 1996. After the International Accounting Standards Committee completes its accounting standards, foreign companies will be able to sell securities in the United States following these standards, even if they are different from the tiresome accounting principles required in the United States. However, such standards must be deemed adequate for American markets to satisfy the investors confidence and not too lax, as is the case with German and British standards.

The performance of the world stock markets was impressive during 1996. The percentage increase (in U.S. dollars) of the stock market was 22.5 for the United States, compared to 27.5 for Canada, 16.8 for Mexico, 20.7 for Britain, 17.8 for France, 13.7 for Germany, and as high as 32.9 for Sweden. However, the stock market of Japan declined by 16.5 percent in 1996. With the rapidly improving telecommunications, investors are tempted to look overseas for more profitable equities and for the help of mutual funds to gain exposure abroad.

The fact that many blue-chip foreign companies trade in the United States with ADRs (more than 1,500 in 1997), indicates that ADRs may be a realistic alternative to mutual funds. The Standard and Poor's 500 stock index was up 22.9 percent in 1996 and Dow Jones 28.2 percent, but foreign stocks were undervalued (e.g., the German market was up 17.2 percent in 1996 in local currency).[15]

Mutual funds is becoming a giant industry. Some 37 percent of the U.S. households invest in mutual funds, compared to 31 percent two years ago. Furthermore, more than 40 percent of 401k money is in mutual funds, compared to 10 percent in 1988. The question, though, is this: If the stock market takes a breather and funds, with 12 to 15 percent return, face losses, how will investors react?

In February 1997, the Dow Jones passed 7,000, compared to 6,000 in October 1996, 5,000 in November 1995, 4,000 in February 1995, 3,000 in April 1991, 2,000 in January 1987, 1,000 in November 1972, 500 in March 1956, 100 in January 1906, and 40.9 in May 1896.

In order to provide a pan-European stock market, the EASTDAQ came into operation in September 1996 in Brussels. Its rules are based on NASDAQ rules as well as on the information disclosure requirements of the Securities and Exchange Commission (SEC) of the United States. High growth companies can gain access to capital sources without the problems and costs associated with cross-border share transactions. EASTDAQ, which is backed by the commission and the European Parliament, operates under the supervision of the Belgian authorities and is recognized in all EU countries under the

Investment Services Directive. Membership is open to both EU and non-EU companies with assets of at least 3.5 million ECU and capital and reserves of at least 2 million ECU and conform to the International Accounting Standards. It is expected that about 350 small high-growth companies would be listed by the turn of the century and contribute to the Single Market and employment of the EU.[16]

Retirement savings channeled into pension funds by millions of people spread capital ownership to many pensioners. A sizable part of pension funds are invested in stocks, the new ownership of which comes to large segments of society in all the EU and NAFTA countries. Millions of professors, physicians, lawyers, and other professional people as well as workers are contributing huge amounts of money to these pension funds, which in turn use the money to buy stocks, thereby spreading ownership to all contributors.

For example, in the United States, millions of teachers and university staff and their related institutions contribute to teachers' insurance funds known as Teachers Insurance and Annuity Association (TIAA) and College Retirement Equities Fund (CREF). TIAA invests mainly in government bonds and other securities and real estate, whereas CREF invests primarily in corporate stocks. This means that all the contributing members of CREF are indirect shareholders of corporations, according to their accumulated premiums. Such an indirect ownership of capital among millions of professors and other employees spreads employee capitalism and makes the economy more stable with greater growth potential.

American pension assets in other, mainly EU, countries are rapidly growing, spreading ownership to many other countries. It was estimated that U.S. pension assets invested in non-U.S. equities have grown to more than $140 billion annually. Australia, Canada, France, Germany, Italy, Japan, Switzerland, and the United Kingdom are some of the main countries where U.S. pension funds invest.

Chapter 8

Investment and Joint Ventures in NAFTA

The merger mania and the buy-out resurgence have appeared in record numbers. The main reasons for the recent boom of mergers and acquisitions are low interest rates that have lowered the cost of financing takeovers, high bank liquidity that stimulates cash acquisitions, the issuing of new shares to pay for deals boosted mainly from booming share prices, the managerial policies of reorganization and cost-cutting innovations, and pressures from foreign competition. Moreover, technological and regulatory changes and the relaxation in the implementation of the antitrust legislation intensifies the boom of mergers and acquisitions.

Government regulations on both sides of the Atlantic are used for the protection of the public. Such regulations deal primarily with highway and airline safety rules, banking establishments, housing, insurance coverage, and a host of other measures of protection. However, too much regulation acts as a drawback to productivity and stifles the economy. That is why criticism against economic regulation led to the introduction of deregulation, especially since the 1980s. However, extensive deregulation and relaxation of the antitrust legislation encourages monopolization and discourages competition.

Nevertheless, the "dog-eat-dog competition," caused by excessive deregulation and laxity in safety inspection, led to business concentration or monopolization and improper standards of maintenance and other protective measures. From that point of view, a distinction should be made between services for the protection of the public, which are a function of the government, and production and distribution operations in the economy, which should as much as possible be left out of regulation. This is because bureaucrats have proved to be less efficient managers in making resources work productively.

If enterprises are natural monopolies, regulations are introduced to prevent unjustified price raises and other monopolistic practices which work against the consumer. Although deregulation and competition are good from the standpoint of efficiency and consumer betterment, short-term self-interest groups may consider them beneficial to society if they are imposed on others. However, competition may be considered a form of necessary, therapeutic hardship to encourage innovations and increase productivity.

Comparatively speaking, there is very limited government intervention in the United States, in contrast to Canada, Britain, and other EU economies. However, there are regulations in the United States on mergers and acquisitions, power utilities, and to some extent on telephone companies concerning rates charged to customers, returns on shareholders' capital, and matters of service quality. Regulations on airline and other industries were mostly abolished in the 1980s and later.

In the Canadian economy there are both U.S.-style regulations and state (Crown) ownership, although the largest part of the economy belongs to the private sector. Nevertheless, the manufacturing sector is dominated by a few firms in the oligopolistic fashion. However, in the United States, there are stronger antitrust laws and over-concentration is discouraged.

Because of the growing importance of the airline industry, the degree of government regulation or deregulation plays a significant role in the economies of NAFTA and the EU. The influence of the U.S. government on aviation started with the Air Mail Act of 1925 which provided for the transportation of mail by airplanes. Because of a lack of faith in the free market in the 1930s, the airlines were subject to regulation mainly by the Commerce Department and the Interstate Commerce Commission. In 1928, the Civil Aeronautics Act (CAA) was passed to increase passenger safety, which was compromised from over-competition according to the supporters of this act. The CAA gave power to the Civil Aeronautics Board (CAB) to regulate fares, provide subsidies, and to control entry in the industry. Such measures have influenced the EU and other countries as well.

In order to coordinate ticket prices and costs, a deregulation process started in the 1970s which abolished controls on entry and exit, as well as on prices, but kept control on airline safety and support for access to international routes. As a result, ticket prices dropped and the number of miles flown by passengers increased significantly. Nevertheless, weak economic conditions, oil price increases, employees' retirement costs, lower communication costs, and a rise in excise tax on airline tickets led the industry to turbulent years on both sides of the Atlantic.

With the exception of sleeping monopolies, concentration of capital through mergers and other monopolistic practices generally leads to innovations and average cost reduction. Although the merger-mania of the 1980s has calmed down, there is a current rising merger trend, particularly for small companies. Investors try to capitalize on mergers in over-the-counter markets and shareholders in order to reap hefty rewards. Potential merger targets are family-owned companies with aging leaders, mainly in telecommunications, health care, banking, and personal computer sectors in the NASDAQ exchange market.

INVESTMENT AND JOINT VENTURES IN CANADA

U.S. investment in Canada was $72.8 billion in 1995, $35 billion of which was in manufacturing, $12 billion in finance, and $9 billion in petroleum. Canadian direct investments in the United States amounted to $43.2 billion in 1995, with $17 billion in manufacturing, $3.4 billion in finance, $2.6 billion in petroleum, and the remaining $20.3 billion in other ventures.

There are many U.S. firms operating in Canada in a number of sectors. Automotive companies have big factories in both Canada and Mexico. Two of these companies, General Motors and Chrysler, have had serious labor problems from time to time. Some 26,000 General Motors union workers went on stike recently in Canada which affected American workers as well. Thousands of workers were laid off from temporary factory closings in Canada and across the Midwest. The workers were demanding that General Motors not sell two Canadian automobile parts factories or buy parts from outside vendors. A similar contractual ban was accepted by Chrysler after the strike of its Canadian labor union.

To be successful in the midst of expected strong competition, the Manufacturers Life Insurance Company, a leading international insurance firm which operates in Canada, the United States, and the Asian–Pacific area, and the North American Life Insurance Company, one of the top ten Canadian insurance firms with a Boston-based subsidiary, agreed to merge. Both companies are based in Toronto and are owned by policyholders, not stockholders. Manulife Financial is the expected name of the new company, which will be the largest life and health carrier in Canada, with assets of C$47 billion (U.S.$35.15 billion) and 6,000 employees. However, as a result of the merger, it is expected that a number of jobs will be eliminated.

Ontario-based General Motors of Canada Ltd., a unit of the General Motors Corporation, was awarded a contract by the Canadian Government for 240 armored cars worth C$552 million, or U.S.$407 million.

American Airlines, a U.S. money-losing company, took a $194 million stake in Canadian Airlines International Ltd., another money-losing carrier. American Airlines, which acquired a 25 percent voting interest in Canadian Airlines, expects to make about $2 billion over the life of the twenty-year contract. In exchange, Canadian Airlines will acquire new technology, mainly for its accounting and data-processing functions.

To acquire Alberta's Czar Resources Ltd. and Orbit Oil and Gas Ltd., Gulf Canada Resources Ltd. is offering about C$147 million (U.S.$108 million). Czar, which is affiliated with Orbit, is also the target of a hostile takeover by Ranger Oil Ltd., whereas Gulf acquired Manniville Oil and Gas Ltd. in June 1995 for

C$140 million. Gulf is offering one of its shares for every 4.5 Czar shares and for every 5.9 Orbit shares. Also, it plans to offer Czar holders the option to take C$1.40 and Orbit holders C$1.10 in cash, up to a maximum payout by Gulf of C$20 million for Czar holders and C$10 million for Orbit holders.

The Toronto's Bronfman family is in a strong position to acquire Olympia and York Development Ltd, U.S.A. (O&Y), which owns several office towers, including the Twin Towers of the World Financial Center and a Los Angeles office tower. At the same time, Apollo Real Estate Investment Fund, which holds 60 percent of O&Y, and Tishman Speyer Properties Inc., which holds 20 percent, press for the early restructuring of a $5 billion debt.

Labatt Company, taken over by Belgium's Interbrew, and Molson, the world's biggest producer of malted barley, each with 19.7 percent interest in Canada Malting, agreed to tender their shares to Con Agra, the U.S. food processor. The takeover bid, subject to acceptance by at least 70 percent of Canada Malting, is for C$390 million, or C$20 per share. Canada Malting, a producer of about 900,000 tons of malt with annual sales of C$367 million, has business centered mainly in North America and the United Kingdom but is expected to expand in Europe and the Asian–Pacific Rim.

The Royal Bank of Canada, the largest financial institution in Canada, agreed to sell under-performing loans and real estate mostly in Toronto and originally valued at $374 million to Whitehall Street, a New York–based fund managed by Goldman, Sachs & Company.[1]

To pay off part of its debt, Norcen Energy Resources Ltd. plans to sell some Canadian oil and gas properties, along with other assets in Canada and the United States, worth about $180 million. Additional sales of property in Australia, New Zealand, and Indonesia, valued at about $75 million, will take place later.

International Business Machines (IBM) Canada Ltd. offered C$157 million (U.S.$118 million) to buy DMR Group Inc., an information–technology services firm in Montreal. This offer was 22 percent higher than BDM's bid and 33 percent higher than that of Amdahl Corp. DBM is a McLean, Virginia, provider of similar services. Both IBM and DMR handle many computer services for Air Canada.

AT&T Corporation took a stake of United Communications Inc., Canada's second largest long distance telephone company, which was rescued from a mountain of debt. In addition, the Bank of Nova Scotia, the Royal Bank of Canada, and Toronto Dominion Bank will invest some C$250 million in Unitel in exchange for equity, and Rogers Communications Inc. and Canadian Pacific Ltd. will give up the shares they hold from the partnership with Unitel.

In response to a joint venture, MCI Communications established a consortium with Stentor that includes Bell Canada. AT&T invested $150 million in Unitel, an upstart long distance company in Canada.

Service Corporation International, a large, Houston-based funeral company, is in the process of a hostile bid to take over Loewen Group, based in

Vancouver. The all-share offer for its rival is worth U.S.$2.7 billion. The two firms have a 15 percent share of the North American funeral business, with 600 cemeteries and 3,750 funeral homes.[2]

Petro–Canada, a large oil and gas producer, sold its personal card business to GE Canada, a subsidiary of the General Electric Company of Connecticut, for C$110 million (U.S.$80.6 million).

American Resource Corporation, a gold exploration and development company in California, agreed to merge with Rea Gold Corporation, a Canadian mining company. Each American Resource share would be exchanged for 2.24 shares of Rea.

The Chicago-based Celestica plant of IBM agreed to sell a Canadian factory that makes memory chips to the Onex Corporation for $540 million. Onex is based in Toronto and has 34,000 employees, conducting business that includes construction products, automotive parts, and airline catering.

Coca-Cola Enterprises Inc., the world's largest bottler of nonalcoholic drinks based in Atlanta, offered $117 million to purchase the Canadian bottled water producer Nora Beverages, based in Montreal. Nora has about 1 percent of the U.S. market for bottled water, with wholesale sales of about $3.5 billion a year. However, the support of the Nora's shareholders is needed for the deal to materialize.

The Abraxas Petroleum Corporation, an oil and gas company based in San Antonio, plans to buy the Canadian Gas Gathering Systems for about $85 million. Canadian Gas owns natural gas sites and processing plants in western Canada.

Ranger Oil Ltd., based in Alberta, agreed to buy about 50,000 acres of land and 46 billion cubic feet of natural gas reserves in British Columbia from Gulf Canada Resources, Ltd., a unit of Olympia and York Developments, Ltd., for $21.7 million.

Samuel Manu-Tech Inc., a steel and plastic scrapping company in Canada and the United States based in Ontario, agreed to buy the packaging business of the Interlake Corporation, based in Illinois, with sales of $141 million. The businesses include Interlake's Acme Gerrard and Pakseal operations in Canada and the United Kingdom.

Before 1993, retired Canadians living in the United States were covered by the government insurance system. Thereafter, they are covered only for serious accidents and heart attacks. Consequently, many Canadians left the United States and returned to Canada, especially from Florida where the Organization of Health, Insurance, and Pension (OHIP) of Canada used to pay millions of dollars each year for medical insurance to Florida's hospitals and doctors for the treatment of Canadians there.

Kruger Inc., a large pulp and paper company based in Montreal, agreed to acquire Scott Paper Ltd. based in Ontario for C$451 million, or about U.S.$330 million. In 1995, Scott merged with the Kimberly–Clark Corporation in a $9.4 billion transaction, but the Canadian Government required that Kimberly sell some of its Scott operations.

Domtar, a forest products company of Canada, will merge its packaging division with the container-board operations of Cascades to create a venture with assets of U.S.$674 million.

Philip Environmental Inc., an environmental remediation and recycling company in Ontario, agreed to buy a Reynolds Metals Company processing plant in Richmond for an undisclosed amount.

Cameron Ashley Building Products Inc., a building products distributor in Dallas, agreed to purchase Bois Daigle, a Canadian distributor of similar products, from Simard–Beaudry Inc., Quebec, for an undisclosed amount.

Remington Energy Ltd., an Alberta-based oil and gas company, agreed to acquire B.C. Star Partners, an oil and gas firm with assets that include reserves of 300 billion cubic feet of natural gas and about six million barrels of oil and natural gas liquids. B.C. Star is a partnership between Texaco Canada Petroleum Inc. and Edison International, a utility-based company in California.

The Phoenix Canada Oil Company based in Toronto offered to buy the Box Energy Corporation based in Dallas for $239 million. The offer includes $12 per share for 3.25 million class A voting shares, and $11.4 per share for 17.55 million class B nonvoting shares. The new company is expected to focus on drilling oil and gas wells.

The Brio Industries, a bottler and distributor of juices and soft drinks in Vancouver, British Columbia, sold certain assets to the Cott Corporation in Toronto for $20 million.

Cinar Films, Inc., specializing in television programming and based in Montreal, agreed to buy Filmfair Ltd.'s library and animation unit from the Carpian Group of Britain for $17.14 million.

Holliger International Inc., which publishes newspapers and magazines in the United States, Canada, Britain, Australia, and Israel, acquired eight million shares of Southern, Inc., the Toronto-based publisher, for C$160 million (U.S.$118 million). As a result, Holliger International, which also owns *The Chicago Sun-Times*, raised its stake in Southern, Inc. from 41 percent to 50.7 percent.

An affiliate of the London-based Shell International Chemicals, Ltd. bought a major Alberta styrene plant in Ontario for C$635 million (U.S.$467 million).

To expand its oil production into the British section of the North Sea, Gulf Canada Resources, Ltd. offered £432 million or $722 million to buy Clyde Petroleum P.L.C. Increases in oil prices have increased the value of exploration for companies like Clyde, and they are expected to expand further in the future.

Rogers Cantel Mobile Communications, a Canadian wireless telephone company, and AT&T Corporation formed an alliance to provide long distance and other wireless and digital personal communication services.

A joint venture of Hilton Hotels Corporation of Beverly Hills, California, and ITT Corporation, bought Circus Enterprises, Inc., which operates a casino in Windsor, Ontario. The terms of the purchase were not disclosed.

Agrium, Inc. based in Alberta agreed to take over Viridian based in Toronto and create one of the largest fertilizer companies in North America for C$1.2 billion (U.S.$887.4 million), with more than $2 billion in revenue.

A thriving gray market for satellite dishes, the size of garbage can lids, has been developing in Canada during the last few years. So far Canada has been unable to offer its own satellite service to Canadians, who consequently illegally subscribe to pirated services from the United States. Canadian television owners pay a monthly fee to a dealer who pays the U.S. satellite television provider. Canada tries to limit the leakage of television and radio services, books, magazines, and films, not only for cultural protectionism, but also to preserve some space for domestic competition.

INVESTMENT AND JOINT VENTURES IN MEXICO

U.S. Investment in Mexico

From 1876 to 1910, under Porfirio Diaz, Mexico was open to foreign investors. However, because of the exploitation of natural resources such as oil and minerals, and the transfer of monopoly profits abroad, the Mexican Revolution of 1910 led to the nationalization of many industries, particularly after the Constitution of 1917. Thus, the foreign oil companies were nationalized in 1938, and later, foreign investments were permitted for import substitution and to gain hard currency and technological expertise. As a result of the reforms of the 1980s, the value of flowing foreign investment mounted to $4 billion in 1991, and has continued to grow.

Although there are problems in labor, finance, and environment, the momentum of NAFTA cannot be stopped. However, Mexico needs a strong inflow of capital investment that NAFTA could facilitate, thereby creating a surge of Mexican jobs. About two-thirds of total foreign investments in Mexico comes from the United States. U.S. direct investment in Mexico was $16.4 billion in 1995, mainly in manufacturing ($10.7 billion) and finance ($2 billion).

By implementing the provisions of NAFTA, Mexico increased reliance on privatization and competition, reduced trade barriers, and enhanced efficiency and productivity. The encouragement of free market forces and institutions unleashed further entrepreneurial initiatives and attracted foreign investment. The economic success of Mexico, due mainly to the divestiture of public enterprises, a rapidly expanding role of the private sector, and an externally oriented economy, sets an example for its neighbors in Central and South America, as well as for many other developing countries.

As a result of NAFTA, Delta Airlines Inc. agreed to pursue code-sharing in reservations and flight schedules with Aeroméxico, as well as to arrange mutual use of a block of seats in flights between Mexico City and the United States. In addition, they are considering opportunities for further joint programs.

The implementation of NAFTA is expected to increase the exchange of Mexican stocks in the NYSE. Teléfonos de Mexico, Cementos Mexicanos Telmex, and Consorcio G Grupo Dina are among the most attractive companies, the shares of which are seriously considered by long-term American and other investors. However, the implementation of NAFTA would lead to a reduction of the current 20 percent Mexican tariffs on European and other foreign trucks, thereby making Dina's and other related shares less attractive.

The Bell Atlantic Corporation agreed to buy a 42 percent share of Grupo Iusacell of Mexico. For the initial 23 percent share, Bell paid $520 million. With the new wireless telephones, the network will compete with Teléfonos de Mexico or Telmex, a state-owned monopoly under privatization since 1990. Regardless of progress under NAFTA, this will greatly improve the telecommunications system of Mexico, where only 8 percent of the people have telephones compared to 85 percent for the United States and Canada.

A joint venture between AT&T Corporation and Grupo Alta S.A. of Mexico, named Alestra, plans to invest $1 billion for the construction of a 5,000-mile telephone cable network in Mexico to connect thirty-four cities. Moreover, the host Marriott Corporation announced its plans to enter into an agreement with Grupo Situr, a Mexican tourist and hotel company, to acquire two hotels in Mexico City worth $133 million. Also, it would buy the Delta Meadowvale Hotel and the Conference Center in Toronto.

The Teléfonos de Mexico (Telmex), in competition with AT&T and MCI Communications, plans to file with the FCC for permission to offer its own long distance, cellular, and other services to Spanish-speaking customers in the United States.

Shell Oil Company agreed to the construction of a new refinery worth $450 million with Petroleos Mexicanos (PEMEX). The refinery, to be established in Salina Cruz, Oaxaca, is expected to process 150 million barrels of crude oil a day.

Kmart Corporation, the U.S. department store chain, and its counterpart in Mexico, Grupo El Puerto de Liverpool, announced a joint venture of $500 million to establish one hundred stores, thereby generating 35,000 jobs. Kmart, with about 4,000 outlets primarily in the United States and Canada, and purchasing offices in Germany, China, and other countries, targets different markets than the existing markets of Liverpool and the province-based Fabrica de Francia outlets. The new Super Centros Kmart is expected to become one of the most modern department stores in Mexico City, Acapulco, and other Mexican locations.

With the establishment of NAFTA, Canadian and U.S. commercial and investment banks will enjoy lucrative markets in Mexico. From that standpoint, NAFTA banks and other investment companies could strengthen their reorganization toward effective joint ventures and intense competition.

Panamerican Beverages, Inc., the largest Coca-Cola bottler outside the United States operating in central Mexico, filed with the Securities and Exchange Commission for an 11.5 million share offering, worth more than $300 million, to pay for capital expenditures and previous debts. About 9 million shares will be sold in the United States and Canada and the rest to other countries.

U.S. Filter Corporation of California agreed to build and operate a plant in Cuernavaca, Mexico, to treat waste water.

Despite NAFTA's provision that bus lines have the right to carry passengers across the Mexican border, Greyhound Lines Inc., the Dallas-based company, and other bus companies face problems because Mexico presents obstacles to U.S. companies using bus terminals or starting new routes.

Morgan Stanley and Company agreed with Grupo Posadas, the largest operator of hotels in Latin America, to buy a number of Mexican hotels worth about $200 million. This is an indication of investment flow into Mexico since the peso devaluation on 20 December 1994 stabilized the economy and led to successful bond issues in German marks (with 10.42% interest), U.S. dollars, and Japanese yens.

Mexico signed an agreement that allows satellite service from the United States to Mexico and vice versa. There are only limited restrictions that require public interest programs and some programs in Spanish, and that keep out obscenity. Mexican broadcasters, therefore, would enjoy full access to the lucrative Spanish-speaking market in the United States, unlike the bureaucratic stubbornness which Canadians face.

European Investment in Mexico

NAFTA could benefit the old and new industries that have been established in Mexico by other non-NAFTA countries, mainly Germany and Japan. Such industries primarily serve the domestic Mexican markets because of U.S. border restrictions. For example, as the author observed during a recent visit in Mexico, many cars and taxis in Acapulco, Mexico City, and other cities, are small Volkswagen automobiles that are manufactured in Mexico by the Volkswagen A.G. Company of Germany.

It is expected that Mexico, with its cheap labor and close proximity to the rich U.S. market, will attract many industries from Japan, Germany, and other EU countries. This will discourage regional trade and investment restrictions and stimulate international competition in accordance with WTO rules.

Mercedes-Benz, the German vehicle producer and Mexico's leader in the truck sales market, invested $125 million for the expansion of its plant in Santiago Tianguistengo, State of Mexico. Moreover, it is expected that another $100 million will be invested in a new bus plant that will produce 2,000 to 3,000 buses annually. Monterrey and Veracruz are among the leading areas considered for the new plant because of their geographic closeness to export markets and labor availability.

MERGERS AND ACQUISITIONS IN THE UNITED STATES

Gigantomania

Since 1991, U.S. mergers and acquisitions (M&As) have been on the upswing. Some 5,237 M&A deals worth $273 billion occurred during the years of 1992 and 1993, and the trend continues. About 17 percent of these M&As were in finance, 11 percent in health care, 5 percent in telecommunications, and 4 percent in defense and technology. These four industrial sectors accounted for about half the total asset value at that period. The Justice Department and the Federal Trade Commission (FTC) have not challenged many mergers (more than 95% for hospitals) because they improve management, stimulate innovations, and lower costs without largely undermining competition.

The gigantomania of the 1980s, with an enforcement moratorium on antitrust laws, seems to have reappeared. The short-run speculative capitalism is gaining more importance than long-run productive capitalism. The economy is moving more toward merger financing than real investment financing. The justification of giantism through acquisitions is to create big corporations able to compete with their foreign counterparts and, thus, enable the United States to recapture its preeminence in international markets.

The Securities Data Company, a research firm, announced record M&A deals. The total of U.S. M&A transactions in 1994 and 1995 were 7,600 and 7,300 respectively, compared to 3,900 in 1988.[3]

In summary, M&As reached $182.6 billion in 1990, $341.9 billion in 1994, $518.8 billion in 1995, and as high as $658.8 billion in 1996. Of the plethora of M&As that take place every year, some of the important ones are presented in the following paragraphs.

The Bell Atlantic Corporation based in Philadelphia offered $33 billion to acquire the Tele-Communications, Inc. and the Liberty Media Corporation. This is the biggest takeover in Wall Street history, and compares to the 1989 leveraged buy-out of RJR Nabisco Inc. by Kohlberg, Kravis, Roberts and Company for $25 billion.

In the telecommunications industry, the largest M&As are: NYNEX and Bell Atlantic in April 1996 (worth $22.1 billion); Disney and Capital Cities/ ABC in August 1995 ($19 billion); McCass Cellular Communications and AT&T in August 1993 ($18.9 billion); SBC Communications, Inc. which agreed to buy Pacific Telesis Group for $16.5 billion, forming the second largest telecommunications firm in the country and providing service to more than thirty million residential and business telephone lines; U.S. West domestic cellular business and AirTouch Communications in July 1994 ($13.5 billion); U.S. West and Continental Cablevision ($11.8 billion); NYNEX's cellular business and Bell Atlantic in June 1994 ($13 billion); and Time Warner and Turner Broadcasting in September 1995 ($7.4 billion).

The megamergers of recent years continue to grow in numbers and in size. Thus, in more details, the Bell Atlantic Corporation, headquartered in Philadelphia with $13.4 billion in revenue in 1995, and the NYNEX Corporation, headquartered in New York with about the same revenue, agreed to merge and create the largest local telephone company in America. With about two million stockholders and 127,600 employees, NYNEX–Bell Atlantic is offering local telephone, long distance, wireless, internet, and even video services to 36.9 million customers in sixteen eastern seaboard states from Maine to Virginia. The NYNEX–Bell Atlantic megamerger created the second largest phone company in the United States (after AT&T) with a stock market value of $51 billion. It is expected to produce economies of scale which will lead to more research and development. Also expected is the loss of thousands of jobs, including those of corporate executives. Already, New York State regulators approved the merger but as a condition ordered NYNEX to spend $500 million for improvement and to hire more employees, and the Justice Department and the FCC are expected to approve it in the near future.

AT&T, which dominates long distance telephone services, proposed a $12.6 billion merger agreement with McCaw Cellular Communications. Also, AT&T is discussing a merger with GTE Corporation worth $48 billion.

In addition to the merger of the two regional Bell telephone companies (SBC Communications and Pacific Telesis Group), U.S. West agreed to acquire Continental Cablevision, the third-largest cable operator in the nation, for $5.3 billion. Nevertheless, the Consumer Federation of America and other consumer advocates argue that such mergers pose severe threats to competition.

Lockheed Martin, the largest defense company with 165,000 employees based in Maryland, announced that it will buy most of Loral Company, based in New York with 38,000 employees, for $7 billion. This acquisition is in addition to the $10 billion merger between Lockheed and Martin Marietta. Annual revenue is expected to be $30 billion (about one-fourth that of the military). With the end of the Cold War, mergers of defense companies have increased. Other companies expected to buy or sell all or parts of defense divisions include Rockwell International, General Electric, Chrysler, United Technologies, Texas Instruments, Litton, Allied Signal, and the mega-deal between Boeing and McDonnell Douglas.[4] Because of the heavy trading in Loral stock options, federal regulators and officials at the Chicago Board Options Exchange are examining the repercussions of the takeover by Lockheed Martin.

After twenty-two previous mergers in the defense industry (mainly by the two mega-companies, Lockheed Martin Loral and Boeing McDonnell Douglas, and three other major companies, Hughes, Raytheon, and Northrop), the Boeing Company offered $13.3 billion to acquire the McDonnell Douglas Corporation at the end of 1996. Such mergers are expected to reduce competition in the production of commercial jets and military aircrafts.[5]

In 1996, Worldcon acquired MFS Communications for $13.36 billion, U.S. West Media Group acquired Continental Cablevision for $11.4 billion, and Nationsbank acquired Boatmen's Bancshares for $9.47 billion.

The largest banking merger in U.S. history took place between Chase Manhattan Corporation and Chemical Banking Corporation, involving $297 billion in assets and 2,000 offices. This banking giant, retaining the Chase name, placed a $10 billion unsuccessful bid for First Interstate Bancorp of California, and many other banking deals with smaller bids are on the forefront.

Also, Western Resources, in alliance with Chase, currently is trying to acquire ADT Inc. in a hostile $3.5-billion bid.

Wells Fargo and Company became the eighth largest banking company in the United States when it completed its $11 billion acquisition of First Interstate Bankcorp. As a result of the merger, more than 7,000 employees were to be laid off. The Banc One Corporation based in Columbus, Ohio, agreed to buy First USA, Inc. Bank based in Dallas for $7 billion.[6] Nevertheless, CoreStates, the largest bank in Philadelphia, turned down an offer from Mellon Bank of Pittsburgh for about $18 billion, which would have led to the largest banking acquisition in U.S. history.

Morgan Stanley Group and Dean Witter, Discovery and Company agreed to merge into the largest security company worth $10.2 billion. Paine Webber and other securities and brokerage firms are also considered targets of takeovers.

First Bank System, the Minneapolis banking company, agreed to buy U.S. Bankcorp of Portland, Oregon, for $9 billion in stock.

Washington Mutual, a Seattle firm with close to 2,000 banking and finance offices, in competition with H. F. Ahmanson and Company, agreed to acquire Great Western Financial of Los Angeles for $6.6 billion. The deal would create the largest savings and loan institution in the United States.

Merck & Co., a drug manufacturer, agreed to acquire Medco Containment Services, a wholesale drug distributor, for $6 billion. The CVS Corporation, based in Woonsocket, Rhode Island, agreed to acquire Revco D. S. Inc., based in Twinsburg, Ohio, for about $2.8 billion, creating the second largest drug store chain behind Rite Aid Corporation.

The Travelers Corporation, an insurance company, accepted the Primerica Corporation's $4 billion merger offer which will create one of the largest financial companies in the country.

QVC Network, Inc., in competition with Viacom, Inc., proposed a $9.5 billion merger with Paramount Communications, Inc.

Kmart Corporation agreed to merge its Builders Square chain with Waban Inc.'s HomeBase chain, which would form the third-largest retail home improvement chain in the country with 250 stores.

The Aetna Life and Casualty Company agreed to acquire U.S. Healthcare, Inc. for $8.9 billion which would create the largest managed-care provider in the United States, with over twenty million members in fifty states. The Columbia Healthcare Corporation and the HCA Hospital Corporation of America agreed to merge in a tax free exchange of shares. The merger, which would create a 190 hospital chain mostly in the South, is expected to reduce costs in the new health care system. From four hospitals in 1987, Columbia/HCA Healthcare Corporation has reached 339 hospitals and 118 clinics in 1996. Although regulators have objected to some previous acquisitions, the chain owns about 6 percent of U.S. hospitals, with the largest share in Florida. Columbia/HCA Healthcare Corporation is presently talking with 150 hospitals for new acquisitions. More large mergers are expected in the near future, particularly with hospitals and other health care providers after the implementation of the Health Managed Organization (HMO) recently introduced in America.[7]

The Gillette Company, a consumer products firm based in Boston, acquired Duracell International Inc., a battery manufacturer based in Bethel, Connecticut, for $7 billion. This represents a windfall for Kohlberg, Kravis, Roberts and Company, the biggest U.S. leveraged buy-out firm, with a controlling 34 percent stake in Duracell, which it bought in 1988 for $1.8 billion. Gillette realizes about 30 percent of its sales in the United States and 36 percent in Europe, compared to 55 percent and 28 percent, respectively, for Duracell, whose shareholders would receive 0.904 shares of Gillette stock for each Duracell share owned.[8]

The Duke Power Company, a large utility company which maintains a partnership with Louis Dreyfus Electric Power, agreed to merge, in a $7.7 billion stock swap, with the PanEnergy Corporation.[9]

For another mammoth merger, that of Time Warner with Turner Broadcasting System in 1995, the FTC put its seal of approval on the $6.7 billion deal in September 1996. The merger of these two cable and distribution giants was made in accordance with the new Telecommunications Act of 1996.

The 3COM corporation, based in Santa Clara, California, agreed to acquire the U.S. Robotics Corporation in a $6.6 billion stock swap. U.S. Robotics, with headquarters in Chicago, supplies Internet service providers.

Union Pacific Corporation has proposed the acquisition of Southern Pacific Rail, worth around $3.9 billion. However, the Justice Department said this deal would hurt competition and could result in price increases by rail carriers in the western region of the United States.

The Newmont Mining Corporation, outbidding the rival Homestake Mining Company, agreed to acquire the Santa Fe Pacific Gold Corporation for $2.43 billion, and similar takeover efforts are made in other gold industries. To break up the merger agreement between Santa Fe and the Homestate Mining Company, the Newmont Mining Corporation based in Denver raised its offer for the Santa Fe Pacific Gold Corporation from $2.04 billion to $2.15 billion. If the acquisition is completed, Newmont, with an annual production of about 3.5 million ounces of gold and exploration projects in the former Soviet Union, will be the second-largest mining company in the world, after the Barrick Gold Corporation of Canada.

Raytheon Corporation agreed to acquire Texas Instruments–Electronics for $3 billion.

American General Corporation acquired U.S. Life Company for $2.4 billion.

Allegheny Ludlum Corporation agreed to buy Teledyne, Inc., another steel manufacturer, using a $2.04 billion stock swap.

Texas Utilities Company based in Dallas would acquire ENSERCH Corporation for $1.7 billion and blend its electric operations with those of a top gas distributor. Through joint operations, such utility industries can lower costs by reducing their staff.

ITT Sheraton, a subsidiary of ITT, and the Hilton Hotel Corporation are each considering a possible merger with the Bally Entertainment Corporation. In 1993, ITT acquired Desert Inn Properties in Las Vegas for $160 million, and in 1994, paid $1.7 billion for Caesars World, which has casinos in Las Vegas and Atlantic City, among other places.

Moreover, in 1997, Hilton Hotels Corporation made a hostile takeover bid of $11.5 billion for the acquisition of ITT Corporation. However, there may be problems with antitrust and gambling laws. The bid may be higher as a result of ITT's decision to sell its one-half interest in Madison Square Garden to Cablevision Systems Corporation for $650 million in cash and the assumption of $115 million of debt.

The Republic Industries, Inc. agreed to acquire the National Car Rental Systems, Inc. for a $600 million stock swap and the assumption of $1.7 billion debt. Two months earlier, the Republic Industries had acquired Alamo Rent-A-Car.

Cigna Corporation agreed to acquire Healthsource Inc., another health company, for $1.45 billion.

Westinghouse Electric Corporation agreed to acquire Nashville Network and Country Music Television operations in the United States and Canada for $1.55 billion. These operations are owned by Gaylord Entertainment Company.

McAfee Associates Inc., dealing with computer networking software, agreed to buy the Network General Corporation for $1.3 billion in stock.

Masco Corporation agreed to sell its furnishings' unit for $1.1 billion to a group of investors which include Citibank.

Corporate Express, based in Broomfield, Colorado, agreed to buy the Houston-based U.S. Delivery Systems, a large delivery company, for $410 million. Annual revenue of the newly created company is expected to be $1.6 billion annually. The stockholders of U.S. Delivery will receive 1.2 shares of Corporate Express, which provides office products, for each of their shares.[10]

Hicks, Muse, Tate, and Furst Inc. agreed to merge with Evergreen Media Corporation to form the largest independent radio broadcaster to then buy the ten stations owned by Viacom Inc. The deal is worth more than $1.6 billion.

NGC Corporation, a seller of natural gas, agreed to buy Destec Energy, an operator of power plants, for $1.27 billion.

McGraw Hill Inc., which publishes *Business Week* magazine in addition to books, and owns four television stations, acquired another 50 percent stake in its partner, Macmillan Publishing Company, a unit of the Maxwell Communication Corporation, for $337.5 million.

Although hostile takeovers result in quick deals, they account for only about 10 percent of all deals. Major investment banks such as Morgan Stanley, CS First Boston, Goldman Sachs, Merrill Lynch, J. P. Morgan, and Lazard Frères have the largest share of the M&A advising market. The fees of advisors vary widely, but on the average, they are around 0.7 percent of the value of the deals.

The Brooklyn Union Gas Company and the Long Island Lighting Company (LILCO) worked out a merger in which Brooklyn Union, with 3,300 employees, would take over LILCO, with 5,600 employees and 2.5 million customers. The New York Public Service Commission is expected to approve the merger in order to reduce Long Island's energy costs, which are the highest in the United States. The merger would create a big utility firm with $4.5 billion in revenue. It is expected to reduce costs by trimming the work force through attrition and other economies.

Microsoft, Inc. engaged in twenty-one acquisitions between 1994 and 1996, the largest with Vermeer Technologies, Inc. for $130 million, and it continues to look for new acquisitions to promote its healthy growth.

Spinoffs

Although the trend is high concentration through M&As, there are cases of ownership and business splits through spinoffs.

Some conglomerates in America and Europe, with a number of enterprises acquired in previous times of diversification, are anxious to spinoff such businesses either because they are difficult to manage or they drag earnings down. They want to rid themselves of volatile businesses that reduce profits or increase losses. For example, ITT Corporation, with 106,000 employees in sixty-three countries, and interests in hotels, insurance, automotive, and forest products, announced that it would spinoff its subsidiary, ITT Rayonier Inc., founded in 1926 and acquired by ITT in 1968. Rayonier, with an annual revenue of more than $700 million, produces and sells timber, wood products, and pulp. Under the plan, ITT shareholders would get one share of Rayonier common stock for every four shares of ITT common stock, or 3.16 preferred stock. No taxes have to be paid on the transaction.

Dun & Bradstreet (D&B), the 155-year-old firm, announced that it will split into three publicly traded companies. D&B would become Dun & Bradstreet Information Services; Moodys Investors Service (for bond ratings); publisher Reuben H. Donnelley; A.C. Nielson, a provider of consumer information; and Cognizant, which would include IMS International, Gartner Group, and Nielson Media Research. Already, the D&B board approved the split, which would increase the shareholders' value.[11]

In anticipation of the AT&T split into three independent units, AT&T Global Information Solutions decided to change its name back to NCR, as it was known in 1991 when AT&T acquired it in a hostile takeover for $7.5 billion. After heavy losses, AT&T abandoned NCR's personal computer business in Dayton, Ohio, reducing the payroll by 8,500.

Lucent Technologies, Inc., the AT&T Corporation spinoff, sold 112 million shares worth approximately $3 billion. As a result of the AT&T plan to divide itself into three parts, the deregulated telecommunications industry became more competitive.

In 1995, ITT carried out a three-way spinoff, creating an independent insurance company, an industrial manufacturer, and a hotel and casino company. If Hilton Hotels Corporation is successful with its $11.5 billion takeover offer for the ITT Corporation, this acquisition would make Hilton the largest hotel and gambling firm in the world.[12]

Loral Corporation spun off Loral Space and Communications, Ltd. when Lockheed Martin Corporation acquired two-thirds of Loral's 180 million shares worth $9.1 billion. However, Lockheed Martin bought a 20 percent stake of Loral Space worth $344 million.

In order to settle Federal Trade Commission's antitrust concerns about reduction in competition, Praxair Inc., the largest supplier of industrial gases, agreed to divest itself of four production plants it had acquired in a $2 billion acquisition of CBI Industries.

The National Semiconductor Corporation based in Santa Clara, California, agreed to sell a majority interest in Fairchild Semiconductor, which makes high volume commodity chips, to a group led by Fairchild Management and Sterling L.L.C., a unit of Citicorp, for $550 million. National will retain a 16 percent stake in Fairchild, and management and employees of the new firm will take a similar share.[13]

Westinghouse Electric Corporation agreed to sell its military and electronic systems to the Northrop Grumman Corporation for $3 billion. The main reason for this sale by Westinghouse was to reduce the debt it incurred with the $5.4 billion acquisition of CBS, Inc.

As mentioned previously, AT&T spun off NCR Corporation, the world's leading maker of automated teller machines because of heavy losses (NCR's value was reduced to about one-half its acquisition value). As part of its three-way breakup, AT&T earlier spun off Lucent Technologies, the successful telecommunications equipment company.

As part of the acquisition deal of Providian Corporation of Louisville, Kentucky, by Aegon N.V., a Dutch insurer in The Hague with some 20,000 employees and operations in Britain, Spain, and Hungary, Profidian Bancorp, a subsidiary of Providian, was spun off as an independent bank company concentrating on issuing VISA credit cards, securing credit card loans, and underwriting second mortgages.

In a move similar to AT&T's three-way split, General Instrument Corporation, the cable industry based in Chicago, plans to spinoff its coaxial cable and semiconductor operations into Next Level Systems Inc., a manufacturer of equipment for internet/data, modems, and other services, with $1.7 billion in revenue; Commscope, Inc., a cable business with $560 million in revenue; and General Semiconductor Company with $360 million in revenue.

Motorola Inc., a maker of semiconductors, advanced electronics systems, and wireless communications equipment based in Schaumburg, Illinois, split into two parts. One part sells Macintosh clones, portables, and servers, whereas the other part sells components to different manufacturers. Each part will be responsible for its own human resources, finance, and profitability.[14] Motorola also has an 18.7 percent stake in Groupe Bull, a French computer company.

WMX Technologies Inc. announced that it would sell $1.5 billion in assets so it can concentrate primarily in domestic waste management operations.

Raytheon Company based in Lexington, Massachusetts, plans to sell its appliance operations for about $1 billion in the wake of its $12.5 billion purchase of military-contracting businesses. Among the potential buyers are Maytag Corporation, Electrolux A.B. of Sweden, and Bosch–Siemens Hausgeräte G.m.b.H. of Germany.

Digital Equipment Corporation announced that it is setting up an independent company, Tracepoint Technology Inc., to produce software tools for computer programs using Microsoft Corporation's Windows 95 and other operating systems.

In some cases, firms bid for divisions rather than for entire companies, while other firms offer certain divisions for sale (mainly unsuccessful ones) to avoid bankruptcy or to acquire cash. Moreover, spinoffs, similar to those that followed the previous M&A boom of the 1980s, seemed to appear after the new M&A boom of the 1990s. Nevertheless, concentration through M&A deals continues with high speed, while spinoffs are relatively limited.

Chapter 9

Cross-Atlantic and Intra-EU Acquisitions

ACQUISITIONS OF EU FIRMS BY NAFTA COMPANIES

In order to increase their share in a unified EU market, American multinationals are aggressively opening more branches in Europe or acquiring EU firms. This increases investment in the old continent and improves economic conditions on both sides of the Atlantic.

Nevertheless, nationalistic politics remain strong in some EU member-nations as they are in a number of cases in the NAFTA countries. Politicians in France, Italy, and other EU countries present objections to acquisition deals over management control of certain industries. However, outside of strategic industries such as automotive companies and airline carriers, the number of acquisitions of EU firms by NAFTA corporations, mainly from the United States, continues to increase.

Harmonization policies in the EU are changing the complexion of NAFTA bilateral agreements with EU countries, as NAFTA firms and affiliates adjust their operations to new conditions before the doors of opportunity are closed. However, the countries of foreign-owned affiliates should provide reciprocal treatment to EU service and other companies.[1] From that point of view, related U.S. laws such as the Glass–Steagall Act, which prohibits banks from selling insurance, should change and adjust to those of the EU. On both sides of the Atlantic, changes in trade services' rules should be made in the context of the Uruguay Round, under the umbrella of the WTO, so that international harmonization standards prevail for all nations concerned.

From the standpoint of investment, it seems that American corporate executives and investors are more enthusiastic and aggressive in their expansionary policies than their European counterparts. A number of U.S. companies are entering joint ventures with European firms. Many U.S. firms establish subsidiaries or offices in the EU member-nations as well as in the Eastern European nations, while others try to enhance their European positions through mergers and acquisitions. The aim is to take advantage of the barrier-free market of the EU, regardless if integration plans are at times bogged down in debates over tax harmonization, exchange rate coordination, and other common regulations. The feeling is that there is a no-lose situation in preparing for Europe's attractive market. That is why American top management is soliciting advice from its overseas counterparts.

The rush of Japanese investment in Europe is another reason that American corporations are being forced to invest in the EU. Already, U.S. direct investment in the EU increased from about $70 billion in 1984 to more than $200 billion at present. Britain absorbs the largest proportion of such investment (about 40%), followed by Germany (20%), France (10%), and the rest of the EU countries with lower percentages. However, there is skepticism that American firms well established in Europe may support protectionism against Japan and even the United States. Such efforts may include limits of imports not only in the EU, but eventually in the reformed Eastern European countries, which are expected to conclude association agreements toward eventual membership with the EU.

From the standpoint of investment, it seems that America discovers the Old World in its new path of integration. Many NAFTA companies, mainly in the United States, have already moved into the EU and are exploiting the new opportunities. A number of executives are rushing to learn French, German, Spanish, and other EU languages in order to conduct business more effectively. Europe is considered one of America's hottest places of investment, and future operations are expected to increase dramatically.

An effective way to reduce and even eliminate barriers, not only between NAFTA and the EU but among many other nations in the world including the Eastern European countries, is through the rapidly growing cable networks. Already Cable News Network (CNN) of the United States airs in more than eighty nations including Britain, Germany, Greece (Hellas), Italy, and other EU countries as well as in some non-EU nations such as Hungary and Poland. As can be observed from visits to various European nations, such cable networks provide a very efficient means of cross-cultural influencing and liquidating various barriers among nations. However, there are major hurdles in the process of expansion such as lack of a common language and a homogeneous market, high costs for satellite time, obstacles from state-owned television operations, and shortages of homes with cable hookup.

Other U.S. cable operators in Europe include American Television and Communications, a subsidiary of Time Warner, concentrating its efforts in Britain, France, and Ireland; Cox Cable Communications, which owns half of Denmark's largest cable company; Pacific Telesis, U.S. West, and United Artists Entertainment, all with cable franchises, mainly in Britain, France, and Ireland.

Paramount Pictures Corporation, MCA, Inc., and MGM/UA Communications Co., all U.S. movie firms, set up a joint distribution subsidiary, United International Pictures, to avoid administrative duplications in Europe. However, the Treaty of Rome, which founded the EU, outlaws agreements among enterprises that restrict or distort competition in the community. Nevertheless, exceptions can be made as long as they benefit the consumers. Thus, the EU's executive body approved this venture by these three major U.S. movie companies after they complied with antitrust rules.

The Omnicom Group, the American parent company of DDB Needham and BBDO Worldwide, merged BMP Davidson Pearce, a Boase agency in London, with Needham's office in London into a new advertising company named BMP–DDB Needham. This friendly takeover was announced after Boulet Dru Dupuy Petit, a French advertising agency, dropped its bid for Boase's agency in London. Boase is the parent of Ammirati and Puris, a marketing research company in New York.

To overhaul its antiquated telephone network, Italy spent about $30 billion on telephone equipment. To achieve that goal, Italtel S.p.A., the Italian state-owned telecommunications company, formed a partnership with AT&T, which would have a large portion of Italtel's new equipment. This was quite an achievement for AT&T, which had difficulties putting a foot in Europe because of severe competition from Siemens A.G. of Germany, Alcatel N.V. of The Netherlands, and Ericsson Telefon of Sweden. The equal partnership of AT&T is expected to improve technological development and joint marketing in selling switches and other Italtel products outside Italy, particularly in other EU countries. Racing to build a global presence, Sprint has formed an alliance with Deutsche Telekom of Germany and France Telecom, in competition with British Telecommunication which agreed to acquire MCI of the United States.

To globalize its operations, Ford Motor Company of the United States is investing heavily in new plants in Western Europe, mainly in Spain and Portugal. Such investments concern the production of sophisticated electronic engine management systems, car audio equipment, on-board computers to manage engine performance, fuel economy and emissions control, and other automotive-related products. Ford is also considering a joint venture with Mazda Motor Corporation to produce vehicles in Europe, mainly compact cars in Germany. It owns about 25 percent of Mazda, which builds the Ford Probe at a Michigan plant.

In competition with General Motors Corporation (GM), the Ford Motor Company acquired the Jaguar P.L.C. of Britain for $2.38 billion. It plans to use its advanced technology to modernize the luxury, gas-guzzling Jaguar and to promote its top notch European products through Jaguar's network without competing directly with it. Ford also plans to buy a major share of Saab–Scania, a Swedish automotive and aerospace company. This linkup would enhance Ford's position in Europe regarding the production of cars for young professionals. Smaller moves during the past few years include Ford buying 75 percent of Aston Martin Lagonda; GM linking up with Group Lotus; and Chrysler buying Maserati and Lamborghini and linking up with Fiat S.p.A. of Italy.

To provide access to the European market, the Chrysler Corporation announced a joint venture with Renault, the French automotive maker, to build a sports utility vehicle in Europe. This youth-oriented, small vehicle (J.J.), to be built either in Spain or Portugal, will compete with the Suzuki and Samurai vehicles of Japan, and the Geo Tracker of GM. In this venture, advanced manufacturing technology would be used to reduce complexity and weight and save costs so that competitiveness would be raised. The venture is expected to increase the sales of jeeps and passenger cars in Europe's tough and demanding market which absorbs about 35,000 Chrysler cars per year. Germany, Austria, Switzerland, and France mainly provide the customers for these cars, which are guaranteed for 110,000 kilometers or three years. Chrysler also agreed with an Austrian firm to produce minivans for the European markets.

Avis Europe P.L.C., which became a separate unit after its U.S. parent company, Avis, Inc., was bought by investors and managers in 1986, agreed to be acquired by a consortium which includes GM and Avis. Avis Europe has more than 70,000 vehicles operating in Europe, the Middle East, and Africa, with annual revenues of about $1 billion. The deal, considered as a step in reuniting Avis Europe with its parent Avis, Inc., is expected to increase the number of GM cars sold in Europe.

In contrast to the European banks and large corporations, American big banks and companies are in a good position to serve a continental market. GM, Unisys, Digital Equipment, Ford, IBM, Citicorp, and American Express are some of the American companies already operating in all or in almost all EU countries. Volkswagen, Peugeot, Renault, Fiat, and many other large European companies primarily operate in their own national markets.

Although computers and office equipment production in the EU grows rapidly, U.S. computer companies sell more computers in every EU country than their European counterparts. IBM, Digital Equipment, Unisys, and Hewlett Packard are among the most successful and growing U.S. companies in the EU. Motivated by the fear of Japanese domination of semiconductor markets, IBM joined Siemens A.G. of Germany to develop memory chips capable of storing sixty-four million bits of information, or the equivalent of ten large novels, in a fingernail sliver of silicon. With this transatlantic collaboration, IBM participates in the operations of Project Jessi Consortium which includes Siemens, Philips N.V., and Thomson CSF.

Compaq Computer Corporation, a Houston-based company that makes business computers, is a fast-growing, major American enterprise in Europe. The surging European demand for modern marketing techniques is responsible for Compaq's success, evidenced by their surpassing of Olivetti and Apple and trailing only IBM in supplying business computers to Europe.

Compaq and other U.S. computer companies still have a technological edge over their European counterparts and are more successful in promoting faster and more flexible computers by setting up their own subsidiaries managed by European nationals instead of using distributors.

Coopers and Lybrand and Price Waterhouse, two of the world's leading accounting firms, with revenues of more than $13 billion, plan a global merger.

Moreover, the Morgan Stanley Group, Inc., Solomon Brothers, Inc., and other American investment banks expanded their operations in Paris, Madrid, Milan, Frankfurt, and other EU cities to help with M&As and other financial dealings throughout Europe. Also, Citicorp, with some 18,000 employees in Europe, introduced credit cards in Belgium, Germany, and Greece, and is acquiring banks all over Europe.

Furthermore, leveraged buy-outs are considered by the Great Atlantic and Pacific Tea Company (A&P), a leading American supermarket chain, and by Kohlberg, Kravis, Roberts and Company, an active investment banker, to acquire Gateway Corporation, a British retail food chain.

Also, KLP, an international sales promotion firm, acquired agencies and affiliates in some fourteen countries. Its holdings in the United States include Comart–KLP with clients Kraft General Foods, Field Research, Inc., and other research and development companies. Serious efforts are being made by this firm to reinforce its position in the EU, especially in Britain, France, and Germany, in order to put teeth into its pan-European marketing.

Two European companies, Philips N.V. of The Netherlands and Thomson CFS of France, formed a consortium with the National Broadcasting Company (NBC), which is owned by the U.S. General Electric Company, to develop a new television system that would produce detailed, high resolution pictures similar to those in movies. This joint venture or consolidation was considered better than the existing fragmentation in meeting the Japanese challenge in future competition in television technology.

To establish a solid European base, Pepsico, Inc. bought two British firms, Walker Crisps and Smiths Crisps, which were acquired from BSN, a French firm. BSN had purchased these two and three other companies recently from RJR Nabisco, Inc. Moreover, Pepsico, a worldwide corporation dealing with snack foods, Kentucky Fried Chicken, and Pizza Hut restaurants, as well as Pepsi and other soft drinks, already has snack food operations in Greece (Hellas), Italy, Portugal, and Spain. With these new purchases, and probably others in the future, it is expected that Pepsico will strengthen its position in Europe.

The subsidiaries of Pepsi Cola Company in Hellas (in Marousi, Loutraki, and Solonika) introduced an investment program for improvement and modernization of production and distribution. The program, which has been extended for twelve years, will introduce the production of metallic cans (at present imported from Holland) and plastic bottles, as well as embarking on advertising campaigns not only for Hellas but for Bulgaria, Serbia, Bosnia, and other Balkan countries.

The Coca-Cola Company, based in Atlanta, Georgia, acquired Societe Parisienne de Boissons Gazeuses of France in order to market Coca-Cola in France. In addition, it is building a large canning factory in Dunkirk, France.

General Electric Company, in addition to acquiring a large medical equipment company in France, is in the process of forming joint ventures in Britain for appliances and electronics, and in Spain for building plastic factories.

Owens–Illinois Inc., a glass and plastic container company based in Toledo, Ohio, agreed to buy Avir S.p.A., a glass container firm of Italy, for about $580 million.

The Whirlpool Corporation formed a joint venture with Philips N.V. of Holland to enlarge its appliance and electronics markets in Europe.

Also, Donald Trump, the New York developer, agreed to acquire a 20 percent interest in the Wilshire Center Partnership of Power Corporation, P.L.C. of Ireland.

Recent cross-border M&A deals of U.S. companies in the EU include Federal-Mogul Company targeting T&N, a British auto supplier worth about $2 billion; Carnival Corporation targeting Airtours of Britain, a travel company worth $309 million; Chiron Company targeting Unit of Hoechst of Germany, a biotechnology firm worth $118 million for a 49 percent stake; Advent International targeting Docter-Optic of Germany, an industrial optics firm worth $12 million; and Stratton Group targeting AOOT, a Russian paper firm. Another cross-border M&A deal involves Fairfax Financial of Canada which is targeting unit of Skandia of Sweden, an insurance company worth $290 million.

Moreover, Robert Bosch acquired the hydraulic and antilock braking businesses of Allied Signal for $1.5 billion. Total sales of Allied Signal are about $14 billion a year, more than $2 billion of which belonged to the businesses sold to Bosch.

Among the fourteen nations to which U.S. West Company provides telephone, advanced wireless communications, and other cable and switching services are a number of EU countries, including Britain, France, The Netherlands, Spain, and Sweden. The Central and Southwest Corporation, an electric company in Dallas, agreed to pay $2.6 billion to buy the Seaboard P.L.C., a utility company of Britain. Service Corporation International, America's largest chain of funeral homes, bought Lyonnaise des Eaux in France, Europe's largest funeral business, and Service Corporation bought two British funeral chains, introducing a competitive zeal in these industries.

Magna International Inc., a Canadian automotive parts company, will sell 80 percent of its two German units to TRW Inc., based in Cleveland.

The TrizecHahn Corporation, a large Toronto-based developer that was formed in 1996 from the merger of the Horsham Corporation and the Trizec Corporation Ltd., agreed to buy commercial real estate in Germany and Britain from Advanta Management A.G.

Raleign Corporation of Vancouver agreed to acquire the Keg Restaurant chain from Whitbread P.L.C. of London.

The New Corporation of Rupert Murdoch is negotiating with the Olympic Games Committee to buy the European rights to broadcast the Olympic Games from 2000 to 2008 for $2 billion, as is the European Broadcast Union as well. In December 1995, General Electric Company agreed to pay $2.3 billion for the U.S. rights to broadcast the Olympics in 2004, 2006, and 2008.

Merrill Lynch and Company of the United States is negotiating to acquire F. G. Inversiones Bursatiles, the largest brokerage company in Spain. F. G. Inversiones controls about 7 percent of trading operations in Spain's four stock exchanges.

Morton International, Inc., the leading salt producer in the United States and Canada, acquired Cie. des Salins du Midi et des Salines de l'Est, a French salt company, for $290 million. Also, Morton combined its air bag operation, with $1.4 billion in annual sales, with that of the Swedish rival, Autoliv AB, so that Morton's chemical and salt business sales would be about $2.8 billion annually.

Allied Signal Aerospace, a maker of wheels and aircraft parts in California, purchased the remaining stake from two French companies, Paribas, which owned 4 percent, and SA des Usines Chausson, which owned 8 percent.

DePuy Inc., a maker of orthopedic supplies based in Warsaw, Indiana, agreed to buy an 89.6 percent interest in Landanger–Camus, another orthopedic products maker in France.

Dana Corporation, an auto parts firm in Ohio, has warehouse distribution operations in Portugal, The Netherlands, and Britain, and plans to sell some of them to Partco Group P.L.C.

Interim Services Inc. of Florida, with some 1,000 offices in North America and Europe, agreed to buy Michael Page Group of Britain. They both deal with staffing and employment services worldwide. Moreover, Hicks, Muse, Tate, and Furst Inc., a Dallas-based leveraged buy-out specialist, plans to buy Forward Group, a British electronics manufacturer.

The Sylvan Learning Systems, Inc. in Columbia, Maryland, agreed to acquire Wall Street Institute International, a franchise of English language learning centers in France, Germany, Italy, Spain, Mexico, and other countries, for $26 million.

Midland's Electricity of the United Kingdom accepted an all-cash bid from General Public Utilities (GPU) of New Jersey for £1.7 billion, in partnership with U.S. Utility Cinergy of Cincinnati.[2]

Attracted by favorable tax rates and lower labor costs, a number of U.S., Canadian, German, Japanese, and South Korean companies, among others, are investing in new or old factories all over Britain. They include Compaq, Black and Decker, and Johnson Controls of the United States; Northern Telecom of Canada; Siemens of Germany, which is building a huge $1.7 billion semiconductor plant; NEC, Fujitsu, Nissan, and Toyota of Japan. Between 1986 and 1993, the United States invested 7.5 times as much in Britain than it invested in Germany, and in 1993, U.S. direct investment in Britain was 35 percent of total investment in Europe and 17.4 percent of worldwide investment.

The Hersey Foods Corporation of North America agreed to sell its European candy lines to the Finnish Food Company, as well as to the German praline manufacturer GuBor, and the Italian Sperlari companies to Huhtamaki Candy Company.

During the period of 1951–1991, U.S. direct investment in Britain amounted to 36.1 percent of that in the EU, whereas Japanese direct investment in Britain, in the period of 1982–1991, was 40.9 percent of that in the EU. Moreover, German net direct investment in Britain between 1982 and 1991 was 12.6 percent of German investment abroad.[3]

Alongside the British industrial dinosaurs such as coal mines, shipyards, and steel mills, which helped develop the Industrial Revolution, a number of foreign projects have been established (434 in the 1995 fiscal year alone, creating 88,000 jobs). This investment growth was a result of the structural reforms initiated by Margaret Thatcher in 1979 and by John Major in 1991, as well as the cooperation of labor unions, companies, local government agencies, and universities. Also, policies resisting EU regulations protecting labor, as well as government intervention, encouraged free market forces and foreign investment. Moreover, the use of English as the first or second language by international companies has helped foreign investment in Britain, which is starting to resemble the United States from the standpoint of financial and investment reforms.

The fever of joint ventures, mergers, and acquisitions is expected to continue in the future as the EU and other non-EU European nations move toward closer economic cooperation and integration.

ACQUISITION OF NAFTA FIRMS BY EU COMPANIES

Not only are American firms establishing subsidiaries in the EU, but Western European companies are also moving into the NAFTA markets. Fat with cash and credit, EU companies initially search for acquisitions within Europe, and afterward, move to NAFTA countries and the rest of the world.

Among the largest EU acquisitions of U.S. corporations during the last decade are as follows: Standard Oil Company by British Petroleum Company; Pillsbury Company by Grand Metropolitan P.L.C. of Britain; Farmers Group by BAT Industries of Britain; Shell Oil Company by Royal Dutch/ Shell Group of The Netherlands; Chesebrough–Ponds, Inc. by Unilever N.V. of The Netherlands; Texas Gulf, Inc. by Société Nationale Elf Aquitaine of France; Celanese Corporation by Hoechst A.G. of Germany.[4]

Hanson P.L.C., a British conglomerate, has a number of operations on each side of the Atlantic. It produces various products from greeting cards, bricks, tobacco, and fertilizer in Britain to fish processing, whirlpool baths, building products, chemicals, and Smith Corona typewriters in the United States. It has at its disposal large amounts of cash, and consequently is searching for big takeovers, especially leveraged buy-outs. Generally, Hanson has been using debt, secured against the assets of the companies bought, and not junk bonds, to buy the new companies. Its annual profits are estimated at $1.5 billion, about half of which comes from the United States.[5]

After the unsuccessful offer by Minorco S.A., Hanson P.L.C. acquired Consolidated Gold Fields P.L.C., the world's second largest gold producer. This was the largest takeover in British history. Consolidated Gold Fields, which opposed a hostile takeover by Minorco and won a U.S. court suit prohibiting the takeover on the grounds of lessening competition, owns 49 percent of Newmont Mining Company, the largest gold producer in America.

Hanson Industries, the British conglomerate's American arm, is also buying shares of other companies, primarily for takeovers of other firms and also for investment purposes, such as consolidated Gold Fields P.L.C., which owns 49 percent of Newmont Mining Company the largest gold producer in America, Cummins Engine Company of Indiana, SCM Corporation of California, and Kidde, Inc. of New Jersey. At times, Hanson buys shares and sells them later for a profit, as happened with Milton Bradley, Gulf Resources, Avon Mills, and Dan River, and it also invests in companies that are under attack by other takeover aggressors.

Faced with labor unions and weakened management, EU companies have moved investment primarily into the fertile U.S. markets. With European integration, further investment in the EU is expected. Similar mutual movements can be observed in the law profession, as lawyers are eager to follow the rapidly growing financial investment dealings of their clients on both sides of the Atlantic. For instance, Italian lawyers played an important role in the partial financing of Kohlberg's acquisition of Duracell.

Sir James M. Goldsmith, the buccaneering Anglo–French financier, after a decade of raiding and breaking U.S. conglomerates, launched a series of bids for London-based BAT Industries P.L.C., the owner of Saks Fifth Avenue, Farmers Group Insurance, Kool and Barclay Cigarettes, Marshall Fields, and Horten, as well as other firms in North America, Europe, and elsewhere. Part of the financing consisted of debt, distributed by Drexel Burnham Lambert, Inc. and Bankers Trust Company. The BAT deal is forcing European companies to rethink their survival strategies and their independence from hostile takeovers. Moreover, regulators worry that EU companies will be too debt-laden to compete effectively in the integrated EU market and that corporate raiders may squeeze companies for short-term profits, and not for investment and a more competitive standing.

In the BAT deal, joining in were Banque Paribas, Rothschild, Gie Banque of France, General Electric Company P.L.C. of Britain, Pargesa of Switzerland, and the Agnelli family of Italy.

WPP Group P.L.C., a large British advertising firm, bought the Thompson Company and the Ogilvy Group, two famous American advertising firms. Its operations have been expanded to public relations, market research, sales promotion, graphic design, business entertainment, and audio–visual communications. Through friendly and hostile takeovers, WPP has invaded America's Madison Avenue, which is gradually losing its long-unchallenged global advertising domination. WPP, together with Saatchi and Saatchi P.L.C., another British advertising firm, control about $30 billion or 10 percent of the world's spending on marketing.

Harrisons and Crosfield Company, which operates the Harcros building business in Britain, shifted its interests away from commodity trading and plantations to chemicals, timber, and builders of merchant markets. In its effort to expand, it bought Moore's Business Forms from Grossmans, Inc., which has some fifty-nine outlets primarily in the states of Maryland, Ohio, Pennsylvania, and Virginia. Harrisons and Crosfield, which also has interests in Australia, first moved into the United States in 1988 when it acquired Woodburys Company, a timber and building supplies firm with operations in New York and Vermont. A new holding company, Harcros Lumber and Building Supplies, was formed for the enlarged U.S. market.

To cope with the competitive market of the EU and the growing global route networks, European airline carriers prefer more links with American carriers. The limit permitted under U.S. Transportation Department regulations is 25 percent for foreign ownership of American airlines. Already, British Airways, a profitable carrier since its privatization in 1987, is a partial owner of Apollo, a computer reservation system of United Airlines that facilitates customers for both carriers. Also, KLM Royal Dutch Airlines acquired a large stake of Northwest Airlines, while the Scandinavian Airlines Systems acquired close to 10 percent of Texas Air Corporation. Nevertheless, such transactions and takeovers of large U.S. airlines raise the concern of the U.S. Department of Transportation to reduce or stop too much control by foreign interests.

Cadbury Schweppes P.L.C., a British soft drink company, agreed to buy Crush International, a beverage branch of Proctor and Gamble Company, a Cincinnati-based firm. With this acquisition, Cadbury expands business not only to North America and Europe, but also to the Middle East, Latin America, and Africa. Thus, the share of the company in the U.S. soft drink market is estimated at 5 percent, and in Canada, 15 percent.

One of the fastest growing companies in telecommunications is British Telecommunications P.L.C. (BT). It acquired ITT Dialcom, Inc., a leading U.S. electronic mail service, and 51 percent of Mitel Corporation, a Canadian supplier of telephone equipment. Also, it bought 80 percent of Metrocast, a U.S. national paging system; 22 percent of McCaw Cellular Communications, a U.S. mobile telephone operator; Tymnet; and other McDonnell Douglas data communications operations. Furthermore, BT is also expected to move aggressively into Germany and other EU countries.

Recently, BT announced its $20 billion acquisition of the MCI Communications Corporation, turning this utility into the world's fourth largest telecommunications enterprise. BT, with 120,000 employees, would absorb 57,000 employees of MCI. After its privatization in 1986, it still has some 87 percent of the British market and after the EU deregulation beginning 1 January 1998, BT is expected to obtain licenses and partners in Germany, Sweden, The Netherlands, and other European countries. On the other side, AT&T Corporation plans to win a significant share in the European Internet market.[6] However, Worldcom Inc. offered $33.9 billion for MCI, which is far more than the amount agreed on with BT. If this bid succeeds, it will deprive BT of a prize U.S. catch, whereas similar European firms will face severe competition. Furthermore, GTE Corporation offered $28 billion in cash for MCI and the takeover battle continues.

On the other hand, Vendex, the largest retail firm in The Netherlands, invested in the U.S. Dillard Department Stores, which expanded from 44 to 150 stores. Dillard, the nation's largest family-owned retail firm, wants to buy back Vendex's stake of 41 percent out of the fear that it may lose its majority position to this Dutch company, which already owns 50 percent of B. Dalton Booksellers, the U.S. book chain and computer programming retailer. Similar fears that foreign investment in the fertile market of NAFTA may lead to takeovers are expressed by other American managements.

Marks and Spenser, Britain's largest retailer, bought Brooks Brothers, the oldest U.S. clothing retailer. Further expansion of this firm, with 550 stores worldwide and $7.8 billion in annual sales, is planned with new stores in Paris, London, and Dusseldorf, as well as in the United States. The focus will be on women's classic fashions, mainly flannel skirts, tailored shirts, and blazers.

Siebe P.L.C., a British engineering firm, agreed to acquire Foxboro Company, a Massachusetts industrial controls firm.

Ladbroke Group P.L.C., a London operator of resorts and hotels, is interested in managing contracts for some American hotels of the Hilton Hotels Corporation based in Beverly Hills, California.

Bass P.L.C., a British brewer with many pubs and other food and drink interests in Europe and elsewhere, agreed with the Holiday Corporation to buy its Holiday Inn hotel chain. Previously, Holiday Corporation borrowed heavily to pay the stockholders in order to avert a takeover by Donald Trump, the New York developer. This deal with Bass would help Holiday Corporation pay back part of its debt. Bass will pick up fifty-five Holiday Inn hotels and franchises and other agreements covering some 1,400 hotels in North America.

Grand Metropolitan, a British food and drinks firm, recently acquired Pillsbury, the owner of Green Giant Vegetables and Burger King, and also purchased Mont La Salle, a large vineyard in California.

Suter P.L.C., a British holding company, acquired a 6 percent stake in Sudbury Inc., a Cleveland manufacturer, for investment purposes. It appears that, because of favorable tax and accounting rules, there is a wave of British acquisitions of American companies, particularly in advertising and other service industries.

BTR, the industrial conglomerate, plans to accelerate divestment of its nonmanufacturing operation in North America, including polymers and construction operations.

Unilever Group, the British–Dutch giant of consumer goods, agreed to buy two U.S. cosmetics firms, Fabergè, Inc. and Elizabeth Arden. The deal is the biggest transatlantic takeover of this sort by European firms and makes Unilever a close rival of Avon Products, Inc. of the United States, L'Oréal of France, and Shisieido Co. of Japan.

Mark IV Industries, Inc., a New York company, agreed to sell its Blackstone Corporation subsidiary to Valeo S.A., the second largest automotive parts firm in Paris. In its aggressive takeover policy, it plans to use the money for additional acquisitions.

Axa Midi Assurances of France filed applications in nine American states to acquire Farmers Group, Inc. Hoylake Group agreed to sell Farmers Group to Axa if the hostile takeover of BAT Industries, the parent of Farmers Group, is concluded.

Pechinery, a French aluminum company, bought the American Can Company from Triangle Industries, Inc. and, as a result, became the number one packaging company. Other similar moves are expected from Groupe Bull, a French state-controlled computer company, and from many other EU firms. From that standpoint, corporate Europe may soon become equivalent to corporate America on an international level.

Carrefour S.A., a French chain of hypermarkets, moved with aggressive marketing into Philadelphia, Cincinnati, and other places in the United States. Carrefour, which means crossroads in French, also has a 22 percent share in the Costco Wholesale Corporation which has a number of discount warehouse stores on the West Coast, in addition to a number of stores in Spain, Brazil, and Argentina. The company expects rapid growth through product diversification and international expansion in the EU and other countries.

Compagnie de Saint-Gobain, a French conglomerate, agreed to acquire Norton Company, an engineering materials firm in Massachusetts. Hachette S.A., a large French publishing firm, acquired Grolier, Inc., a publishing company in Connecticut. Moreover, the U.S. government decided to permit the acquisition of three divisions of Fairchild Industries, dealing with communications and electronics control systems and space, by Marta S.A. of France. The decision was based on the results of an investigation by the Committee on Foreign Investment in the United States concerning foreign ownership. Furthermore, Sodexho Alliance, the French contract catering group, and Marriott International agreed to combine their North American businesses in a deal worth about $2 billion.

Owners and executives of Fiat, Olivetti, Feruzze, Fininvest, and the Gartini Group of Italy are expanding their operations not only in Europe but in the United States as well. Thus, Fiat, in cooperation with Chrysler Motors Company, is promoting its luxury car, the Alfa Romeo, in the U.S. market.

Pirelli S.p.A., a large Italian tire company, acquired the Armtek Corporation tire operations, and plans to buy Goodyear Tire and Rubber Company of the United States. Finmeccanica Società Finanziaria per Aziona, a high technology holding company in Italy, agreed to buy the Bailey Controls operations of a Babcock and Wilcox unit which belongs to McDermott International, Inc. Bailey supplies diagnostic and computer system to chemical, paper, and electric utility industries. Bennetton Group S.p.A. of Italy formed a joint venture with Sports, Inc. of the United States and Marubeni Corporation of Japan to produce and market shoes for women all over the world.

Henkel, a German firm, acquired the Emery division of America's Quantum Chemical, which is only one of more than forty acquisitions it has made within the last few years.

To strengthen its position in American and international markets, Siemens A.G. of Germany agreed with IBM of the United States to develop advanced computer memory chips for the 1990s. Also, Siemens acquired a 10 percent stake in the U.S. automotive supplier Breed Technologies Inc. by buying newly issued shares.

A Belgium supermarket, GIB, was permitted by American authorities to buy the remaining 42.7 percent of the share of its U.S. subsidiary known as Scoty. There are some 160 Scoty stores in Florida alone. Scoty chain stores in other places sell tools, construction material, woodwork, and other products.

The Algemain Bank of The Netherlands acquired the Cancorp of Chicago.

L. M. Ericsson A.B., a large Swedish telecommunications firm with units in Spain, Denmark, and other European nations, agreed with General Electric Company, a giant U.S. firm with many manufacturing and distribution units in North America, to form a joint venture called Ericsson–G.E. Mobile Communications, in which Ericsson will hold a 60 percent stake. With this deal, both companies would have access to the huge digital cellular technology and communication systems markets of Europe and North America.

To slow the pace of mergers and buy-outs and to put a damper on stock prices, the U.S. Congress is considering legislation to eliminate the corporate tax deduction for non-cash interest payments on junk bonds which sometimes are termed fake wampum. Also, the U.S. Congress granted a three-year takeover protection to Conrail, a railroad company, which lately is under takeover consideration by CSX Corporation in competition with Norfolk Southern Corporation.

On the other hand, the U.S. Congress is also considering repealing the Glass–Steagall Act of 1933 that prevents banks from owning securities companies as concern grows over greater European and Japanese competition.

Some recent important acquisitions are as follows: Aegeon N.V., an insurance company of The Netherlands, bought the insurance business of the Providian Corporation of the United States in Louisville, Kentucky, for $2.62 billion. Strong competition from banks and mutual funds for Cife insurance customers is forcing consolidations not only domestically but internationally as well.

Incentive A.B., a Swedish holding company that controls 58 percent of the votes in Gambro A.B., a medical equipment company, offered to buy the rest of Gambro for $1.56 billion (10.3 billion kronor). The offer was $23.47 for each B share and $25.82 for each A share, which are controlled by the Grafoord family heirs, the founders of the company. The American depository receipts of Gambro soared to $23.125, or 20 percent higher, as a result of the offer.

Luxottica, an Italian eyewear company, acquired U.S. Shoe in a successful $1.4 billion hostile takeover. In contrast to Nine West, a U.S. shoe retailer that made an unsolicited offer for the footwear division of U.S. Shoe Company, Luxottica bought the whole company.

John A. Benckiser G.m.b.H., a German private cosmetic firm founded in 1823 with annual sales of around $3.4 billion, offered to buy Maybelline Inc., the American cosmetics company, for more than $660 million, which L'Oréal S.A. of France had offered previously. However, L'Oréal, the world's largest cosmetics company, already has a binding agreement with Wassestein Perella and Company, a merchant bank in New York, to buy 30 percent of its stake in Maybelline, which complicates the deal.[7]

Germany's Hoechst A.G. and Rho–Poulenc Rorer of the United States combined their plasma protein businesses in a new fifty–fifty venture, which is based in King of Prussia, Pennsylvania, and known as Centeon. It became the largest provider of plasma protein products with sales of about $1.2 billion annually.

Reckitt and Colman, the London-based maker of Woolite, has consolidated $230 million in advertising with McCann–Erickson Worldwide in New York.

Breaking with Spain's patriarchal tradition, Banco Santander, the largest bank in Spain with assets of about $150 billion, is expanding to former colonies in the Western Hemisphere. Thus, in October 1996, Banco Santander took control of Mexico's fourth largest bank, Banco Mexicano, for $425 million.

The Lucas Varity P.L.C. of Britain, an automotive and aerospace parts manufacturer, acquired S.B.C. Ltd. and Kinefic Parts Manufacturing Inc., a distributor of replacement automotive parts, for an undisclosed sum. Lucas Varity, recently formed by a merger of Lucas Industries P.L.C. and the Varity Corporation of Buffalo, has annual sales of about $7 billion.

In competition with twelve other shipping companies from the United States and Canada, the Hellenic shipping company Sotiris Emmanuil acquired the shipyards of Quinsi of Boston for $55 million, which had not been in operation for a decade. The new shipyards, partially subsidized by the federal government, would apply modern technology to the construction of commercial ships, creating about 2,000 jobs. Already, Mr. Emmanuil, a graduate of M.I.T. and former president of Elefsina Shipyards, has agreed to construct six ships for the Papalexis Company of London.

Several European automakers have established subsidiaries in the United States. BMW is building a factory near Greer, South Carolina, worth $400 million to produce small sedans and sports cars. Mercedes-Benz has a factory near Vance,

Alabama, where sport-utility vehicles are manufactured. Volvo, the Swedish automobile maker is considering sites for factories in Georgia and the Carolinas. High wages demanded by labor in their home countries, weak unions in the southwestern United States and large NAFTA markets are the main reasons for movement to the United States by the European automakers.

Camas, Britain's large aggregate and concrete block supplier, continues its expansion in the United States with the purchase of Model Stone, worth $30 million. Model Stone operates four U.S. mixed concrete plants in addition to one in Minneapolis.[8]

HSBC Holdings P.L.C., a bank holding company based in London, agreed to acquire a 19.9 percent stake in Grupo Financiero Serfin of Mexico, worth $300 million.

Sabena S.A. (the Belgian national airline), Austrian Airlines, and Swissair A.G. agreed to deepen their pact with Delta Air Lines of the United States in order to increase their share in the transatlantic market. Swissair owns a 49.5 percent stake of Sabena and 10 percent of Austrian Airlines.

ACQUISITIONS AMONG EU COUNTRIES

As global competition stiffens, corporate Europe is tuning up, through restructuring and takeovers, in order to be able to compete with NAFTA and the Asian–Pacific Rim. British, French, Italian, and German companies are issuing new equity or debt to carry out ambitious acquisition plans similar to those in the United States. The waves of deregulation and privatization in Europe will intensify M&As and the number of giant companies in Europe is expected to rise significantly.

The merger mania, which has prevailed in the United States for some years, has struck Europe. The number of M&As by EU companies has been increasing dramatically year after year. The removal of internal barriers and the growing competition from American and Japanese firms encourage European companies to merge with or acquire other companies in order to keep and increase their competitive edge against their external counterparts.

There are many mergers and acquisitions of major companies in Europe and even more involving small- and medium-sized companies, mainly in Britain and Germany. As American companies invest heavily in Europe, EU corporations, from London and Madrid to Rome and Athens, use the growth-by-acquisitions strategy, instead of investing in new plants the old-fashioned way.

It seems that the spillover effect in Europe from big LBOs is growing. Such buy-outs embrace telecommunications, power generation, consumer electronics, military contracts, and many other products and activities. To support friendly or hostile takeovers and LBOs in general, American-style debt financing has been introduced. Not only bank loans but junk bonds are used to fuel big corporate takeovers.

Yet EU member-nations have their own laws and regulations regarding protection of competition against monopolization of the market and unfair price fixing and quantity restrictions. To supervise the implementation of these laws, they have special institutions or public commissions, such as the Monopolies and Mergers Commission of Britain, that do not permit takeovers and mergers if they reduce competition and lead to monopolistic practices.

Although there is no specific control provision in the Treaty of Rome, Articles 85 and 86 of the Treaty, which deal with competition, can be applied to M&As, in addition to national competition laws of EU member-nations.

Recently, the EU Commission put forward a proposal to amend the Merger Control Regulation of 1989, which deals with lowering the economic threshholds to 3 billion ECUs (combined worldwide turnover) and 150 million ECUs (EU-wide turnover of at least two parties), compared to 5 billion ECUs and 250 million ECUs, respectively, up to now. Regarding the multiple filings, merger control review in more than two member-nations would also fall within the exclusive jurisdiction of the Commission with thresholds of 2 billion ECUs (worldwide turnover) and 100 million ECUs (EU-wide turnover). A number of M&As between EU members as well as EU and non-EU members have been cleared or are under consideration by the commission under the Merger and Control Regulations.

More than fifty directives have been issued by the EU that affect internal services industries. They include financial services (banking, securities, insurance, and investment consultancy); transport services (air, shipping, and roads); information services (computer programs, broadcasting, and advertising); tourism, educational, and professional services (training, research, medical practice, engineering, and accounting). Other directives deal with government procurement services (including public works), residence permits, and the mutual recognition of college diplomas.

Under the pressure of large U.S. and Japanese companies, the EU policymakers are trying to develop a common policy of cross-border takeovers to have member-nations surrender much of their individual power on industrial policy. Although Britain and Germany argue that such power may be abused by the EU commissioners to the detriment of competition in related industries, France and other EU members prefer to have the commissioners' approval of large mergers as well as to have them monitor the incursions from other countries, notably the United States and Japan. Such policies are related to present trends of deregulation and privatization in the EU industries, particularly in aviation, where many airlines now operate mainly in the public sector.

To catch up with American and Japanese technology, Europeans are forming cooperative ventures and consortiums to build planes, missiles, advanced computers, new television systems, and other competitive products. Thus, a four-nation consortium of the EU-developed Airbus Industries, the second-largest aircraft company in the world after Boeing. Also, three semiconductor firms (Siemens of Germany, Philips of Holland, and SGS–Thomson, a French–Italian company) launched a program to build the most advanced computer chip in the world, with more megabytes of capacity, compared to those of the United States and Japan. Because antitrust laws in Europe are looser than in the United States, cooperation in research and other ventures is more effective in avoiding duplication by individual national projects.

Through effective management, acquisitions, and creations of new enterprises throughout the EU, European company owners and successful managers (Euro-capitalists) speed up business expansion not only in the EU but in Eastern Europe as well. They are more successful in promoting economic development and making European integration a reality. They achieve better results than politicians, who have been trying for decades to realize integration. Competition from big firms in the United States and Japan push Euro-capitalists into innovation, better business organization, and modernization.

In the EU, Articles 1, 9, 21, and 22 of the Merger Regulation deal with concentrations between undertakings and do not permit mergers and acquisitions which restrict competition. A concentration exists where two or more previously independent undertakings merge and where one or more undertakings acquire direct or indirect control of the whole or parts of other undertakings. The Commission, subject to review by the Court of Justice, has sole competence to make related decisions, and not the member-nations.

Thus, the European Commission fined Bayer A.G., the German drug maker, $3.9 million because it held back supplies of *adalat*, a drug used in cardiovascular treatments, from French and Spanish traders to prevent them from exporting the drug to Britain where prices are higher. The Commission ruled that this is a violation of the antitrust law.

To facilitate traveling and encourage competition, the EU is gradually eliminating airline monopolies over the skies of member-nations. Thus, Alitalia, the Italian airline, started flying over France when France opened its skies to competition on 2 January 1996.

Intra-EU cross-investment and acquisitions are expected to increase significantly. For example, Volvo A.B. of Sweden and Renault Company, a French state-owned automotive firm which has become partially privatized recently, each agreed they own 45 percent of the truck operations of each other. Volvo and Enasa (an equivalent Spanish firm) recently agreed to a similar joint venture. Electrolux A.B. of Sweden agreed to acquire up to 20 percent of the shares of AEG Hausgerate A.G., a unit of Daimler–Benz A.G. of Germany, for expansion in the production of washing machines, dishwashers, and other appliances. However, such M&As may lead to the concentration of economic power and monopolistic capitalism, away from the "democratization of capital" and people's capitalism.

As the EU gradually removes trade and investment barriers, French companies and banks adjust themselves to new competitive conditions through joint ventures, mergers, and other corporate arrangements. Thus, there are efforts to rearrange and modernize the Société Générale, France's largest non-state bank, with $150 billion in assets, by selling a portion of the shares to other investment groups including state-owned companies. Although there are allegations of insider trading, this bank, which was privatized in 1987, is expected to improve and expand operations not only in France but also in other EU countries.

British Airlines, which was privatized in 1987, and KLM Royal Dutch Airlines, which is 38 percent owned by the Dutch government, each plan to buy 20 percent of the shares of Sabena Airlines, 54 percent of which is owned by the Belgian government. This consolidation of three major European airlines will be the largest cross-border alliance in the airline industry on the old continent.

It is recognized that, through cooperation, the EU computer industries may advance and survive competition from their American and Japanese counterparts. Although a joint venture of French, German, and Dutch computer companies did not succeed in the 1970s, expectations are that, under the EU's common esprit program of a single European market, they will reorganize and be more competitive in the future.

Through standardization and systems integration, the new computers (mainly of the Unix operating system) would allow software from different firms to run on them. According to the Yankee Group, a company of U.S. computer analysts, European companies making medium-sized computers would be able to withstand competition by non-EU companies, especially in data and telecommunication systems.

To overcome the antimonopoly regulations of the British government, General Electric Company P.L.C. of Britain and Siemen A.G. of Germany revised their joint bid for a hostile takeover of Plessey Company of Britain. Under the new bid, a number of Plessey military and telecommunications businesses would be owned by one bidder, not jointly by the above bidders. Also, Daimler–Benz of Germany has acquired Freightliner, and Renault of France has 45 percent ownership of Mack Trucks.

In addition to the acquisition of the British Rowntree P.L.C. and the Italian Buitoni S.p.A. by Nestlé, Rhône–Poulenc, a French pharmaceutical firm, acquired Nattermann, another pharmaceutical firm, of Germany. This is one of six other acquisitions in Europe and another six in the United States (including Stauffer Chemical) over the last few years.

The BAT Industries of Britain, with an American insurance subsidiary, and the Zurich Group of Switzerland plan to merge their insurance and financial service business into a new firm worth $30 billion. Also, Guinness P.L.C., the beverage giant, and Grand Metropolitan P.L.C. moved closer to their planned $20 billion merger after they gained approval from the European Commission. Reed Elsevier, a British–Dutch publisher, plans to merge with its Dutch competitor, Walters Kluwer.

The Compagnie de Suez and the Lyonnaise des Eaux S.A. plan to merge and create a giant industrial company in France worth $14 billion. Moreover, Axa

S.A. and Union Assurances de Paris, France's two big insurance companies, united in a $10 billion merger. AGF of France is under a $9 billion hostile bid by Generali, a large Italian insurance company. Lafarge S.A., a French building-materials company, bid $2.8 billion for a British rival, Redland P.L.C.

The Thomson Group in France acquired Telefunken, the German electronics powerhouse, and Mostek, a U.S. semiconductor firm. Also, the Thomson Group bought Thorn–EMI of Britain and formed a semiconductor joint venture with S.G.S. Microelectronics S.p.A. of Italy. On the other hand, Alcatel Alsthom S.A. and Dassault Industries plan to bid for the state's majority stake in Thomson–CSF, as does Lagardène Company of France.

Schneider S.A., a French construction and electronics company, acquired Télémecanique Electrique S.A., a French electronics firm. Also, the German Rheinisch–Westfoelisches Elektrizitaetswerk A.G. bought Deutsche Texaco A.G., a German subsidiary of Texaco.

The trend toward acquisitions is supported by European banks, such as the Banque Paribas and Banque Indosuez in Paris, Mediobanca in Milan, as well as U.S. banks, such as Morgan Stanley. Moreover, banks themselves, such as Banco Central and Banco Español de Credito (the largest banks in Spain), practice M&As or have large holdings in industrial companies, especially in Germany. To avoid conflicts with national antitrust laws, the EU is moving toward introducing common regulations on disclosures of shareholdings above certain percentages as member-nations have, except Italy, Spain, and Greece (Hellas). Moreover, in their efforts toward democratization and industry privatization, Eastern European countries are introducing similar regulations.

The Hypo-Bank and Vereinsbank of Germany merged and created a $412-billion behemoth, second only to Deutsche Bank.

In order to survive international competition, Krupp–Hoesch, a German steelmaker, plans a takeover of Thyssen A.G. for $8.1 billion. There are fears, though, that the result would be the loss of some 30,000 jobs in such a merger of these two companies, which control about 70 percent of German steel production. Moreover, the German firm Mannesmann A.G. agreed to join forces with Olivetti S.p.A. in the Italian mobile phone market.

The Angelli and Marzotto families are merging assets to create the Gruppo Industriale Marzotto (G.I.M.) with 21,000 workers and $4.84 billion revenue. In this large conglomerate of mainly clothing, publishing, and banking industries, Fiat S.p.A., which is controlled by the Angelli family, will hold a 17 percent stake, and the Marzotto family will take 12.4 percent and Mediobanca.[9] Moreover, Ifil S.p.A., an Angelli company of Italy, and Assurances Générales de France S.A. bid $5.4 billion for Worms & Cie, the French sugar, paper, and insurance company.

The Irish Distillers Group P.L.C., almost a monopoly in Ireland's whisky market, was considering a friendly takeover by Pernod–Ricard S.A., a famous wine company in France. Grand Metropolitan P.L.C., a large British hotel and liquor company, was also in competition for the takeover of Irish

Distillers. However, the European Commission, which is the executive branch of the EU, blocked this effort as monopolistic since it aimed to fix the market price of Irish Distillers' products.

In the tourist sector, the European integration is encouraging tour operators to expand across borders, leading to M&As in that industry. Thus, TUI, the major German package tour operator, acquired 40 percent of ARKE, the largest tour company in The Netherlands. Earlier, it had acquired control of Robinson Club, another German tour company, and it has interests in Touropa, a French tour agency. In France, Club Aquarious teamed up with Go Voyages, which Havas merged with Wagons Lits Tourisme. They plan to build vacation villages to compete with Club Med Inc., which pioneered the industry back in 1960. Because of troubles at its 74 percent-owned U.S. subsidiary, Club Med turned to expansion in Europe and acquired a 34 percent stake in Nouvelles Frontières Touraventure to build new villages and to start a joint airline venture. In any case, competition among large tour operators may lead to price wars in Europe and across the Atlantic to the benefit of EU and NAFTA vacationers. Such competition has been intensified with the opening of the fertile Eastern European tourist markets.

Intra-European mergers and business concentrations are encouraged by the EU for industries that are expected to be competitive against similar U.S. and Japanese industries. At the same time, existing small- and middle-sized firms are supported by the EU through subsidies and loans primarily from the European Investment Bank.

Daimler–Benz A.G. acquired Messer–Schmitt–Bölkow–Blohm G.m.b.H, both in Germany. This acquisition and the restructuring of Daimler–Benz transformed it from the maker of Mercedes cars and trucks into a high technology aerospace and armaments conglomerate in competition with Aerospace P.L.C. of Europe and United Technologies and Boeing of the United States.

Campagnie Financière de Suez of France is considering a takeover bid for Gie Industrielle, a French holding company. Minority stakes of Gie Industrielle and its main asset, a 40 percent stake in insurer Groupe Victoire, are considered by Ferruzzi Finanziaria S.p.A. of Italy. Groupe Victoire had already acquired Colonia Versicherung A.G., the second largest German insurer company. Other companies such as Gie Financière de Paribas, Gie de Navigation Mixte, and Gie du Midi may ally with Gie Industrielle against Suez for the possible cancellation of that takeover bid. However, Suez, the Paris-based banking group that financed construction of the Suez Canal in 1858 (which was nationalized by Egypt in 1956), won control of Groupe Victoire for $4 billion.

French firms have become aggressive in acquiring companies in other EU countries. Abielle Groupe acquired 50 percent of Prudential Holding S.p.A. from Edizione Holding S.p.A. of Italy; RSCG Group S.A. agreed to buy KLP Group P.L.C. of Britain; and Thomson S.A. entered joint ventures with the British Aerospace P.L.C. and Philips N.V. of Holland.

Peugeot Company, the largest French automotive company, expressed interest in acquiring the Porsche Company of Germany. Such an expansion would make Peugeot, a well-known European auto firm, able to compete with its American and Japanese counterparts on a worldwide scale.

Britoil, Harris Queensway, and Ross Youngs of Britain were acquired by British Petroleum, Lowndes Ventures, and United Biscuits, respectively, all of Britain. Moreover, G. H. Mumm of France acquired Martell of France, and Royal Dutch/Shell of The Netherlands acquired Tenneco of Colombia. Ritz, a British firm, acquired British Petroleum Company for $4.3 billion, while Compagnie Bancaire, the French group of economic services, acquired Hyberclyde Investment, a British company.

Dresdner Bank A.G. of Germany acquired Kleinwort Benson Group P.L.C. of Britain for $1.63 billion in 1995.

Some of the most recent intra-EU border M&A deals include: Gehe of Germany, targeting Lloyds Chemists of Britain, a pharmaceutical distribution company worth $990 million; Polypipe of Britain, targeting Meridionale des Plastiques of France, a building products company worth $38 million.

Pitsos Company of Hellas, which belongs to the Siemens–Bosch Company of Germany, was merged with the Elinta Company of Hellas. Both produce refrigerators, kitchen ovens, and washing machines mainly for Hellas and, to a limited extent, for the Balkans and the Middle East. Elinta produces Izola and Eskimo products (180,000 pieces annually) and represents Kelvinator Leonard and the Luxor companies. The relatively low labor cost in Hellas will make Siemens–Bosch products competitive not only for the domestic market but for the export market as well.

BSN, a French holding company, agreed to buy Henninger Hellas, a beer company in Hellas. BSN, producer and distributor of such products as Evian mineral water, Dannon dairy products, and Kronenburg beer, acquired the trademark of Henninger of Germany for Hellas. Expectations are that the beer market will be important in tourist Hellas. The strategy of BSN is to expand and control important trade in other European countries as happened with the Maes Company of Belgium, Peroni of Italy, and Mahou of Spain.

Hoechst A.G., a chemical group in Frankfurt, agreed to acquire Bribos Sinteticos S.A. of Portugal.

In order to control big mergers, the EU empowered the European Commission to review mergers with the EU for firms (including those of the United States and other nations) having revenues of more than five billion ECUs ($5.85 billion). Companies with less revenue would be reviewed by individual member-nations. However, regardless of the new controls and regulations, M&As and joint ventures are expected to increase in Western as well as Eastern Europe. Encouraged by the end of trade barriers, big financial firms such as Wasserstein, Parella Group Inc., and Drexel Burnham Lambert Inc. (still operating in Europe but collapsed in the United States) are establishing investment funds in Europe to facilitate large takeovers. Also, other American firms in coordination with similar financial corporations, such as Banque Paribas of France, Commerz-Bank of Germany, Ambro Bank of The Netherlands, and other investment firms from Italy, Spain, and Japan, created huge funds for industrial restructuring and buy-outs in Europe.

ABN AMRO Bank, the major bank of The Netherlands, acquired a 70 percent stake of Axios Chrimatistiki AE, one of the largest financial companies of Hellas, with shares in the Athens Stock Exchange since 1990 and many domestic and foreign customers. The new company, named ABN AMRO Axios Chrimatistiki AE, became a subsidiary of the international network of ABN AMRO Bank, which was established in Hellas in 1974 and now has nine offices in Athens and Thessaloniki.

Bank Austria, the major bank of Austria, won control of Creditanstalt, Austria's second largest bank, for $1.55 billion (Sch17.2 billion), in competition with EA–Generali, the Austrian arm of an Italian insurer, and other financial institutions. This brings to an end the process of privatization which started in 1990.[10]

Lear Corporation of Sweden, a supplier of car interiors, agreed to buy Borealis Holding A.B. of Denmark, which manufactures door panels and other components for the European car and truck industry. Also, Nordbanken, a state-controlled Swedish bank, and Merita, Finland's largest bank, agreed to merge to a giant firm worth about $10.5 billion.

In order to be able to compete in the production of jetliners with Boeing Company of the United States, which recently acquired McDonnell Douglas Corporation, the four European partners of Airbus Industry reached an accord to restructure the airplane manufacturer. The four partners, Daimler–Benz Aerospace A.G. (with 37.9%), a unit of Daimler–Benz A.G. of Germany, Aerospatiale of France (with 37.9%), British Aerospace P.L.C. (with 20%), and Construcciones Aeronauticas S.A. of Spain (with 4.2%), said that the consortium must adopt a corporate structure to absorb part of the nearly 70 percent of the world market of Boeing–McDonnell, with some $48 billion sales. After two decades of losses of some $8 billion, Airbus has become profitable, receiving sizable orders from China and Singapore, as well as orders for 400 airplanes worth some $18 billion from U.S. Air, Inc., the largest civilian order in history. In order to increase its share, Airbus plans to invest in the NAFTA markets. It also aims at producing super-jumbo jets to compete with the 747 Boeing airplanes.[11]

Chapter 10

Relations with
Other Countries

INVESTMENT, GROWTH,
AND ECONOMIC FLUCTUATIONS

From time to time, supply shocks and economic fluctuations occur in international trade and investment which lead to new inventions and technological progress. For example, the higher prices of oil instituted by the OPEC oil cartel of the 1970s led to the production of more fuel-efficient cars, as well as the development of solar, wind, and other alternative forms of energy. Such supply shocks have punctuated world history. In ancient Greece (Hellas), for example, the transition from the Bronze Age to the Iron Age around 1000 B.C. occurred mainly because tin, a component of bronze, became very expensive, probably because of the wars with Persia (Iran) from which tin was imported and the trade disruption in the Eastern Mediterranean region by the Phoenicians (1025 to 950 B.C.). As a result, the need for a less expensive metal became apparent, and the Greek (Hellenic) smiths learned how to produce iron (though they had a knowledge of iron-making dating back to 3000 B.C., and continued to use it thereafter). This means that supply shocks and crises may contain the seeds of progress in NAFTA, the EU, and the world over. Nevertheless, modern forecasters, due to economic fluctuations and human behavior, may face making Cassandra's pessimistic predictions. It seems though that Polyanna's optimistic predictions could prevail presently on matters of economic and stock market performance on both sides of the Atlantic.

To improve economic and geopolitical relations among the NAFTA and EU countries, investment from the richer to the poorer member-nations is needed so that the per capita income could be enhanced, and closer cooperation would be the outcome. The per capita GDP growth per year (g) depends on the rate of investment (j), the incremental capital-output ratio ($v = \Delta K / \Delta Q$) and the rate of population growth (n). That is, $g = j/v - n$. For example, if the rate of investment is 15 percent ($j = 0.15$) of GDP, v is constant and equal to 3 (three units of capital are required per unit of output) and population growth is 2 percent ($n = 0.02$), then the per capita growth is 3 percent ($g = 0.15/3 - 0.02 = 0.05 - 0.02 = 0.03$).

Figure 10.1 shows the relationship of annual per capita real GDP growth rate to investment as a percentage of GDP (on average from 1970–1990). Most of the EU member-nations' investments varied from 21 to 24 percent of GDP in the period of 1970–1990. Austria, Finland, Luxembourg, and Portugal had investment above 25 percent, and the United Kingdom around 18 percent, whereas Canada had close to 22 percent and the United States close to 19 percent. Also, most of the EU countries had per capita real GDP growth above the middle (regression) line, and varying from 2 to 3.5 percent, compared to 2.5 percent for Canada and close to 1.5 percent for the United States. Japan and Norway, with high rates of investment (above 28%), had also high per capita real growth rates (above 3%). The up-sloping regression line shows the positive relationship of per capita real GDP growth to investment as a percent of GDP ($g = 1.6 + 0.11j$), and the correlation is relatively good, in that it is not a large variation. This means that for each percentage change in GDP growth, about 11 percent investment was used, during that period.

Although Vladimir Lenin described foreign investment as economic imperialism, and developing economies as neo-colonialism, almost all countries of the world invite such investment. In this investment intercourse, Europe (considered "Fortress Europe" some years ago, particularly during the Charles de Gaulle period), currently absorbs most of the U.S. investments.

Direct U.S. investments abroad, running at a record $75 billion per year, help to create jobs and wealth at home, although some foreign investments shift U.S. jobs abroad, mainly in the apparel, automobile, and electronic industries. After the collapse of socialism, anti-Americanism (and the slogan "Yankees go home") was largely eliminated.

During the 1980s, foreign investment was flowing into the United States from Europe, the Arab oil countries, and Japan, and properties such as Rockefeller Center, the Pebble Beach golf area, and Hollywood Studios were bought. However, now the trend has reversed and U.S. investment abroad has become popular.

British, French, and other European universities teach American management skills, and many foreign students and business executives take management and related courses in American universities. At the same time, EU countries are establishing independent or private nonprofit universities, similar to those in the United States, that are more flexible and modern compared to the inflexible and arteriosclerotic public or government universities widespread in Europe.

It is expected that global investment will shift away from the United States and Western Europe, which absorbed about 85 percent of direct investment in

Figure 10.1
Investment and Productivity Growth

Average annual per capita real GDP growth rate, 1970-90 (percent)

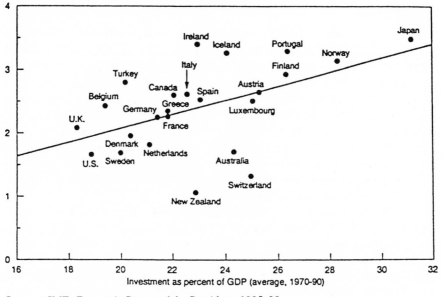

Investment as percent of GDP (average, 1970-90)

Sources: IMF; *Economic Report of the President, 1995*, 28.

recent years, to Latin America and Eastern Europe. These countries offer encouraging investment prospects because of deregulation, privatization, and improved economies.

It seems that the pressure of foreign competition for NAFTA countries will continue because U.S. companies and institutions do not pay as much attention to research and development as foreign firms do, tending to be interested in short-run results at the neglect of long-run improvement. Consequently, they are pushed aside in quality competition. Thus, Japanese companies utilize more than five times the number of robots used by American firms, and competition is severe mainly in consumer electronics, steel, and automobiles. Toyota, for example, is using only 10 percent of the labor that General Motors is using to produce the same number of cars.

Furthermore, American firms are interested in short-term profits and diversification instead of paying more attention to eliminating waste, driving costs down, and improving quality. Moreover, there is not a comprehensive industrial policy with connections between business and government in the United States as exists in Japan. This leads to Japan's dominance (*Pax Nipponica*) in technology, trade, and investment, although a reverse trend has been evident of late. Already, some American manufacturing firms and banks and other assets are owned by Japanese and EU firms.[1]

INVESTMENT AND TRADE IN THE
WESTERN HEMISPHERE

Investment

The tide of direct foreign investments in the United States of the 1980s turned around in the 1990s. U.S. direct investments abroad reached $93 billion in 1995, $53 billion in 1994, and $77 billion in 1993. Total direct investments (excluding portfolio investments) around the world by all countries rose to a record $226 billion in 1994, a 9 percent increase from 1993. A large part of direct investment (about $60 billion per year) is attracted by the U.S. economy. Developing countries attract about $70 billion net foreign direct investment and $90 billion portfolio investment per year. The EU membr-nations, the United States, and other industrial countries contribute ever-growing amounts of investment to developing countries, which absorb about 30 percent of total world foreign direct investment.[2]

Enjoying high profits abroad, NAFTA corporations, mainly in the United States, which were regarded as pirates until recently, continue to buy companies, open offices and stores, and build factories in other countries of the Western Hemisphere, in some cases shutting down factories at home. Reduction or elimination of protectionist measures, sales of state-owned enterprises, and economic growth encourage such investment.

European companies are the top investors in the United States, supporting six million jobs. The United States and Europe, enjoying the world's largest commercial relationship, had $776 billion in cross-investment and $412 billion in two-way trade in 1995, compared to $500 billion cross-investment and $224 billion two-way trade in 1994.

Foreign assets in the United States amounted to $4.127 billion in 1995 (with direct investment at market value), compared to $3.353 billion of U.S. assets abroad; therefore, the net international position of the United States was negative and equal to $774 billion. Foreign direct investment in the United States was $1.019 billion and Treasury securities owned by foreigners amounted to $389 billion in 1995, compared to $533 corporate and other bonds and $465 billion corporate stocks. U.S. assets abroad include $1.301 billion (at market value) in direct investment, $722 billion in foreign securities, and $411 billion in corporate stocks.[3]

Out of the $560.1 billion foreign direct investment in the United States during 1995, $360.8 billion came from Europe, $108.6 billion from Japan, $46 billion from Canada, $22.7 billion from Latin America and other Western Hemisphere countries, and $5.1 billion from the Middle East. The largest amount of European investment came from Britain ($132.3 billion), followed by The Netherlands ($67.7 billion), Germany ($47.9 billion), and France ($38.2 billion).

From the total U.S. direct investment abroad of $711.6 billion in 1995, $363.5 billion went to Europe, mainly to Britain ($119.9 billion), Germany

($43 billion), The Netherlands ($37.4 billion), and France ($32.6 billion). U.S. investment in the amount of $122.8 billion went to Latin America and other Western Hemisphere countries, and $81.3 billion went to Canada.

The Expansion of NAFTA

Chile is expected to be among the first countries of the Western Hemisphere to join NAFTA, having already signed a trade pact with Canada in November 1996. In bypassing Washington, D.C., which hesitates to expand NAFTA to include Chile mainly because of strict capital requirements, Canada has made a good interim step in helping to speed up the process of Chile's admission to NAFTA. Prime Minister Jean Chretien of Canada and President Eduardo Frei of Chile said after they signed the agreement in Ottawa that they want to keep pushing the United States to rapidly extend NAFTA and include Chile.

This agreement removed tariffs on three-quarters of all imports between Canada and Chile, and in five years all import duties will be eliminated. This will increase trade between the two countries, which is more than $500 million per year, or more than double since 1988. Canada primarily exports machinery, grain, minerals, and paper products to Chile, and imports fruits, wine, nuts, and fish.[4]

Furthermore, businesses in both countries have formed more than fifty joint ventures, and more are expected after the signing of the accord, particularly in the mining industry. If Chile removes the regulation that requires all foreign investors to deposit one-third of the capital they bring into the country with the Central Bank of Chile for at least a year, then large amounts of investment could flow to Chile from Canada, and particularly from the United States. This capital requirement was imposed by Chile to avoid an over-reliance on speculative capital and leveraged deals, which damaged the economy of Mexico before the devaluation of the peso.

Chile has had an average annual growth rate of 7 percent over the past decade, an unemployment rate of only 5 percent, and an inflation rate of less than 10 percent, as well as surpluses in foreign trade. With such economic performance and the continuation of privatizations and reforms, Chile will soon be ready to join NAFTA, and could serve as a benchmark for the integration of the Western Hemisphere.

Depending on the success of NAFTA and the performance of other Central and Latin American countries, other nations of the Western Hemisphere may join NAFTA. In a meeting with thirty-three Western Hemisphere leaders in 1995, U.S. President Bill Clinton promised a Free Trade Area of the Americas from Alaska to Argentina by the year 2005. This is anticipated to be the largest market of the world. Expectations are that, after Chile joins NAFTA, many other Latin American and Caribbean nations will apply for membership.

In the meantime, four nations—Argentina, Brazil, Chile, and Uruguay—forged a new common market called Mercosur with more than 240 million people and are in negotiations with other neighboring groups, such as the five-member Andean Pact, and the EU. Also, Chile signed agreements with Canada and Mexico, which have similar free trade agreements with Colombia and Venezuela. As the Chileans say, the bride waits for the groom (or the United States) to arrive, but after a while, she will take off the wedding dress and go find another suitor. Later, if the NAFTA partners desire, they can join Mercosur or any other group.

For closer cooperation, important conferences have taken place in the Americas. The fifth annual United States–Latin America Resort Development Conference, held on 26–28 January 1997 in Costa Rica, dealt with finance, investment, and joint ventures in Latin America.

The Mercosur trade group has not been very successful mainly because the trading products are mostly capital-intensive goods which cannot be exported to outside competitive markets. From that standpoint, productivity-sapping trade diversion may outweigh productivity-enhancing trade creation, and the overall welfare of the countries involved may decline as this preferential group diverts trade from more efficient outside producers.

As a sign of protest against Washington regarding the Helms–Burton Law—which aims at punishing foreign companies that invest in Cuba—Canada's Foreign Minister, Lloyd Axworthy, visited Cuba in January 1997 and signed joint declarations with Fidel Castro on foreign investment, human rights, and environmental problems. Canada is now Cuba's largest foreign investor, and this visit, the first in twenty years, is expected to encourage more trade and investment from Canada to Cuba, and probably from the EU and other countries as well.

Although investment and exports among the NAFTA countries are booming, those with other neighboring countries, particularly in the Caribbean, are reeling. It is estimated that about one-third of the Caribbean's $12.5 billion exports to the United States will be replaced by Mexican trade. As a result of NAFTA, apparel plants in Jamaica, sugarcane fields in Trinidad, and other industries face job losses and the pulling out of investment as the United States increases trade with Mexico. This trend suggests that Washington should extend similar trade preferences to other neighboring nations. From that standpoint, the Caribbean Basin Initiative, put in place by the United States fifteen years ago, should be updated so that Jamiaca, with 2.3 million people and a 16 percent unemployment rate, and other nations of the region, could improve their economies and move toward NAFTA membership.[5]

Joint Ventures

In an effort to modernize public utilities and improve efficiency, many countries, including those of the Western Hemisphere, are in the process of denationalizing state enterprises by selling them, totally or partially, to the private sector. Initially, the government of Argentina retained 51 percent control of Aerolineas Argentinas, while 9 percent of the shares were distributed among employees, and the remaining 40 percent were sold to Scandinavian Airlines. More or less, the same arrangement occurred with Entel, 40 percent of which was sold to Telefonica de España S.A., a Spanish state company, for $900 million. This move was necessary to reduce the losses of public enterprises that count for more than 50 percent of Argentina's budget deficit, to reduce inflation, and to implement austere measures suggested by the IMF because of the country's heavy external debt.

Recent investment in Latin American countries include Rio Algon, the Canadian-based international mining and metals group. It is estimated that production of copper in northern Chile will increase from 240 million pounds to about 900 million pounds a year, and as a result, Rio Algon stock rose from C$2.30 to C$34.30 in Toronto, a new record high.[6]

Aetna Inc., the Hartford, Connecticut-based insurance company, formed a joint venture with Sul America Seguros S.A., a Brazilian insurance company, to offer life and health insurance in Brazil.

Another investor in Brazil is Lloyds TSB Group P.L.C. of Britain, which decided to buy assets from its Brazilian joint venture, Banco Multipic S.A. The assets, worth $600 billion, belong to Multiplic Empreendimentos of Brazil.[7]

Viasa, Venezuela's flagship, was sold in 1991 during a wave of privatizations, partially (60%) to Iberia Airlines of Spain, and partially (20%) to its employees. Viasa paid $74.3 million for a 45 percent stake, and has invested $274 million in improving the company. However, because of misgivings over training, maintenance, and inspection of Viasa, the U.S. Federal Aviation Administration heightened surveillance, and the airline is now close to bankruptcy, despite the reduction of one-third of its 3,400 ground staff and other cost-cutting measures.[8]

The State of Sao Paulo in Brazil sold 60 percent of the shares of VASP Airlines to employees and other private groups.

Also, the Banco Santander acquired 51 percent stake in Banco Osorno y La Union of Chile, and majority control of other large banks in Colombia, Venezuela, and other Latin American countries. Furthermore, the Banco Bilbao Vizcaya, the second largest Spanish bank, took over Banco Provincial of Venezuela, and the acquisitions continue. Telefonica de España S.A., Spain's telecommunications giant, and Television España S.A., a large producer of Spanish-language programming, are forging joint ventures of local companies, not only in Mexico but in other Latin American countries as well.

The fear among Europeans of being pushed out of the Latin American markets by the extension of NAFTA forged a cooperation agreement between the EU and the Mercosur trade group in Madrid on 15 December 1995. It is expected that the two groups will sign a free trade agreement by the year 2001, as the Europeans worry about America's aggressive efforts for increasing exports in the area.

Already EU investment has started flowing into Latin American countries. For example, Bayer A.G., the German chemicals company, agreed to take over the majority stake, for $51.6 million, in Central de Polimeros de Bahia S.A., the Brazilian plastics company that makes shock absorbers for computers and automobiles.

INVESTMENT AND TRADE IN EASTERN EUROPE

Reforms in Eastern Europe

The effects of the integration of Western Europe on the rapid opening of Eastern Europe and the former Soviet Union are expected to dramatically change mutual trade and investment with the EU and NAFTA. The new trend toward privatization and democratization in the previously planned economies of Europe make joint ventures and acquisitions attractive and profitable, particularly in Hungary, Poland, and in the Czech and Slovak Republics, as well as in the former Soviet Union.

The removal of technical, monetary, and trade barriers within the EU, and the liberalization of the economies of Eastern Europe and the former Soviet Union would be beneficial not only for Europe but for NAFTA and the whole world.

The former east bloc countries, only recently coming out of long and painful central controls, are trying to catch up economically and politically with Western countries. The end of the Cold War, the unification of Germany, and the drastic reforms in the former Soviet Union are important elements of peaceful coexistence, under which economic and political cooperation can flourish, not only among European nations but between them and other nations, particularly the NAFTA countries and Japan. Furthermore, the structural economic reforms and the political openness in the former planned economies of Europe may lead to further cooperation and eventual integration of the EU and Eastern European countries, including Russia. The EU integration programs and the upheavals in Central and Eastern Europe present fertile pastures and are attracting many European and NAFTA companies as new markets for direct and financial investments. National interests, in the context of a rapidly changing European system, are gradually being subordinated to common regional systems and eventually to a global economy. The growing interdependence of trading nations requires a shift from isolated and hierarchical decision making to negotiations and common domestic and foreign economic policies.

Poland, Hungary, the Czech and Slovak Republics, and the Balkan countries (Albania, Bulgaria, Romania, and the remnants of Yugoslavia) want to be members of the EU as well. However, their per capita GNP is far lower than that of the current EU member-nations, which means that a transition period will be needed before they are able to join. All these countries have engaged in drastic economic reforms resulting in more trade with the EU, which currently accounts for more than half of their foreign trade. In the meantime, agreements have been signed by each country and the EU to facilitate gradual adjustment toward full membership.

Similar desires toward EU membership can be observed in the European republics of the former Soviet Union, mainly Belarus, Moldovia, and the Ukraine, as well as the Baltic countries, Estonia, Latvia, Lithuania, and to a lesser extent, Russia. Privatizations of state enterprises and other reforms are used by these countries to adjust to the market economies of the EU and the West, and negotiations between the EU and these countries are underway. All agreements and negotiations with the Eastern European countries need to be ratified by the parliaments of the EU and the partner countries.

The enlargement of the EU toward the Eastern European countries, including the Balkans, and eventually Russia and other former Soviet republics, is related to the stability and growth of their economies. The instability of their currencies makes the convertibility into hard currency difficult, and trade and investment with the EU, NAFTA, and other countries problematic. To avoid the problems created for Germany in the 1920s, which left it unable to trade with its neighbors, financial and other support is needed. This may take the form of a strategy similar to the Marshall Plan, or a policy of establishing currency advisement committees by the EU similar to the currency boards of John Maynard Keynes for Russia in 1918.

Like Germany and Japan, as "late starters," the former east bloc countries should look to the most advanced technology, such as fiber optics and digital communications, computers, and other inventions and innovations which bolster entrepreneurship. A well-educated and cheap work force, available natural resources, expected high demand, and a marketplace joined with incoming new technology are likely to lead to a high level of development, equivalent to that of the EU.

There is skepticism, and to some extent, a setback in the movement for EU expansion mainly due to the instability in the countries of the former Soviet Union and other areas. However, the member-nations of the EU, particularly Germany, seem to favor both closer unity and enlargement of the union. There is no better alternative to EU expansion, which could create a Federation of Europe, promoting large-scale production, market expansion, and peaceful coexistence freed from the eliminations of chauvinism and old-fashioned nationalism. A stage-by-stage pan-European confederation, with the member-nations maintaining their role in internal matters, would reduce the possibility of excessive concentration and a huge bureaucracy in Brussels.

To make enlargement feasible and successful, the EU should accommodate other European countries that aspire to join it. However, cohesion of the EU should not be strained by bringing on new members that might overload the EU budget. This means that priority should be given to countries at the same level of development and with homogeneous institutions. Furthermore, adaptations are needed regarding the numerical proportions of the EU institutions, particularly the Commission, so that new members contribute to the effective decision making and governance of an enlarged EU.

Because of the closer relationship of the Eastern European countries with the EU and the United States, as a result of the cosmogonic economic and political reforms recently implemented, a brief review of the fiscal system is needed.

The tax system of the Eastern European nations relies heavily, as before, on turnover taxes to provide revenue and to balance supply and demand. When policymakers want to avoid shortages, they impose turnover taxes to move prices close to the equilibrium of supply and demand and to collect revenue to finance government expenditures. The turnover taxes therefore play a distribution role by discriminating between necessary goods (housing, transportation, medical care, education, and books) for which there is a small or no turnover tax, and luxury goods (cars, videos, and liquor) which have higher taxes. Usually manufacturing is favored over the agricultural sector, as are other social services (health, education, and the arts) through inexpensive credit, tax reduction, and undervalued foreign currency. To correct severe shortages of some goods and sectoral imbalances, *tax-cum-subsidy* measures are used, which avoid extensive productivity losses due to misallocation of resources and effective protection of imports.

To encourage domestic and foreign private enterprises, the tax laws of Eastern European countries have been changed. Not only turnover and other indirect taxes were reduced, but progressive income or direct tax rates, which are as high as 90 percent, were changed and adjusted to those of the EU.

Total direct taxes in the Eastern European countries are relatively small. As percentages of government revenue, they are around 30 percent, while indirect (mainly turnover) taxes account for around 70 percent. The ratio of direct and indirect taxes is only about 40 percent compared to 80 to 90 percent in the EU and the United States. Although recent reforms tend to reduce the fiscal role of turnover taxes in favor of new taxes on income, profits of enterprises, and capital changes, they still continue to be relatively large, mainly because it is easier to collect them compared to other forms of taxation. General government tax revenues in the Eastern European countries are around 60 percent of national income compared to about 35 percent for the United States and 45 percent for the EU. In order to adjust to the EU system, the value-added tax is gradually being introduced in all these countries.

The Eastern European countries, including Russia, are undergoing drastic changes in their economic systems as they try to imitate the Western market economies and attract foreign investment. As the author of this book observed in a recent trip, the new policies of privatization and democratization in the previously centrally-planned economies of Europe create challenges and opportunities from the standpoint of investment, trade, and economic growth.

The end of the Cold War and the profound reforms in the Eastern European countries are important elements for peaceful coexistence under which economic and political cooperation can flourish between the nations of the EU and the United States. [9]

The main variables which affect foreign investment in the recently liberalized Eastern European countries, including Russia, involve changes in investment policies, incentives and productivity, joint ventures and acquisitions, and problems of capital and profit repatriation.

As a result of the mass privatization in Russia which started in the fall of 1991, more than two-thirds of the Russian industry is privately owned and more than forty million Russians own company shares. Through the privatization process, Russian firms became responsive to market rather than political influence, thereby attracting EU and U.S. investments.

On 16 December 1995, the fifteen leaders of the EU met in Madrid and agreed to begin negotiations for the admission of ten Eastern European countries to the union. Although it is not clear exactly how much time will be required for these countries to be ready for full membership, it seems that five or more years, after the beginning of the negotiations, will be needed.

Bulgaria, Estonia, Hungary, Latvia, Lithuania, Poland, Romania, and Slovakia have formally applied for EU membership, as have Cyprus and Malta for which negotiations will soon begin. Also, the Czech Republic and Slovenia want to join the EU. Germany favors the quick entrance of its neighboring countries, that is the Czech Republic, Hungary, and Poland, as their economies are closer to the EU markets, but this preference may create division and instability in the region.[10] Also, an agreement was signed between the EU and a few Latin American countries (Argentina, Brazil, Paraguay, and Uruguay) to work toward free trade after four years.

The enlargement of the EU to include Eastern Europe would cost about $13 billion in additional subsidies to farmers. Currently, the EU pays $47 billion in subsidies to the farmers of the member-nations. Moreover, other kinds of assistance for poorer regions would increase to $90 billion, almost double the $40 billion in other subsidies the EU currently provides.

Investment Potential and Joint Ventures

There is a high potential for growth in the former planned economies of Europe, particularly in Russia with its oil, gold, and other valuable resources. For example, only 40 percent of the 4,000 oil wells are operational in Russia, and large reserves of oil and gas exist in Siberia and other areas. EU companies such as Royal Dutch/Shell, British Gas, Total, AGIP, British Petroleum, Statoil, as well as automobile and other firms may be considered the pioneers of EU enlargement.

A number of EU enterprises expand operations in the former Soviet bloc countries. For example, institutions such as the Banque Nationale de Paris of France and the Dresdner Bank of Germany, in a joint venture, as well as Credit Lyonnais, opened subsidiaries in Russia. Many other companies producing various goods and services in manufacturing, transportation, mining, housing, finance, and trade services have moved aggressively into the former planned economies of Europe, which provide cheap labor and resources as well as a huge market.

In competition with the Cable and Wireless P.L.C. of Britain, Deutsche Bundespost Telecom and Ameritech Corporation became fifty–fifty partners in the Hungarian company, Matav. The new firm, named MagyarCom, will provide wireless telephones which work through radio-wave links and are cheaper than the cellular telephones in installation and maintenance. This deal, which was one of the biggest privatizations in Eastern Europe, may set the pace for expansion to all the former Soviet bloc countries where the number of telephones, compared to televisions, are very low because of the fears held by communist regimes of the spread of rumors and rebel organizing through telephones. As the joke goes, half of the population is waiting for a telephone and the other half for a dial tone.

Other state telephone companies expected to be privatized are the TP SA of Poland and the SPT Telecom of the Czech Republic. The development of the telephone system would create business opportunities for EU and other countries, thereby propelling the European economies to higher growth rates.

Comparatively speaking, Poland was the first country to introduce drastic "shock therapy" in 1990 for the transformation of its economy into the market system, followed by the Czech and Slovak republics and the former Soviet republics. Hungary began introducing reforms earlier in 1968 through the New Economic Mechanism. The other former planned economies of Eastern Europe are at a slower pace of economic liberalization and openness.

Along with the democratization of Russia and other former communist countries, there should be an establishment of proper institutions for property titles and mortgages for credit, as well as patent and copyright laws, to ensure an orderly transfer of ownership. Such efforts can be financed and supported by Western countries and world institutions while international mutual funds can capitalize on Eastern Europe's dramatic changes and invest in productive ventures. As government subsidies, prices, and unemployment are reduced, Eastern Europe will need Western support because it is difficult to implement such drastic changes alone. It is important to remember that in the long run, such a policy is expected to be beneficial to the Western economies as well.

In any case, the transformation from communism to capitalism remains the "Gordian knot" of the European former communist countries. Karl Marx and other socialists wrote about the transfer of ownership from the private to the public sector, but there is no experience, and not enough studies exist, regarding the transformation from communism to capitalism.

Adjusting from a totalitarian to a democratic and competitive system is difficult. To a large extent, people in a totalitarian society do not understand the workings of capitalism and fear the free market system because of its association with unemployment and inequalities. From that standpoint, economic policies suggested by economists become nightmares for politicians. Laws introduced by politicians without related customs are worthless, as Roman writers suggested centuries ago.

The reforms of economic management and political democracy increase expectations for more consumer goods and an improved standard of living. Such expectations are intensified through exposure to Western ways of life via tourism and rapidly spreading communications. As a result, complaints about shortages persist and the rationing of meat and other consumer goods continues in some former planned economies. Long waiting lists for housing, cars, and telephones, as well as goods, even of poor quality, add to consumer frustration and despair, even while rapid improvements occur.

The privatization process, including the transfer of state-owned firms to workers and employees in Eastern European countries and the former Soviet Union, is reinforcing the system of people's capitalism. Selling state enterprises to individuals and making workers whole or partial owners of the firms in which they work, with special discounts, seem to be effective alternatives to public or private sector monopolies. The saying that "in capitalism man exploits man, in communism it is the other way around" may not be relevant to people's capitalism, practiced to some extent in these nations as well as in the EU and NAFTA.

People's capitalism perpetuates the widespread ownership of shares in enterprises, mainly by low-income people. It shifts indirect ownership in public sector firms to direct legal ownership by individuals. By privatizing public enterprises, the government tries to maximize the number of shareholders. People's capitalism, primarily used for the political support of privatization, may not be successful enough if the shares are resold by large segments of shareholders, especially by low-income people. That is why the governments of these countries provide incentives or bonuses to people who retain their shares for a specified period.

The low level of cooperation and advancement in foreign trade in the Eastern European countries under communism was primarily due to duplication of industrial production. Trade among these countries was basically conducted on a bilateral basis. Each nation planned its own development, and included an increase in trade with other partners. There was not an integrated planning body or a common economic policy for multinational allocation of resources, or to take advantage of specialization and economies of large-scale production.

The dismantling of Western European trade and other barriers and the economic and political reforms of Eastern Europe are gradually becoming a reality. A unified market of Europe is expected to benefit business, workers, and consumers alike. In spite of some opposition, mainly from left-wing parties, politicians, economists, and the citizens in general support a unified Europe and talk about the creation of the United States of Europe, with prospects of advancing it to the level of the United States of America. Already, campaigns to alert citizens and businesses in the European countries have begun by almost all governments. They include conferences and seminars and even the creation of special ministries and other institutions to deal with the implications of a "border-free Europe." It seems that what once was regarded as a dream, a utopian concept, is becoming a reality.

The EU, with a population of 370 million and total GDP of about $8 trillion, is almost equivalent in economic power to NAFTA, with a population of 380 million and a GDP of more than $8 trillion. All European nations should prepare individually for the race among themselves, and together for the race with NAFTA and the Asian–Pacific Rim, particularly Japan. The gradual approach to a single market may be accompanied by a further political unification, and in time the European Parliament may become more influential and powerful than national parliaments. Through the expansion of the EU to Eastern Europe, and NAFTA to Latin America, global competition and technological improvement will be enhanced.

German investments are moving to Eastern Europe and other countries mainly because of lower cost, reaching $35 billion in 1995 compared to about $25 billion in 1994 and around the same in 1993. Foreign investment in Germany increased from $700 million in 1991 to $9.1 billion in 1994. An important Germany investment in Eastern Europe was that of the Deutsche Telekom group which won the bid for the Czech GSM Digidal, a mobile telephone company. Also, Hoechst of Germany plans to separate its drug and chemical businesses, after the merger of Sandoz and Ciba of Switzerland, and expand into Eastern Europe. In addition, ING of The Netherlands is targeting Dunabank of Hungary, a banking company.

U.S. investment in Eastern Europe is growing, primarily in telecommunications, computers, and other high-technology ventures. Domestic investment and M&As are largely associated with transfers of control, but foreign investment and acquisitions are used as bridgeheads for the expansion of American markets and the main avenues of economic growth. Moreover, saturated markets and strong competition at home, as well as less protection and more deregulation abroad and exchange rate differentials, are some of the reasons for investing abroad, including in Eastern Europe.

The EU and NATO

Western ideals of freedom, democracy, and laissez-faire economics inspired, to a large extent, the recent revolutionary changes in Eastern Europe and particularly in the former Soviet Union. As the Berlin Wall which confined such ideals collapsed, the ice of the Cold War gradually melted and suspicions that prevailed for decades have evaporated. These changes are challenging established defense organizations such as NATO, which has begun to remodel accordingly.

During the post–World War II period, Western and particularly American policies of NATO and the former Warsaw Pact of the Soviet Union were built on the fear of war; and with the end of the Cold War, the question now became how to overcome that long legacy of suspicion and mistrust. The support for rapid reforms to shift these precommunist countries into market economies, with privatization and people's capitalism, by a consortrium of the trilateral powers (EU, NAFTA, and the Asian–Pacific Rim) would lead to mutual economic and geopolitical gains.

With the profound economic and political reforms toward free markets and pluralistic democratic systems in Eastern European countries and the former Soviet Union, the Warsaw Pact lost its importance and was dissolved. On the contrary, NATO, protecting the ideals of freedom and democracy, has survived, and acquired more importance.

The purpose of NATO in Western Europe, after embracing Germany as a junior partner, was to prevent the former Soviet Union from regional expansion and Germany from new militaristic adventurism. In other words, the main goal of the U.S. centered alliance in Europe was to "keep the Americans in, the Russians out and the Germans down." This is known as the strategy of double containment. However, the new order created through mutually accepted dependence in the EU mitigated the revival of militarism and weakened security dilemmas in Germany. In a democratic and federal Germany, anchored to an integrated EU, militarism and nationalism do not carry as much importance, particularly as a result of a gradual synchronization and solidarity with Eastern Europe and the former Soviet Union. It seems that economic cooperation between Europe, North America, and Japan will be needed to provide socioeconomic stability and growth in these regions and on a global scale.

On the other hand, the increasing preoccupation of the United States with Latin America and the Middle East results in fundamental changes in economic and security matters that were established after World War II. France, Germany, and other EU member-nations, and eventually all of Europe, are considering plans for their own defense strategy. This became obvious with the removal from Europe of U.S. medium-range missiles, the expected reduction and the eventual removal of U.S. ground forces, as well as the weakening of the U.S. atomic unbrella that protects NATO.

Other Eastern European countries may join NATO in the near future. However, NATO needs drastic change as well. Emphasis should be placed not so much on defense, as long as the former Soviet threat does not exist anymore, but on economic, political, and cultural affairs of the nations. Initially NATO was established as a commonwealth of nations that shared the same democratic ideals. After the Korean War, and when West Germany became a member in April 1955, it became a U.S.-led military bloc.

Perhaps there might be no need for the existence of NATO as long as there are no more adversaries, unless a new enemy is created to justify such an organization. Such may be the case with China, or with a united front of Islamic fundamentalists. However, there are fears that after the unification of Gemany, an American–German axis may leave the other European nations, particularly Britain and France, out in the cold. In any case, it seems that for some time to come and until the complete emancipation of Europe, U.S. engagement is essential to the stability of Europe. On the other hand, Western countries, mainly those in the EU and the United States, can help the East form a constructive transition toward a pan-European security system and a rapid economic growth via investment ventures, managerial expertise, and technological dissemination. Moreover, for the stability of Europe, NATO expansion should include not only Eastern Europe, but Russia as well.

In Brussels, on 10 December 1996, NATO announced that it is going to expand to include Eastern European and possibly the Balkan countries. However, there are questions, particularly on the part of the United States, about the automatic commitment to go to war for these countries. Article 5 of NATO, established in 1949, states that an attack against one or more of the members in Europe or in North America shall be considered an attack against them all. Also, in the Treaty of Rio de Janeiro in September 1947 of mutual defense and essentially more than a century before (1823) through the Monroe Doctrine, the United States pledged to defend the entire Western Hemisphere. Nevertheless, defending the fued-prone Eastern European countries is more risky than the neighboring countries in the Americas, and present problems with Russia because such an expansion may revive Cold War policies.

By expanding the EU to engulf the whole of Europe, the role of NATO should be changed and adjusted to new geopolitical conditions. Perhaps its role would be to resist the siren songs of ethnic conflicts in Europe, and discourage by not reconciling itself with military dictatorships in its members as it did with Spain, Portugal, Hellas, and Turkey in the past, and as it does now with the Turkish military occupation of about 40 percent of Cyprus. Most probably, the extreme Islamic fundamentalists will be the future enemies of Europe and NATO. Nevertheless, the enlargement of NATO, parallel to that of the EU, should include not only the Visegrad countries of Poland, Hungary, and the former Czech and Slovak Republics, but other Eastern European countries and eventually Russia.

To help Eastern Europe and Russia move forward, the different nations and nationalities should moderate their nationalist tempers and try to improve cooperation among themselves, and with the EU, which should ultimately be their objective. However, this requires proper training of the people concerned to shed their nationalist prejudices and accept democratic national equality and federalism. As Europe enters a new age, cooperation agreements on matters of security such as those of Helsinki (August 1975) and Helsinki II (November 1990) promote détente and reforms in the rapidly changing old order of Europe.

The three centers of economic power—NAFTA, the EU, and the Asian–Pacific Rim—should combine economic resources to rebuild the new democracies of Eastern Europe. New capital investment, accompanied by modern technology and efficient management, and a reduction of trade and investment barriers would help elevate these economies from the vicious cycle of low performance to stability and economic growth. It is in the interest of all the countries of NATO, particularly those of Europe, to help avoid a collapse of the former Soviet republics, which could devastate the economies of Europe and negatively affect the world economy. It would seem that free market democratic systems, such as those of the United States, Japan, and the EU, exhibit a path to success that other countries could emulate. On the other hand, the failure of the former Soviet and Eastern European economies has proved that communism is a long, hard path from capitalism to capitalism.

From an economic standpoint, Germany and Japan have become the main competitors of the United States. Under the American defense umbrella, both countries, which were the main U.S. rivals during World War II, managed to develop rapidly and challenge American supremacy in international trade and finance. It is time then that they take a larger share of the defense burden, instead of relying on the United States.

In their effort to integrate the Western European Union (WEU), a military arm of the EU, member-nations, particularly France, have proposed that an official representative of the EU, or a "Mr. Europe," be appointed to speak on behalf of its defense policy and foreign affairs. However, Germany has rejected this idea and suggests that the use of majority voting would make the WEU more efficient. So far, Austria, Finland, Ireland, and Sweden have not joined the WEU. There is skepticism that the appointment of Mr. Europe to deal with foreign and defense policy may lead to more bureaucracy and concentration of power, as well as to the dissatisfaction of Eastern European countries.

THE BALKAN COUNTRIES AND THE EU

Economic and Political Reforms

After many wars and disturbances throughout history led to their economic deterioration, the northern Balkan countries, primarily Albania, Bulgaria, Romania, and the former Yugoslavia, came under the political and economic influence of the former Soviet Union after World War II, when central planning, collectivization of farms, and nationalization of industries were imposed. The pressure for reforms led to the gradual privatization of state enterprises and the free market system, similar to that of the EU.

Previous proposals and conferences for Balkan economic and political cooperation and for a confederation has not succeeded. The Balkan countries produce competing primary products, and so a closer economic cooperation or integration is difficult. From a political standpoint, the conflicting interests of outside powers acted as drawbacks to movement toward a confereration. As the saying goes, "When elephants quarrel, the grass is destroyed."

The Balkan countries, which for centuries were under Turkish occupation and subject to internal conflicts, introduced reforms similar to those of the other Eastern European nations. The former Yugoslavia, which has practiced the self-management system for the last four decades, has split into independent republics after severe ethnic conflicts and is in the process of economic and political adjustments.

The winds of freedom and democracy in Eastern Europe are blowing through the Balkan region as well. However, the region, which experienced four costly wars during the first half of this century, was recently troubled again by ethnic and religious conflicts.

The Balkan countries, Albania, Bulgaria, Greece (Hellas), Romania, Turkey, and the former Yugoslavia, are following different economic systems in the process of their development. Currently, there is a trend toward greater cooperation between these countries which may eventually lead to their economic convergence.

The dilemma of unemployment and inflation recently faced by the economies of Hellas and Turkey, as well as low production incentives in the former centrally planned economies of the other Balkan countries, may force more decentralization and further movement toward the free market mechanism. Such concurrent trends may justify some of the conclusions of the theory of convergence among these economies.

The Balkan countries are in a stage of dramatic political and economic changes, and Western investments are needed to revitalize their economies so they will be able to join the EU. By helping them, the West would be helped as well in the immediate future. Such an EU enlargement does not necessarily lead to a weak and chaotic Europe but to a prosperous Europe and more stable world. As Chancellor Helmut Kohl of Germany said, "Poles and Hungarians, Czechs and Slovaks, and many other people and nations in Central, Eastern, and Southeastern Europe place their hopes in the Community. We cannot disappoint them."[11]

Closer relations between the EU and the Balkan countries would reduce or eliminate disturbances and improve the socioeconomic conditions of these countries. In a letter to the leaders of the major EU and Balkans nations, the author suggested that they pursue vigorously the entrance of the Balkan countries in the EU at the present time. The cost from tariff reduction and other assistance would be less than the ongoing military involvements through the United Nations, NATO, and other groups or countries. Membership of the Balkan countries in the EU could force out ethnic and religious conflicts, increase the EU–Middle East trade and investment, and give hope for economic and sociopolitical improvement to the people involved.

The office of the British Prime Minister's answer to said letter was that "Mr. Major has asked that your letter and the closure be passed to the Department with particular responsibility for the matter you raise so that they, too, are aware of your views."

The office of the President of France answered that the President "has always stated that in time, the Central and Eastern European countries would become part of the union, in an integral way and without shortcuts or compromises" (translated from French). However, it was emphasized that probationary periods can be introduced, as in the case of Britain and Spain, for the Balkans and other European countries, including Cyprus and Malta, which are ill-prepared to be thrown into this grand union without borders. In that way, enlargement would not be contradictory to deepening, in that it would avoid emptying, little by little, the existing EU content, structure, and strength. At the same time, the other countries must share objectives and respect the guidelines of the EU.

The main problem for the EU in incorporating the Balkan countries is the price support of farmers. Already more than $60 billion per year is paid, mainly to Hellas, Portugal, and Spain, primarily by Belgium, Britain, Germany, and The Netherlands. But such subsidies can be converted to income supplements instead.

The expectations of Poland, the Czech and Slovak Republics, and Hungary to join the EU create favorable conditions for the inclusion of the Balkan countries. Moreover, such an enlargement would be advantageous geographically not only for the Balkans, through providing more efficient transportation networks, but for all EU countries that could use the Balkan Peninsula as a natural bridge for mutual trade and investment with the Middle East countries.

Investment and Joint Ventures

The flow of foreign investment, mainly from industrial countries, provides overhead capital, jobs, and technology for the recipient Balkan countries in exchange for raw materials, as well as returns for the investing nations. In order to have the flow of foreign investment and the accompanying technological transfer continue, favorable conditions, including guarantees against administrative controls and the assurance of profitable opportunities, must prevail.

All the Balkan countries offer attractive terms to foreign investors and multinational corporations in return for the introduction of new technology and know-how. Despite criticism that such corporate "beasts" influence and even threaten the economic and political life of the host countries, at the same time they are considered agents of technological innovation that provide managerial expertise, capital investment, and employment.

A number of foreign enterprises have established themselves in Balkan economies for trade and investment. This economic exchange has been intensified during recent years. The Balkans are willing to forsake certain controls over incoming foreign investors in return for the hard currency so desperately needed to pay for imported Western equipment and technology. The Intercontinental Hotels Corporation operates and continues to build new hotels in Balkan cities, including Bucharest, Zagreb, and Belgrade. A Japanese consortium that includes the Nippon Steel Corporation and the Mitsui and Mitsubishi groups has created trade centers in a number of Eastern European countries, including Bulgaria.

Romania, following the example of Hungary to some degree, has introduced special legislation for joint ventures with the West, especially for investment involving new technology.

For the financing of exports and trade transactions among Eastern and Western European countries, a number of joint banks have been established in Eastern European countries. They include the French–Romanian Bank, the French–Yugoslavian Bank, and the International Bank of Central Europe in Budapest, in which Balkan economies share up to 50 percent.

Although joint investment ventures among the Balkan countries have been limited, a number of joint enterprises and investment projects have been established primarily on a bilateral basis. Such joint ventures between Bulgaria and Hellas include the Chemiport–Bilimport Company, in which Unifert Company of Lebanon participates for the production of chemical products; the Machine Export Industry (MEVET); the DKW, which cans vegetables and fruits at Almyros, Hellas, and in which the Bulgarian Plont Export, the Greek Kanaris Company, and Uink–Konk of Holland participate; and the Kopelouzos–Balkan Car Impex Company, which manufactures and repairs buses. More joint Hellenic–Bulgarian ventures are in the process of development for the production and trade of fish products, meat products, and sausages, and the manufacturing of leather products.

Joint investment ventures can be planned and implemented on hydroelectric dams and irrigation projects, especially in border areas such as Samoritz–Islaz near the Danube and the Iron Gate on the Yugoslavian–Romanian border. Other joint investment may include mining enterprises for the extraction and processing of iron, lead, zinc, bauxite, petroleum, and other subsoil resources. Also, bilateral agreements may be conducted for transportation, communications, electricity, banking, tourism, and manufacturing. However, careful feasibility studies are needed to overcome the limited or nonexistent research, and the lapses and lacunae of statistical information prevailing in this region.

In the context of Partnership for Peace, the countries of the Balkan Peninsula enter into bilateral agreements for economic, technological, environmental, and defense cooperation with the EU and the United States. At the same time, efforts are being made for multilateral agreements among Albania, Bulgaria, Hellas, Romania, and the former Yugoslav republics.

A growing number of investments are taking place in the ex-Socialist Balkan countries, mainly by Hellas, Italy, and Germany, among other EU countries. The Bank of Macedonia–Thrace of Hellas opened a branch in Sofia, Bulgaria, to help finance EU joint ventures. Moreover, a large number of private investments in Albania are subsidized by the Hellenic government. They include Rekor Albanias AE, a shoe factory; Areziro Tabaccutex GR Company Ltd., a cigarette producer; Market Petra, a construction material producer; and many other firms dealing with cloth, furniture, fish breeding, dairy products, and minerals, primarily in the Argyrocastro and St. Saranta areas.

From a bilateral standpoint, the fulfillment of the educational and human rights of the large Hellenic minority in Albania creates a bridge of friendship between the two countries. Moreover, Hellenic support for Romania's entry in the EU and NATO creates an axis of stability.

Furthermore, the tripartite plan involving Russia, Bulgaria, and Hellas for the construction of the oil pipeline from the Black Sea in Russia to the port of Alexandroupolis in Thrace, Greece (Hellas), would necessitate closer relations among these countries.

In addition, the agreement between Hellas and Bulgaria regarding the administration of the waters of the River Nestos would improve the relations between these two countries. As a result of this project, the economies of the neighboring areas would also be significantly developed.

The advantageous location of Hellas in the Balkan Peninsula, and its membership in the EU make its northern region an important base for trade with and investment into the other Balkan countries. It is estimated that Hellenic entrepreneurs are involved in some 2,000 mainly bilateral joint ventures in Albania, Bulgaria, and Romania. Hellas holds the first place in Bulgaria, in terms of the number of foreign firms, the second in Albania (after Italy) and the twelfth in Romania. Although they are mostly small, such enterprises open the way and encourage large European and American companies to invest in these countries, mainly in manufacturing, agriculture, tourism, and other service sectors. Canadian companies such as Teleglobe, Bellacanada, Bombardier, and Hydro Quebec have expressed interest in investment in Hellas for further expansion in the Balkans.

The city of Thessaloniki with its seaport and airport facilities, as well as the projected stock exchange, is the second-largest city in Hellas after Athens, and is expected to attract domestic and foreign investment for Balkan operations. The Thessaloniki Stock Exchange, with a projected capitalization exceeding $30 billion, could be an important market for providing capital to finance Balkan businesses. It is expected that it will eventually be supplemented by a commodities exchange, which will acquire great importance when manufacturing-free zones, a permanent Balkan trade center, and the Black Sea Trade and Development Bank are established. The Eurobank and the Interbank merged recently to create a powerful bank to finance expansion from Thessaloniki into the northern Balkan countries. Other initiatives for Balkan investment are taken by Hellenic shipowners and entrepreneurs such as Kapelousos, Kounalis, Latsis, and Vardinogiannis.

In addition to the economic penetration of Hellas into the neighboring Balkan countries, other countries also invest in the region. Germany invests mainly in Bulgaria and Turkey, France and Britain invest in Romania, Italy invests in Albania, and the United States invests in all the Balkan countries. The EU is financing, to some extent, such investment expansion into the Balkan countries, mainly for land transportation through the countries that once made up Yugoslavia, and sea transportation through the Adriatic Sea.

The improvement of the Hellenic and other Balkan economies, through partial or complete denationalizations of inefficient public sector enterprises and organizations, would create a favorable environment for domestic and foreign investment, mainly in manufacturing and tourist industries but also in other services. Such improvements or denationalizations would reduce budget deficits and inflation and prepare the nonmember Balkan countries to join the EU, and Hellas to fulfill the Maastricht requirements to join the common currency.

Former Yugoslavia, an important region in the Balkans, faces severe economic and geopolitical problems. When Yugoslavia collapsed in 1991, total foreign debt to commercial banks was $4.2 billion. Negotiations between the so-called London Club of 400 commercial banks, led by Chemical Bank of the United States and the former Yugoslav republics, are in the process of debt allocation among these republics. It is expected that Croatia will assume 28.4 percent of the debt and Slovenia 18 percent.[12]

Serbia asked Slovenia, the richest republic of the former Yugoslavia, to assume more than 18 percent of the debt, but Slovenia argues that this amount is double what is required according to the relative proportion of the population. Moreover, Slovenia and Croatia argue that Belgrade confiscated part of the reserves they transferred to the central bank of Serbia, and ask for the allocation of the remaining $1 billion reserves. At the same time, Serbia went to court for $90 billion in claims against the other republics of former Yugoslavia dating back to 1918. Nevertheless, the banks of the London Club continue negotiations with Croatia, Slovenia, FYROM (the former Yugoslav Republic of Macedonia), and Bosnia, as well as Serbia, for its debt portion of about 40 percent.

EU companies are investing in the profitable Balkan economies. The Robert Bosch G.m.b.H, an automobile and electronics company in Stuttgart, Germany, acquired 80 percent stake in the Turkish brake manufacturer Transturk Fren Donanim Endustrisi A.S., worth $21 million.

Since the collapse of communism, Hellenic and other EU companies are returning to Romania. Many Hellenic–Romanian joint ventures have been established, and direct Hellenic investment in Romania is more than $100 million. As before World War II, when expatriate Hellenic families controlled trade and shipping, Hellenic entrepreneurs are focusing on shipping, trade, construction, food processing, and the banking sectors of Romania. Although Hellenic trade has grown more rapidly with Albania and Bulgaria, it did increase to more than $200 million per year with the larger market of Romania, an increase of about 40 percent over the previous years. Taking advantage of the burgeoning private economy, which accounts for more than half of Romania's GDP, entrepreneurs like Yiannis Alafouzos pioneered joint shipping ventures with Petromin, the state shipping company, after a similar deal with Forum Maritime, another Hellenic group, was called off by the privatization agency and the Romanian Parliament. Hellenic owners, who proved to be effective managers, operate some forty tankers of petroleum through joint ventures, with the help of loans from Alpha Credit Bank, the largest private Hellenic bank, and Banca Bucaresti. The latter bank is controlled by Alpha Romanian Holdings, a group established by Alpha Credit Bank, in which large Hellenic companies active in Romania also have equity participations, as does the European Bank for Reconstruction and Development, with a 20 percent stake.[13] Also, Ion Chryssovelonis, whose family had large banks in Romania in the 1930s, plans to start the production of cigarettes together with the Papastratos company of Hellas. The Apostolopoulos Group, in joint ventures in Montenegro, established off-shore companies dealing with aluminum, shipping, hides, timber, mobile telephones, insurance, and even banking operations.[14]

The East Power Corporation, a Hellenic–Russian company, agreed with the Electrostopanstvo of FYROM to construct a hydroelectric project of 100-megawatt capacity, worth $115 million, close to Skopja. The majority of shares belong to the Hellenic Energiaki Techniki AE Company.

Intracom, a Hellenic telecommunication and information company, and Gazprom, a Russian natural gas company with capital double that of Shell, plan to cooperate for the modernization of telecommunications in these two and other neighboring countries. Also, Prometheus Gas, a Hellenic company, agreed with Asea Brown Boveri (A.B.B.) of Russia, in cooperation with Salzguter and Linde, two German polyethylene equipment companies, to establish a production unit of polyethylene in Siberia worth $1 billion, and eventually in other regions.[15]

Loans have been provided by international institutions. Romania, Turkey, and the former Yugoslavia received loans from the World Bank for the construction of the Danube–Black Sea Canal for structural adjustments to improve irrigation, and for highways and agricultural credit.

In light of further trade and investment cooperation between the northern Balkan countries and the EU nations, the question of what problems may appear in the future remains. It would seem that the trend toward more economic transactions between these two groups of countries does not represent a new movement toward integration, but rather, a policy of gradually abandoning autarky in favor of reliance on the EU countries, especially Austria and Hellas.

OTHER REGIONAL GROUPS

For more investment and trade liberalization, and as a response to the creation of a free trade Europe, a new bloc, the Asia Pacific Economic Cooperation (APEC), was inaugurated in November 1989. It includes Australia, Brunei, Canada, China, Hong Kong, Indonesia, Japan, South Korea, Malaysia, New Zealand, the Philippines, Singapore, Taiwan, Thailand, and the United States.

The twelve members of APEC arrange periodic meetings in order to regenerate the group and eventually to integrate this vital dynamic area of the world economy. The revitalization of this transpacific bloc and the progress with

NAFTA are expected to improve competition with Europe and enhance the chances for further reductions in trade and investment restrictions. Such regional groups initiate global liberalization and show that regionalism is not a new form of mercantilism or colonialism. Already, 60 percent of the world trade takes place within free trade agreements.[16]

APEC aims at a gradual dismantling of trade barriers, increasing investment, and improving the standard of living of the population for the member-nations, which count for 40 percent of the world's population. The total GDP of the group is more than $13 trillion, and the U.S. exports to other member-nations are about $350 billion a year, compared with $270 billion to Canada and Mexico and $230 billion to Western Europe. Nevertheless, the bloc is in its embryonic stage, and some countries, which are also members of the Association of Southeast Asian Nations (ASEAN), such as Malaysia, worry that the large economies of the United States and Japan will dominate the region. In any case, APEC is still a weak bloc and it may take a long time to be effective.

APEC absorbs the largest U.S. exports of information technology products ($53.5 billion in 1995), followed by the EU ($23.6 billion) and other countries ($11.6 billion, including Brazil with $2 billion). As a result of the recent international agreement in Singapore to reduce tariffs on a broad range of information technology products, exports of computers, software, and various types of electronic equipment would increase not only among APEC members but among other countries as well.

In another conference of the WTO on 20 December 1996 in Geneva, representatives of 160 countries reached an agreement to extend copyright law to cover material that can be copied and distributed over computer networks, including music, movie, and on-line distribution of copyrighted materials. It is estimated that piracy costs the U.S. software industry $13 billion each year. However, the tradition of allowing individuals to make a limited number of copies of material downloaded from the Internet for noncommercial purposes or fair use would still apply in cyberspace.

Cooperation of the EU with the Lomé Convention of seventy African, Caribbean, and Pacific countries, created in 1975, will end in the year 2000. One of the main reasons is the collapse of the former Soviet Union and the shift of EU support to Eastern Europe and also the desire not to support friendly despots, previously considered to be "our sons of bitches." With the agreement, signed in Nuritius on 4 November 1995, the Lomé group will get better terms for their exports than before and financial aid (13.3 billion ECUS), on par with previous levels until 2000. The EU has spent more than 30 billion ECUS, or $39 billion, for the group up until now.

Regional groups such as the EU, NAFTA, the Asian–Pacific Rim, and the Commonwealth of Independent States (CIS) of the former Soviet republics help stabilize the free market system and diffuse wealth and income to more countries and more people. The fear that fortress regions will be created that may move against each other are gradually put to rest by similar international agreements.[17]

The recent pact of the WTO, which was concluded after seven years (1986–1993) of negotiations during the Uruguay Round, shows that the spread of the free market system, and the expected participation of more and more people in the efforts to promote progress and economic growth, takes on worldwide dimensions. In this world accord on trade and investment, concluded on 15 December 1993 and effective in July 1995, 117 member-nations of the WTO agreed to reduce tariffs by one-third on the average over six years and boost investment and business activity. Tariffs on manufacturing goods would average only 5 percent worldwide. This world trade accord, the largest ever, the first since 1979 (Tokyo Round), and the second since the 1960s (Kennedy Round), opens markets for goods and services for all countries involved and promotes specialization and productivity. It elevates national economics to international economics, reduces or liquidates nationalism and other regional conflicts, and introduces new trade and investment rules into the next century, not only for industrial goods and capital movement but for agricultural goods and financial and other services as well. Particularly, the EU and U.S. tariffs will be reduced by half on the average, and less for the rest of the world, and agricultural tariffs will be cut by 36 percent in industrial countries and 24 percent in developing nations.

Both NAFTA and the EU can be more effective by moving out of narrow national borders, where established monopolies and oligopolies as well as labor unions, property owners, and other special interest groups stifle competition and react negatively to innovative changes. By expanding the economic borders, production or labor collisions can be avoided, and global business activity can stimulate competition by increasing the number of producers, property and business owners, consumers, and labor interests. On the contrary, concentration of national markets and protectionism can lead to economic stagnation and backwardness, as was the case with Argentina, whose per capita income was the same as the United States in the 1890s, but, after a century of protectionism, found its per capita income to not even be one-third that of the United States. It seems that free trade is an effective vehicle for technological transfer and an engine of growth and socioeconomic development.

Regional trade agreements are the pioneers and the catalysts to international agreements. They open the way for cooperation among nations instead of generating isolationism and conflict. Regional pacts are normally the forerunners of global liberalization, and they set the foundation for worldwide accords. As long as they reduce tariffs for producers inside as well as outside the region, they create trade regionally and internationally. It seems that they do not divert more trade from low cost outside producers than they create because of the reduction of tariffs and other restrictions through international negotiations.

All the regional unions, and primarily NAFTA and the EU, are not expected to create fortress groups which may move against each other. Rather, through gradual enlargement, they diffuse wealth to more countries and prepare the ground for worldwide free trade agreements through the WTO. The establishment and growth of NAFTA, as well as the Asian–Pacific Rim and the little-known APEC, necessitate the enlargement of the EU.

The CIS of the former Soviet republics is not strong enough to be competitive with the EU or NAFTA. Consequently, the whole group, or some of its members, particularly the Eastern European ones, are expected to apply for EU membership. In a similar fashion to the EFTA countries, the CIS members, and the Baltic nations seem to prefer association with and eventual membership in the EU.

Likewise, the obscure Union of Euxene Countries of the Black Sea nations—namely Armenia, Bulgaria, Georgia, Hellas, Romania, and Turkey—is not expected to have much impact. However, Hellas has been a full member of the EU since 1981 and Turkey an associate member since 1964, and currently the other countries of the Black Sea are willing to join the EU. This group, as well as other possible groups in Central Europe such as the Danube basin countries, may be considered complimentary and not antagonistic to the EU. Likewise, the Mercosur and Ande regional groups are not antagonistic to NAFTA and are expected to join it.

With the new agreement of sixty-eight countries under the WTO to open their telecommunication markets to foreign competition, protection for telephone and satellite monopolies would end before the year 2000. The pact, endorsed by NAFTA and the EU, would lead to liberalization and steep price reductions in many segments of the $602 billion worldwide telecommunications market.[18]

Technological innovations in telecommunications minimize distances and improve economic cooperation among nations and groups of nations such as the EU and NAFTA. The Internet already makes available courses taught by professors at distant places, simulated archeological digs of actual sites dating back to ancient Hellas, and book-based information from libraries around the world. Such information may be available not only in classrooms but in homes as well, thereby democratizing education, creating investment opportunities, discouraging nationalism, and encouraging cooperation.

Notes

CHAPTER 1

1. For more details, see Henriette Mertz, *The Wine Dark Sea: Homer's Heroic Epic of the North Atlantic* (Chicago: H. Mertz, 1964), Chaps. 12–14. Ms. Mertz argues that Scylla and Charybdis were in Nova Scotia, not in the Straits of Messine (between Sicily and Italy), as tradition suggests, the Sirens between Cuba and Haiti, and Cyclops in the Azores Islands. For an English translation, see Homer, *The Odyssey*, trans. Robert Fagles (New York: Viking, 1996). For a brief review, see *The New York Times Book Review*, 22 December 1996, 1, 7.

2. For such pessimistic predictions, see Harry Browne, *The Economic Time Bomb: How You Can Profit from the Emerging Crises* (New York: St. Martin's Press, 1989); see also Paul Kennedy, *The Rise and Fall of the Great Powers: Economic Change and Military Conflict from 1500 to 2000* (New York: Vintage, 1988).

3. For the fears of some Europeans that the reunification of Germany might create a "Fourth Reich," see "One Germany? First, One Europe," *The New York Times*, 25 November 1989, A22.

4. For such evaluations, see Jane Kramer, *Europeans* (New York: Farrar, Straus, and Giroux, 1988).

5. "Achtung, Europe," *The Wall Street Journal*, 9 January 1977, A9.

6. Nicholas V. Gianaris, *Contemporary Public Finance* (Westport, Conn.: Praeger, 1989), Chap. 9.

7. J. Monnet, *Memoirs*, trans. R. Mayne (New York: Doubleday, 1989). see also Winston S. Churchill, "The Tragedy of Europe," in *The European Union: Readings on the Theory and Practice of European Integration*, ed. Brent F. Nelsen and Alexander C-G. Stubb, (London: Lynne Rienner Publishers, 1994), 5–9; Jacques Delors "A Necessary Union," idem, 51–54; Robert Schuman "The Schuman Declaration," idem, 11–12; Charles De Gaulle, "A Concert of European States," idem, 25–41; Margaret Thatcher, "A Family of Nations," idem, 45–50.

CHAPTER 2

1. Anne Merrian Peck, *The Pageant of Canadian History* (New York: David McKay, 1963), Chap. 1.

2. Ibid., Chap. 9.

3. Gerald S. Graham, *A Concise History of Canada* (New York: Viking, 1968), 103.

4. Ibid., Chaps. 1–4.

5. Andrew H. Malcolm, *The Canadians* (New York: Random House, 1985), 191.

6. For more details, see Bernal Diaz del Castillo, *The Discovery and Conquest of Mexico* (New York: Farrar, Straus, and Cudahy, 1956), Book 2, Chaps. 1, 4, and 11; Nigel Davies, *The Aztecs: A History* (New York: G. P. Putnam Sons, 1974), Chaps. 8 and 9; William H. Prescott, *History of the Conquest of Mexico and History of the Conquest of Peru* (New York: Modern Library, 1936), Books 2 and 3.

7. Robert E. Quirk, *Mexico* (Englewood Cliffs, N.J.: Prentice-Hall, 1971), 55–56.

8. For more details, see Morko Voljc and Joost Draaisma, "Privatization and Economic Stabilization in Mexico," *The Columbia Journal of World Business* 18, 1 (1993): 123–132.

9. Elizabeth Weiner, "Mexico: Will Colosio Be a Kinder, Gentler Salinas?" *Business Week*, 13 December 1993, 62.

10. Peter Jones, *An Economic History of the United States since 1783* (London: Routledge and Kegan Paul, 1969), Chap. 1. For economic conditions during colonial times, see Susan Lee and Peter Passell, *A New Economic View of American History* (New York: W. W. Norton, 1979), Chap. 1. For the Treaty of Peace with Great Britain, see Henry Commager, ed., *Documents of American History* (New York: Crafts, 1928), 117–119.

11. Edward Humphrey, *An Economic History of the United States* (New York: The Century Co., 1931), Chap. 14. More details in Chester Wright, *Economic History of the United States*, 2d ed. (New York: McGraw Hill, 1949).

12. Elizabeth Gilboy and Edgar Hoover, "Population and Immigration," in *American Economic History*, ed. Seymour E. Harris (New York: McGraw Hill, 1949).

13. For related information, see George Soule and Vincent Carosso, *American Economic History* (New York: Dryden Press, 1957), Chap. 19; Merton Peck, "Transportation in the American Economy," in *American Economic History*, ed. Seymour E. Harris, Chap. 12.

14. Frank Tuttle and Joseph Perry, *An Economic History of the United States* (Cincinnati, Ohio: South-Western Publishing, 1970), 117–118.

15. Peter Jones, *An Economic History of the United States since 1783*, Chap. 11.

16. U.S. Bureau of the Census, *Historical Statistics of the United States, 1789–1945* (Washington, D.C.: The Bureau, 1949), 246.

17. Gary Walton and Ross Robertson, *History of the American Economy*, 5th ed. (San Diego, Calif.: Harcourt Brace and Co., 1983), 474–478; Lee and Passel, *New Economic View*, 146–152.

18. For more details, see Norman Angell, *The Story of Money* (New York: Frederick A. Stokes, 1929), Chaps. 4 and 9; Walter Haines, *Money, Prices and Policy* (New York: McGraw Hill, 1961), Chaps. 5 and 6.

19. For more details, see Robert C. Puth, *American Economic History* (Chicago: Dryden Press, 1981), 342–348; Peter Jones, *An Economic History of the United States since 1783*, Chap. 13.

20. A useful statistical presentation in John M. Keynes, *Economic Consequences of the Peace* (San Diego, Calif.: Harcourt Brace and Co., 1919); U.S. Department of Commerce, *The United States in World Economy* (Washington, D.C.: U.S. Government Printing Office, 1943).

21. Bureau of the Census, *Historical Statistics* 65 (Series D 52–76) and 216 (Series K 158–167); Walton and Robertson, *History of the American Economy*, Chap. 24.

22. American businesses and farm groups initially supported the program but, with the recession of 1949, many firms demanded discouragement of imports from Europe. For more details, see William F. Sanford, Jr., *The American Business Community and the European Recovery Program 1947–1952* (New York: Garland Publishing, 1952).

23. Walter Lippmann, in *The Herald Tribune*, 1 April 1967, reprinted in Stephen Rousseas, *The Death of a Democracy: Greece and the American Conscience* (New York: Grove Press, 1967), 84; Nicholas V. Gianaris, *Greece and Turkey: Economic and Geopolitical Perspectives* (Westport, Conn.: Praeger, 1988), Chaps. 3 and 10.

CHAPTER 3

1. For more details, see Terrot Glover, *The Challenge of the Greeks and Other Essays* (New York: Macmillan, 1942), Chaps. 1–3; C. Stanley, *Roots of the Tree* (London: Oxford University Press, 1936), Chap. 1; S. Todd Lowry, "Recent Literature on Ancient Greek Economic Thought," *Journal of Economic Literature* 17 (March 1979): 65–86.

2. Further valuable information is provided in Frank Tenny, *An Economic History of Ancient Rome* (Baltimore: Johns Hopkins University Press, 1933), Chaps. 1–2; Paul Louis, *Ancient Rome at Work* (New York: Alfred A. Knopf, 1927), Chaps. 1–3.

3. Roman merchants used the Aegean Islands for the transport and exchange of commodities and slaves from east to west. Some 10,000 slaves were sold in a single day on the island of Delos alone. See Jules Toutain, *The Economic Life of the Ancient World* (New York: Alfred A. Knopf, 1930), 232. Spartacus, a slave from Thrace, revolted against the slavery of Rome (71 B.C.) but finally, he and some 90,000 slaves who followed him in the area of Vesuvius were crucified by the Roman army.

4. J. Carey and A. Carey, *The Web of Modern Greek Politics* (New York: Columbia University Press, 1968), 35. See also Barbara Ward, *The Interplay of East and West* (London: Allen and Unwin, 1957), 22.

5. Frances Nicholson and Roger East, *From the Six to the Twelve: The Enlargement of the European Community* (London: St. James Press, 1987), Chaps. 8–11; Paul Taylor, *The Limits of European Integration* (New York: Columbia University Press, 1982), Chap. 2.

6. Evropaikis Enosis (European Union), *Ta Organa tis Evropaikis Enosis* (The Organs of the European Union) (Athens: Vassi-Lissis Sofias 2, 1995). See also Juliet Lodge, "The European Parliament," in *The Impact of European Integration*, ed. George Kourvetaris and Andreas Moschonas (Westport, Conn.: Praeger, 1996), 233–251.

7. For further details, see Anna Michalski and Helen Wallace, *The European Community: The Challenge of Enlargement* (London: Royal Institute for International Affairs, 1992), Chap. 3.

8. Ibid., 127–129.

9. Athanasios Kanellopoulos (Euvoulos), "I Evropi kai o Horos tou Mellontos mas (Europe and the Place of Our Future)," *To Vima* (Athens) 5 July 1992, A14.

10. For more information, see Loukas Tsoukalis, *The New European Economy: The Politics and Economics of Integration* (New York: Oxford University Press, 1993).

11. For the performance of the EU nations, see Nicholas V. Gianaris, *The European Community and the United States: Economic Relations* (Westport, Conn.: Praeger, 1991), Chap. 4; Theodore Hitiris, *European Community Economics* (New York: St. Martin's Press, 1991).

12. For problems of integration, see the valuable papers in Bella Balassa, ed., *European Economic Integration* (Amsterdam: North Holland, 1975); Michael Emerson, ed., *Europe's Stagflation* (Oxford: Clarendon Press, 1984); Desmond Dinan, *Ever Closer Union? An Introduction to the European Community* (London: Macmillan, 1994), Part 1.

13. For more information, see Nicholas V. Gianaris, *Geopolitical and Economic Changes in the Balkan Countries* (Westport, Conn.: Praeger, 1996), Chap. 8; and his "The Limits of the European Union: The Question of Enlargement," in *Political Sociology of European Integration*, ed. George Kourvetaris and Andreas Moschonas (Westport, Conn.: Praeger, 1996), Chap. 13.

14. For further comments, see Nicholas V. Gianaris, *The European Community, Eastern Europe, and Russia* (Westport, Conn.: Praeger, 1994), Part 2; and his "Helping Eastern Europe Helps the West," *The New York Times*, 6 February 1990, A28.

CHAPTER 4

1. For more details, see Thomas Hobbes, *Leviathan* (London: J. M. Dent and Sons, 1934).

2. Adolph Wagner, *Financzwissenschaft*, 3d ed. (Leipzig, 1890). However, the Stoic and Epicurean philosophers (fourth century B.C.), as well as Thomas Hobbes (1588–1679), John Locke (1632–1704), Jean-Jacques Rousseau (1712–1778), and the classical economists supported the limits of the central authority.

3. Arthur C. Pigou, *A Study of Public Finance*, 3d ed. (London: Macmillan, 1951), 31. See also Alan T. Peacock and Jack Wiseman, *The Growth of Public Expenditures in the United Kingdom* (New York: National Bureau of Economic Research, 1961).

4. Plato, *Laws*, in *The Dialogues of Plato*, trans. B. Jowett (New York, 1876), 765.

5. Adam Smith, *An Inquiry Into the Nature and thr Origin of the Causes of the Wealth of Nations*, ed. Edwin Cannan (New York: Modern Library, 1937), 689.

6. J. A. Kay and D. T. Thompson, "Privatization: A Policy in Search of a Rationale," *The Economic Journal* 96 (March 1986): 18–32. See also Emanuel S. Savas, *Privatization: The Key to Better Government* (Chatham, N.J.: Chatham House Publishers, 1987), Chap. 9.

7. It is estimated that federal regulations in the United States are responsible for 12 to 21 percent of the slowdown in the growth of labor productivity in manufacturing. Gregory Christiansen and Robert Haveman, "Public Regulations and the Slowdown in Productivity Growth," *American Economic Review, Proceedings* 71, 2 (1981): 320–325.

8. Janet Smith, "Canada's Privatization Programme," in *Privatization and Deregulation in Canada and Britain*, ed. Jeremy Richardson (Aldershot, U.K.: Dartmouth, 1990), Chap. 3.

9. "A TV Coup in Mexico," *Business Week*, 2 August 1993, 43. For more information on privatization, see Pedro Aspe, *Economic Transformation the Mexican Way* (Cambridge: MIT Press, 1993); Bradford De Long et al., "The Case for Mexico's Rescue," *Foreign Affairs* 25, 3 (May–June 1996): 8–14.

10. Conner Middelmann, "State Sales Set for $53 Billion Record," *Financial Times*, 13 January 1997, 18.

11. Howard Banks, "Tomorrow, The World," *Forbes*, 18 December 1995, 178.

12. "France to Open to Investors Merged Aerospace Firm," *The Wall Street Journal*, 9 January 1997, A8.

13. For more information, see Joseph Blasi, *Employee Ownership: Revolution or Ripoff?* (New York: Ballinger, 1988), Chaps. 1–3; Carey M. Rosen, Katherine J. Klein, and Karen M. Young, *Employee Ownership in America: The Equity Solution* (Lexington, Mass.: Lexington Books, 1986), Chap. 2.

14. For information about employee ownership in Hellas, see Irini Hrysolora, "Measures of People's Capitalism," *Kathimerini* (Athens), 25 October 1987, 7; Nicholas V. Gianaris and Constantine Papoulias, "Participation of Employees in Enterprises," *Oikonomikos Tahydromos*, 2 January 1986, 73–74 (in Hellenic).

15. For Aristotle's aspects of labor, see James B. Murphy, *The Moral Economy of Labor: Aristotelian Theories in Economic Theory* (New Haven: Yale University Press, 1993).

16. For relaxed pioneering proposals, see Martin L. Weitzman, *The Share Economy: Conquering Stagflation* (Cambridge: Harvard University Press, 1984), 73–74; and his "The Simple Macroeconomics of Profit Sharing," *American Economic Review* 75 (1985): 937–953.

CHAPTER 5

1. Adolph Wagner, *Financzwissenschaft*, 3d ed. (Leipzig, 1890).

2. The limits of central authority were supported by the Stoic and Epicurean philosophers (fourth century B.C.) as well as by Thomas Hobbes (1588–1679), John Locke (1632–1704), and Jean Jacques Rousseau (1712–1778), in addition to the classical economists.

3. For more data, see Nicholas D. Kristof, "Aging World, New Wrinkles," *The New York Times*, 22 September 1996, E2.

4. For more details, see Nicholas V. Gianaris, *Contemporary Public Finance* (Westport, Conn.: Praeger, 1989), Chap. 6; and his "Making It Progressive," *The New York Times*, 29 April 1993, A22.

5. Peter Norman, "CDU Aiming for 35% Top Tax Rate," *Financial Times*, 1 October 1996, 3. For suggestions for a flat tax, see Robert E. Hall and Alvin Rabushka, *The Flat Tax*, 2d ed. (Washington, D.C.: Hoover Institution Press, 1995).

6. For a brief review, see Timothy Tregarthen, *Economics at the Margin* (New York: Worth Publishers, 1996), 21.

7. Adam Smith, *An Inquiry Into the Nature and the Origin of the Causes of the Wealth of Nations*, ed. Edwin Cannon (New York: Modern Library, 1937), 79.

8. John Stuart Mill, "Principles of Political Economy," in *Masterwork in Economics*, ed. Leonard Abbott (New York: McGraw Hill, 1973), 1: 164.

CHAPTER 6

1. In 1820 and 1840–1860, about 90 percent of government revenue came from tariffs. Grant Gardner and Kent Kimbrough, "The Behavior of U.S. Tariff Rates," *American Economic Review* 79, 1 (March 1989): 211–218.

2. Patrick A. Messerlin and Geoffrey Reed, "Anti-Dumping Policies in the United States and the European Community," *Economic Journal* 105, 433 (November 1995): 1565–1575.

3. For more details, see Jagdish Bhagwati, *Protectionism* (Cambridge: MIT Press, 1989), Chap. 3; Rudiger Dornbusch and Jeffrey Frankel, "Macroeconomics and Protection," in *U.S. Trade Policies in a Changing World Economy*, ed. Robert Stern (Cambridge: MIT Press, 1989), 107–109.

4. "Trade: Mote and Beam," *Economist* 311, 7601 (6 May 1989): 22–23.

5. For more information on trade problems, see Robert Baldwin, Carl Hamilton, and Andre Sapir, eds., *Issues in U.S.–EC Trade Relations* (Chicago: University of Chicago Press, 1988); "European Plan on Farm Aid," *The New York Times*, 13 June 1988, D6; "A Tale of Eleven Myths," *Europe* 265 (April 1987): 16–18.

6. For a quantification and analysis of protectionism, see related articles in Andrews Stoeckel, David Vincent, and Sandy Cuthbertson, eds., *Macroeconomic Consequences of Farm Support Policies* (Durham, N.C.: Duke University Press, 1989). See also the valuable articles in Baldwin et al., eds., *Issues in U.S.–EC Trade Relations*.

7. "The Economic Impact of the European Community," *American Economic Review, Proceedings* 79, 2 (1989): 288–294; International Monetary Fund, *The Common Agricultural Policy of the European Community* (Washington, D.C.: IMF, 1988).

8. Warren Hoge, "Major, Feeling Political Heat, Plans to Step Up Slaughter of Cows," *The New York Times*, 17 December 1996, A15; George Parker and Robert Peston, "New Cattle Cull Expected to be Approved," *Financial Times*, 11 December 1996, 9.

9. For more details, see David G. Tarr, "The Steel Crisis in the United States and the European Community: Causes and Adjustments," in *Issues in U.S.–EC Trade Relations*, ed. Robert E. Baldwin, et al. (Chicago: University of Chicago Press, 1988), 173–198.

10. For more details, see "American Steel: Plea Bargaining," *Economist* 311, 7603 (1989): 79; Loukas Tsoukalis and Robert Strauss, "Crisis and Adjustment in European Steel: Beyond Laissez-Faire," *Journal of Common Market Studies* 23 (1985): 207–225; Robert Lawrence, "Protectionism: Is There a Better Way?" *American Economic Review, Proceedings* 79, 2 (1989): 118–122. For the hefty work benefits in Germany compared to Britain and other countries, see Edmund L. Andrews, "The Upper Tier of Migrant Labor," *The New York Times*, 11 December 1996, D1.

11. Close to 25 percent of U.S. imports are under special protection, mainly through the trade policy or, more politely, the policy of managed trade during the 1980s. "America's Trade Policy: Perestroika in Reverse," *Economist*, 25 February 1989, 59–60.

12. Karl E. Meyer, "Older, Simpler, Wiser," *The New York Times*, 10 June 1996, A16.

CHAPTER 7

1. John M. Goddard, "Kayaks Down the Nile," *National Geographic Magazine* 107, 5 (May 1995): 713–714; Walter W. Haines, *Money, Prices, and Policy* (New York: McGraw Hill, 1961), 34.

2. Norman Angell, *The Story of Money* (New York: Frederick A. Stokes, 1929), Chap. 5.

3. For additional information, see Nicholas V. Gianaris, *Contemporary Public Finance* (Westport, Conn.: Praeger, 1989), 20.

4. A. R. Burns, *Money and Monetary Policy in Early Times* (London, 1927), 365; Angell, *Story of Money*, 104.

5. Haines, *Money, Prices, and Policy*, 42.

6. For more details on the functions and structure of the Fed in the Board of Governors, see Federal Reserve Bank, *The Federal Reserve System: Purposes and Functions* (Washington, D.C.: The Bank, 1963), 1–29.

7. Nathaniel C. Nash, "Europeans Agree on New Currency," *The New York Times*, 16 December 1995, A1, L40.

8. Anthony Giustini, ed., *European Union Report* 7, 1 (Paris: White and Case Publishers, 1996): 28–32.

9. Simon Kuper and Richard Adams, "Lira Rises on ERM Return," *Financial Times*, 26 November 1996, 1; "European Union to Readmit Lira to Exchange Rate System," *The New York Times*, 26 November 1996, D2.

10. Gillian Tett, "Optimism on Monetary Union Grows," *Financial Times*, 17 September 1996, 9.

11. For more details, see Charles Enoch and Mark Quintyn, "The European Monetary Union: Operating Monetary Policy," *Finance and Development* 33, 3 (1996): 28–31.

12. New York Stock Exchange, *Fact Book, 1995 Data* (New York: NYSE, 1996), 3. See also Benn Steil and Eric Berglöf, *The European Equity Markets* (Washington, D.C.: Brookings Institution Press, 1996).

13. Floyd Norris, "Americans Don't Like Treasury Bonds," *The New York Times*, 3 November 1996, F1.

14. For more information, see Alberti Giovannini, *The Debate on Money in Europe* (Cambridge: MIT Press, 1996).

15. Michael Brush, "As U.S. Giants Soar, Foreign Ones May Be Bargains," *The New York Times*, 29 December 1996, F4.

16. Anthony Giustini, ed., *European Union Report* 7, 4 (Paris: White and Case Publishers, 1996): 18–19.

CHAPTER 8

1. For financial deregulations, see Jill Bodkin, "Deregulation of Canada's Financial Sector," in *Privatization and Deregulation in Canada and Britain*, ed. J. J. Richardson (Aldershot, U.K.: Darmouth, 1990), 153–173.

2. Bernard Simon, "U.S. Funeral Group Raises Bid for Canadian Rival," *Financial Times*, 3 October 1996, 15.

3. "Late Nights in the M&A Lab," *Economist* 337, 7940 (1995): 73; "A Big Day for Mergers in the United States," *The New York Times*, 3 April 1996, D8.

4. Del Jones, "Defense Giant Lockheed to Buy Loral," *USA Today*, 9 January 1996, 1B, 2B.

5. Lawrence J. Korb, "A Military Monopoly," *The New York Times*, 21 December 1996, A25; John G. Auerbach and Jeff Cole, "Suitors for Hughes Unit Are Expected to Raise Bids," *The Wall Street Journal*, 9 January 1997, A3.

6. Saul Hansell, "Banc One Seen in $7 Billion Bid for First USA," *The New York Times*, 20 January 1997, D2.

7. "Columbia Looking to Buy Hospitals," *St. Petersburg Times*, 10 January 1996, 6E.

8. Kenneth N. Gilpin, "Gillette to Buy Duracell for $7 Billion," *The New York Times*, 13 September 1996, D1.

9. Agis Salpukas, "A \$7.7 Billion Union of Gas, Electricity," *The New York Times*, 26 November 1996, D1.

10. "Delivery Merger," *USA Today*, 8 January 1996, 1B.

11. "Dun Deal," *USA Today*, 10 January 1996, 1B.

12. Edwin McDowell, "Hilton Makes \$6.5 Billion Bid for ITT," *The New York Times*, 28 January 1997, D1.

13. Lawrence M. Fisher, "National Semiconductor to Shed Fairchild," *The New York Times*, 28 January 1997, D2.

14. "Motorola Computer Business Splits Into Two Divisions," *The New York Times*, 4 February 1997, D4. For more information on spinoffs or split-ups, see Edward D. Herlihy et al., *Financial Institutions—Mergers and Aquisitions 1996: Another Successful Round of Consolidation and Capital Management* (New York: Sixteenth Annual Institute Securities of Banks, November 1996), 128–136.

CHAPTER 9

1. An affiliate is a company in another country, in which a foreign person has ownership of or controls, directly or indirectly, 10 percent or more of the voting interest.

2. Patrick Harverson, "Midlands Accepts GPU Cash Offer," *Financial Times*, 7 May 1996, 15.

3. Richard W. Stevenson, "Smitten by Britain, Business Rushes In," *The New York Times*, 15 October 1995, 2F, 10F.

4. For more details, see Norman J. Glickman and Douglas P. Woodward, *The New Competitors: How Foreign Investors Are Changing the U.S. Economy* (New York: Basic Books, 1989).

5. "Hanson's Future: The Conglomerate as Antique Dealer," *Economist* 310, 7593 (11 March 1989): 71–73.

6. Alan Cane, "AT&T Plans European Internet Service," *Financial Times*, 25 September 1996, 21; Youssef M. Ibrahim, "Buying MCI Just One Step in British Executive's Plan," *The New York Times*, 25 January 1997, L38.

7. Leslie Wayne, "A Second Suitor Is Pursuing Maybelline," *The New York Times*, 13 January 1996, Y18.

8. Andrew Taylor, "Camas in Further U.S. Acquisition," *Financial Times*, 3 October 1996, 21.

9. "Two Italian Families Form a Conglomerate," *The New York Times*, 11 March 1997, D22.

10. William Hall, "Bank Austria's Bid Chosen in Creditanstalt Sell-Off," *Financial Times*, 13 January 1997, 2.

11. "A Wake-Up Call on the Continent," *Business Week*, 30 December 1996, 40.

CHAPTER 10

1. For further details, see Michael Jacobs, *Short-Term America* (Cambridge: Harvard Business School, 1991).

2. Joel Bergman and Xiaofang Shen, "Foreign Direct Investment in Developing Countries: Progress and Problems," *Finance and Development* 32, 4 (1995): 6–8; Allen R. Myerson, "Investments Abroad Reach Record Pace," *The New York Times*, 24 November 1994, D5.

3. For more details, see U.S. Department of Commerce, *International Investment Position of the United States* (Washington, D.C.: U.S. Government Printing Office, 1996).

4. Anthony Depalma, "Separate Trade Pact by Canada and Chile," *The New York Times*, 19 November 1996, D8.

5. Larry Rohter, "Blows from NAFTA Batter the Caribbean Economy," *The New York Times*, 30 January 1996, A1, A8.

6. Robert Gibbens, "Copper Find Lifts Rio Algon," *Financial Times*, 13 January 1997, 18.

7. "Lloyds Buying Assets of Brazil Joint Venture," *The New York Times*, 6 February 1997, D4. For reforms in Argentina, see Filipe A. M. de la Balze, *Remaking the Argentine Economy* (Washington, D.C.: Brookings Institution Press, 1995).

8. Diana Jean Schemo, "Privatization's Perils: Grounded in Venezuela," *The New York Times*, 4 February 1997, D8.

9. For a review of the reforms in Eastern European countries, see Nicholas V. Gianaris, *Contemporary Economic Systems: A Regional and Country Approach* (Westport, Conn.: Praeger, 1993), Chap. 10. For the problems of EU–Eastern European security, see Noel Malcolm, "The Case Against Europe," *Foreign Affairs* 74, 2 (1995): 52–68. For additional information on problems of security, see U.S. Department of Defense, *United States Security Strategy for Europe and NATO* (Washington, D.C.: U.S. Government Printing Office, 1995), 7–22.

10. For more information, see Nicholas V. Gianaris, *The European Community, Eastern Europe, and Russia* (Westport, Conn.: Praeger, 1994); "Helping Eastern Europe Helps the West," *The New York Times*, 6 February 1990, A28. See also Jeffrey Sachs, *Capitalism in Europe after Communism* (Cambridge: MIT Press, 1991), Chaps. 2–4; United Nations, *East–West Joint Venture Contracts* (New York: United Nations Publications, 1992–1993); David Dyker, ed. *Investment Opportunities in Russia and the CIS* (Washington, D.C.: Brookings Institution Press, 1995).

11. Helmut Kohl, "European Integration," *Presidents and Prime Ministers* 2, 1 (1993): 14. See also Martin Holland, *European Community Integration* (New York: St. Martin's Press, 1993), Chap. 3.

12. Kevin Done, "Creditor Banks Firms on Slovenia Debt Deal," *Financial Times*, 15 March 1996, 2.

13. Kerin Hope, "Greeks Renew Their Romanian Ties," *Financial Times*, 3 October 1995, 8.

14. "Helliniki Ependisi Mamouth Sto Mavrovounio" (Hellenic Investment Mammoth in Montenegro), *National Herald*, 27 December 1996, 1, 10.

15. "Symphonia Intercom Kai Gazprom Ipo Ekkolapsin" (Agreement of Intercom and Gazprom in the Making), *To Vima* (Athens) 19 January 1997, D5.

16. For information on the world trade share by APEC and other regional groups, see C. Fred Bergen, "Globalizing Free Trade," *Foreign Affairs* 75, 3 (1996): 105–120.

17. For more information, see Lester Thurow, *Head to Head: The Coming Economic Battle among Japan, Europe, and America* (New York: W. Morrow, 1992), Chap. 3. See also Dominick Salvatore, "NAFTA and the EC: Similarities and Differences," in *The North American Free Trade Agreement*, ed. Khosrow Fatemi and Dominick Salvatore (New York: Elsevier Science, 1994), Chap. 2.

18. Edmund L. Andrews, "68 Countries Agree to Widen Markets in Communications," *The New York Times*, February 16, 1997, A1.

Selected Bibliography

Andrews, Edmund L. "68 Countries Agree to Widen Markets in Communications." *The New York Times* (16 February 1997): A1.

———. "The Upper Tier of Migrant Labor." *The New York Times* (11 December 1996): D1.

Angell, Norman. *The Story of Money.* New York: Frederick A. Stokes, 1929.

Aspe, Pedro. *Economic Transformation the Mexican Way.* Cambridge: MIT Press, 1993.

Auerbach, John G., and Jeff Cole. "Suitors for Hughes Unit Are Expected to Raise Bids." *The Wall Street Journal* (9 January 1997): A3.

Balassa, Bella, ed. *European Economic Integration.* Amsterdam: North Holland, 1975.

Baldwin, Robert, Carl Hamilton, and Andre Sapir, eds. *Issues in U.S.–EC Trade Relations.* Chicago: University of Chicago Press, 1988.

Banks, Howard. "Tomorrow, The World." *Forbes* (18 December 1995): 178.

Bergen, C. Fred. "Globalizing Free Trade." *Foreign Affairs* 75, 3 (1996): 105–120.

Bergman, Joel, and Xiaofang Shen. "Foreign Direct Investment in Developing Countries: Progress and Problems." *Finance and Development* 32, 4 (1995): 6–8.

Bhagwati, Jagdish. *Protectionism.* Cambridge: MIT Press, 1989.

Blasi, Joseph. *Employee Ownership: Revolution or Ripoff?* New York: Ballinger, 1988.

Board of Governors of the Federal Reserve Bank. *The Federal Reserve System: Purposes and Functions.* Washington, D.C.: Federal Reserve Bank, 1963.

Bodkin, Jill. "Deregulation of Canada's Financial Sector." In *Privatization and Deregulation in Canada and Britain*, ed. J. J. Richardson. Aldershot, U.K.: Dartmouth, 1990.

Browne, Harry. *The Economic Time Bomb: How You Can Profit from the Emerging Crises.* New York: St. Martin's Press, 1989.

Brush, Michael. "As U.S. Giants Soar, Foreign Ones May Be Bargains." *The New York Times* (29 December 1996): F4.

Burns, A. R. *Money and Monetary Policy in Early Times.* London, 1927.

Cane, Alan. "AT&T Plans European Internet Service." *Financial Times* (25 September 1996): 21.

Carey, J., and A. Carey. *The Web of Modern Greek Politics*. New York: Columbia University Press, 1968.

Christiansen, Gregory, and Robert Haveman. "Public Regulations and the Slowdown in Productivity Growth." *American Economic Review, Proceedings* 71, 2 (1981): 320–325.

Churchill, Winston S. "The Tragedy of Europe." In *The European Union: Readings on the Theory and Practice of European Integration*, ed. Brent F. Nelsen and Alexander C-G. Stubb. London: Lynne Reinner Publishers, 1994.

Commager, Henry, ed. *Documents of American History*. New York: Crafts, 1928.

Davies, Nigel. *The Aztecs: A History*. New York: G. P. Putnam Sons, 1974.

de la Balze, Filipe A. M. *Remaking the Argentine Economy*. Washington, D.C.: Brookings Institution Press, 1995.

del Castillo, Bernal Diaz. *The Discovery and Conquest of Mexico*. New York: Farrar, Straus and Cudahy, 1956.

De Long, Bradford, Christopher De Long, and Sherman Robinson. "The Case for Mexico's Rescue." *Foreign Affairs* 75, 3 (1996): 8–14.

Depalma, Anthony. "Separate Trade Pact by Canada and Chile." *The New York Times* (19 November 1996): D8.

Dinan, Desmond. *Ever Closer Union? An Introduction to the European Community*. London: Macmillan, 1994.

Done, Kevin. "Creditor Banks Firm on Slovenia Debt Deal." *Financial Times* (15 March 1996): 2.

Dornbusch, Rudiger, and Jeffrey Frankel. "Macroeconomics and Protection." In *U.S. Trade Policies in a Changing World Economy*, ed. Robert Stern. Cambridge: MIT Press, 1989.

Dyker, David, ed. *Investment Opportunities in Russia and the CIS*. Washington, D.C.: Brookings Institution Press, 1995.

Emerson, Michael, ed. *Europe's Stagflation*. Oxford: Clarendon Press, 1984.

Enoch, Charles, and Mark Quintyn. "The European Monetary Union: Operating Monetary Policy." *Finance and Development* 33, 3 (1996): 28–31.

Evropaikis Enosis (European Union). *Ta Organa tis Evropaikis Enosis* (The Organs of the European Union). Athens: Vassi-Lissis Sofias 2, 1995.

Federal Reserve Bank. *The Federal Reserve System: Purposes and Functions*. Washington, D.C.: The Bank, 1963.

Fisher, Lawrence M. "National Semiconductor to Shed Fairchild." *The New York Times* (28 January 1997): D2.

Gardner, Grant, and Kent Kimbrough. "The Behavior of U.S. Tariff Rates." *American Economic Review* 79, 1 (1989): 211–218.

Gianaris, Nicholas V. *Contemporary Economic Systems: A Regional and Country Approach*. Westport, Conn.: Praeger, 1993.

———. *Contemporary Public Finance*. Westport, Conn.: Praeger, 1989.

———. *The European Community, Eastern Europe, and Russia*. Westport, Conn.: Praeger, 1994.

———. *The European Community and the United States: Economic Relations*. Westport, Conn.: Praeger, 1991.

———. *Geopolitical and Economic Changes in the Balkan Countries*. Westport, Conn.: Praeger, 1996.

———. *Greece and Turkey: Economic and Geopolitical Perspectives*. Westport, Conn.: Praeger, 1988.

———. "Helping Eastern Europe Helps the West." *The New York Times* (6 February 1990): A28.

———. "The Limits of the European Union: The Question of Enlargement." In *Political Sociology of European Integration*, ed. George Kourvetaris and Andreas Moschonas. Westport, Conn.: Praeger, 1996.

———. "Making It Progressive." *The New York Times* (29 April 1993): A22.

Gianaris, Nicholas V., and Constantine Papoulias. "Participation of Employees in Enterprises." *Oikonomikos Tahydromos* (2 January 1986): 73–74.

Gibbens, Robert. "Copper Find Lifts Rio Algon." *Financial Times* (13 January 1997): 18.

Gilboy, Elizabeth, and Edgar Hoover. "Population and Immigration." In *American Economic History*, ed. Seymour E. Harris. New York: McGraw Hill, 1949.

Gilpin, Kenneth N. "Gillette to Buy Duracell for $7 Billion." *The New York Times* (13 September 1996): D1.

Giovannini, Alberti. *The Debate on Money in Europe*. Cambridge: MIT Press, 1996.

Giustini, Anthony, ed. *European Union Report 31*. Paris: White and Case, 1996.

Glickman, Norman J., and Douglas P. Woodward. *The New Competitors: How Foreign Investors Are Changing the U.S. Economy*. New York: Basic Books, 1989.

Glover, Terrot. *The Challenge of the Greeks and Other Essays*. New York: Macmillan, 1942.

Goddard, John M. "Kayaks Down the Nile." *National Geographic Magazine* 107, 5 (May 1995): 713–714.

Graham, Gerald S. *A Concise History of Canada*. New York: Viking, 1968.

Haines, Walter W. *Money, Prices and Policy*. New York: McGraw Hill, 1961.

Hall, Robert E., and Alvin Rabushka. *The Flat Tax*, 2d ed. Washington, D.C.: Hoover Institution Press, 1995.

Hall, William. "Bank Austria's Bid Chosen in Creditanstalt Sell-Off." *Financial Times* (13 January 1997): 2.

Hansell, Saul. "Banc One Seen in $7 Billion Bid for First USA." *The New York Times* (20 January 1997): D2.

Harverson, Patrick. "Midlands Accepts GPU Cash Offer." *Financial Times* (7 May 1996): 15.

Herlihy, Edward, David Neill, Craig Wasserman, Adam Chinn, John Coates IV, and Nancy Clark. *Financial Institutions—Mergers and Acquisitions 1996: Another Successful Round of Consolidation and Capital Management*. New York: Sixteenth Annual Institute Securities of Banks, November 1996.

Hitiris, Theodore. *European Community Economics*. New York: St. Martin's Press, 1991.

Hobbes, Thomas. *Leviathan*. London: J. M. Dent and Sons, 1934.

Hoge, Warren. "Major, Feeling Political Heat, Plans to Step Up Slaughter of Cows." *The New York Times* (17 December 1996): A15.

Holland, Martin. *European Community Integration*. New York: St. Martin's Press, 1993.

Homer. *The Odyssey*, trans. Robert Fagles. New York: Viking, 1996.

Hope, Kerin. "Greeks Renew Their Romanian Ties." *Financial Times* (3 October 1995): 8.

Hrysolora, Irini. "Measures of People's Capitalism." *Kathimerini* (Athens) (25 October 1987): 7.

Humphrey, Edward. *An Economic History of the United States*. New York: The Century Co., 1931, Chap. 14.

Ibrahim, Youssef M. "Buying MCI Just One Step in British Executive's Plan." *The New York Times* (25 January 1997): L38.

International Monetary Fund (IMF). *The Common Agricultural Policy of the European Community*. Washington, D.C.: IMF, 1988.

Jacobs, Michael. *Short Term America*. Cambridge: Harvard Business School, 1991.

Jones, Del. "Defense Giant Lockheed to Buy Loral." *USA Today* (9 January 1996): 1B, 2B.

Jones, Peter. *An Economic History of the United States since 1783*. London: Routledge and Kegan Paul, 1969.

Kanellopoulos, Athanasios (Euvoulos). "I Evropi kai o Horos tou Mellontos mas (Europe and the Place of Our Future)." *To Vima* (Athens) (5 July 1992): A14.

Kay, J. A., and D. T. Thompson. "Privatization: A Policy in Search of a Rationale." *The Economic Journal* 96 (1986): 19–32.

Kennedy, Paul. *The Rise and Fall of the Great Powers: Economic Change and Military Conflict from 1500 to 2000*. New York: Vintage, 1988.

Keynes, John M. *Economic Consequences of the Peace*. San Diego, Calif.: Harcourt Brace and Co., 1919.

Kohl, Helmut. "European Integration." *Presidents and Prime Ministers* 2, 1 (1993): 14.

Korb, Lawrence J. "A Military Monopoly." *The New York Times* (21 December 1996): A25.

Kramer, Jane. *Europeans*. New York: Farrar, Straus and Giroux, 1988.

Kristof, Nicholas D. "Aging World, New Wrinkles." *The New York Times* (22 September 1996): E2.

Kuper, Simon, and Richard Adams. "Lira Rises on ERM Return." *Financial Times* (26 November 1996): 1.

Lawrence, Robert. "Protectionism: Is There a Better Way?" *American Economic Review, Proceedings* 79, 2 (1989): 118–122.

Lee, Susan, and Peter Passell. *A New Economic View of American History*. New York: W. W. Norton, 1979.

Lemco, Jonathan, and William B. P. Robson, eds. *Ties Beyond Trade: Labor and Environmental Issues Under the NAFTA*. Toronto: C. D. Institute, 1993.

Lodge, Juliet. "The European Parliament." In *The Impact of European Integration*, ed. George Kourvetaris and Andreas Moschonas. Westport, Conn.: Praeger, 1996.

Louis, Paul. *Ancient Rome at Work*. New York: Alfred A. Knopf, 1927.

Lowry, S. Todd. "Recent Literature on Ancient Greek Economic Thought." *Journal of Economic Literature* 17 (1979): 65–86.

Malcolm, Andrew H. *The Canadians*. New York: Random House, 1985.

Malcolm, Noel. "The Case Against Europe." *Foreign Affairs* 74, 2 (1995): 52–68.

McDowell, Edwin. "Hilton Makes $6.5 Billion Bid for ITT." *The New York Times* (28 January 1997): D1.

Mertz, Henriette. *The Wine Dark Sea: Homer's Heroic Epic of the North Atlantic*. Chicago: H. Mertz, 1964.

Messerlin, Patrick A., and Geoffrey Reed. "Anti-Dumping Policies in the United States and the European Community." *Economic Journal* 105, 433 (1995): 1565–1575.

Meyer, Karl E. "Older, Simpler, Wiser." *The New York Times* (10 June 1996): A16.

Michalski, Anna, and Helen Wallace. *The European Community: The Challenge of Enlargement*. London: Royal Institute for International Affairs, 1992.

Middelmann, Conner. "State Sales Set for $53 Billion Record." *Financial Times* (13 January 1997): 18.

Mill, John Stuart. "Principles of Political Economy." In *Masterwork in Economics*, vol. 1, ed. Leonard Abbott. New York: McGraw Hill, 1973.

Monnet, J. *Memoirs*, trans. R. Mayne. New York: Doubleday, 1989.

Murphy, James B. *The Moral Economy of Labor: Aristotelian Theories in Economic Theory*. New Haven: Yale University Press, 1993.

Myerson, Allen R. "Investments Abroad Reach Record Pace." *The New York Times* (24 November 1994): D5.

Nash, Nathaniel C. "Europeans Agree On New Currency." *The New York Times* (16 December 1995): A1, L40.

New York Stock Exchange. *Fact Book, 1995 Data*. New York: NYSE, 1996.

Nicholson, Frances, and Roger East. *From the Six to the Twelve: The Enlargement of the European Community*. London: St. James Press, 1987.

Norman, Peter. "CDU Aiming for 35% Top Tax Rate." *Financial Times* (1 October 1996): 3.

Norris, Floyd. "Americans Don't Like Treasury Bonds." *The New York Times* (3 November 1996): F1.

Parker, George, and Robert Peston. "New Cattle Cull Expected to be Approved." *Financial Times* (11 December 1996): 9.

Peacock, Alan T., and Jack Wiseman. *The Growth of Public Expenditures in the United Kingdom*. New York: National Bureau of Economic Research, 1961.

Peck, Anne Merrian. *The Pageant of Canadian History*. New York: David McKay, 1963.

Peck, Merton. "Transportation in the American Economy." In *American Economic History*, ed. Seymour E. Harris. New York: McGraw Hill, 1961.

Pigou, Arthur C. *A Study of Public Finance*, 3d ed. London: Macmillan, 1951.

Plato. *Laws*. In *The Dialogues of Plato,* trans. B. Jowett. New York, 1876.

Prescott, William H. *History of the Conquest of Mexico and History of the Conquest of Peru*. New York: Modern Library, 1936.

Puth, Robert C. *American Economic History*. Chicago: Dryden Press, 1981.

Quirk, Robert E. *Mexico*. Englewood Cliffs, N.J.: Prentice-Hall, 1971.

Rohter, Larry. "Blows from NAFTA Batter the Caribbean Economy." *The New York Times* (30 January 1996): A1, A8.

Rosen, Carey M., Katherine J. Klein, and Karen M. Young. *Employee Ownership in America: The Equity Solution*. Lexington, Mass.: Lexington Books, 1986.

Rousseas, Stephen. *The Death of a Democracy: Greece and the American Conscience*. New York: Grove Press, 1967.

Sachs, Jeffrey. *Capitalism in Europe after Communism*. Cambridge: MIT Press, 1991.

Salpukas, Agis. "A $7.7 Billion Union of Gas, Electricity." *The New York Times* (26 November 1996): D1.

Salvatore, Dominick. "NAFTA and the EC: Similarities and Differences." In *The North American Free Trade Agreement*, ed. Khosrow Fatemi and Dominick Salvatore. New York: Elsevier Science, 1994.

Sanford, William F., Jr. *The American Business Community and the European Recovery Program 1947–1952*. New York: Garland Publishing, 1952.

Savas, Emanuel S. *Privatization: The Key to Better Government*. Chatham, N.J.: Chatham House Publishers, 1987.

Schemo, Diana Jean. "Privatization's Perils: Grounded in Venezuela." *The New York Times* (4 February 1997): D8.

Simon, Bernard. "U.S. Funeral Group Raises Bid for Canadian Rival." *Financial Times* (3 October 1996): 15.

Smith, Adam. *An Inquiry into the Nature and the Origin of the Causes of the Wealth of Nations*, ed. Edwin Cannan. New York: Modern Library, 1937.

Smith, Janet. "Canada's Privatization Programme." In *Privatization and Deregulation in Canada and Britain*, ed. Jeremy Richardson. Aldershot, U.K.: Dartmouth, 1990.

Soule, George, and Vincent Carosso. *American Economic History*. New York: Dryden Press, 1957.

Stanley, C. *Roots of the Tree*. London: Oxford University Press, 1936.

Steil, Benn, and Eric Berglöf. *The European Equity Markets*. Washington, D.C.: Brookings Institution Press, 1996.

Stevenson, Richard W. "Smitten by Britain, Business Rushes In." *The New York Times* (15 October 1995): 2F, 10F.

Stoeckel, Andrews, David Vincent, and Sandy Cuthbertson, eds. *Macroeconomic Consequences of Farm Support Policies*. Durham, N.C.: Duke University Press, 1989.

Tarr, David G. "The Steel Crisis in the United States and the European Community: Causes and Adjustments." In *Issues in U.S.–EC Trade Relations*, ed. Robert E. Baldwin et al. Chicago: University of Chicago Press, 1988.

Taylor, Andrew. "Camas in Further U.S. Acquisition." *Financial Times* (3 October 1996): 21.

Taylor, Paul. *The Limits of European Integration*. New York: Columbia University Press, 1982.

Tenny, Frank. *An Economic History of Ancient Rome*. Baltimore: Johns Hopkins University Press, 1933.

Tett, Gillian. "Optimism on Monetary Union Grows." *Financial Times* (17 September 1996): 9.

Thurow, Lester. *Head to Head: The Coming Economic Battle among Japan, Europe, and America*. New York: W. Morrow, 1992.

Toutain, Jules. *The Economic Life of the Ancient World*. New York: Alfred A. Knopf, 1930.

Tregarthen, Timothy. *Economics at the Margin*. New York: Worth Publishers, 1996.

Tsoukalis, Loukas. *The New European Economy: The Politics and Economics of Integration*. New York: Oxford University Press, 1993.

Tsoukalis, Loukas, and Robert Strauss. "Crisis and Adjustment in European Steel: Beyond Laissez-Faire." *Journal of Common Market Studies* 23 (1985): 207–225.

Tuttle, Frank, and Joseph Perry. *An Economic History of the United States*. Cincinnati, Ohio: South-Western Publishing, 1970.

United Nations. *East–West Joint Venture Contracts*. New York: United Nations Publications, 1992–1993.

U.S. Bureau of the Census. *Historical Statistics of the United States 1789–1945*. Washington, D.C.: The Bureau, 1949.

U.S. Department of Commerce. *International Investment Position of the United States*. Washington, D.C.: U.S. Government Printing Office, 1996.

———. *The United States in World Economy*. Washington, D.C.: U.S. Government Printing Office, 1943.

U.S. Department of Defense. *United States Security Strategy for Europe and NATO*. Washington, D.C.: U.S. Government Printing Office, 1995.

Voljc, Morko, and Joost Draaisma. "Privatization and Economic Stabilization in Mexico." *The Columbia Journal of World Business* 18, 1 (1993): 123–132.

Wagner, Adolph. *Financzwissenschaft*, 3d ed. Leipzig, 1890.

Walton, Gary, and Ross Robertson. *History of the American Economy*, 5th ed. San Diego, Calif.: Harcourt Brace and Co., 1983.

Ward, Barbara. *The Interplay of East and West*. London: Allen and Unwin, 1957.

Wayne, Leslie. "A Second Suitor Is Pursuing Maybelline." *The New York Times* (13 January 1996): Y18.

Weiner, Elizabeth. "Mexico: Will Colosio Be a Kinder, Gentler Salinas?" *Business Week*, 13 December 1993, 62.

Weitzman, Martin L. *The Share Economy: Conquering Stagflation*. Cambridge: Harvard University Press, 1984.

———. "The Simple Macroeconomics of Profit Sharing." *American Economic Review* 75 (1985): 937–953.

Wright, Chester. *Economic History of the United States*, 2d ed. New York: McGraw Hill, 1949.

Index

Accelerator effect, 95
Achaean League, 42
Adriatic Sea, 44
Aegean Sea, 42, 53
Albania, 9, 56–57, 60, 236, 245–246, 248–250
Alexander the Great, 42, 147
American Depository Receipts (ADRs), 185, 187
American Federation of Labor (AFL), 34
American Revolution, 20, 28
Andean Pact, 234
Antitrust laws, 63–64
Argentina, 67–68, 139, 146, 233–235, 239, 253
Aristotle, 7, 25, 42, 44, 57, 72, 150–151
Asia Pacific Economic Cooperation (APEC), 251–252, 254
Asian–Pacific Rim, 9, 14, 15, 59, 221, 242–244, 252, 254

Balkan countries, 7, 10, 56, 236, 244–251
Baltic countries, 10
Black Sea, 37, 57, 249, 251, 254
Brazil, 67, 139, 141, 143–144, 233, 235, 239, 252
Budget deficit, 3, 4, 6, 25

Bulgaria, 56–57, 60, 236, 239, 245–250, 254
Byzantine Empire, 43–44

Capital–labor co-management, 15
Caribbean Basin Initiative, 234
Chile, 130, 146, 233–235
China, 21, 124, 149, 228, 243, 251
Churchill, Winston, 33, 47
Colosio Murrieta, Luis Donaldo, 27
Common agricultural policy (CAP), 140
Commonwealth of Independent States (CIS), 60, 252, 254
Congress of Industrial Organization (CIO), 35
Continental Congress, 32
Crete, 41, 44
Cyprus, 44, 53–54, 60, 90, 239, 244
Czech and Slovak republics, 7, 54, 56, 58, 236, 240, 244, 246–247

Delian League, 42
Delors, Jacques, 50

Employee Stock Ownership Plans (ESOPs), 7, 55, 72–79, 164
Enterprise for the American Initiative (EAI), 9, 15

Euratom, 2
Eurodollar market, 175–176
European Coal and Steel Community
  (ECSC), 37, 48
European Commission, 50, 223
European Council, 6, 50
European Currency Unit (ECU), 150
European Economic Community (EEC),
  37, 48
European Free Trade Association
  (EFTA), 52, 60
European Monetary System (EMS), 58,
  156, 175, 178
European Monetary Union (EMU), 8,
  11, 57
European Parliament, 8, 11, 49–50, 59,
  187, 242
European Payment Union (EPU), 37
Exports, 121–145

Federal Reserve Bank, 32, 152
French Revolution, 23

Gini coefficient, 95
Great Depression, 5, 38, 64, 69
Greece (Hellas), ancient, 1, 2, 3, 4, 41, 229
Greek (Hellenic) Revolution, 28
Guatemala, 26

Hamilton, Alexander, 30, 32, 152
Hapsburg Dynasty, 47
Hellenes, 1, 41–42, 149
Hercules, 1
Hitler, Adolf, 35, 47, 92
Homer, 147, 149
Hormones, growth, 139
Hungary, 29, 54–56, 92, 164, 208, 236,
  239–240, 242, 244, 247–248

Iceland, 19, 52
Immigration, 29
Imports, 121–145
Inflation: cost-push, 164; demand-pull,
  164; and recession, 166
International Monetary Fund (IMF), 27,
  52, 136
Investment and joint ventures, 189, 191,
  195, 247

Islamic fandamentalists, 243–244

Japan, 2, 6, 7, 9, 10, 13, 24, 36, 52, 69,
  81, 90, 93, 122, 124, 128, 130, 134,
  136–137, 139, 141, 143–144, 156,
  163, 188, 197, 208, 213, 222, 230–
  231, 237, 243, 245, 251
Jefferson, Thomas, 28, 32
Junk bonds, 156, 221

Kennedy, John F., 22
Keynesian prescription, 35, 169

Labor Congress of Mexico, 18
Labor–management cooperation, 82
Latin America, 6, 26, 48, 231, 233–235,
  242–243
League of Nations, 4
Leveraged buyouts (LBOs), 163, 215, 221
Lincoln, Abraham, 32

Maastricht Treaty, 8, 51, 55, 57, 180–
  181, 183
Maquiladora program, 18
Marshall Plan, 36
Mediterranean Sea, 42, 146
Mercantilism, 45
Mercosur, 233–235, 254
Mergers and acquisitions (M&As), 136,
  189, 197–198, 227, 242
Mexican *ejidos*, 24, 25
Mexican Revolution, 25, 195
Middle East, 44, 48
Monetarism, 168
Monnet, Jean, 48, 121
Monroe Doctrine, 244
Multiplier effect, 95

Napoleon Bonaparte, 28
Nemean Games, 147
New Deal, 35
North Atlantic Treaty Organization
  (NATO), 2, 21, 37, 56, 58, 146, 242–
  246
Norway, 52–53, 230

Odysseus, 1
Olympic Games, 147, 213

Organization for Economic Cooperation and Develoment (OECD), 36, 99
Organization for European Economic Cooperation (OEEC), 36–37
Organization of American States, 26

Pareto's optimality, 63
People's capitalism, 8, 60, 241
Plato, 62, 65, 150
Poland, 7, 29, 54–55, 60, 65, 164, 208, 236, 239–240, 244, 247
Privatization, 7, 15, 25–27, 55, 60, 65–73, 94, 109, 221–222, 236, 239, 241
Protectionism, 9, 12, 129, 136, 138
Protestantism, 44
Puerto Rico, 23

Renaissance, 44, 46, 151
Rio Grande, 18, 23, 24, 145
Roman Empire, 43, 150–151
Romania, 56–57, 92–93, 236, 239, 245–246, 248–251, 254
Roosevelt, Franklin, D., 24, 35, 48
Russia, 7, 9, 10, 14, 21, 28–29, 53–56, 60, 65, 146, 237–240, 244, 249, 251

Schumpeter, Joseph, 72
Smith, Adam, 70, 88, 116
Social Security System, 35
Soviet Union, 2, 6, 36–38, 52, 60, 91, 94, 175, 236–237, 241–243, 245
Stagnation, 10
Steel industry, 141–143
Stock market panic, 35
Suez Canal, 37

Taxes: consumption, 98, 109, 114–116; corporation, 109; income, 98, 109, 113; payroll, 94; property, 109, 112; sales, 109–110, 113–114; turnover, 238

Thatcher, Margaret, 156, 214
Trade creation, 130–131
Trade diversion, 130–131
Treaty of Paris, 23, 28
Treaty of Rome, 51, 156, 222
Trigger-price mechanism (TPM), 141–142
Trojan War, 1, 59
Truman Doctrine, 37
Turkey, 10, 37, 53–54, 57, 60, 71, 92, 244, 246, 249, 251, 254

Ukraine, 58, 237
United Nations Relief and Rehabilitation Administration (UNRA), 36

Value-added tax (VAT), 112–115
Velocity of money, 152–162, 166
Venezuela, 234–235
Venice, 44

Wagner, Adolph, 61, 87
Warsaw Pact, 52, 58, 242
Washington, George, 28, 32, 152
Worker's Councils, 60
World Bank, 26, 52, 251
World Trade Organization (WTO), 9, 12, 19, 122, 129, 134–135, 137, 140, 144, 146, 207, 252–254
World War I, 4, 5, 10, 30, 31, 33–34, 46, 58
World War II, 2, 4, 5, 14, 21, 24, 30, 33, 36, 41, 46–48, 96, 117, 122, 175, 242–243, 245, 250

Yugoslavia, 9, 56–58, 92, 245–246, 248, 250–251

Zapata, Emiliano, 24
Zollverein, 47

ABOUT THE AUTHOR

NICHOLAS V. GIANARIS is Professor of Economics at Fordham University. Dr. Gianaris is the author of ten books with Praeger, including *Geopolitical and Economic Changes in the Balkan Countries* (1996), *Modern Capitalism: Privatization, Employee Ownership, and Industrial Democracy* (1996), *The European Community, Eastern Europe, and Russia: Economic and Political Changes* (1994), *Contemporary Economic Systems: A Regional and Country Approach* (1993), and *The European Community and the United States: Economic Relations* (1991).

ABOUT THE AUTHOR

NICHOLAS V. GIANARIS is Professor of Economics at Fordham University. Dr. Gianaris is the author of ten books with Praeger, including *Geopolitical and Economic Changes in the Balkan Countries* (1996), *Modern Capitalism: Privatization, Employee Ownership, and Industrial Democracy* (1996), *The European Community, Eastern Europe, and Russia: Economic and Political Changes* (1994), *Contemporary Economic Systems: A Regional and Country Approach* (1993), and *The European Community and the United States: Economic Relations* (1991).

ISBN 0-275-96167-2

90000>

EAN

9 780275 961671

HARDCOVER BAR CODE